THE LIE OF THE LAND

English Literary Studies in India

THE LIE OF THE LAND
English Literary Studies in India

edited by

RAJESWARI SUNDER RAJAN

DELHI ·
OXFORD UNIVERSITY PRESS
OXFORD NEW YORK
1992

Oxford University Press, Walton Street, Oxford OX2 6DP

New York Toronto
Delhi Bombay Calcutta Madras Karachi
Petaling Jaya Singapore Hong Kong Tokyo
Nairobi Dar es Salaam
Melbourne Auckland

and associates in
Berlin Ibadan

Computerset by Resodyn, New Delhi 110030
Printed at Rekha Printers Pvt. Ltd., New Delhi 110020
and published by S.K. Mookerjee, Oxford University Press
YMCA Library Building, Jai Singh Road, New Delhi 110001

Contents

Acknowledgements

Some of the essays in this volume were originally presented at a UGC-sponsored seminar, 'The Study of English Literature in India: History, Ideology and Practice', organized by the English Department of Miranda House, University of Delhi, in April 1988.

Lola Chatterji's generous assistance in various aspects of the compilation of this volume, and Svati Joshi's involvement in the early stages of its production, are gratefully acknowledged.

Grateful thanks also to Suvir Kaul, for permission to use 'The Lie of the Land' from his essay in this volume, as the title of this book.

Note on Contributors

RUKUN ADVANI is an editor with Oxford University Press, New Delhi. His Cambridge Ph.D. appeared under the title *E.M. Forster as Critic* (London: Croom Helm, 1985). Now he writes jacket blurbs, academic parodies, sardonic reviews and funny stories.

TAPAN BASU teaches English at Hindu College, University of Delhi. He was a Fulbright Visiting Fellow at Yale, 1988-9. His research interests are in the areas of American literature and Indian literature in English.

RIMLI BHATTACHARYA is engaged in a project on nineteenth-century Bengali theatre actresses. She taught English at Jawaharlal Nehru University, New Delhi, and has worked on translation and comparative literature studies. She studied Comparative Literature at Jadavpur University and Brown University.

LOLA CHATTERJI taught English at Miranda House, University of Delhi. She is the editor of *Woman/Image/Text: Essays in Feminist Literary Criticism* (New Delhi: Trianka, 1986), and runs an academic publishing concern, Trianka Publications.

MANJU DALMIA teaches English at Miranda House, University of Delhi. She has published an essay on Emily Bronte, and writes poetry in English.

SUVIR KAUL taught English at Khalsa College, University of Delhi. He has a fellowship at Cornell University, to be followed by teaching English at Stanford University. His book on Thomas Gray will be published by Oxford University Press.

ANIA LOOMBA teaches English at Jawaharlal Nehru University, New Delhi. She is the author of *Gender, Race, Renaissance Drama* (Manchester: Manchester University Press, 1989, forthcoming as an Oxford India Paperback). She has also published essays on feminism, theory, and colonial discourse.

YASMEEN LUKMANI teaches English at the University of Bombay. She specializes in applied linguistics and the teaching of English, and has taken a leading role in developing English language studies and literature-cum-language studies at her university.

MEENAKSHI MUKHERJEE teaches English at Jawaharlal Nehru University, New Delhi. She is the author of *Twice Born Fiction* (1971), *Realism and Reality: The Novel and Society in India* (1985), and *Jane Austen* (1991). She was editor of the literary journal *Vagartha* from 1973 to 1979.

RUKMINI BHAYA NAIR teaches English and Linguistics at the Indian Institute of Technology, New Delhi. She has also taught these subjects at the National University of Singapore, following upon a Ph.D. in Linguistics from Cambridge.

TEJASWINI NIRANJANA teaches English at the University of Hyderabad. Her book, *Siting Translation: History, Post-Structuralism and the Colonial Context*, will soon be published by the University of California Press. She is also co-editor of an anthology of essays on studying culture in India, as well as of a reader of feminist criticism in Kannada (both forthcoming).

RAJESWARI SUNDER RAJAN teaches English at Mother Teresa Women's University, Madras. She is currently preparing a book on feminist critical essays as well as a critical work on Dickens.

ANURADHA MARWAH ROY teaches English at Zakir Husain College, University of Delhi. She has worked on Salman Rushdie's *Shame* (M.Phil.). She writes and reviews extensively in Hindi and English.

GAYATRI CHAKRAVORTY SPIVAK has taught English and Philosophy at a number of American universities, her current appointment being at Columbia University, New York. She is the author of *In Other Worlds: Essays in Cultural Politics* (London and New York: Methuen, 1988), and *Master Discourse, Native Informant: Deconstruction in the Service of Reading* (forthcoming). She is also the translator of Jacques Derrida's *Of Grammatology*.

RUTH VANITA teaches English at Miranda House, University of Delhi, and co-edits *Manushi: A Journal about Women and Society*. She has published essays on Shakespeare, and is currently working on Virginia Woolf.

GAURI VISWANATHAN teaches English at Columbia University, New York. She is the author of *Masks of Conquest: Literary Study and British Rule in Inda* (New York: Columbia University Press, 1989, copublished London: Faber and Faber).

Introduction

THE essays in this volume address the issue of English literary studies
in India, most specifically in the Indian university. The official study
of English in India has a history of over a hundred and fifty years; in the
majority of Indian universities today English continues to be a compulsory subject and the medium of instruction, as well as an optional
Honours undergraduate programme leading to postgraduate and research studies. In view of this long history, and of the number and size
of English departments in India's universities, it is not surprising that
English literature should continue to be part of the academic establishment. Traditional pedagogic methods and assumptions about its
study are still maintained largely intact. The present volume is an
attempt to challenge this *status quo*.

Several recent developments—the fall in the student enrolment in
English Honours courses, the regional/political opposition to English-
medium education, informally expressed doubts and anxieties among
younger teachers everywhere, as well as an increasing number of formal
seminars, articles, and books on the subject—all suggest that this challenge is representative of the historical moment. In a central way, the
present volume engages with the politics of the English text in a post-
colonial society. In a more indirect way it also contributes to the study
of the disciplinary formation of English literature in a context very
different from, and yet necessarily part of, its country of origin. The
contributors, nearly all of them university teachers of English, are uniquely positioned to respond both to the local pressures of language
politics and the rapid changes in government education policies in
recent years, as well as to developments in the metropolitan (Anglo-
American) academy. Indeed, even the 'expatriate professors of English'
among them—Gauri Viswanathan and Gayatri Chakravorty Spivak (the
latter quotes this journalistic description of herself self-deprecatingly)—

deploy the double advantage of earlier connection and continuing involvement with the Indian university in order to achieve the perspective of the alienated insider in their contributions.

This book should therefore prove of interest to all educationists in the country, both policy-makers and professionals in the field. It is also intended as a contribution to the field of English Studies, already a well-established meta-critical and disciplinary area of investigation in the Anglo-American university, but one that has yet to take fully into account the historical consequences of the discursive formation of 'English' in the 'world'. Its address to questions of post-colonial culture and society, in line with the concerns that engage intellectuals in Africa and the Indian subcontinent today, renders it a contribution to third world studies as well.

The section headings given in the table of contents broadly suggest the areas covered by the essays. While the majority of these are concerned with the contemporary situation of English in the Indian university, the larger issues regarding its historical and social context inform the discussions. These contextual areas are briefly sketched in the background essays of the opening section. While my essay ('Fixing English') does little more than position English in terms of nation ('of England'), language, and subject (the literature of England / literature(s) in English), Viswanathan's essay, 'English in a Literate Society', connects the issue of English literary studies in India with two notable facts in the contemporary educational scene: the strikingly high national illiteracy rate, and the recent establishment of Navodaya schools—elite 'centres of excellence'—in rural areas.

In the next section, 'The Colony and the Text', Manju Dalmia's essay on Derozio examines the complex ways by which the English text was inserted into the cultural and educational mainstream of the colony, but equally the ways in which it was resisted, subverted, or selectively appropriated by its recipients among the native intelligentsia. Dalmia represents Derozio as a victim of the first stages of this cross-cultural encounter. As a 'native' teacher of English Literature (and History) of exceptional ability, Derozio was instrumental in creating the very changes the British discreetly sought to make in the socio-intellectual make-up of the upper classes—and, at the same time, served as 'a convenient buffer for absorbing the adverse consequences that such radical changes were bound to unleash'. Dalmia goes on to speculate about the radical possibilities of English in the Indian context today, and the implications these have for the role of present-day teachers of English.

The essays in the next section, on pedagogy and criticism, describe and analyse the academic situation of English in its most visible and immediate context, the classroom. Ania Loomba's essay uncovers the complicity between classroom lectures, 'mainstream' literary criticism, and the ubiquitous *kunji* or Indian bazaar guide, an alliance that has successfully maintained the *status quo* of English literature teaching in Indian colleges for over a century. The short contributions to the discussion on the English text in the Indian classroom, by Ruth Vanita, Anuradha Marwah Roy, and Tapan Basu, approach three prescribed texts in the Delhi University BA syllabus—*Mansfield Park, A House for Mr Biswas,* and *Nectar in a Sieve*—from the analytic perspectives, respectively, of gender, nation, and class. They reveal how Indian classroom responses can both conform to and be skewed from the accepted, and expected, critical (primarily western) responses, and touch upon the teacher's mediating role between the two.

If the classroom is the central arena for the formation of an academic discipline, its institutional context crucially determines its features, even as it itself develops in support of them. Both publishing and foreign cultural agencies enter into this mutually defining relationship with English literature teaching in India. The position taken by Rukun Advani, editor at Oxford University Press, in his essay ('Master English, Native Publisher') exemplifies the importance attached to English *language* teaching in India and the relative triviality and irrelevance of indigenous English *literary* criticism. Therefore it is the English literary anthology, widely used in undergraduate language courses, which is the coveted object of the publisher's desire, with the critical monograph coming a poor third (after critical editions of canonical texts) in the field of publishing for English Studies. (Loomba's examination of the less exalted form of indigenous criticism—the kunji, or study-aid, that accompanies the prescribed text-book, and whose ideology—if not idiom—closely conforms to mainstream British literary criticism, provides a useful counterpoint to Advani's defence of the foreign university press operating in India.) My essay, 'Brokering English Studies', offers a description of the British Council's contribution to English studies in India in terms of a watchdog role—that of preserving and promoting Indian academic interest in English, as well as an 'expert's' role—that of providing resources (books, films, etc.), authorities (visiting professors), and incentives (scholarships, grants).

The two essays in the fourth section, on English teachers and students, attempt a sociology of English Studies in India: who studies and who teaches English literature, and why. Yasmeen Lukmani's report, 'Attitudinal Orientation towards Studying English Literature in India', is based on tests conducted with final-year English literature students in Bombay University, in order to determine the nature of their motivation for studying the subject. The results she obtained did not bear out the hypothesis she began with: the students, contrary to expectations, were imbued with a predominantly *instrumental* rather than *integrative* orientation towards English. Their detachment from the 'values' and experiences represented in English literature must lead us to conclude that the traditional humanistic motives behind teaching it need to be re-examined. Rimli Bhattacharya's 'Siting the Teacher', in the same section, foregrounds the teacher in an attempt to relate teaching modes (e.g. canonical readings) to teaching mores (the teacher/student relationship, systems of evaluation, etc.), and goes on to describe the exigencies of a livelihood with interests other than English literature. In Bhattacharya's view the viability of English literature in India today depends largely on the extent to which teachers are prepared 'to critique, to be critiqued, and to learn, even at the cost of re-siting themselves in unfamiliar territory'.

Suvir Kaul's essay in 'The Question(s) of Theory' marks the distance that must be maintained between theory 'there' and practice 'here'. His scrupulous critique of essays by Paul de Man, Jonathan Culler and Homi Bhabha identifies the strategically useful openings they provide for resistant reading; but ultimately Indian teachers of English must opt for the specificity of the historical method to discover their relationship to English texts. Kaul's essay is therefore a plea for 'a genuine *resistance* to critical theory' and for 'the establishment thereby of a critical dialectic that respects the protocols of theory' even as it responds to the urgencies of pedagogical practices in the Indian situation.

The last section, titled, with conscious irony, 'Post-colonial "English"', includes four papers suggesting alternative enterprises that may be undertaken within the space of English Studies: Meenakshi Mukherjee describes a postgraduate course she devised, consisting of Indian novels in English translation; Tejaswini Niranjana presents the challenges that African and Carribean literature pose in the Indian classroom to the traditional assumptions of English literature; Rukmini Bhaya Nair invokes the methodological tools and ideological assumptions of linguistics in an effort to 'contaminate' the 'pure' enterprise of literary studies; and Gayatri Chakravorty Spivak argues that 'the teaching of English literature can become critical only if it is intimately yoked to the teaching of the literary or cultural production in the mother tongue(s)'. In all these essays, not only is the canonical English text sought to be replaced by 'other' objects of study, but the politics of the enterprise of English studies itself is thereby given a new charge in the post-colonial context.

Meenakshi Mukherjee's paper, 'Mapping a Territory', is based on the belief that in a multilingual society literary studies should make students aware of 'this very important dimension of our cultural existence rather than shut them off from it'; at the same time Mukherjee dwells on and speculates about the difficulties of finding adequate English translations of Indian texts. Focusing on the revision in the (post-colonial) understanding of history that emerged from the reading of Derek Walcott's works in the classroom, Niranjana discusses the 'empowerment' that this literature provides, and the other social and political conditions that now allow students to 'talk back' to the hegemonic text.

Rukmini Bhaya Nair's 'Dissimilar Twins: Language and Literature', suggests that the ideological presuppositions of linguistics, as well as its analytic tools, may be used to teach English literature in India in 'a more precise, conscious, and therefore politically liberated space'. After distinguishing between the methods of the two disciplines, she identifies the areas of convergence between the ideologies of linguistics and literary studies in an attempt to delineate the space of a common curriculum. The 'radical renegotiation of the gap between ordinary language and literary language, between English literature and other literatures' which linguistics undertakes is, she argues, enormously enabling in the English literature classroom in India.

Gayatri Chakravorty Spivak, in 'The Burden of English', begins from the observation that the goal of literary studies is 'at least' 'to shape the mind of the student so that it can resemble the mind of the so-called implied reader of the literary text, even when that is a historically distanced cultural fiction'. This leads to an alienating (though admittedly anachronistic) 'cultural indoctrination'. Spivak examines a handful of literary 'figures' of such alienation in the texts of Tagore ('Didi' and *Gora*), Kipling (*Kim*), Mahasweta Devi ('The Hunter'), Binodini Devi (*Amar Katha*), Hanif Kureishi (*The Buddha of Suburbia*), and Nadine Gordimer (*July's People*). In the 'asymmetrical intimacy' of these texts, she suggests, 'the *topos* of language learning, in its various forms' can become 'a particularly productive site'.

In the annexure Lola Chatterjee provides a compendium of facts and figures relating to official education policy and the spread of English in India.

The scope of this volume is, admittedly, limited: the full dimensions of English studies in India must include, for instance, a fairly detailed scrutiny of English education in schools. The present enterprise seeks chiefly to advance the debate over English in India among those who are involved in teaching and learning it. It tries to identify 'the lie of the land', both as a polemical flourish and as a survey of the territory, as a way of confronting the contradictions of our pedagogic practice as well as correlating them with the social, civil and educational institutions of the country.

1

Fixing English: Nation, Language, Subject

RAJESWARI SUNDER RAJAN

> *English*: Of or belonging to England or its inhabitants; . . . as the
> designation of a language . . . the English language; . . . the
> English classics (Macaulay)
> ——*The Shorter Oxford English Dictionary*

T HE academic study of English literature as a subject in Indian
universities is, in its present form, virtually indistinguishable from
the curriculum shaped for it in the metropolitan university in the west.
The corpus of English literature is divided by period or genre, each
exemplified by its representative half-dozen canonical texts. These are
explicated and annotated more or less thoroughly in the classroom.
Standard secondary sources—'criticism'—produced by western scholarship are invoked to provide the paradigms of knowledge about the
texts in question. Annual examinations, centralized and set to a pattern,
consolidate these forms of knowledge.

Given this, it should be possible to treat 'English' in India as a quaint
historical relic, or as another post-colonial 'mimic' activity.[1] But several
reasons prevent that sort of perspective: the subject is studied in this
form (rather than within the contours of 'area' studies) because it presupposes the student's intimate and long-standing familiarity with the
English language; the English language itself has been taught, through

---

[1] In an earlier essay I hinted at the subversive possibilities of our students'
(mis)appropriation of the English 'book', in line with Homi Bhabha's
theorization of colonial mimicry. See 'After "Orientalism": Colonialism and
English Literary Studies in India', *Social Scientist 158*, July 1986, 23-5, and
esp. 33.

many years of schooling, via the English literary 'classic'— so that there is a profound imbrication of the issues of literature and language; and this 'mimic' mode is not simply the peculiarity of the particular subject, English, but an aspect of the entire structure of Indian higher education.

The disciplinary formation of English in India therefore needs to be contextualized within at least three broad areas: its history; language politics; and the socio-cultural scene of education. By framing it within these larger issues—which, in a sense, provide the fixes for its location— we are also enabled to see from where resistance to it is mounted, and what forms it takes.

THE COLONY AND THE NATION

The introduction of English education in India in the nineteenth century, and even specifically of English literary studies, has been extensively researched and commented upon by various scholars.[2] The recent researches of Chris Baldick, Gauri Viswanathan and Franklin Court have disclosed the multiple purposes that the study of English literature was intended to serve, both in England and the colonies, in terms of social reform and social control.[3]

[2] See D.J. Palmer, *The Rise of English Studies: An Account of the Study of English Language and Literature from its Origins to the Making of the Oxford English School* (London: Oxford University Press, 1965); Chris Baldick, *The Social Mission of English Criticism 1848-1932* (Oxford: Oxford University Press, 1983); Terry Eagleton, *Literary Theory: An Introduction* (Minneapolis: University of Minnesota Press, 1983); Franklin E. Court, 'The First English Literature Professorship in England', *PMLA 103*, October 1988, 796-807; Gauri Viswanathan, *Masks of Conquest: Literary Study and British Rule in India* (New York: Columbia University Press, 1989); Svati Joshi, ed., *Rethinking English: The Cultural Politics of Literature, Language and Pedagogy in India* (New Delhi: Trianka, 1991).

[3] All are agreed on the purpose and function of English literary studies as an ideological force. Baldick and Viswanathan, however, stress the social *control* effected by it (chiefly on the English working-classes, women, and 'natives'), while Court argues that it was motives of political reform rather than social control that lay behind the institution of English literature courses in London University in 1828. The development of the reading habit among the masses would politicize them, and lead them to demand reforms — and thereby avert revolution. Marilyn Butler is also inclined to stress the reformist impulses of English literary studies in the early nineteenth century. See her 'Revising the Canon', *Times Literary Supplement* 4-10 December 1987.

Thomas Babington Macaulay's education minute of 1835—which recommended to the Governor General in Council that Britain officially support English education in India and withdraw support to Arabic and Sanskrit education—is generally regarded as a crucial document in this history. Macaulay argued that 'English is better worth knowing than Sanskrit and Arabic'; that 'the natives are desirous to be taught English'; and that 'it is possible to make natives of this country thoroughly good English scholars'.[4] These arguments about the superiority of English in an absolute sense, its political uses, and its teaching have set the terms within which the question of English continues to be viewed.

The official introduction of English in Indian higher education, which Macaulay's minute announces, was preceded by the complex history of its consolidation as a recognizable body of knowledge and as a collection of texts in the eighteenth and early nineteenth centuries, and of the attendant notions of 'literature', national language, textuality, and interpretive authority that were developed in this project. A recognizable 'English' literature—marked by scholarly editions of texts, literary histories, critical works, biographies of writers—took shape in Britain concurrently with the project of imperialism, within a common social and historical configuration.[5] Among other things, both were impelled by a nascent British nationalism. At the same time, it is important to bear in mind that, from the start, this consolidation was countered by the contestation of the canon by Britain's own local colonies—Wales, Scotland, Ireland.[6] Away from the scene of its production, Britain, English

---

[4] 'Indian Education', Minute of 2 February 1835. See *Macaulay: Prose and Poetry*, ed. G.M. Young (Cambridge, MA: Harvard University Press, 1967), 729.

[5] See Butler, 'Revising the Canon'. Eighteenth-century criticism and scholarship (Addison, Johnson) was a significant forerunner of the formalization of English literary studies. Court cites Palmer to show that Scottish universities in the late eighteenth century had already introduced courses in English under the rubric of 'rhetoric' and 'belles lettres'.

[6] Butler remarks thus on the more 'contentious', democratic English literary tradition that was invoked in the eighteenth century—'a more British, non-Latinate literary past, including ballads, gothic tales, Elizabethan lyric and drama, and (for the learned like Cambridge's Thomas Gray) Anglo-Saxon, Celtic and Old Norse.' It was the nineteenth-century 'professionals' who made the canon 'harmonious . . . nationalist . . . individualist or pluralist' and uniform. Colin MacCabe also asserts that 'English' as 'an accepted canon

literature could, in the colonies, assume a fixed and more homogeneous nationalist cast.

Second, the Anglicist advocacy of English as the language of education for Indians was by no means the first colonial intervention in these spheres. Large-scale linguistic engineering had been engaged in from at least the end of the eighteenth century, involving a long process of standardization of the Indian classical and vernacular languages and literatures, through the production of 'authentic' texts, translations, lexicons, grammars, prose writings, etc.[7] The analogy that the Orientalists and Fort William missionaries drew on most often for their modernization of the vernaculars was Dante's endeavours on behalf of the European vernaculars during the Renaissance. Further, the vernacularists' attempts to develop 'a simple, referential prose in Indian languages'—an explicit aim of the Asiatic Society—was based upon the ideals of the British Royal Society, and was part of the evolutionary goal proposed for these languages.[8]

Notions of the secular text and its interpretation were being simultaneously developed in Europe and its colonies in this period; and though these proceeded along different paths and were aimed towards different ends in the two locations, they were consolidated in the common project of Orientalism. Edward Said reminds us that modern Western philology—as typified in the work of Ernest Renan—was allied to the projects of religion (the Higher Criticism) and Orientalism, and directly subserved the ends of colonialism. By reducing languages to 'language groups, historical and racial theories, geographical and anthropological theses', Renan was able to argue the inferiority of Semitic languages, hence of their religious texts, and, by extension, their cultures and histories. 'What comes to replace divine authority is the textual

---

of works in a clearly defined national language' never existed: 'All such fables of a past unfissured by division and contradiction are, of course, deeply suspect.' See 'The State of the Subject (I) English', *Critical Quarterly* 29, 5-8, esp. 5.

[7] The relationship between Orientalist translations and the introduction of English in India is explored by Tejaswini Niranjana in 'Translation as Subjectification: English in India', in Joshi, ed.

[8] Gita Wolf-Sampat, 'English in India', unpublished paper. See also David Kopf, *British Orientalism and the Bengal Renaissance* (Berkeley: University of California Press, 1969).

authority of the philological critic.'[9] In India British Orientalists were extrapolating and codifying the laws of the land from the Hindu shastras and the Islamic shariat, in collaboration with native scholars, to serve the ends of colonial administration.[10]

It is against this background of the disciplinary formation of English as a branch of knowledge, and the early history of colonialist interventions in Indian education, language and literature, that the establishment of English as the medium of educational instruction and as a subject for study must be viewed. This 'pre-history' shows that neither the formation of a discipline nor the implementation of a national education policy is achieved by fiat. The policies themselves were by no means unambiguous or consciously directed towards clear-cut goals; as Gauri Viswanathan has shown, they were subject to frequent shifts of direction.[11] There was, further, the inevitable gap between policy and actual practices on the ground.[12] Above all, there was the fact of resistance from the native intelligentsia, more properly formulated as a responsiveness to English education on their own terms and not solely on the terms set by colonial educationists.[13] The two chief purposes of English education, which may be broadly distinguished as the 'instrumental' and the 'integrative', were forwarded by Macaulay in his minute with no consciousness of contradiction in such doubleness of purpose. The native elites too had no difficulty in accepting, and in fact

[9] Edward Said, 'The World, the Text and the Critic', in *The World, the Text and the Critic* (London: Faber, 1984), 46-7.

[10] Lata Mani has demonstrated this in her argument about the British abolition of sati. See 'The Production of an Official Discourse on Sati in Early Nineteenth Century Bengal', *Economic and Political Weekly*, XXI, 7, 26 April 1986, 32-40.

[11] Gauri Viswanathan, 'The Beginnings of English Literary Study in British India', *Oxford Literary Review* 9, 1987, 2-26. Also her *Masks of Conquest*.

[12] See Robert E. Frykenberg, 'The Myth of English as a "Colonialist" Imposition upon India: A Reappraisal with Special Reference to South India', *Journal of the Royal Asiatic Society* 2, 1988, 305-15. Frykenberg argues that Macaulay's minute 'signalled no change in previous policy'. Bentinck hesitated to intervene in traditional education, 'Oriental' studies continued, and there was no dramatic increase in state funding for English education (313-14).

[13] For an interesting argument about colonial resistance in the context of the debate over English education, see Jenny Sharpe, 'Figures of Colonial Resistance', *Modern Fiction Studies 35*, Spring 1989, 137-55.

demanding, English education for the first purpose, as a means to securing employment in the colonial bureaucracy or—more broadly—acquiring knowledge of western sciences; the second they negotiated in various ways—through outright resistance to any trespass upon indigenous religious belief, as in the case of Hindu College patrons; or by more subtle forms of appropriation and a subversion of the values that were intended to mould them as subjects.[14] The westernized intellectuals' shift of focus from reformist to nationalist activities towards the end of the nineteenth century came about as a consequence of their recognition that their 'modernity' had to contend with the continuing influence of the traditional conservative classes, and that political struggle alone could grant them influence over the larger constituencies they sought'.[15] Thus, though the overt purpose of English education—which was to create an amenable native elite population that would be impressed by, conform to, and propagate the values of the secular English book— was undoubtedly served, the English text was also, in complex and mediated ways, appropriated within native arguments for political representation, for articulating demands, and for questioning the rulers.[16] But *in either case*, as Gauri Viswanathan has shown, the English book remained uncontaminated by the material practices of colonialism:[17] in other words, English *literature* was not indicted on ideological or historical grounds by association with the English ruler. Rather it became the surrogate—and also the split—presence of the Englishman, or a repository of abstract and universal values freely available to the colonized as much as to the colonizer.

It is this dissociation of English literature from its national origins that has made possible its unproblematic retention and continuance in the post-Independence education syllabus in India.[18] At the same time,

---

[14] The case of Derozio illustrates the attitudes of Hindu College patrons in the 1830s. See Manju Dalmia's 'Derozio: English Teacher', in this volume.

[15] Michelguglielmo Torri, '"Westernised Middle Class" Intellectuals and Society in Late Colonial India', *Economic and Political Weekly*, 27 January 1990, PE2- PE11, esp. PE7.

[16] See Jashodhra Bagchi, 'Shakespeare in Loincloth: English Literature and the Early Nationalist Consciousness in Bengal', in Joshi, ed.

[17] Viswanathan, 'The Beginnings of English Literary Study', 22-3. See also, as an example, Tagore's remarks about English literature, quoted in Dalmia, 'Derozio'.

[18] This is well illustrated in R.K. Narayan's *The English Teacher* (Mysore: Indian Thought Publishers, 1955), published in 1946 on the eve of inde-

however, British patriotism could invoke English literature as the specific historical, social and cultural product of Britain to advance its nationalist ideology during various historical crises.[19] The recognition of a 'national' literature carries a different charge for liberal critics in contemporary Britain. Colin MacCabe, for instance, has argued that it no longer makes sense for Britain to aggrandize a national culture 'in an era which sees a growing internationalisation and localisation of cultural production.'[20]

In India recent historical researches have initiated more critical investigations of colonial education policies and the effects that followed from them. In many of the former colonies, cultural movements of resurgence and nationalism have also led to the position that the hegemony of English language and literature in these societies is a form of continuing cultural imperialism.[21] The conditions that promote such post-colonial critiques are complex and various. Among them must be included such historical developments and political positions as the diminution of Britain's global power; the increase in India's economic and military status; the consequent tokenism of such post-colonial affiliations as the Commonwealth; the formation of significant third world alliances such as the Non-Aligned Movement (NAM) and the South Asian Association for Regional Co-operation (SAARC); global support for the anti-apartheid movement; third world vigilance against economic exploitation and neo-colonization by multinational corporations and international funding agencies; and, significantly, the anti-English propaganda of certain national political parties in response to internal divisive tendencies within the country.

The earlier unproblematic conversion of English literature into, simply, 'literature', something possessing universal and trans-historical

---

pendence. The eponymous hero, Krishna, even as he rebels at the methods of English *teaching* ('a whole century of false education'), venerates English literature itself: 'What fool could be insensible to Shakespeare's sonnets or *The Ode to the West Wind* or "A Thing of Beauty is a joy for ever"!' (220, 221)

[19] See Terence Hawkes, *That Shakespeherian Rag: Essays on a Critical Process* (London and New York: Methuen, 1966).

[20] MacCabe, 'The State of the Subject', 8.

[21] Michael Thorpe labels the 'revisionist literature and history' produced by intellectuals in newly liberated nations 'biased', and 'intimidating' to 'guilt-stricken whites'! See 'Calling the Kettle Black: Some Thoughts on "Cultural Imperialism"', *Encounter*, December 1989, 40-4, esp.41.

values which could form a component of the 'humanities' (in education) and of 'culture' (in society), is qualified by the recognition—historical or simply polemical—of its specific and circumscribed origins in a nation that has ceased to be an empire. Simultaneously, the English language, despite its imposition upon the colony, has developed into an international commodity with merely a privileged connection with the English nation.

THE LANGUAGE DEBATE

The position of English in different third world countries, or even among Britain's former colonies, is not identical. In India, English is only a second language in most states, after Hindi or the regional languages; but it also shares the status of the official national language with Hindi, and hence is the language of state administration and the law courts. The chief importance of English in India—as in other non-English-speaking nations—is its global currency; as the language of technology and international commerce it serves as an important communication link. While its widespread use, prestige, and even expansion in India in recent decades are rationalized by this development—which is more properly attributable to the post-war hegemony of the United States than to the British empire—the preserve of English in India is guarded by interests predominantly defined by ideology, region and class.

Therefore 'English'—not simply the language, but the locus of a set of values loosely termed 'westernization'—must be viewed within an essentially *conflictual* social dynamics. I identify the chief parties to the conflict in three areas: the first is between the opposed advocates of a national language; the second is between linguistic regions; and the third is between the privileged and the less privileged classes.

For advocates of Hindi, the use of English is *anti*-national because it displaces the 'rashtrabhasha', Hindi. The colonial origins and the undeniable foreignness of English obviously validate this argument. But English is precisely claimed by *its* advocates as the pan-Indian, the link, the *national* language, the logic being that it is not the first language of any specific Indian region,[22] as well as that it is the language of ad-

---

[22] English is the state language of four states in the north-east, Manipur, Meghalaya, Nagaland, and Tripura, and of all the union territories except Delhi. But it cannot be called the 'native' language of any of these regions.

ministration: the 'nation', as Aijaz Ahmad points out, is in this argument 'co-terminal with the state itself.'[23]

More crucially, English figures in the conflict between linguistic regions as the 'lesser evil'. While Hindi is the language of roughly half the Indian population, the other half speaks a multitude of languages unrelated to it.[24] Therefore the continuation of English in these states ensures that there will be no imposition of Hindi. 'If English, which protects us like a shield, is banished, the Hindi sword will cut us to pieces', warned M. Karunanidhi, chief minister of Tamilnadu.[25] Major language riots took place in Tamilnadu in 1965, exiling the Congress party from power in the state and bringing in the DMK and AIADMK parties on anti-Hindi planks. The much-touted three-language formula was evolved soon afterwards as a solution to the language problem in school education, but it was never implemented with any vigour. With this curious function—of imposing an equality of handicap on learners from all regions—English finds perhaps its most powerful *raison d'etre* in India.

Finally, and in a sense subserving these opposed interests, is the fact that English is the asset enjoyed by the English-speaking upper classes; the lack of it is a handicap suffered by the rest, traditionally known as the masses. It has thus constituted the most visible divide between the ruling classes and the ruled. In an acute and penetrating essay, D.L. Sheth argues that the recent anti-English crusade in the Hindi belt must be located in the context of the more recent changes in social structures:

the debate reflects a conflict over power in society between two elite groups: the nationally entrenched English-educated elite and the new but ascendant elite sans the trappings of an English education. The former have successfully managed to continue and tighten their hold on the levers of power at the national level since independence. They control the higher echelons of politics, bureaucracy, armed forces, corporate business and the professions.

[23] Aijaz Ahmad, '"Third World Literature" and the Nationalist Ideology', *Journal of Arts & Ideas*, 17-18 June 1989, 117-36, esp.125.

[24] The claim that Hindi is the 'majority' language has been questioned by C. Rajagopalachari, among others. According to the linguistic census of 1961, only 23 per cent of the population knew Hindi well (this number is likely to be much higher now). Hindi is spoken in only fifteen states, and even in many of these there are several dialects unrelated to Hindi. See K.V. Lakshmana, 'Looming Threat of a Language Divide', *The Hindu*, 26 August 1990.

[25] Quoted by V. Jayantha, 'A Ploy to thrust Hindi', *The Hindu*, 26 August 1990.

The members of the latter group have, as a result of democratic politics, risen at the regional level and come to exercise power in the states for the last three decades. They are now attempting to create for themselves spaces in the power structure at the national level. (They are known by various names: regional elite, rural elite, mofussils or simply kulaks.) The differences between the two are indexed in terms of their urban–rural and caste backgrounds. While there is some overlap between them in economic terms, the sharp differences between them in socio-cultural terms are marked by the language divide. In the life-world of the former, English occupies a central role; for the latter its role is at best marginal . . . the regional elite . . . because of the numbers they represent . . . are seeking to change not only the terms of discourse on the language issue in their favour but are generally proceeding to challenge the role the English-educated elite have been playing since independence, both as norm-setters and pace-setters of India's public life.[26]

Given that English is the site of these several and overlapping conflicts between ideologies, linguistic regions and classes, it is necessary to be clear about the material consequences of the choice of national language. Language in society can be hegemonic in two spheres: culture and education. Though the distinction between them is not an absolute one, in India we may usefully, if broadly, distinguish between the spread of *Hindi* in the cultural arena, and the influence of *English* in education.

In spite of its central importance, English in India is less widely perceived as a cultural and linguistic threat to indigenous literatures and languages than it has been, for instance, in Africa, where its colonial imposition displaced or marginalized entire cultures. The languages and literatures of India, many of them older and better developed than English, did not altogether languish in the shadow of a hegemonic English; and the phenomenon of bilingualism (and even trilingualism) has divided up the spheres of actual language use in such a way that English and Indian languages co-exist in a fairly natural way within social discourse.[27] In post-Independence India the reorganization of states on a linguistic basis, the vigorous development of print media in the regional languages, and the rise of new socio-cultural groups that have been educated through the medium of a regional language are all factors that have contributed to the influence of Indian languages.[28]

[26] D.L. Sheth, 'No English Please, We're Indian', *The Illustrated Weekly of India*, 19 August 1990, 34-7, esp.35.

[27] Amitav Ghosh, 'The Novel in a Multilingual Society', unpublished paper.

[28] Sheth, 36.

All this is not to deny the profound and pervasive influence of English literature on colonial and post-Independence Indian literatures and criticism. This history, and features of this influence, are matters too vast to be gone into here.[29] Periodic crises of conscience occur among writers seeking to write 'as Indians'; but, as U.R. Anantha Murthy has pointed out, no simple option to re-write history exists for Indian artists. Even when the contemporary writer seeks to write for 'the masses', he is confronted with the issue of literacy before that of language. The small reading public that exists is one 'whose sensibility [has been] formed by a study of English literature'—and it is within 'the defined frameworks of the cultural and literary expectations' of this group that the writer is obliged to create —unless he can resurrect an oral tradition.[30] Therefore the forms of fiction, the metrics of poetry, the conventions of theatre— the very sensibility and politics of Indian literature—are often derivative, even when the language is Indian.

Beyond the influence of the high cultural product—literature—there is also the widespread use of English in journalism—a fifth of all newspapers are English language dailies; and in academic publications—a third of all Indian publishing is in English. Entertainment productions from the west—the best-selling paperback, the video film—Western music, Hollywood cinema, the western theatre, the local imitations of all these—are also popular and influential, the reach and speed of their transmission being enormously increased by the advances in telecommunication and print technology.

But it is the more striking popularity of Hindi cinema and television programmes that is responsible for the significant development, in recent years, of something like a pan-Indian culture, dubious and contested though it may be. These 'ground level forces', as Sheth terms them,[31] are likely to eventually assure Hindi a cultural hegemony, with the consequence of a reduction in the importance of English as a cultural resource. Regional cultures, even as they seem to resist the imposition of

---

[29] For an account of the influence of western 'realism' on Indian fiction, see Meenakshi Mukherjee, *Realism and Reality* (Delhi: Oxford University Press, 1985). See also Harish Trivedi, 'Reading English, Writing Hindi: Indian Writers and English Literature', in Joshi, ed.

[30] U.R. Anantha Murthy, 'The Search for an Identity: A Kannada Writer's Viewpoint', in *Dialogue: New Cultural Identities*, ed. Guy Amirthanayagam (London: Macmillan, 1982), 66-78, esp. 78.

[31] Sheth, 36.

national TV in Hindi and the hegemony of commercial Hindi cinema, neverthless inevitably succumb to their influence.

The combined and contested hegemonies of English and Hindi in the arena of culture have resulted in a form of hybridization that the popular columnist Jug Suraiya has lampooned as an aspect of Indian 'postmodernism':

In post-modern India, there is a resurgence of nationalism . . . It is a nationalism of ethnic chic. . . . a neo-indigenous identity based on mirror-image mimesis, containing element of self-consciousness, if not self-parody . . . This mirage of a mirage is a refraction largely caused by the electronic distortion generated by television, the intangible, all-pervasive rainbow bridge between post-modern India and unregenerate Bharat. The contemporary battle of Kurukshetra is being waged in the televisionary ether, whizzing with the missiles that are the message of conspicuous commercialism.

In the new mythology, the Janus face of India has found an appropriate double-speak in 'Hinglish' or 'Hindlish' . . . This pseudo-demotic idiom, claimed by its advocates to be a linguistic triumph of post-colonial India, gives voice to our national split personality . . . So-called 'Hindlish' lacks both reach and resonance, except within its own solipsistic context.[32]

This hybrid linguistic product may be defended of course, both as the historically inevitable indigenization of a foreign language (in line with the assimilation of Sanskrit and Persian in India's earlier history), as well as a creative enrichment of both the Indian and English languages.[33]

This postmodern hybrid culture is, as Suraiya stresses, the product of the new middle classes and, specifically, of their consumerism. The phenomenon of a vastly expanded middle class, formed by the entry of new upwardly mobile social groups into the traditional ruling elites, has resulted in a change in the cultural outlook of this class. They are perceived to be 'more in tune with the global metropolitan world', out of touch with regional cultures, and incapable of the kind of bilingualism that earlier educated elites (Gandhi, Tagore, Tilak) possessed. In short 'they lack the cultural basis to their political power.'[34]

[32] Jug Suraiya, 'The chips are down for post-modern Hindi', *The Times of India*, 19 June 1990.

[33] See Braj Kachru, 'Indian English', *Seminar 359*, July 1989 (Special Issue on Literature and Society), 30-5. For a disquisition on the 'amazing mix, the English we speak', see the opening pages of Upamanyu Chatterjee's *English, August: An Indian Story* (New Delhi: Rupa, 1989).

[34] Sheth, 36.

But it is primarily because English is the chief, even sole, language of official administration in the country that knowledge of it is crucial for white-collar job-seekers. It therefore remains a major component of Indian higher education. This demand and supply situation is hard to destabilize through political intervention alone. Though state governments have on occasion removed the English requirement in their schools and colleges as a populist measure, the proliferation of bazaar institutes, private English medium ('convent') schools, and—in extreme instances, as in Nepal—even the emigration of students to areas offering English education, are indications of the pursuit of English by aspiring white-collar job-seekers. What exacerbates the elitism of English speakers is the prevalence of what Sheth has termed the 'dual system' of education: the existence of (a small number of) expensive public schools where English is the medium of instruction from the lowest classes, along with (a preponderance of) regional-language schools, for the most part run by governments or municipalities, where English is taught—badly—as a subject for a few years.[35] The continuing availability of, and recourse to, English has also prevented the sustained and systematic development of Indian languages for technical and higher education purposes, and even of viable translation schemes.

All this has implications for how English is taught. Clearly it must be taught 'better'. Since the demand for functional, specific, goal-directed language pedagogy is reflected only in a few school and university syllabi—in most cases it is the 'classic' texts, including Shakespeare, that are used for imparting language skills—there is a trend towards such teaching moving out of the academic arena of schools and colleges. The mushrooming of bazaar institutes offering crash courses in spoken English and for a variety of other 'real life' communication purposes—interviews, exams, business correspondence—is an indication of the marketplace response to this need.

The radical move would be the universal adoption of an Indian language as the medium of instruction in *all* schools, with English taught uniformly as a second language, or as a subject.[36] English literary studies would then lose some of their rationale as language courses.[37]

---

[35] Sheth, 37.
[36] Various educational committees, from the nineteenth century onwards, have been recommending this step, without success.
[37] Yasmeen Lukmani concludes, on the basis of a study she conducted, that English literature is studied primarily as a means of acquiring language

They might then move—if they do not wish to continue as the cloned version of Eng. Lit. in the Anglo-American academy—more meaningfully into the area of cultural studies.

Any consideration of the teaching of English, however, cannot confine itself only to the conflictual language situation in the country; it must also take into account the scene of education—which partakes of the conflict but extends beyond its dimensions.

THE SCENE OF EDUCATION

In a country where more than half the country's population lacks basic literacy skills, where only 3 per cent of the national income is spent on education, and where (compulsory) primary education receives only 10 per cent of this amount, the place of English—as it is framed within the humanities in the structure of university education—must seem a consideration of infinitesimal importance. But the other side of the picture is the disproportionate emphasis and consequent expenditure on higher education in the country (85 per cent of the total outlay, on 2 per cent of the population).[38] University education is so highly subsidized as to be virtually free, and there are no minimum admission requirements except a high school pass. This situation has been attributed to the pressures exerted by the middle class lobby in the country.[39] As higher

---

proficiency. See her 'Attitudinal Orientation towards Studying English Literature in India', in this volume.

[38] A recent study conducted by the Operation Research Group reveals that 57 per cent adults (15 years plus) in the country are illiterate. The situation is worse in the Hindi belt (80 per cent illiteracy), among rural areas (twice that in urban areas), and among women. Illiteracy levels are higher even than poverty levels. See 'Illiteracy level higher than poverty', *The Times of India*, 17 December 1990. The amount spent on higher education has been computed in several ways. Badri Raina, quoting from the *Challenge of Education* report of 1986, says that Rs 4775.3 crores would be allotted for general education during the annual plan for 1990-1, of which only Rs 1830.45 crores would be intended for elementary education. See 'Education Old and New—A Perspective', *Social Scientist* 17, 9-10, September-October 1989, 4-13, esp.9. See also Amrik Singh, 'Higher Education is a White Elephant', *The Times of India*, 22 April 1989. Singh is scandalized at the budgeted expenditure of Rs 4000 crores on higher education in the eighth plan.

[39] Amrik Singh, 'Pressure Groups set Educational Pattern', *The Times of India*, 13 January 1990.

education empowers the bourgeoisie, the latter inevitably influence the shape of Indian education. Amartya Sen sees in the 'injustice of keeping a large majority of the people illiterate while the elite enjoys the benefits of a vast system of higher education . . . the firm grip of the elite'. This is visible in practically every sphere of social activity in India, so that while 'dramatic deprivations and new sufferings' (such as starvation) are prevented, the 'quiet continuation of an astonishing set of persistent injustices' is allowed.[40]

What large-scale illiteracy at one end, and large-scale unemployment among college-educated youth at the other, indicate is that university education exists in a kind of limbo unconnected with the realities of either word or world.[41] From among the privileged few who acquire a higher education, there is an even smaller elite which finds suitable employment.

Vinod Sena has diagnosed the major post-Independence development in higher education that has, paradoxically, accompanied the enormous expansion in student enrolment and in the number of new colleges and universities to accommodate them—the narrowing down of the *conception* of the university. As research, specialization, and 'development'-oriented studies have grown in importance, technology, medicine, management, economics, statistics, and the pure sciences and mathematics have moved into autonomous institutions *outside* the ambit of the university. The university has, as a consequence, shrunk to the location of undergraduate and postgraduate science and arts courses. Not only are most of the available funds for research directed towards these prestigious institutions, the university also loses that exchange of ideas across disciplines which is its traditional hallmark.[42] As one college teacher puts it feelingly, the university, 'reduced to the status of a

---

[40] Amartya Sen, 'How is India Doing', in *The Indian Economy and its Performance since Independence*, ed. R.A. Chaudhury *et al.* (Delhi: Oxford University 1990), reprinted in *Express Magazine*, 17 June 1990.

[41] V.A. Pai Panandikar, 'Paradox of Unemployment: Failings of the Educational System', *The Times of India*, 1 May 1989. Panandikar quotes a figure of 2.8 million university graduates registered with employment exchanges in India. He blames not so much the shortage of jobs for this situation, but (a) the mismatch between the demand in the employment sector and the supply of suitably qualified students, and (b) poor educational standards.

[42] Vinod Sena, 'University Grants Commission: Maker or Undertaker?' *The Hindustan Times Magazine*, 24 January 1988.

pseudo-industry . . . is expected to accept without protest the satellite role of a caretaker institution or creche',[43] absorbing social unrest among the young and semi-educated, mostly urban, youth.

The politics of the university is as crucial as its structure. Those who berate the elitism of higher education in India demand either a reduction of expenditure on universities (read: teachers' salaries), or a privatization of colleges (read: cost-effectivity through higher fees),[44] but rarely urge an *overall* increase in the budgetary allocation to education, which is still among the lowest in the world. The conflict between the state and the university is a more or less vexed feature of all contemporary societies—and in post-Emergency India it has been an exacerbated one. The progressive centralization of education was initiated by the transfer of education from the state to the concurrent list, then strengthened by the introduction of the repressive Hospitals and other Institutions Bill (1979) in Parliament, the devolution of powers to the University Grants Commission as a central bureaucratic regulatory body, and, most recently, by the recommendations of the New Education Policy 1986 for accreditation and autonomy of colleges.[45]

Thus we have the paradox of the seemingly privileged situation of higher education coexisting with ceaseless government attempts to control, trivialize, and bureaucratize it. The university is perceived as a place that both *contains* social unrest (hence vast enrolments and subsidies), as well as *foments* it (hence the threats to privatize it, regulate teachers' and students' unions and control the content of education).

The humanities—fast developing into the major branch of learning offered by the typical university—occupy the same confused and contested ground. The emphasis on technology and science in a developing country, the greater employment opportunities for those opting for professional courses, the irrelevance, obsolescence and trivialization of most arts courses—all this marks the devaluation of the humanities.[46]

---

[43] Amrit Srinivasan, Letter to the Editor, *The Times of India*, 10 September, 1987.

[44] Amrik Singh, 'Vested Interests of College Teachers', *The Times of India*, 24 March 1990, and 'Higher Education is a White Elephant'. Raina agrees that elementary education is neglected, but stresses the need to raise the *total* expenditure on education from the present 2.5 per cent of the total public outlay to 10 per cent of GNP (9,13).

[45] Raina, 8.

[46] For a survey of student preferences among college courses at admission time, see Rajdeep Sardesai, 'Arts *vs* Science *vs* Commerce', *Sunday Review*, 27

The largest numbers of students, however, still fill undergraduate arts classes on account of undemanding admission and performance requirements in these areas.[47] The courses themselves proliferate effortlessly, partly because they require little investment in hardware or equipment beyond blackboards and desks,[48] and partly because token acknowledgements are still periodically made in official policy to the need for the nourishment of the 'spirit' through the encouragement of the humanities.[49] We must also note that for a small intellectual and class-conscious elite who *opt* for the humanities (instead of entering it as a last resort like the majority), its very 'irrelevance' represents the privilege of a liberal education, and a mode of entry into the generalist but highly influential fields of bureaucracy, law, journalism, communications and academia.[50] Consider also that the *content* of the humanities, however diluted—even as it functions to transmit a hegemonic 'culture'—is also potentially critical, subversive and radical. Together, these

----

May 1990. Sardesai points out that out of 165 colleges affiliated to Bombay University, 32 colleges offer only commerce, 43 have arts, science and commerce courses, while a further 22 colleges hold arts and commerce classes. Commerce has therefore become the 'dominant degree'. Arts is favoured by girl students because it is perceived as a more 'comfortable' degree, while science and commerce 'are associated with long-term careers'. In a typical Bombay college, there were 575 girls in the degree arts course, as opposed to 86 boys.

[47] Panandikar bemoans the fact that arts students rarely attend classes. Most employers hold standardized recruitment tests of their own since university degrees have become a farce.

[48] See Alok Rai, 'Out There: An English Teacher in the Provinces', in Joshi ed.

[49] Raina quotes the first University Education Commission's report (1948): 'If we wish to bring about a savage upheavel in our society, a *raksasa raj*, all that we need to do is to give vocational and technical education and starve the spirit' (8). Subsequent reports, including the 1986 Challenge of Education report, make the same point.

[50] Thus, Sardesai makes the point that humanities students have an edge in the public service examinations, and that company executives are frequently 'generalists, not specialists'. There are also 'growth' fields like tourism, hoteliering and advertising which absorb arts graduates. These observations are exemplified in *English, August*, where the hero, Agastya Sen, an IAS officer, has an English degree from Harvard; and his friend Dhrubo, who works in a multinational bank, has a doctorate from Yale!

qualifications of the overall situation of the humanities serve to invest a university arts degree with a small measure of significance.

What this fluid situation indicates is that the humanities in Indian university education cannot, without severe contradiction, be enshrined as the repository of humanist values, culture, and spirit in the way they have been in the countries of the industrial developed west; but neither will they simply go away as relics of the past or as recrudescences of the changed present.

To identify English in the Indian university curriculum unproblematically with the humanities, we would have to ignore its genealogical and ideological import. As Suvir Kaul warns in his essay in this volume, for us to reproduce the preservation and propagation of the central texts of the humanist tradition that Anglo-American literary studies calls for is to 'shut our eyes to the historical complicity of philosophy and politics, pedagogy and ideology, culture and imperialism.'[51]

This partakes of the larger debate over the indigenization of Indian education. Both the structure and the content of university education in India are, of course, based upon the British model, and have remained largely unchanged in the post-Independence decades. While the need for a greater responsiveness to contemporary Indian realities is urgent, the option of a return to the past through an idealization of ancient Indian centres of learning and systems of education is as ideologically suspect as it is impractical.[52] The fossilization of the study of English literature is part of the overall resistance to the forces of change visible in higher education as a whole. Further, since a high degree of specialization prevails in the Honours degree programmes, English literature, like other subjects, is studied in a relatively isolated and hence largely irrelevant way. The equivalent of a liberal arts programme is available only in the devalued 'Pass' courses. Any notion of interdisciplinarity would find resistance from both the structure of the system as it currently exists as well as the disciplinary rigidity of 'English' itself. There is a conspicuous refusal of alliance between English and other language departments in colleges. Many English Honours courses have no second language requirement; and the study of a 'subsidiary' subject is more honoured in the breach than in the observance.

[51] Suvir Kaul, 'The Indian Academic and Resistance to Theory'.

[52] Dharam Pal's pioneering research work, *The Beautiful Tree: Indian Education in the Eighteenth Century* (New Delhi: Biblia Impex, 1983), is, nonetheless, guilty of such an idealization of pre-colonial education.

What the larger scene of education reveals therefore is the anomalous position of university education in a context of large-scale illiteracy, as the site of both privilege and state controls; the simultaneous importance and devaluation of the humanities within this structure; and the retention of 'English' within the humanities in imitation of the western model without a matching rationale for such incorporation.

With a narrowing of focus upon the university as providing one of the major *institutional contexts* for the study of a subject, we shall be able to see how it works by both authorizing as well as excluding what might be counted as knowledge (here, by framing the syllabus, or course content); by stipulating the ends or purposes for which it shall be imparted (here, by devising the means of testing and evaluating the knowledge acquired); and finally by determining who shall learn, and who shall teach it, and under what conditions (here, admission requirements, the employment of teachers, the material conditions of work, pedagogic practices). It is the workings of the university as an institution in this sense, as well as the support provided to it by publishing houses, the foreign cultural agency, and the metropolitan university, that are explored in the following essays.

The location of English studies within its institutional context in this country, which this volume attempts, does not, admittedly, take into sufficient account the variety of colleges within the country, and even within a single city; the high degree of stratification that exists between undergraduate colleges and post-graduate university departments; regional differences among universities; the differences of status and standards between older ('presidency') universities and more recent ones, between central and state universities, between the metropolitan cities and the 'mofussil' towns—and is therefore guilty of a number of generalizations. But as striking as the heterogeneity of educational institutions in the country is the remarkable *homogeneity* of syllabi, examination systems and teaching practices. This is the result both of centralized system-making as well as the unresponsiveness and inflexibility of education to local circumstances and historical changes on the ground. Thus, while there is scope for a more nuanced analysis of specific disciplines and universities, it is nevertheless possible, without falsification, to talk of a certain 'English' in 'the Indian university'.

CONCLUSION : CRISIS IN ENGLISH STUDIES?

There are at least two objections that could be raised at any announcement of a crisis in English studies in India. One would be simple disagreement about such a reading of the situation; as a college teacher remarked at a seminar on the subject, the only crisis in English studies in India is that there is no crisis. And indeed the powerful hold of the *status quo* in English departments—the counter-resistance to resistance —is remarkable. Arguments that the colonial past of English is an irrelevant consideration, and hence/or that English literature is a repository of universal values—or even a simple disregard of the whole issue—are still current and influential positions.[53] Nevertheless universities—and still less postgraduate departments within it—are not the only places to look to for change. The winds of change blow from and across the entire national scene. The essays in this volume are premised upon a felt need for change, if not the actual perception of it, among a portion of the English-teaching community responding to the pressures upon English in India.

The second objection could be a more cynical observation to the effect that 'our' crisis is only a (characteristically) belated imitation of 'theirs'. While happenings in the Anglo-American academy have their inevitable impact on the study of English elsewhere in the world, we might broadly distinguish between the *internal* destabilization of the discipline there, and the factors—which I have been at some pains to identify in the preceding pages—which bring it to crisis from the *outside* here, in India. Eng. Lit. in America (and to a smaller extent in Britain) has been problematized, in the immediate institutional context, by a radical rethinking of issues of textuality and interpretation emerging from two locii, continental theory and feminist politics—themselves, of course, aspects of a larger historical situation,[54] but not reducible to it. In India the specific features of post-colonial issues, language politics, and the state of higher education provide a different context for viewing the situation of English studies.

No contributor to this volume—or anyone who engages with the issue elsewhere—envisages a simple abolition of English as a solution to the problem, even when she questions its privileged status in the curriculum. The reasons why the issue cannot be addressed in the more straightforward polemical tone employed by Ngugi wa Thiongo in the

[53] See Suvir Kaul's essay for illustrative 'anecdotes' of the 'resistance to theory' among senior faculty members—which is equally a resistance to all threats of change.

[54] This historical area has been usefully marked out by Aijaz Ahmad (118-25).

essays in *Decolonizing the Mind,* or the contributors to *Toward the Dec-olonisation of African Literature,*[55] and why a more cautions and nego-tiated approach seems to be called for, require some consideration. I shall state the most obvious—and indeed perhaps the most prag-matic—of them first. This is with regard to the stakes which we, as professional teachers of English literature in the university, have in the continuation and perpetuation of the subject in our educational institu-tions. The somewhat farcial situation of English teachers resigning *en masse* as a result of a crisis of conscience is not envisaged.[56] A second and less self-serving motive for wishing to change, rather than abolish, the face of English lies in the implicit understanding that *English* literature is, theoretically and technically, the most developed of the disciplinary literary studies we have in the Indian academy, and that, for better or worse, it stands in for the humanities by providing (however meagrely) the equivalent of a liberal education. For many teachers of English the subject seems to be worth retaining because the values associated with 'culture' as a whole are found in the curriculum (at present only) in English.[57] Several contributors to this volume express yet another and similarly pragmatic reason for not calling for radical changes—that teachers of English themselves are in no position to effect them, being only part of a larger system that authorizes the structure of English studies, and which is too large, monolithic and bureaucratic to respond to pressures from below.[58]

But the single most crucial reason for wishing not to jeopardize the position of English goes beyond the constraints of the academy and is linked to the politics of language and region in the country. Elsewhere I spoke of the dangers of a certain kind of critique of colonial history:

[55] Ngugi wa Thiong'o, *Decolonizing the Mind and Other Essays* (London: Heinemann, 1986), and Chinweizu, *et al., Toward the Decolonization of African Literature* (Washington, D.C: Howard University Press, 1983).

[56] Ania Loomba defends her advocacy of an 'alternative pedagogy' which 'appropriates' the book instead of 'throw[ing] it out'. Any other position would be unrealistic, she argues, because we are teachers 'who are not about to resign our jobs *en masse'.* See *Gender, Race, Renaissance Drama* (Manchester: Manchester University Press, 1989), 33.

[57] This, of course, is a distinctly Arnoldian position, and one that Alok Rai would appear to subscribe to, in 'Out There'.

[58] See the essays by Tejaswini Niranjana and Ania Loomba in this volume. Rimli Bhattacharya, in contrast, makes the teacher's role more central to the active process of change.

It is all too easy to proceed from our awareness of our historically—and ideologically—enshrined colonialist relationship to English literature, to a search for 'roots' and origins and the recovery of a 'lost' native tradition. Such a simple either/or alternative seeking can be misleading. We are historically constituted to the extent of not being able to afford 'self-marginalization' (the phrase is Spivak's), by alienating ourselves from all western knowledge. More crucially, in our country and in the present political conditions, nationalistic anti-imperialism takes the form of a particularly violent Hindu revivalism whose backlash is generally felt by the nation's minority communities.[59]

For many English teachers the removal/reduction/alteration of English as a *response* to fundamentalist nationalistic, demands for Hindi or regional language study—translated into a revival of 'Hindutva'—is likely to seem counterproductive and a capitulation. This dilemma, at the same time, cannot serve as a rationalization for leaving the situation of English untouched, and embalming the *status quo* .

Given these complexities, teachers of English engaging with the issue of English are limited to strategic moves and counter-moves. In this volume the contributors variously address themselves to the possi- bilities of radical pedagogy, the expansion of the canon of 'classical' English literary texts (to include literatures in English by 'Common- wealth' and other third world writers, English translations of Indian texts, etc.), the study of comparative or world literatures, interdiscipli- nary cultural studies, and theory, as ways out of the impasse of English literary studies—even as they recognize that teaching strategies, finally, only beg the question of the legitimacy of the English text in our literary curriculums.

The question of alternatives, in any case, can never be resolved once and for all: the packaging of such solutions would precisely foreclose the essential debate, discussion and consultation among those concerned, which is the crucial preliminary step. The title of this volume makes transparent the politics and purpose of this book—the one issuing out of the shared experience of the inauthenticity of teaching English in our land, and the other announcing the intention to chart the territory of text and world that will begin the search for alternatives.

---

[59] Sunder Rajan, 32.

2

English In a Literate Society

GAURI VISWANATHAN

I could not help being overcome by a sense of *déjà vu* on reading some of the essays in this collection. Institutional apathy, inflexible syllabi, cynical students, demoralized teachers: these are uncannily familiar echoes of laments heard tragically too many times before. I pulled out my old file of minutes, reports, and observations from a workshop for college teachers of English in Delhi that I helped organize in 1981 under the auspices of the Department of Education, and was startled to see the structural continuity of diagnosis, rhetoric, and argument between the two sets of papers. My initial reaction was one of unalleviated depression: has there been so little change over the years?

All the same, there is one heartening difference, and that is the much greater acceptance today of education as a subject worth talking about. I recall that, ten years ago, for every English teacher (usually from the so-called peripheral colleges of Delhi) who was deeply concerned about the teaching of English in a multilingual, pluralistic society such as ours, there were five who felt discussions of pedagogy, curriculum, and 'national' and 'local' needs were irrelevant to their own scholarly interests, and that these were better left to sociologists and specialists in education, whose expertise in school education presumably made them more equipped to deal with the 'practical' requirements of English instruction.

What then has changed in the last decade in India to produce the sense of 'crisis' and 'embattlement', so much so that it has engendered a spurt of conferences and seminars recently on English studies? What has brought about a new-found interest in issues of pedagogy and educational reform, especially by members of 'elite' colleges and universities? If one were to answer in terms of 'post-colonial consciousness', one would still have to explain why such a sensibility (assuming that there is such a monster) should make its presence felt on English teaching more strongly within the last decade than at any other time in the last four decades of Indian independence. Is the sense of crisis itself a foreign import, a reflection of the contestations and upheavals that English studies are undergoing elsewhere?

Cynical critics might respond in the affirmative in order to launch a crusade against the techniques of reading that have become associated with these contestations—which increasingly find adherents among younger Indian academics. Undoubtedly, this is a reactionary response of the most dangerous kind, substituting complacency and condescension for reflection and dialogue. But the fact that such a criticism can be made at all heightens the urgency of rooting our critiques in the present historical and political situation, rather than treating issues of English pedagogy and criticism as somehow divorced from other, related trends in Indian education—trends such as the increasing divergence between centre and state on policies relating to English, the disparate allocation of resources for teaching English and other vernacular languages in rural and urban areas, and the splitting of Indian education into vocational and liberal arts streams.

All this is a preliminary way of saying that I am somewhat worried that the (much needed) challenges to English studies currently being made in India seem not to have any identifiable reference point in recent Indian history, politics, or sociology. One looks in vain for references to proposed or actual legislation mooted in various Indian states to abolish English altogether; to the (pernicious) effects of the National Educational Policy of 1986; to the introduction of select Navodaya schools in specific districts and their implications for perpetuating elitist education; to the demand for English education by the new rural rich; to the declining rate of literacy in the country at large; to the expansion of higher education at the expense of primary education; to the increasing voices on behalf of 'merit' and against reservations. The diagnoses of the ills of English in terms of institutional inertia, outmoded critical and pedagogic practices, and a rigid, archaic syllabus are too restricted; but also, the sense of crisis in English studies recorded in recent discussions appears not to emerge out of any specific conjuncture of historical events or policies.

In this essay I want to direct attention to two recent developments—the setting up of Navodaya schools and the decline in literacy across the nation—which I think bear significantly on English studies today. At first glance it would appear that neither development is particularly relevant in the present volume, which focuses mainly on literary studies at the university level. How can teaching at the school level, and even more so at the primary-school level, have any relation to the teaching of academic specializations in universities? This sense of the unrelatedness of school education, however, drastically undermines the potential usefulness of critiques of higher education, which suffer from a continued neglect of, and indifference to, the education that precedes it at the primary and secondary level.[1] The disseverance of school from university education, which is so readily accepted by many today, is yet another colonial legacy that we shall have to come to terms with at some point or the other. Prior to the founding of the Indian university system in 1857 on the model of the University of London, Indian schools and colleges were more organically connected, the curriculum of the one usually extending into the other. But when the university system was introduced, it was specifically established as an examining rather than teaching body, a centralized mechanism for bringing to the attention of the British government those students of 'merit' who might be inducted into government service. Because of their function as instruments of bureaucratic selection, these centralized university examinations virtually made teaching subordinate, if not irrelevant, in the larger educational enterprise. University education bore little continuity with the aims of secondary education, and university degrees, linked as they so closely were with employment, acquired an autonomous value. Learning, knowledge, inquiry: these were no longer the motivating principles in the education of Indian youth. Rather, a nebulous concept of 'excellence' was promoted that was best measured in terms of the distinctions that the university examinations and a university system percolated down to the secondary-school level, which too became an instrument for selection and advancement, in this case to the tertiary level of education.

If the linking of employment with education explicitly created an elitist bias in recruitment processes, the disseverance of the two would appear to be an obligatory post-colonial response. And indeed the 'delinking' of jobs from degrees is one of the slogans bandied about since independence to give a more egalitarian thrust and meaning to the

---

[1] Incidentally, for those who are curious about such things as 'generic rupture' and 'generic transformation', it has always seemed to me an interesting and worthwhile question to ask how 'reading comprehension', which is the name that the study of English goes by in schools, metamorphoses into 'literature' in the university study of English, and how linguistic understanding gets transformed into literary criticism.

content of Indian education, even as it sought a more positive reconceptualization of education as an end in and for itself. But the whole idea of 'education for its own sake' has turned out, in many instances, to be no less exclusionary. The Navodaya schools are a good example of such misguided ventures that attempted to decontextualize 'excellence', only to enthrone it even more firmly in a selective, competitive system transplanted to rural areas.

In the wave of educational promises and dreams that flourished in the years immediately following independence, equalization of educational opportunity and universal literacy were consistently the two ideals to which every education commission set up in those years routinely expressed its full commitment. The National Educational Policy of 1986, however, abruptly reversed the goals of the earlier commission reports. Its most controversial proposal remains to date the setting up of the Navodaya schools as model institutions of learning for rural India. In the original proposal mooted by the Rajiv Gandhi government, 433 Navodaya schools were to be built, one in every district of the country. Admission to these schools was based on examinations taken by students who had passed the fifth class from every district, all of whom would be competing for eighty seats in the sixth class of every Navodaya school. Each school was intended to be residential, situated in a large verdant stretch of land, and fully equipped with technological aids, computers, audio-visual supplements, trained teachers, and new syllabi characterized by a distinctly social and cultural orientation. To promote national integration, sixteen students from each school were to be relocated to a school in another part of the country where they would live in residence and interact with a different cultural and regional environment.

On the surface this sounds very utopian—a state-supported school system that banishes arbitrary distinctions between rural and urban, rich and poor, regional and national. However, its promise is belied by the 'Challenge of Education' document that preceded the National Education Policy. A monument to pious posturing, the document claimed to eliminate the urban bias in 'quality' education even as it reproduced its very inequalities in rural education. That posturing comes out most tellingly in the section of the manifesto that dealt with the self-selection of students from urban schools to prestigious professional degree colleges. Without even a trace of irony or self-scrutiny, the document claimed that urban schools automatically guaranteed success to their graduates because they offered education in English, which by its very definition—or so we are told—gives students greater exposure to a whole host of formative influences and to a more competitive environ-ment. The 'Challenge' report asks us to believe that if rural and/or economically deprived students are to reclaim the world, the instrument for such recovery has necessarily to be an education in English. The colonial distinctions between a worldly, empirically derived knowl-edge, such as that provided by English studies, and a narrower, self-ab-sorbed learning, as the indigenous languages were thus characterized, have not merely left traces on contemporary policy; they virtually dic-tate it.

Parenthetically, I can't help noting a strange encounter I had recently with just such colonial reasoning. I had gone to visit a large residential school about 40 kilometres outside Madras. This was a much touted school (significantly, now run by the corporate sector), English-medium of course, offering the best of moral, ethical, cultural, and philosophical traditions—as the school's brochure put it. I was interested in talking to some of the English teachers there, as well as to the students, about the kinds of reading materials they were using and the way they structured the English curriculum to adapt to the school's much-publicized cul-tural agenda. Instead, I was taken around by an earnest school official to see their computers, swimming pools, squash courts, and horse stables. When I protested, saying I wanted to know more about how English literature and language were taught there, the man looked blankly at me and then muttered, 'But this is how our students learn English—they learn about the world!'

The Navodaya schools are an example of how, in the post-inde-pendence period, education still continues to grow in the framework of the old structures. This growth has not only accentuated contradictions but brought them into mutual conflict. The result is that the English-medium public school phenomenon no longer remains confined to urban areas but has also spread to rural areas with the support of state governments, especially in those states where a leadership of the rural rich has come to power. Far from blurring the urban–rural divide, the Navodaya schools can more accurately be described as the govern-ment's capitulation to pressures from the rural rich, who have become fully conscious of the value of English education in consolidating their own hegemony, not unlike the Bengali bhadralok more than a century earlier. With the Navodaya schools, the terms of educational discourse are changed: the rich–poor and urban–rural dichotomies are replaced by the bright–mediocre dichotomy, the model schools having absorbed and neutralized a larger conflict of interests between rich and poor, urban and rural. It would appear that, given the choice between mass education and the reconciliation of rural and urban interests, the government has chosen to forge a compromise among the educational interests of different ruling classes.

With the establishment of the Navodaya schools, the state sector has appropriated the English-dominated public-school model, but now under the banner of equalization of educational opportunity. There is no greater proof of the false allure of egalitarianism put forward by the model-school concept than the facile projection of the mass examinations that students take to gain admission to these schools as ideologically pure. Here too there is continuity with an earlier colonial era. Holding out the promise of uniform standards, mass examinations during the colonial period reassured the rising middle classes that the educational system was an essentially fair one, that status could indeed be attained through competitive performance. In his essay on 'The Chinese Literati', Max Weber has brilliantly shown how, in both ancient and modern systems of education, the examination system enjoys unassailable credibility precisely because it is so highly ritualized. The Indian situation is no different. It is ironic that the very things one reviles about our present examination system also ensure a semblance of equality and democratic parity. The elaborate ceremony surrounding anonymous paper setting, invigilation, and evaluation—the exaggerated self-importance of both those who set and evaluate examinations and those who take them—fuels and sustains the expectations of the bulk of people that in this impersonally-directed world of learning they too have a chance to achieve. No wonder the concept of autonomous schools and colleges does not enthuse people as much as one would expect. Autonomy entails deregulation, and deregulation casts uneasy shadows over the guarantee of equality because of the constriction of the public base upon which mass ceremonies, such as examinations, are conducted. Indeed, as some educationists argue, autonomy may be yet another code-word for further stratification and inequalities in the system.

I have singled out the Navodaya schools for special discussion, not necessarily because I think they are more pernicious than other educational designs (the fact that the Navodaya schools never really took off in a big way is worth noting), but because they exemplify the peculiar contradictions of any scheme that attempts reform of the educational system while preserving English in its present disciplinary form as the agency of such purportedly egalitarian transformations. In the Navodaya schools we come face to face with the central challenge of teaching English in India: English is asked to serve as an avenue to educational opportunity even as it creates a separate constituency. Elsewhere I have discussed this dual tendency as a 'paradox of power' in British educational policy in India.[2] There the conflict lay in the fact that education in Western culture and Western knowledge was represented as a source of greater equality, whereas the social stratification that the British policy of differentiated education endorsed produced a contrary effect of inequality. At this point I want to add only one or two observations. For the British rulers this conflict was manageable as long as it did not create additional stresses that exposed the moral pretensions of British colonialism. From our post-colonial perspective, however, the conflict cannot be allowed to remain tractable, for the very reason that a palpable irreconcilability of conflictual objectives may be the only way of laying bare the inegalitarian foundations upon which, following its colonial forebear, the present educational system rests. It is a truism to say that the longer an absolute standard is promoted as the desired object to be attained, the more invisible become the discrepancies of the system. To break out of the cycle of contradictions that is part of the history of English in India, we may very well have to court the imprecisions, distorted readings, and idiosyncratic responses that many contributors of this volume have meticulously recorded as their daily experience of teaching.

Regardless of how one might feel about the prevalence of English in India, there is a tacit acceptance by many that possessing English is the surest means of advancement. Denying people the opportunity to learn English—both its language and literature—is in many respects as presumptuous and arrogant as the Macaulayan project of enjoining its compulsory study *en masse*. As is only too well known, expressions of frustration with the teaching situation can easily camouflage resistance to the extension of education to broader segments of the population. Frustration and exasperation may indeed be coded versions of subliminal antagonisms to the effects of mass education, to the shifts in educational clientele from what Hugh Kearney calls 'scholars and gentlemen' to first-generation learners, for whom English language and literature are impossible hurdles.[3] But the sharp vibrations along the quality-equality axes—the philosophical twin poles of English education—caused by efforts to diffuse English more broadly, also force a

---

[2] See my *Masks of Conquest: Literary Study and British Rule in India* (New York: Columbia University Press, 1989; London: Faber and Faber, 1990), Chapter 6, 'The Failure of English', 142-65.

[3] See Hugh Kearney, *Scholars and Gentlemen: Universities and Society in Pre-Industrial Britain 1500-1700* (London: Faber and Faber, 1970).

recognition of the limits of a pedagogy drawn exclusively from the critical parameters of the discipline itself. From this point of view, hybridized, imperfect approximations of standardized responses are not so much the price that must be paid for unfreezing English from its pristine status as the possession of a select few, but the markers of a conflict made newly visible—of contradictions that can neither be contained nor rendered malleable by a skills-oriented, corrective pedagogy.

Linguistic 'errors' sometimes reveal far more about what is sought to be illuminated than the most careful attempts to achieve precision in language. Marshall McLuhan is said to have been so struck by the unexpected conceptual possibilities released by a typographical error, turning the word 'message' into 'massage' in the title of one of his books, that he decided to retain the 'error' in the final version. That book, of course, is *The Medium Is the Massage.*

Likewise, I have at times seen 'literary education' quietly slip into 'literacy education' in the hands of unsuspecting printers, but it occurs to me now that the error may have far more to say to the Indian educational scene than the corrected version. For, after all, the history of modern Indian education can be said to have evolved between these two poles, the conflation of 'literary' and 'literacy' being one of the ideological achievements of a discipline functioning as the carrier of both secular and religious culture. This is a relevant piece of information, especially for those critics who may be nettled by the phrase 'English literary education' when it is used in India, as it sometimes seems to signify more than just the study of English literature and embraces English-medium education and even Western education as a whole. This blurring of meanings is intrinsic to the formation of the discipline itself, which has never been particularly clear about its identity or relations to other disciplines, including the empirical sciences.

Initially, the study of English was rooted in a study of rhetoric. When English was first introduced in India, the rhetorical approach was readily adapted to an existing indigenous curriculum that employed a language-based approach to instruction in Arabic and Sanskrit. The more literary emphasis that English studies subsequently came to acquire results directly from the actions and efforts taken by missionaries to challenge what they saw as the harmful effects of teaching English for its own sake, without any reference to morals or values.[4]

[4] Some of these arguments are presented in my *Masks of Conquest,* specifi-

It is ironic that the missionaries should have been the group of people to have most directly contributed to the formation of the discipline of English literature as we know it today—ironic because of their extensive involvement in literacy work. The missionary role in precipitating the moral and cultural study of English literature prompts one to ask a set of questions related to such discursive shifts from 'literacy' to 'literary': can there be literacy in a language (let us take English for the time being, though in India it is an unreal choice) that is not just a mechanical study of words, an acquisition of structures and sounds (which missionaries termed a secular approach), but is also a vehicle of acquiring and expressing ideas, feelings, and values? At the same time, can literacy in the latter skills evade appropriation by more formalized, institutionally determined critical approaches, such as that offered by literary study? In other words, the broad question I am asking in ever so tentative a fashion is this: How can societies such as ours attain levels of functional literacy without necessarily being bound by predetermined, externally motivated programmes of linguistic or literary training?

These questions acquire some urgency when one considers that the literacy percentage in India, in all languages, has crawled at the rate of less than one point per year since independence. At a time when three out of five students drop out before they reach the fifth standard, when another fifteen per cent fail to reach the high school stage, and when more than fifty per cent of those who do manage to go to secondary schools fail to matriculate, the declining literacy rate is cause for considerable alarm. Furthermore, the decline has to be set against the mushrooming growth of schools offering an education in English language and literature. Far from encouraging the spread of literacy, the growth of such schools has virtually stymied it. This it has done by promoting a restrictive meaning of literacy as the passive acquisition of the mechanics of language and structured ways of thinking. The filter-down effect has diluted whatever creative potency literacy programmes in other Indian languages might have.

As Paulo Freire has consistently pointed out, most recently in *Learning to Question: Pedagogies of Liberation* (1989), literacy is reducible neither to mastery of language structures nor internalization of institutionalized systems of thought and ways of knowing. In his earlier work Freire had

---

cally in chapters 2 and 3. For a survey of educational practices and uses of language instruction from Vedic times, see also my 'Education in South Asia', in *the Encyclopedia of Asian History* (New York: Macmillan, 1987).

coined a new word, 'conscientization', to describe the self-generated, self-motivated literacy programmes developed by the popular masses with whom he worked in Brazil. Freire views literacy as a mode of acquiring cultural power, not by appropriation of power from the state but by what he calls 'rediscovery' of it in the language one knows and the culture that surrounds one:

Intellectuals are mistaken when they maintain that power is located only in the state, and that, therefore, to gain power means to take over the power of the state. I regard the state—its administration, its coercive power, and its ideological apparatus—as the point from which power is distributed. Thus teachers, educationists, and politicians possess a portion of power because they receive it from the state . . . To identify power with the state, and so lay down that in order to change society you must begin by taking over the power of the state (since state and power are identical) is a mistake—epistemologically, politically and even psychologically. Power must be rediscovered. And if power is to be rediscovered, then the struggle to achieve power also needs to be rediscovered . . . [And] just as we shall have to rediscover power, we shall have to rediscover language and culture.[5]

The emphasis that Freire lays on subject-constitution through questioning, invention, and dramatization fortifies his vision of basic literacy as a programme that creates rather than acquires its texts in the process of learning. In the Indian context it is possible that when we too start asking questions about literacy that do not delimit it to passive acquisition of either language structures or structured modes of feeling and thought, then we might also begin to find a place and a use for English studies in India—a function that complements rather than obstructs the development of literacy levels in other Indian languages.

Several years ago I worked with English teachers in a predominantly residential, Hindi-medium school in Tis Hazari, Delhi. Many of the students who attended this school were orphans from nearby villages. Theirs was in many ways a contradictory world: taken out of one environment and placed in another, and quite literally dislocated from any sense of filiation, they were patently confused by the plethora of prescribed texts delineating an unfamiliar world which students in other learning situations seemed to be able to accept with much greater ease. My designated task was to help teachers teach the assigned material drawn from the Central Board syllabus. But the sheer futility of

---

[5] Paulo Freire and Antonio Faundez, *Learning to Question: A Pedagogy of Liberation* (New York: Continuum, 1989), 63, 82.

presuming to address either the experience of these students or the skills they already possessed caused us to abandon altogether any illusions that we could manage the impossible. It was not even so much that the English language posed an obstacle, or that the students were being introduced to it in a form, such as the lyrical poem, that was 'unnatural'. Indeed, their responses to a poem like Yeats's 'An Irish Airman Foresees His Death' (taught entirely through paraphrase and translation, and in which every possible—and implausible—interpretation was thrown in by the students, including glosses that invoked karma and reincarnation), were anything but passive or sluggish. Rather, the problem was that these texts, in their institutional framework, offered a predetermined, manufactured world that effectively excluded the students from creative participation in its meanings.

Because of the extreme conditions of the situation, where no one could really fault us for not teaching the syllabus because there was no way the syllabus could be learnt, we—that is, both teachers and students—decided instead, co-operatively, to design our own lessons in English. Using something akin to the 'Manipravalam', or gem-coral, method developed in eleventh-century South India (which involved a free admixture of Tamil and Sanskrit in commentaries and glosses on Sanskrit works), we began with some of the most wildly improbable responses students made to the literary selections read in class and asked them to improvise on the situation that they thought a given work referred to. The written improvisations took on a life of their own. It was an exercise that virtually asked the students to move from reading other people's work to writing their own lessons—their own stories, as it were. In ever so humble a way, there grew a feeling among them that this was *their* literature, their perception of the world.

Whatever the failings of Gandhi's theory of basic education (and there are many), his contention that the boundary walls of the school must be coterminous with its surrounding community resonates in the experience of many who have studied or taught English and tried to recover the local features of a generalized English pedagogy.[6] When the

---

[6] An unconscious echo of Gandhi's basic education plan reverberates in the British classroom, as presented by Roger Bromley in his essay 'Dreaming the local: teaching popular cultural forms', in Peter Brooker and Peter Humm, eds., *Dialogue and Difference: English into the Nineties* (New York: Routledge, 1990). Bromley wants to recover the 'local' in the English curriculum, defining it as a 'field in which possible meanings are generated and shared' (156),

cultural milieu of students cannot be invoked into their readings of literary texts because that milieu contradicts the construction of a homogeneous universe of meaning, one reaches a pedagogical impasse, a radical turning-point of sorts, where either the syllabus or the students have to be thrown overboard. Whatever else may happen, it is clear that a harmonious integration of the two simply cannot, or perhaps ought not to, be orchestrated.

If elitism in education can be defined as the enforced gap between social reality and the world of learning, then obviously English is not alone in cultivating elitism. Nor is it the only subject that produces a sense of estrangement from lived daily experience. Nonetheless, it is the experience of many students of English literature in India that they are uncomfortably alienated and, as I discovered when I talked to groups of students around Madras and elsewhere, at the same time not quite sure what they are alienated *from*. For some, it is the sense of the local; for others, an identification with something much larger that they might be inclined to name 'Indianness'. In either case, dislocation prevails—a dislocation that is acutely experienced because 'the real' is what is thought to be apprehended through English education, that belief itself being rudely contradicted in everyday interactions.

I close with what has been for me a haunting reminder of the power we are believed to possess as students and teachers of English. A couple of years ago in Madras, I was returning home late one afternoon, my arms laden with books from libraries and bookstores. At that time there was a lot of construction work going on in the locality where I lived, and that day as I walked past one particular site, where a large house was coming up, I saw a young woman, not more than sixteen or seventeen years of age, carrying a large vessel of water on her head. I had seen her several times before around the same place, where she would often stop to ask me the time. As she approached the makeshift boundary wall that I was then passing, she again called out to me to ask the time. On this particular day, however, she looked at me with a little more curiosity, especially at the books I was clutching in my hands. I had already moved well past the site when I heard the young woman's voice calling out

---

and in which a community-based, rather than national, set of meanings provides the organizing principle of the English curriculum. 'It is in this "common belonging" that aspiration and possibility *culturally* become "reality", symbolically overcoming alienation, difference, hierarchy, and distance.'

again. 'Akka, do you know English?' I turned around, startled by the question, and replied that I did. She then excitedly asked, 'Can you teach me English? Can you teach me how to read nice books like the ones you're holding?' This time I was visibly astonished and asked her why she wanted to learn English so badly. Her answer shook me up then, and continues to do so even now when I recall it: 'Because I want to live in these houses rather than help build them.'

3

Derozio:
English Teacher

MANJU DALMIA

Forty years after Independence, English language and literature continue to hold their dominant position among the liberal arts subjects offered at Indian schools and universities. English was the main language I was brought up in, the language I was taught to think and read in. I became an English teacher, but the earlier unquestioning acceptance of English as my own language has over the years been replaced by ambivalence. This ambivalence has grown in the process of teaching, through the years of trying to bring fundamentally alien texts closer to students who can best understand them as imaginative constructs. I am not able, any longer, to universalize the books I teach without falsifying the situations I deal with in the classroom; to do so is to ignore obvious cultural, social and linguistic differences between text and student. Instead I am increasingly driven to situate English as part of a foreign literature, often with no obvious relevance to us. This paper, then, grew out of a desire to understand my own position as an English teacher in India. If history is a route to self-knowledge,[1] then history could help me come to terms with my uneasiness about a subject I grappled with every day in the classroom.

This case study of Derozio seeks to locate, in a limited and small way (for I am not equipped to deal with all the historical and political

[1] 'The starting-point of critical elaboration is the consciousness of what one really is, and is "knowing thyself" as a product of the historical process to date which has deposited in you an infinity of traces, without leaving an inventory.' Antonio Gramsci, *Selections from the Prison Notebooks*, ed. and trans. Q. Hoare and G. Nowell Smith (New York: International, 1985).

complexities of the original situation), some of the anomalies inherent in being a teacher of English literature in a colonial situation. In focusing on Derozio I take for my example one of the first Indian college teachers of English, an early victim of the politics of pedagogy in the years of British rule. English literary studies in India were used to achieve diverse goals, such as moral upliftment, political control, religious enlightenment, and social stratification. Derozio's history illustrates some of the contradictions that governed such an enterprise.

References to Derozio fall into two categories. He is classified as the first Indo-Anglian poet, one who brought into his writing on Indian themes a wide variety of metres, rhythms, forms and images from English poetry. He is also considered a teacher and journalist who wielded a cultural and ideological influence that made itself felt in Bengal for the next fifty years. Behind the Young Bengal movement, noted for its rationalist philosophy, its radical thinking, its patriotism, idealism, and impatience with superstition, bigotry and religious ritual, can be seen those minds who had come into contact with Derozio in one way or another. He is regarded as a proto-nationalist, one who created a critical awareness of modes of government and representation, but at the same time reflected the contradictions surrounding English higher education at the time. The Young Bengal activists have been castigated as rootless intellectuals who were culturally alienated from their own tradition,[2] and who failed to establish meaningful contact with India.[3]

In focusing on Derozio as an English teacher, I examine him in a capacity which enabled him to function not merely as teacher but also as speech-maker, visionary, guide, radical, leader and public figure. In the Calcutta of the 1830s, circumstances combined to make his position particularly significant. Derozio taught a syllabus of Western literary and historical texts in the rational, humanist spirit which had been stressed in his own education. Introducing this spirit into an Indian context created a tension between the subject matter and the recipients of the knowledge, there being a mismatch between social and religious conditions of the students' home lives and what they were told to read. This situation is of particular interest to English teachers today. Pedagogic attitudes influenced by the Western tradition, and then brought to

[2] See David Kopf, *British Orientalism and the Bengal Renaissance* (Calcutta: Firma K.L. Mukhopadhyaya, 1969), 253.

[3] See Niranjan Dhar, *Vedanta and the Bengal Renaissance* (Calcutta: Minerva Associates, 1977), 162.

bear upon texts which are treated as utterances of universal truth, rather than as historically specific creations, have antecedents in Derozio's methods.

Here it seems necessary to examine some of the political motivations that led the British to promote English education, as well as the manner in which this was done in India.

After the early nineteenth century, Calcutta was where jobs and wealth were possible through contacts with Europeans. Knowledge of English was a very valuable asset, and the English text therefore became an object of increasing importance. This trend received publicity from both Englishmen and those Indians who saw their interests in the spread of Western education. Writing to Rev. Henry Ware of Cambridge on 2 February 1824, Ram Mohan Roy felt 'fully justified in stating that two-thirds of the native population of Bengal would be exceedingly glad to see their children educated in English learning'.[4] By 1838 Charles Trevelyan could point to the virtual demise of the classical Indian languages under the impact of English:

Indeed, books in the learned native languages Arabic and Sanskrit are such a complete drug in the market that the school book society has for some time past ceased to print them; twenty-three thousand such volumes, most of them folios and quartos, filled the library, or rather the lumber room, of the education committee at the time when their printing was put a stop to, and during the preceding three years their sale had not yielded quite one thousand rupees.[5]

Bentinck indirectly encouraged this situation when he began to employ Indians in various administrative posts to cut costs. The market link with a 'useful' education was too obvious to be ignored by middle-class Indians. The Hindu demand that English usage should spread even to the language used in the courts had its roots in British policy on education. In a letter dated 26 June 1829, the secretary of the Persian department suggests the government declare that 'English will be eventually used as the language of business', and that after three years preference 'be given to candidates for office' who know English, and that English become 'the language of our Public Tribunals and Correspondence'.[6]

[4] Ramesh Chandra Mitra, 'Education', The History of Bengal: 1757-1905, ed. N.K. Sinha (Calcutta: University of Calcutta, 1967), 434.

[5] Charles Trevelyan, On the Education of the People of India (London: Longman, 1838), 79.

[6] Ibid., 146.

According to British official thinking, jobs linked to education would be incentive enough for Indians to pursue a learning that would provide government with a class of men to support their rule, as well as cheap manpower. As early as 1825, Captain Sutherland of the 3rd Light Cavalry had 'submitted a plan for the education of native youths in such branches as would qualify them to serve the Company in the revenue line, in which department of the service the greatest want of efficient agents was experienced'.[7] Despite such strong and unequivocal recommendations, the Governor-General favoured the discreet approach characteristic of the official British attitude to education in the first thirty-five years of the nineteenth century. He was not prepared to give any 'distinct and specific pledge as to the period and manner of effecting so great a change in the system of our internal economy', preferring 'the gradual and cautious fulfilment of our views'.[8]

The government was very aware of the possibly negative political consequences of openly advocating English education. It wanted educated Indians to feel that the British respected Indian traditions, learning and manners. In September 1780, Hastings stated that a Calcutta madrassa would help 'soften the prejudices excited by the growth of British dominions'.[9] In 1792 Johnathan Duncan similarly asserted that the Benaras Sanskrit College would 'endear our Government to the Native Hindoos'.[10] In 1824, the Committee for Public Instruction exhibited the same regard for treading softly on Indian sensibilities:

We must for the present go with the tide of popular prejudice . . . the course is by no means unprofitable. At the same time we are fully aware of the value of those accessions which may be made from European science and literature to the sum total of Asiatic knowledge, and shall endeavour, in pursuance of the sentiments and intentions of Government, to avail ourselves of every favourable opportunity for introducing them when it can be done without offending the feelings and forfeiting the confidence of those for whose advantage their introduction is designed.[11]

---

[7] See A.N. Basu, ed., *Indian Education in Parliamentary Papers*, pt I (1832; Bombay: Asia, 1952), 58.

[8] Trevelyan, 146-7.

[9] See Bernard Cohn, 'The Command of Language and the Language of Command', *Subaltern Studies IV*, ed. R. Guha (Delhi: OUP, 1985), 317.

[10] Ibid., 318.

[11] A.F.S. Ahmed, *Social Ideas and Social Change in Bengal* (Leiden: Brill, 1965), 140.

Even people not particularly noted for their Orientalist sympathies could be found to voice the same caution in the politics of control. Thus we find, on 2 January 1835, Adam writing to Bentinck while on the point of starting his commission to report on the state of education in Bengal:

To labour successfully *for* them we must labour *with* them; and to labour successfully *with* them, we must get them to labour willingly and intelligently *with* us. We must make them, in short, the instruments of their own improvement.[12]

The method of working behind the scenes ensured that the British did not come to the forefront in any controversy regarding English education. Though they encouraged English education from the point of view of political expediency, their policy ensured that as far as possible they were not held responsible for any adverse social and cultural effects it might have.

HINDU COLLEGE

Among the institutions which came up to provide English education to Indians in Calcutta, the most successful was Hindu College. Its origins reveal the middle-class Indians' desire for modern Western learning, but one offered under orthodox supervision. The earlier association of this learning with missionary endeavours, and the consequent loss of caste and religion suffered by Hindu students resulted in the Indians' desire for this education on their own terms.[13] The people associated with its inception were traditional Hindus, whose contacts with the English had brought them money and official positions, and who wished their sons to gain the practical advantages of a Western education.[14] Most prominent among these were Radhakanta Deb and Ramkamal Sen, whose

[12] Arabinda Poddar, *Renaissance in Bengal: Quests and Confrontations 1800-1860* (Simla: Institute of Advanced Study, 1970), 104.

[13] The initial foreign impetus for teaching Indians English came from the missionaries. In fact it was not till the 1830s that the state assumed a public role in education. The missionaries thought that a knowledge of English amongst the Indians would make their conversion easier. The Serampore College, founded in 1818 by Carey, Marshman and Ward to train native evangelists, combined the religious courses of study with a training in Western science, English language and English literature.

[14] Even Ram Mohan Roy could not participate in the establishment of Hindu College, because of the antagonism with which he was viewed by the

work in the field of education did much to make Western learning acceptable to Hindu society. The aims of Hindu College, as laid down in its charter, stress the fruitful combination of Eastern and Western learning: 'the primary object of the institution is the tuition of the sons of respectable Hindoos, in the English and Indian languages and science of Europe and Asia'.[15] Sir Edward Hyde East records his impressions of a meeting held on 14 May 1816 by the people involved in the founding of Hindu College. He was 'struck with the enthusiasm of the prominent pundits, Sanskrit scholars, for the introduction of Western literature and science', as well as by the fact that they associated the new knowledge with a revival of their own literature:

the head pundit, in the name of himself and the others, said that they rejoiced in having lived to see the day when literature (many parts of which had formerly been cultivated in this country with considerable success, but which were now extinct) was about to be revived with greater lustre and prospect of success than ever.[16]

By May 1827 the building that was to house Hindu College and the new Sanskrit College was completed. By 1828 there were 400 boys on the rolls of Hindu College, out of whom a hundred were scholarship students with a supply of free books. The School Book Society and the Committee of Public Instruction paid for a further 5000 books that had been recently imported from England. The classes of the senior section were devoted to Western history, literature and the natural sciences. W.H. Carey reports that Sanskrit was discontinued early, the Persian class abolished by 1841, while English and Bengali continued to be taught.[17] Greek and English history, grammar, arithmetic and geography, were all on the syllabus. Such was the rapid progress in Western learning that the Committee of Public Instruction could say of Hindu

---

Hindu orthodoxy. Radhakanta Deb and his associates refused to have anything to do with Ram Mohan Roy on the grounds that 'he had chosen to separate himself from us and to attack our religion . . . he has publicly reviled us and written against us and our religion'. See M.K. Haldar, trans., *Renaissance and Reaction in Nineteenth Century Calcutta*, by Bankim Chandra Chattopadhyaya (Calcutta: Minerva, 1977), 11.

[15] Kopf, 182.
[16] Ibid.
[17] W.H. Carey, *The Good Old Days of Honourable John Company* (Calcutta: Quins Book Co., 1882; abridged edn. 1964), 178-9.

College in 1830 that 'a command of the English language, and the familiarity with its literature and science have been acquired to an extent rarely equalled by any schools in Europe'.[18]

British observations on Hindu College suggest that it came to be regarded as the showpiece of Western education in India, and as a justification for greater emphasis on English language and literature. Holt Mackenzie's evidence before the Parliamentary Committee which examined the Company's affairs between 1830-2 focuses on Hindu College to show the progress of English education in Calcutta. The students show 'an astonishing proficiency in language, writing it, many of them, with purity quite equal to that shown by the lads of the same age in an English school'.[19] Significantly, only a hundred out of the 436 pupils were provided scholarships, while most of the students of the vernacular institutions were paid stipends to study their subjects.

The rapid development of Hindu College provided a convenient pretext for various British official and non-official agencies to extend patronage and support without overtly appearing to influence the course of Indian education. European Professors were appointed to raise standards, and Hindu College became the focus of attention of the British India Society, formed in England by retired Company officials and English philanthropists for 'the intellectual and moral improvement' of Indians.[20] They advanced the cause of science in India by donating laboratory equipment to the College for the teaching of physics. The press also followed the progress of English education with great interest:

This is truly a most interesting Institution, and will, we have no doubt, prove a very effective engine of improvement. The youth educated at this College will acquire a taste for European literature which cannot fail of leading to more important results, and of greatly ameliorating the state of society. [21]

At one prize-giving function, recitation from Shakespeare, with special mention of a rendering of Brutus' speech, was commented on: 'it could not but be a matter of pleasing surprise to see a Hindoo boy personating the noble Roman, and giving utterance with good emphasis

[18] Trevelyan, 18.
[19] Basu, 280.
[20] Ahmed, 144.
[21] *Calcutta Monthly Journal*, 11 January 1827, quoted in B. Ghose, ed. *Selections from English Periodicals : Nineteenth Century Bengal, 1815-1833*, I (Calcutta: Papyrus, 1978), 8.

& good discretion' to the sentiments of Shakespeare'.[22] The examinations of January 1828 took place before high officials in Government House. Governor-General Amherst and his wife were present, along with Members of Council and the Supreme Court judges. Those students who performed exceptionally well were lauded by name, in this case Krishnamohan Banerji, Rasik Krishna Malik and Radhanath Sikhdar, all pupils of Derozio. The *India Gazette* of 16 February 1832 describes in detail the Hindu College exam, the guests present and the Shakespeare recitations, and compares the students' progress with that of the year before. These public functions, according to the editorial, were meant to give people the means to gauge 'the progress of the Hindoos in the acquisition of literature and science'.[23] Such publicity, mostly shed on progress in English learning, conveyed a corresponding sense of gain in intellectual advancement and modernity which is not to be found in contemporary accounts of vernacular studies.

Although the occasions do not seem to have been numerous, it is significant that any indifference on the part of the official administration towards native English education was noted with displeasure. The 5 September 1827 letter from the Court of Directors to the Governor-General in Council in Bengal states:

We desire it may be notified to the parties concerned that we have taken particular notice of the following passage in your letter: 'We regretted to observe that some unexplained circumstance had prevented the attendance of the local committee at the disputations and distributions of prizes, at the Hindu College of Benaras and deeming it to be of vital importance to the efficiency of all the public seminars that the European officers appointed to their control should take every opportunity they conveniently can, of openly manifesting an active interest in the institutions over which they preside, we directed that the attention of the local committee should be called to these several points by the General Committee of Public Instruction'.[24]

The emphasis the British laid on the popularity of their education had an additional underlying message: not only did Indians benefit from their presence in India, but also, in order to continue the good work in the Utilitarian tradition, it was necessary to establish this education even more firmly. Social reform, as defined by British culture could be better effected by changing native perceptions through the medium of English

[22] Ibid., 10.
[23] Ibid., 118.
[24] Basu, 156-7.

literature. James Sutherland in his evidence before the Parliamentary Committee of the affairs of the East India Company, makes explicit this connection. He says that the size of the English-speaking native population has 'wonderfully increased', and English manners are increasingly imitated so 'that very few of the great number of the well-educated Hindoos any longer adhere to the superstitions of their countrymen'. Several literary societies have sprung up in Calcutta and there is a great familiarity among College youths with 'the merits of English literature'.[25] And Macaulay writes in 1836: 'No Hindu who has received an English education, ever remains sincerely attached to his religion . . . It is my firm belief that if our plans of education are followed up, there will not be a single idolater among the respectable classes in Bengal thirty years later.'[26]

To facilitate their administration, the British relied on educated Indians, particularly those who had gone to Hindu College. They were well aware of the uses to which the native Indian could be put.

DEROZIO

One of the earliest Indian teachers of English literature in an institution of higher learning was Henry Louis Vivian Derozio. Born of Eurasian parents in Calcutta, his birth and education made him easily susceptible to Western influences. His habits, dress, taste, manners, speech, and intellectual preoccupations were closely modelled on those of the colonial rulers. At the same time, his Indian nationality, his patriotism, and his perception that English language and literature were the essence of civilization and the way to progress, gave his teaching a zeal and enthusaism that, for political considerations, no Englishman could have so openly exhibited. Derozio's position as a teacher in a college which catered to the most elite and influential section of Bengali society resulted in an influence that extended considerably beyond the brief three years of his tenure there. He functioned both as a medium and a catalyst of changes that reached further than he had intended. His influence extended into the movement known as Young Bengal, spearheaded by many of his students, but it also persisted, in a more general way, because many of those he taught later held public positions as teachers,

[25] Ibid., 284.
[26] Arthur Mayhew, *The Education of India* (London: Faber and Gwyer, 1926), 15.

journalists, editors, and preachers. Paradoxically, it was this very position as a teacher in Hindu College that made Derozio vulnerable. For Hindu College was unique. The focal point of both Indian and British academic endeavours, it was positive proof that natives possessed the ability to absorb and master the intricacies of a Western education, a political asset for Indians and British alike. Derozio, instrumental in creating the very changes the British had so discreetly sought to make in the socio-intellectual make-up of the upper classes, was also a convenient buffer for absorbing the adverse consequences that such radical changes were bound to unleash. Derozio's life illustrates the anomalies that surfaced when opposed purposes were at work; while Indians accepted Western learning for material, practical purposes of their own, the British viewed it as a means of establishing their cultural, political and even religious hegemony.

Derozio was born in April 1809, in Calcutta, of mixed Portuguese, British and Indian parentage. At six he entered Dharamtola Academy, run by David Drummond, one of the best schools in Calcutta at the time. At fourteen he finished school and joined Messrs. J. Scott and Co., his father's place of work, as a clerk. At sixteen he left for his aunt's indigo plantation in Bhagulpore, Bihar. Here he spent the next three years and wrote most of his poetry, including a lengthy romantic epic, 'The Fakir of Jungheera'. He sent his poems to the *India Gazette* under the pen name of Juvenis, and, with the encouragement of the editor, John Grant, decided to collect and publish his poems. In 1827 he came to Calcutta, was appointed assistant editor of the *India Gazette* by Grant, and on the release of his volume of poetry achieved fame and recognition at the age of seventeen. Such was his repute and such his fluency in English that he was considered qualified enough to be appointed master of the senior department in English literature and history at Hindu College when he was only twenty. In April 1831 he was dismissed from Hindu College, and for the remainder of his short life returned to journalism. On 17 December 1831 he was stricken by cholera. Six days later he died.

The major influence on Derozio in his formative years was the head of his school, David Drummond, a follower of David Hume. Hume's emphasis on the 'organic relationship between personal moral decision and the social process' can be seen reflected in Derozio's belief in the connection between personal values and social commitment.[27] Drummond's rationalism was described thus:

[27] See Raymond Williams, *Writing in Society* (London: Verso, 1977), 141.

He would believe nothing, accept nothing, unless it could be made evident and reasonable as a mathematical axiom. Tradition and antiquity were to him no authority, and he built up his system of faith and the universe on a basis not much broader than the *cogito ergo sum* of Descartes.[28]

Drummond was also apparently the source of Derozio's love of literature and philosophy, his liking for Burns, and his faith in English radicalism and the French revolution.[29] The emphasis on reason and individual thinking later became one of the major appeals of Derozio's teaching.

By 1828, the year Derozio was appointed to Hindu College, English literature and the natural sciences as curricular subjects had already shown a steady increase in popularity. Although the subjects were not compulsory, almost half the student body chose to study them. The syllabus that Derozio taught was one that emphasized the positive value of rational thinking. It was fixed by the Committee of Management, which consisted of three Hindus and two Englishmen, Horace Wilson and David Hare. Wilson, as Secretary for the Committee of Public Instruction, was the government representative, and both Hare and he were liked and trusted by the Indian community. Their efforts to help Indians get the kind of education they wanted were well known, and anything they recommended would have been accepted without reservation. The texts for the English history and literature component of the syllabus were Goldsmiths's *History of Greece, Rome and England*, Russell's *Modern Europe*, Robertson's *Charles the Fifth*, Gay's *Fables*, Pope's version of the *Iliad* and *Odyssey*, Dryden's version of the *Aeneid*, Milton's *Paradise Lost*, and one of Shakespeare's tragedies.[30]

Notably, literature and history were taught in one composite unit and, in this case, by a man whose strengths were literary rather than historical. From the reactions of Derozio's pupils, it would appear that the study of both together tended to historicize literature, so that the heroism perceived in the works cited captured the imagination and became desirable norms of behaviour in a social system very different from the one in which the works originated. By placing the history of Greece, Rome and England together, the syllabus gave England a paral-

[28] Thomas Edwards, *Henry Derozio* (Calcutta: Riddhi India, 1884, rpt. 1980), 19.

[29] Susobhan Sarkar, *Bengal Renaissance and Other Essays* (New Delhi: Peoples Publishing House, 1970), 109.

[30] Edwards, 6.

lel status as a global civilizing influence, and it is significant that, in fact, the British often did compare themselves to the Greeks and Romans in their role as torch-bearers of Western civilization. As Tagore was to say in his *Reminiscenses*:

> When I was young, we were full of admiration for Europe, with its high civilization and its vast scientific progress, and especially for England, which had brought this knowledge to our own doors. We had come to know England through her glorious literature, which had brought a new inspiration into our young lives. The English authors whose books and poems we studied were full of love of humanity, justice and freedom. All this fired our youthful imagination. We believed with all our simple faith that even if we rebelled against foreign rule, we should have the sympathy of the West. We felt that England was on our side in wishing us to gain our freedom.[31]

In this sort of context, criticism would be rendered unlikely in the classroom, given the authority of the Western text and the glamour of a young and well-known public figure as a teacher.

The inclusion of four epic poems in this syllabus accorded with the belief of the eighteenth-century literary establishment that the epic was the highest form of art. Greek, Latin, and the 'classics' in these languages were required study for the upper classes in England, while the lower classes were given texts with strong moral and religious overtones to study. By prescribing Milton, and translations of the classics by Pope and Dryden, the dual purpose of moral and classical education was combined for the Indian middle classes, filtered in the latter case through eighteenth-century British notions of propriety.

Between Virgil and Homer, both Pope and Dryden were agreed in considering Virgil the more moral and therefore superior writer, though they agreed that he lacked the poetic genius of Homer. In Virgil's *Aeneid* the ideal of a public figure is presented, a man with a mission, with all the heroic qualities of leadership. Such a hero, the British no doubt felt, would provide a useful model for Indians setting out to reform their own society, and as such the text would provide a valuable and subtle blueprint for social engineering. Homer's *Iliad* and *Odyssey* were more problematic. The anthropomorphic Greek gods and goddesses indulged in the kind of sexual activity and malicious petty behaviour most detrimental to the Christian notion of a judicious deity. Pope wrote elaborate footnotes to the text, excusing these lapses as aspects of a rude

---

[31] Quoted in Ganesh Prashad, *Nehru: A Study in Liberal Colonialism* (Delhi: Sterling, 1976), 29.

and pagan age. The fact that these texts, conveyed through the medium of eighteenth-century enlightenment ideology, were constructed as the noblest expressions of civilized man and given universal value—rather than located in a culturally specific context—meant that the valuation of one kind of literary work implicitly took place at the expense of other kinds, in this case the religious texts of the Hindus. That an ostensibly secular education was successful in affecting the religious sensibilities of at least some of the Hindu students is evident from Edwards' account of Derozio's pupils, who 'instead of repeating prayers to deities which their enlightened reason and awakened conscience told them was merely the distorted mythic creation of former days and earlier men, chose to repeat some noble passage from the *Iliad*'.[32] The ideological thrust that might have lain behind the choice of texts was voiced by one of the syllabus-makers: 'Only when we initiate them into our literature, particularly at an early age, and get them to adopt feelings and sentiments from our standard Writers, can we make an impression on them, and effect any considerable alteration in their feelings and notions.'[33]

With the eighteenth-century rise in literary scholarship and criticism, both Shakespeare and Milton became firmly entrenched in the literary canon. Since English literature was not part of higher education in Britain at the time, we can observe here, upon the Indian academic scene, both the process and the effects of canon-formation in the choice of texts exported to the colonies.

Derozio, who had himself been educated in the tradition of eighteenth-century rationalist thought, proved enormously effective in conveying his learning. From all accounts he brought to his teaching a dedication that extended well beyond the classroom. Numerous testimonials exist to the influence he wielded, and certainly some of the radical actions of his students testify to the fundamental change that came about in their personal lives while they studied in Hindu College. The manuscript history of Hindu College by Baboo Hurro Mohun Chatterji, a clerk in the college, testifies to the close relationship Derozio had with his pupils:

They loved him most tenderly; and were ever ready to be guided by his counsels and imitate him in all their daily actions of life. In fact Derozio acquired such an ascendancy over the minds of his pupils that they would not

---

[32] Edwards, 69.

[33] See Gauri Viswanathan, 'The Beginnings of English Literary Study in British India', *The Oxford Literary Review*, vol. 9, 1-2, 1987, 14.

move even in their private concerns without his counsel and advice. On the other hand he fostered their taste in literature, taught the evil effects of idolatry and superstition; and so far formed their moral conceptions and feelings as to make them completely above the antiquated ideas and aspirations of his age.[34]

Thomas Edwards, Derozio's nineteenth-century biographer, describes the qualities that made him a messianic figure:

the force of his individuality, his winning manners, his wide knowledge, his own youth, which placed him in close sympathy with his pupils, his open, generous, chivalrous nature, his humour and playfulness, his fearless love of truth, his hatred of all that was unmanly and mean, his ardent love of India.[35]

The interaction between Derozio and the student body continued beyond the college. The most significant of these encounters took place at the Academic Association, a debating club started by Derozio, the first of its kind in the city. Meetings were regularly held, in a garden house in Maniktola, Calcutta. Derozio was the president, Umacharan Bose the secretary. Although a non-official body, the Academic Association generated enough interest to attract British attention and encouragement. The meetings were frequently attended by David Hare, who participated actively in the Association. Other Europeans who attended occasionally were from the educational field, and from administration—Colonel Benson, Bentinck's private secretary, and Colonel Beatson, afterwards Adjutant-General. Subjects such as free will, fate, faith, virtue and vice, the existence of God, idolatry, and priesthood were placed in the perspective of a rational discourse. Papers were read, and issues discussed and debated without fear of alienating Hindu orthodoxy. The hierarchy of the classroom was replaced by the equality of intellectual interchange. Critical attitudes to traditional social, literary, moral and religious customs grew, as the Young Bengal intelligentsia applied to them critical perspectives derived from the thought of Bacon, Locke, Hume, Paine, and Bentham.

Derozio did not confine his teaching abilities to his students, but gave 'weekly moral and intellectual lectures' to the pupils of Hare's school. Heard by some four hundred young men, he cast a 'spell that bound his pupils around him which served to animate them to almost superhuman exertions'.[36]

---

[34] Edwards, 67.
[35] Ibid., 65.
[36] Poddar, 95.

DEROZIO'S DISMISSAL

From around 1830 the westernized habits of the young men educated at Hindu College became a source of controversy. Although English dress and living styles were not unknown among Indians in Calcutta, they had previously reflected money and social status rather than radical changes in religious and cultural identity. The founding fathers of Hindu College, Radhkanta Deb, Ramkamal Sen, and other Hindu conservatives, had imagined that English language and scientific knowledge could be taught without any serious disturbances being created by the ideas conveyed through them. This attitude to Western education concealed an anomaly which began to surface partly as Derozio's teaching caught the students' imagination in ways anticipated by the British, but which took the Indians by surprise. Hurro Mohun records the debates Derozio's pupils held in May 1829, which focused on precisely those issues that the British had highlighted in their memos when advocating Western education for the natives:

The principles and practices of the Hindu religion were openly ridiculed and condemned, and angry disputes were held on moral subjects; the sentiments of Hume had been widely diffused and warmly patronized ... The most glowing harangues were made at debating clubs, then very numerous. The Hindu religion was denounced as vile and corrupt and unworthy of the regard of rational human beings. The degraded state of the Hindus formed the topic of many debates; their ignorance and superstition were declared to be the cause of such a state, and it was then resolved that nothing but a liberal education could enfranchise the minds of the people.[37]

These views were expressed by Derozio and his pupils in print as well. Sometime in 1829-30, they started a journal called *Parthenon*. No known copy of this exists, but the first issue apparently contained articles on the importance of educating women, condemned idolatry and superstition among the Hindus,[38] and strongly advocated the colonization of India by Europeans, thus 'echoing the voices of the English free-traders and the radicals'.[39] The first issue of *Parthenon* aroused a great deal of opposition from the more orthodox parents of the students; the second issue was not allowed to appear, even though it was in type.

[37] Edwards, 68.

[38] Gautam Chattopadhyaya, ed., *Bengal: Early Nineteenth Century (Selected Documents)* (Calcutta: Research India Publications, 1978), VI.

[39] Ahmed, 71.

Public opinion against Hindu College radicals was on the rise among Indians. Newspapers such as *Samachar Chandrika* and *Sambad Prabhakar*, which expressed the orthodox view, criticized the 'atheist beasts' who imitated the 'vagabond Firingis', and blamed this on the teachers of Hindu College.[40] Even at the height of the controversy over the new education, the usefulness of English was never questioned. Its ill effects were seen to reside in the style of teaching, in particular the style of Derozio. Early in 1830 steps were taken by the managers of Hindu College to stop religious discussion. Hurro Mohun relates that they passed a resolution:

as the students of the Hindu College are liable to lose all religious principles whatever, it is resolved that Mr. D'Anselm (head master) be requested to communicate with the teachers, and check as far as possible all disquisitions tending to unsettle the belief of the boys in the great principles of Natural Religion.[41]

This had little effect, and was followed in February 1830 by another order from the management forbidding any discussion among the students on religion, especially the Hindu religion, further warning that any eating and drinking in the classrooms would result in dismissal. Attempts were made to control the movements of the students outside the college premises.[42]

Even this did not have much effect. Duff, who had been giving lectures on 'natural and revealed religion' in his house on College Square, opposite Hindu College, was forced to stop for a while, but the Academic Association continued to hold their meetings. The *India Gazette* published an article maintaining the right of the students to 'private judgement on political and religious questions'. The changes the new learning had generated had begun to create public alarm, and both the British and the Indians tried to avoid things coming to a head.

In April 1831 Ramkamal Sen convened the meeting that ended in Derozio's dismissal. By this time the life of the institution was felt to be in danger, the institution that had been so carefully nurtured by Hindus and British alike. For the first time, parents began withdrawing their children from Hindu College. As many as 25 left, while the attendance dropped dramatically, with 160 students staying away,[43] their intention

---

[40] Sarkar, 112.
[41] Edwards, 69.
[42] Ibid., 70.
[43] Ahmed, 47.

being to drop out unless some action was taken. Giving these facts, Ramkamal Sen stated that the object of the meeting was to check 'the growing evil and the public alarm arising from the very unwarranted arrangements and misconduct of a certain teacher'.[44] The proposals Ramkamal Sen made to save Hindu College consisted in dismissing Derozio and those 'publicly hostile to Hinduism and the established customs of the country'. He furthermore advocated a return to a system of greater distance between pupil and teacher, and suggested that 'a separate place be fitted for the teachers to dine in; and the practice of eating on the school table be discontinued'. Books injurious to the morals of the students should not be 'taught, brought, or read in the College'. Attendance of the students at any meetings or lectures would result in dismissal. And *whenever Europeans are procurable*, a preference shall be given to them, their character and religion being ascertained before admission'. In the discussion that followed, both Wilson and Hare defended Derozio's competence and ability as a teacher, but in the vote afterwards both declined to participate, on the grounds that this was an issue concerning native feelings alone. Although most of the Hindu management did not question Derozio's abilities as a teacher, in the interests of the college it was considered best to dismiss him. The boys, they felt, could not be stopped from attending meetings.

Derozio's passionate letter written on 25 April 1831 to the managing committee of Hindu College shows his complete innocence about the politics of the situation.[45] Protesting the injustice to him, he presents certain facts which 'did not appear on the face of your proceedings'. No charge had been brought against him, and if they were any accusers he was not called upon to face them. No witnesses were examined on either side, nor was he given a chance to defend himself. And finally, despite his acknowledged merits as a teacher, it was decided, 'unbiased, unexamined, and unheard', to dismiss him 'without even the mockery of a trial'. Wilson's pragmatic response to Derozio's letter shows a very different understanding of the situation. He excuses 'the native managers whose decision was founded merely upon the expediency of yielding to popular clamour, the justice of which it was not incumbent upon them to investigate'. By saying that there was no trial because there was no specific accusation, Wilson reveals the vagueness of the dissatisfaction against Derozio. The distinctions between teacher and text are

[44] Ibid.

[45] The Derozio–Wilson correspondence is in Edwards, 77-89.

blurred in a conjunction so powerful that any attempt made by Derozio to free himself from the effects of his teaching would have been useless. As Wilson goes on to say: 'An impression had gone abroad to your disadvantage, the effects of which were injurious to the College, and which would not have been dispelled by any proof you could have produced that it was unfounded.'

The extent of the threat that the orthodox community had begun to feel is illustrated by the nature of the rumours circulating about Derozio. His influence, embodied in the new learning, was seen to be destructive of religious values, parental authority, and sexual morality. Wilson mentions three charges that had been brought against Derozio: that he did not believe in God, that he encouraged rebellion against parents, and that he believed in incest.

Derozio's reply, vindicating himself, clarified that he only encouraged an open appraisal of both sides of moral and religious questions. On the charge of atheism, Derozio maintained that it was not for him to have made his students 'pert and ignorant dogmatists, by permitting them to know what could be said upon only one side of grave questions.' Where the question of the existence of God was concerned, when he had given them Hume's arguments against Theism, he had also provided Dr Reid and Dugald Stewart's replies. The other charges Derozio refuted indignantly, saying 'For the first time in my life did I learn . . . that I am charged with inculcating so hideous, so unnatural, so abominable a principle.' But this was to no avail, and reveals how immaterial Derozio's actual ideas were in the face of a perceived threat to traditional values. A mythology had been created in which Derozio stood at the heart of a devilish enterprise that struck at religion, morality, and the sanctity of home and family. No proof to the contrary was going to be believed, and thus Derozio became the casualty of the learning he had been encouraged to spread. Though Wilson earned Derozio's gratitude by speaking up for him in the Committee, the fact remains that, by advising him to voluntarily resign, he was also accepting the convenience of having Derozio as a buffer to absorb the fallout of a larger strategy to acculturize and dominate the Indian mind.

The alarm that English education had created was so widespread that even the Anglo-Indian press took exception to the amount of negative publicity the Hindu College radicals were attracting. The *India Gazette*'s editorial on educated Hindu youth on 21 October 1831 mentions that the radicals of Hindu College 'have our warmest wishes in their favour', but while expressing wholehearted approval of their object 'to make a stand against the folly, the vice and the impiety of idolatry, and to vindicate for themselves and others the right of conscience, the right of exercising their own judgement on moral and religious truths', it had reservations about the way in which this was being achieved. Violations in regard to caste rules of eating and drinking will only alienate, and alienation creates opposition, not change:

most of those of whom we are speaking despise the rules of caste and refuse all conformity to them, by which means they not only banish themselves from Hindoo society and lose all influence over it, but even supply their enemies with a handle against themselves, as if their only purpose in rejecting the religion of their country was to obtain the gratification of their appetites.[46]

In fact, Derozio's departure from Hindu College could not, by its very nature, contain the effects of Western education. British policy made sure that the new learning had come to stay, though the face of it might be modified to suit the circumstances. As Pradip Sinha puts it, there was initially no real place for the class of people created by the introduction of an English education, and the uncertainties of their position led to an exaggeration of social tensions. Sir Edward Ryan recognized this when he wrote to Bentinck, the Governor-General, about the condition of the radicals. He says that for Hindu boys 'of very considerable acquirements' there was 'no honourable or appropriate employment' and that

it cannot be a right state of things, that under British Government, moral and intellectual improvement should be to those subject to that Government, rather a curse than a blessing, and that abandoning a debasing and vile superstition should be rewarded by poverty and disgrace; and yet such is the condition of these Hindoo boys.[47]

It was only after official recognition by the government of the pre-eminence of English education, with English coming into use in administration and as the language of the courts, that the social status of the English-educated Indian became more assured. By the second half of the century the original Indian impetus for learning English, as a means to further mercantile and career interests, no longer provided the sole reason for using it.

The forces that converged and manifested themselves in Derozio's dismissal had their roots in the contradictions governing the early stages of English education in colonial India. The British attempt to establish political domination through cultural hegemony was reflected in their

---

[46] Ghosh, 64-5.
[47] Ahmed, 45.

early educational policies. That Derozio embodied this trend could be seen in his assumptions, certainly not unique to him, that Western texts contained certain universal truths. The ahistorical acceptance of the absolute value of these texts had a radical effect on his students, and in praising the changes he saw in them Derozio foresaw the dawn of a brave new age, where 'truth's omnipotence' would flourish.[48] In the rhetoric he used about the new learning, variously seen as the coming of dawn, light breaking on darkness, the shedding of shackles, etc., the amount of truth realized was also measured by the distance the mind had travelled from its original state. To what extent the change was a welcome or an alienating one is still a subject of debate, but the critical awareness which this change brought about undoubtedly resulted in a transformation of (Western) educated Indian perceptions on a number of social issues.

In what way is this history of Derozio, English teacher, relevant to us? English—as the harbinger of modernity, civilization, innovation and change—served a social and political need in early-nineteenth-century education, and contributed to its importance in a way that, obviously, cannot be paralleled today. But English teachers, it seems, can act as Derozio did, as catalysts of far-reaching changes even under these changed circumstances.[49] In order to recover a radical or even meaningful position for English literature teaching in our country (bracketing for the moment the question of teaching it at all), it is necessary once again to abstract the 'values' which are of relevance to us.

I speak in a limited way, since the students I teach are women in an 'elite' women's college in the capital (but Derozio was positioned similarly). Lately it has been feminist literary criticism that has provided the cutting-edge to our teaching. It is recourse to the strategies suggested by feminist theory that has allowed us to deconstruct the English text in ways that make it relevant to us as women and as members of the third world.[50] On the other hand, were we to be too successful in bringing our

---

[48] From Derozio's 'Sonnet to the Pupils of Hindu College'.

[49] The English teacher as *agent provocateur* is well handled in Peter Weir's recent film, *Dead Poet's Society*.

[50] See Lola Chatterjee, *Woman / Image / Text : Feminist Readings of Literary Texts* (New Delhi: Trianka, 1986) for some instances of such a 'making sense' by reading 'as women'.

students to an awareness of, for instance, patriarchal structures, the dominance of male bias, and their own oppression in our society, we would be creating a conflict between the pressures of their lives (early marriages, arranged marriages, dowry, 'eve-teasing', harassment, sexual exploitation, etc.), and the assertion of female individuality in other cultures and in other times that our teaching would uncover.

But lacking Derozio's rashness or initiative, we tread carefully in class, because we do not want to rock boats or create storms we cannot handle. Our wariness contributes to the ivory tower stigma that English studies has acquired in most of our universities. Our academic study of English literature implicitly eradicates our position as third world readers and as women, enfeebles rather than enables us.

The only two options available to us—radical destabilization of our social structures, or a safe 'formalism'—themselves reveal the contradictions inherent in the project of teaching English in India.

Derozio's propagation of eighteenth-century western rationalism through the texts of Hume and Paine, and our own celebration of feminist individualism in *Antigone* or *Jane Eyre*, should be comparable enterprises in the context of the gap that exists between our lives and the books we teach and learn.

4

Criticism and Pedagogy in the Indian Classroom

ANIA LOOMBA

In many ways it is far more difficult to talk or generalize about the Indian classroom than about the crisis of English literary studies. We have all been exposed to the elaboration as well as, recently, to critiques of both the institutionalized canon of great writers and the critical tradition shaped, among others, by Arnold, Eliot and the Leavises. But the *pedagogical* effects of this particular disciplinary formation are far more varied than a study of either the literary canon or the critical debates will reveal. For those who teach English literature in India, the 'crisis' goes beyond the challenge to certain critical orthodoxies: to delineate it involves a social and political critique of dauntingly mammoth dimensions. I suspect, moreover, that for all those trained in English literary studies—even that small section whose alienation from the received truths of established criticism has been prompted by the experience of teaching—general discussions of the problem remain easier, more valued, or at least more pleasurable, than venturing into the quasi-sociological analyses demanded by 'the classroom situation'. Training in literary criticism does not equip, and in fact has de-sensitized us towards the pedagogical dimension.

On the other hand, supposedly 'grass-roots' analyses can be offered from within existing parameters of English Studies. At a recent conference on English literature teaching in India, teaching strategies were often discussed without scrutinizing the existing ideological thrust of the discipline in India.[1] Cosmetic changes in student-teacher relation-

---

[1] This was a seminar jointly organized by the British Council and the Centre for Linguistics and English, Jawaharlal Nehru University, and held in New Delhi, 30 March – 3 April 1990.

ships, or in 'approaches' to existing texts, are in order to deflect the challenge made by recent critiques of the discipline, or by pedagogies informed by, say, feminist or marxist theory. Theoretical analysis is accused of being rarefied and 'up there', while conservative teaching practices masquerade yet again as apolitical, down-to-earth and so on. A venerable Shakespearean professor informed me, typically, that theoretical criticism is incapable of 'close readings', of communicating with ordinary students, and so on. In such a situation it becomes all the more imperative to demonstrate the connections between criticism and pedagogy, between policies and classroom realities, and between different sections of those involved in English literary education; and to deny simplistic oppositions between high and low, theory and practice, and indeed colonizer and colonized, which leave the actual 'site' of the discipline unmapped. Having said this, I reiterate that it is a tall order, and that what follows is at best a tentative exercise.

It is by now well established that what became entrenched as critical orthodoxies within the subject were themselves products of the disciplinary, i.e. pedagogic, formation of the subject. A growing body of criticism has substantiated the ways in which the political, ideological and cultural uses of teaching English shaped particular critical approaches; conversely, teaching strategies were determined both by these uses as well as the specific situations in which English began and continued to be taught.[2] Therefore there is no literary criticism that is not pedagogically moulded. Given the colonial history of English literature teaching in India, and especially its intersections with the history of the discipline in the metropolis itself, there are bound to be shared aspects of its current 'crisis'— both the orthodoxies as well as notions of alternative teaching—in the Western and Indian classrooms. In fact the relatively monolithic structure of Indian universities, to which I will return later, is itself a result of colonial educational history, whereby diverse educational and cultural situations were sought to be streamlined into an administrable and thus controllable whole.

---

[2] See e.g. Chris Baldick, *The Social Mission of English Criticism* (Oxford: Oxford University Press, 1983); Franklin E. Court, 'The Social and Historical Significance of the First English Professorship in England', *PMLA*, vol. 108, no. 5, October 1988; Jean E. Howard and Marion O'Connor, eds., *Shakespeare Reproduced: The Text in History and Ideology* (New York and London: Methuen, 1987); Gauri Viswanathan, 'The Beginnings of English Literary Studies in British India', *Oxford Literary Review*, vol. 9, nos. 1-2, 1987, pp. 2-26; Peter Widdowson, ed., *Re-reading English* (London and New York: Methuen, 1982).

However, this situation was complicated by several factors: by the different policies of colonial administrators at various points of time, by the contradictions within colonial administration even during a single given period, by the interaction of English educationists (and the dominant paradigms of literary education in particular) with different sections of the native intelligentsia, by the interpolation of women as the majority of the recepients of literary education at both ends of the colonial spectrum, by the necessary disjunctures between colonial intentions and their actual effects, and so on. On the one hand, the English text was clearly used in the colonial situation as an instrument of social control. On the other, the *interaction* between British education, especially English literature teaching, and those whom it was intended to 'shape', is a crucial area which needs to be explored in order to map the history of the discipline in India. Put together, they constitute a cultural study of the last hundred and fifty years as well as of contemporary society.

This notion of 'interaction' does not deny the locus of power. It does remind us that the recipient of the text crucially affects what its 'truth' or 'meaning' is, as so much recent work in cultural studies has emphasized. 'Real readers', Willemen reminds us, 'are subjects in history, living in social formations, rather than mere subjects of a single text ... the text may be contradicted by the subject's position(s) in relation to other texts, problematics, institutions, discursive formations'.[3] Such contradictions do not automatically result in questioning the received authority of the text or the institutions or traditions within which it is deployed. Often the 'real' subject may herself be party to the smoothening of these fissures, as is discussed later in this essay. But even so, she is the crucial factor which reminds us constantly of the interlocking of criticism and pedagogy, and needs to be examined by anyone writing a history of English literature in India, including the present-day scenario.

Jasodhara Bagchi has argued that sections of the nineteenth century Indian intelligentsia used the English literary text to consolidate their own hegemonic culture. Elsewhere I have suggested that such uses of the canon were double-edged, in as much as they often challenged its dominant Western interpretations, even as they buttressed its claim to universal meaning.[4] It is not surprising that the consolidation of native

[3] Cited in Dave Morley, 'Texts, Readers and Subjects', in Hall, *et al.*, eds, *Culture, Media, Language* (London: Hutchinson, 1980), 167, 169.

[4] *Gender, Race, Renaissance Drama* (Manchester: Manchester University Press, 1989), 20-33.

hegemony and the challenge to colonial authority were often collateral tasks; but the specific working of this process on the site of the English literary text means that reading against the grain can, and maybe always does, paradoxically reinforce the universalist premises of dominant literary education. This is cause for self-reflection in our present efforts to seize the book and Caliban like, curse in the colonizer's tongue. More immediately, it problematizes what is necessarily the first step in exploring the contemporary Indian classroom, i.e. how literary 'power' or 'authority' is constituted in this context.

Where do we locate the 'establishment' of English literary studies? Does it refer to those who frame education policy? Their notions of literature are certainly responsible for a large chunk of the existing problem—the contents of Pass Course and Subsidiary courses of English at the undergraduate level. They are also responsible for the existing examination systems, and more specifically for the confusion between language and literature teaching, which I discuss later. Or is it professors of university departments who are often educated in the West and who largely echo dominant Western critics? They are certainly at the helm of the actual constitution of syllabi, and, crucially, institutional power in terms of research or job conditions. Or is the *status quo* to be identified with writers of cheaply published *kunjis* (mug-books, or, literally, 'keys' to the text) who are the real mediators between student and text? Their views are in a sense the authoritative interpretation of the English literary text and displace the views of the teacher in the classroom; almost anyone trying to teach differently will acknowledge that they are pitted against the power of the kunji. But usually kunji writers are themselves college lecturers—and therefore we have a Jekyll-and-Hyde scenario, where college teachers as kunji writers undermine their own classroom authority. Finally, where do we place the nominal mediators—college teachers of English who have to deal with the privileged upper-class student as well as the humble Pass Course ones, and who may have been educated in either a foreign university and an elite Indian college, or a small town university, or even a rural one? The heterogeneity of this last category makes it also the most difficult to analyse; certainly generalizations about it are impossible. Publishers also play an authoritative role, despite their own assertions that they are merely reacting to existing situations; if alternative critical material were easily available or cheaply priced, it would have a considerable impact on the classroom situation.

All this indicates, clearly, that in the situation today a neat polarization between the goodies and the baddies is difficult to sustain, as is the idea of the student as pure 'victim'. However, I do not intend to suggest either an unanalysable 'system' or a state of affairs for which no one can be held responsible. Instead, I want to identify several overlapping contradictions relating to both the structures and the ideologies of the discipline which constitute the heaving ground on which English Studies has erected its pedagogical tower. It seems to me that it may be useful to locate how critical, pedagogical and institutional factors interact in specific situations. For instance, western critical orthodoxies offered by high-brow dons, the humble kunji or mug-book used by a vast majority of students and paraphrased by many undergraduate teachers, and the ministry of education can be demarcated from each other; at the same time, received notions of categories such as 'literature', 'human nature' (and specially 'female nature'), 'love', or 'morality' are often shared by all of them. Again, a student mouthing established critical platitudes is well equipped, not just for university examinations, but for the entrance tests to the Indian Administrative Service—what is critically upheld is institutionally rewarded, undercutting the apparent unrelatedness of 'Shakespeare as a seer of the human condition' and the Indian bureaucracy or the established examination system. By problematizing too easy dichotomies between 'high' and 'low' or colonial (or western) and indigenous, I hope to indicate how institutional and critical structures penetrate the classroom.

The three basic contradictions that beset English literary teaching in India have to do with the nature of educational institutions, with educational policies, and with the status of the discipline. All three impinge on, even determine, what happens in actual teaching situations. At best one can only gesture at how they do so. For several reasons, this task remains fraught with difficulties—practical, methodological and conceptual. To begin with, the Indian classroom has been far less systematically explored than its Western counterpart, particularly in relation to literature teaching in the university. Empirical work relating to English Studies in India is in its infancy; one of the disincentives for beginning is the general poverty of records and the paucity of documentation. For instance, nowhere in the records or libraries of Delhi University could I locate its question papers in English literature for the past fifty or twenty, or even ten years. Given enormous regional variations in standards, cultural contexts and language, moreover, 'the Indian classroom' is almost a meaningless generalization. The status of English literature teaching, the class, social and linguistic background of students, the conditions of libraries and institutions as well as the social factors that frame the education process and actual classroom practices—all vary enormously, and until such time as these are more fully examined one can only claim to discuss that slice of Indian reality in which one is actually positioned—in my case this is, at present, a constituent college of the University of Delhi.

The difficulty of mapping actual teaching practices has also something to do with the teaching of English literature *per se*. Speaking about the British situation, Tony Davies quite rightly argues that there is a disjuncture between critical theory and 'the humdrum, everyday and generally quite "untheoretical" activity of English teaching [where] the real effectivity of "literature" as a practice is to be found'.[5] This is quite true of India as well. In other words the teaching strategies of this discipline often belie its implicit purpose of imparting culture, resting as they do on the notion of 'feeling', of 'exploring' and 'discussing.' Moreover, teachers in higher education are not, unlike schoolteachers, 'trained, assessed, supervised'.[6] This makes for a wider variation of classroom experiences than in the case of other disciplines.

But there are crucial differences between the British and Indian teaching situations. Davies indicates that the tutorial or seminar, rather than the lecture, is the usual mode of teaching literature in the British classroom: 'Few English teachers would wish to return to the tedious monolithic lecture, the mechanical dictation of parts of speech and figures of rhetoric, the imposition of narrow orthodoxies.' Of course, as he goes on to underline, such a pedagogy

itself constitutes a determinate discursive regime . . . that can be characterized as 'liberal' in so far as it imposes itself not by insisting on the positional authority of the teacher, nor by compelling assent to a given and explicit curriculum of knowledge, but by inviting a voluntary recognition of the existence, purpose and value of a 'subject': Literature itself.[7]

To the extent that this apparent liberalism in teaching methods is derived from the ideological stance of dominant criticism, it probably characterizes the Indian classroom as well. But here the tutorial and seminar system is only a malfunctioning appendage to the business of teaching, which is overwhelmed by the 'monolithic' lecture, where the cruder forms of the teacher's authority are still rampant. A mechanical dictation of class notes, a lack of any discussion or questioning, the

---

[5] Tony Davies, 'Common Sense and Critical Practice; Teaching Literature,' in Widdowson, 34.

[6] Ibid.

[7] Ibid., 37.

imposition of opinions by the teacher—all these are still dominant realities, into which there are obviously multiple inputs. I have not the space nor the necessary research to speculate on whether this situation derived from the fairly strict routine of indigenous learning situations before English education, or whether and how colonial education heightened the disparity between teacher and taught and regimented the lecture routine. Today, however, it is not confined to the university, nor to literature teaching alone. But in literature teaching the apparent opposition between the liberal strategies of established criticism and an extremely orthodox classroom is 'overcome'.

This pedagogic orthodoxy is fuelled by the fact that, despite the enormous variations I have indicated,

The Indian academic system is monolithic in character. All universities, by and large, follow one uniform practice, be it admissions, appointments to faculties, framing of syllabi or examinations. Since the appointment of the first Education Commission, each Commission has said essentially the same thing about all the important matters relating to education.[8]

Therefore one can see why explorations of the state of English literature in the Indian classroom have mainly rested on what happens 'above'—in official policies, statements and institutional procedures; one can also see why these cannot be ignored but need to be related to the different situations 'below'. In that sense, no analysis of 'the Indian classroom' can hope to be representative; yet it derives from a problem that disparate teachers and students will recognize as familiar.

This diversity/uniformity is the most basic structural contradiction that impinges on the actual teaching of English literature: there is no scope for teachers in drastically different situations to cater to the specific needs of their students. Despite this, we all do 'tailor' our teaching to different kinds of students. This makes for a kind of 'adhocism' that accompanies even the most conventional teaching methods on the one hand, and fairly crude forms of ideological imposition on the other, so that the average student remains most hesitant to voice an opinion or even ask a question. This latter paralysis is obviously catalysed by the cultural and linguistic alienation of Indian student from Western text. Finally, experimentation with desired courses remains a distant dream even for those who are arguing for syllabi reform; we have very little

---

[8] D.P. Pattanayak, *Multilingualism and Mother-Tongue Education* (Delhi: OUP, 1981), 131.

actual classroom experience to back up our recommendations. Arguably, a uniform syllabus even for all colleges of Delhi University is untenable, since their students come from different socio-economic and cultural backgrounds. At the same time completely free-wheeling courses may prove to be complicit with a process whereby, as teachers' unions fear, existing differentials in educational institutions (in terms of facilities, the class-background of students, and various privileges) will be bolstered by current attempts of the state to grant 'autonomy' to some colleges. The monolithic character of the university also makes for obvious bureaucratization with respect to evaluation, which impinges on any possible syllabus reform.

The second contradiction, as I said, has to do with educational policy. It is obvious that the conflation of Honours, Pass Course and Subsidiary English teaching in this discipline is the crux of the classroom problem. Arguably, the latter two should cater to the teaching of language, although much Subsidiary teaching can be done away with altogether until some genuine alternative in terms of interdisciplinary curriculi can be envisaged. However, the relationship between language teaching and literary education continues to be confused and unexplored both in the university and by education policy-makers. The dominant assumption in Indian education, following the British model, has generally been that language and literature are 'inextricably connected', and that the language of literacy must be the language of literature. Here, Pattanayak's suggestion that this text-oriented approach to language was not simply imported from overseas, but worked out in the specific context of the existing Indian situation, is worth investigating:

During the medieval period, the study of language meant by and large the study of grammar or of literature. When the British took over the administration it suited their purpose to continue this tradition as regards English education. Thus a study of English remained confined to the study of English literature and students were not prepared for the use of English as a medium of other science and humanistic subjects.[9]

Krishna Kumar makes an analogous case for the predominance of a 'textbook culture' in contemporary India, which he sees as 'a joint product of the soil as it existed and the seed thrown in it by the missionary and the colonial administrator'; this culture erodes the autonomy and creativity of the individual teacher and is tied in with the

[9] Pattanayak, 160-1.

bureaucratic, centralized governance of language.[10] It is worth noting that the result of this textbook culture is not just a prioritization of literary texts in teaching language but also a fear of exploration in critical texts—hence both the teacher and the taught depend on *accepted* criticism and Bradley has the status of a textbook in relation to Shakespearean study. Another result is, obviously, fear of experimentation with texts themselves, so that the textbook culture is more than a dependence on texts—it is an attitude to teaching and learning itself.

Neither the champions nor the opponents of education in English have paid much attention to the question of *literature*. On the one hand the claims of English literature to universal value and culture are not examined either by educationists or by departments of English. On the other hand policy statements privilege the teaching of English as a second language or for technological or library purposes. In 1967 the language controversy flared up, following attempts to switch to the mother tongue as the medium of instruction even in higher education. At the end of much debate on access to information, the merits of our own languages, the colonial heritage, and the 'scientific outlook', English emerged simultaneously devalued and doubly secure: 'The Education Commission has insisted that for a successful completion of the first degree course a student should possess an adequate command over English, be able to express himself in it with reasonable ease and fluency, understand lectures in it and avail himself of its literature'.[11]

But there is an accompanying, never-examined slide from this to the assumption that literature is central to language teaching. So, ironically, language continues to be imparted through the medium of the text. This should not be seen only as a reflection of the view that language is best taught through literature, for theories of teaching language are rarely on the ministerial agenda. Instead, it must be understood as part of the unspoken assumption that the literary text is the means to education, culture and knowledge in general. The contradiction between this assumption and the accompanying devaluation of literature and human sciences generally is apparent.

The report of a study group appointed by the ministry of education,

[10] Krishna Kumar, 'The Origins of India's Textbook Culture', *Occasional Papers on History and Society*, no. XLVII (New Delhi: Nehru Memorial Museum and Library, 1987), 15, 16-17.

[11] A.B. Shah, *The Great Debate: Language Controversy and University Education* (Bombay: Lalvani, 1969), ix.

Government of India, in 1967, is a good example of the confusion that besets Indian educationists with respect to English literature and language. It first states that: 'compulsory English should be taught, not merely in the first and second year of the three-year degree course, but for all the three years. This makes for better comprehension of written materials in English—a skill which is essential as ever at the post-graduate stage'.[12]

The study group goes on to confidently predict that if language and literature teaching is demarcated,

more and more students are sure to opt for language study, for that is the need of the hour. We expect that within the next twenty years or so, most of the departments of English in the Universities will have changed over mainly to a language oriented postgraduate course in English.[13]

There is thus a clear disparagement of literature in favour of functional language teaching, but the study group's own suggestions for the compulsory English courses revert to textual study, and the texts chosen are again canonical 'high' literature, and Western literature at that: Shaw's *Major Barbara*, T.S. Eliot's *Murder in the Cathedral*, Oscar Wilde's *The Importance of Being Earnest*, Shakespeare's *Hamlet*, Robert Bolt's *A Man For All Seasons*, Emily Bronte's *Wuthering Heights*, Dickens' *Great Expectations*, Golding's *Lord of the Flies*, Wells's *The History of Mr Polly*.

As a result, about twenty years after the predictions of the study group, there has been no shift away to real language teaching — at Delhi University the Pass Course syllabus includes Sheridan's *The Rivals*, Golding's *Lord of the Flies* and Shakespeare's *Othello*! Such confusion is the result of the belief that the literary text is not only the highest repository of words but also of 'value'. If such assumptions were at the heart of the introduction of the subject in colonial India, they continue to inform policy-makers today.

Recent discussions indicate that the 'literariness of language' is a questionable concept, and that the same qualities of language which are supposed to be revealed through the literary text can be located in ordinary language — including its most banal usage in jingles and advertisements.[14] On the other hand, literature may be, if judicially

<hr/>

[12] Ministry of Education, Government of India, *The Study of English in India* (1967), 28.

[13] Ibid., 34.

[14] Christopher Brumfit and Ronald Carter, eds., *Literature and Language Teaching* (Oxford: OUP, 1986), 6-15.

selected, extremely useful in teaching language. Sandra Mckay argues that—

Our success in using literature, of course, greatly depends upon a selection of texts which will not be too difficult on either a linguistic or a conceptual level. Ultimately, however, if we wish to promote truly aesthetic reading, it is essential that literature be approached . . . in a manner which establishes a personal and asthetic interaction between a reader and a text.[15]

Our syllabi makers are only too eager to concur with the first proposition; in their assertions about the cultural and spiritual value of literature they are not willing to admit any scrutiny into the heterogeneity of the term, and are hostile to its contextualization either in terms of its production or its reception. In our courses it is simply assumed that *Othello* will equip a Pass Course student to use English in any situation because Shakespeare naturally uses the 'best' English possible; that literature 'touches our common humanity',[16] and is therefore the best repository of language. This 'hidden agenda' of English Studies sets the parameters for pedagogy: I taught Miller's *All My Sons* to a first year Pass Course class, meeting them thrice a week for over eight months. At the end of that period, 22 out of 23 essays written by the class got even the story wrong—they stated that throughout the play Kate really believed that Larry was alive! I later discovered that the kunji states this too. I actually think that the play is fairly 'relevant' to the commercial culture and growing business ethic of Delhi, but this has been impossible to communicate, even within a relatively elite institution.

The relationship between language teaching and English literature is not the subject of this essay; my purpose has merely been to indicate that English literature teaching in India is carried on in this uneasy space, where the subject is officially devalued and yet sacrosanct, where a denigration of literature is implicit in the current 'functionalism' which itself never really takes off.

Clearly, the contradictions of English teaching are not just structural; in the example noted above their ideological implications are evident. One of the most important constituents of such a situation is the status of English literature in India today. (By status I mean how the discipline is viewed by educationists, by students and their families, by the general

---

[15] Sandra Mckay, 'Literature in the ESL Classroom', in Brumfit and Carter, 198. See also J.P. Boyle, 'Testing Language with Students of Literature in ESL Situations' in Brumfit and Carter, 199-207.
[16] Brumfit and Carter, 200.

public, and by its own teachers.) At its apex, English literature as a university discipline appears to have remained nearly inviolate. What is more, give or take a few cosmetic concessions, actual syllabi have remained frozen over the years. But this should not blind us to the heaving of the ground on which English Studies has erected its tower. The post-independence expansion of universities and schools, the debates about English language, and the devaluation of the humanities in recent education frame and qualify this apparent stasis and immutability. Institutionalized Indian criticism has not only treated Western literature as monolithic, but has refused to acknowledge either the heterogeneity of its Indian readers or the educational changes which affect its teaching today. In fact, to read most of it one would not get even a hint about the context in which it is being written.

But I want to suggest that various positions on the spectrum of English Studies—from those that defend the *status quo* to those which interrogate and seek to change it—are constituted by, even if they are not themselves fully aware of, this contradictory status of English Studies and its satellite activities. The critical, pedagogical and institutional stances of departments of English, in particular, are derived from the latter's perception of their own fading centrality, which is not to say that they are less pernicious for that. On the one hand the same old claims are made about the humanizing nature of literary study, and retrogressive political stances are justified with reference to the higher morality of literature teachers who should be 'above' such mundane considerations as increasing bureaucratization in education, pay-cuts, retrenchment, and adverse working conditions. Such stances are bolstered by specific critical orthodoxies: 'human nature' is above 'politics'; a valuable author critiques society but then 'rises above' that to talk about the perennially valid truths of 'the human condition'—and so on. On the other hand, increasing hostility to alternative positions, a marked underlining of bureaucracy in these departments' own functioning, a holding fast to dogmas but a lack of rigour in scholarship, are also signs of a fading power.

Equally, those seeking to establish an alternative pedagogy are caught on the horns of a dilemma shaped by the same reality: a dilemma which shapes the critique of existing education as well as any alternatives we may seek to explore. Both the architects and the critics of established literary education have articulated the cultural and political uses of literature, although from opposing positions. Indeed the connection between 'ways of seeing' and 'ways of being' need not be spelt out here. Oppositional criticism hopes to radically change in both these. The politics of literary theory is again the subject of much discussion; in recent months it would appear that many, too many, voices have registered the disjuncture between radical criticism and radical politics in the Anglo-American academy. I resist the enormous temptation to intervene in this crucial debate in this essay; my point is simply that the effort to make a critical approach become the carrier of a way of seeing the whole world is thwarted, in the Indian academy, by the devaluation of literary education in general. In other words, I will fondly imagine that my re-reading *Macbeth* will persuade my students to change their views on women, on state power, on the connections between the private and the public, and so on. But, and I will come back to this shortly, alternative criticism requires a great deal more work and material than does carrying on with accepted views. Very few students (and indeed teachers) are prepared to invest enough time and effort in this enterprise—those who are, are daunted by poor working conditions, or simply the desire to get on to more 'worthwhile' occupations.

Our university departments of English are, for the most part, the last outposts of Leavisite criticism; not only their critical practice, but much more importantly their attitudes, modes of functioning, even behaviour patterns, are seen to be elitist and influenced by a Western outlook or a hankering after the Western academy. At first glance it appears that the home-grown kunji exists at a far remove from them. Departments of English will all formally deprecate kunjis; in fact howlers from the latter are probably their only source of humour, the incomprehension or malapropisms of students always excepted. Interestingly, while the uses of Dogberry and Verges' malapropisms in Shakespeare's *Much Ado About Nothing* are much analysed, those of our own students are used only to confirm the social and intellectual superiority of those who can use the language 'properly'. The 'higher' the status of the English teacher, the more removed she is from the lowly undergraduate, or the even lowlier Pass Course student. I do not need to underline the reasons for the seductiveness of the kunji, although I will later refer to what a small survey among my honours students revealed. My point is, simply, that its power is complete because the kunji is saying exactly what dominant Western criticism and its Indian practitioners dish out in more 'sophisticated' language. The kunji is a more accessible version, linguistically and materially, of established critical paradigms—thus it and the classroom experience do not usually contradict each other. Where they do, the kunji is still, in my experience, victorious.

The kunji shares with institutional criticism the privileging of literature as the bearer of truth, culture and morality, and of the canonical status of the writer as directly proportional to his/her transcendental status. Consider, for example, the ways in which both Arthur Quiller Couch and John Dover Wilson's introduction to Cambridge University Press's New Shakespeare edition of *As You like It* and Raghukul Tilak's kunji on *Much Ado About Nothing* operate within the Coleridgean paradigm of Shakespeare's universality:

> It may very well be that, as our texts reach us, they were adapted out of Christian to pagan ceremonial in obedience to royal wish or statute. But it matters nothing surely. The gods change, but literature persists . . . [17]

> Shakespearean comedy has been loved and enjoyed in every age and country. Its charm is as fresh as ever today . . . It is like a perfume, all pervasive and delightful. Much water has flown under the Thames, since the top and crown of English humorists lived and created, but none has been equal to him in this respect, as in other respects, upto this time.[18]

Except for variation of language, does it matter which is the Cambridge and which the Rama Brothers publication? Or that they are talking about two different plays? Since the kunji blithely announces its debt to other critics but does not follow any systematic pattern of referencing, there are verbal echoes as well, often distorted: for example, Tilak quotes Raleigh to the effect that 'the world of Shakespearean comedy is a rainbow world of love in idleness', and the New Cambridge edition calls Arden 'a rainbowed island'. Does Tilak derive from Dover Wilson; do both from Raleigh? After all, there is a stock response which circulates among Western critics as well, so Tilak is no more unoriginal than Quiller Couch or Wilson, although he is remarkably innovative in adapting well-worn criticism to a more accessible language and style. Sandwiched between a quote from Marlowe and a quote from Raleigh is his own remark about the absolute and immediate nature of love in Shakespeare: 'Their love is engendered in the eye at first sight.' It is ludicrous, and yet ideologically in tune with the twenty or so other, respectable, Western critics he cites. In its general remarks, the kunji's main accent is on the universality of the canonical text. Its general principles are derivative but the style is completely home-grown: 'Shakespeare was one of the greatest men of genius that have ever been

[17] Arthur Quiller Couch and John Dover Wilson, eds, *As You Like It* (Cambridge: CUP), XVIII.

[18] Raghukul Tilak, *William Shakespeare's Much Ado About Nothing* (New Delhi: Rama Brothers, 1986), 18, 32.

born on this blighted planet of ours'.[19] So there is, at a very basic level, no contradiction between the kunji and canonical criticism; the former's purpose of making a particular kind of criticism available to another specific student community is implicitly sanctioned by the ways texts are dominantly taught in more elite situations.

What is specific to us is that the universality-of-literature approach becomes particularly pernicious when applied to the Western text in the Indian situation because it acquires neo-colonial overtones. If the dominant Anglo-American critical traditions have traditionally emphasized the 'unity' of desirable texts, and have been preoccupied with a unified metaphysical and experiential truth, order and stability, the literary establishment here has gone one step further by attempting to smoothen the contradictions between different established approaches by welcoming them all with open arms. In India, it would appear that there are hardly any tensions between the positions of, say, Bradley, Frye or Leavis. All have been comfortably accommodated by the powers that be. In fact, one of the peculiarities of the literary establishment in India is its insistence (whereby one may suggest liberalism meets the Hindu rhetoric about being large enough to contain multitudes) on accommodating different 'approaches' to literature. There is a method to this madness. Whereas Bradley allows them to indulge in easy character criticism, and Frye to create their own mythical monolith, Leavis restores to literary dons their sense of professional importance. Leavis' seductiveness in India lies in his real achievement in being able to begin to 'professionalize' the discipline and mould English literary studies for what he calls 'the technological age': 'The problem is to *have* an English school that truly deserves the respect of those who are acquainted with intellectual standards in their own fields'.[20] Or again: '"English" suffers by reason of its extreme remoteness as an academic discipline from Mathematics; how to produce and enforce the standards that determine genuine qualification?'[21] The debate provoked by Leavis on education in general finds no echo here, although his view that 'a focus of cultural continuity can only be in English' is adopted out of context by our departments in order to deny their own increasing marginalization. They implicity, and often explicitly, echo Leavis vigorous assertions of the centrality of:

[19] Ibid., 1.
[20] F.R. Leavis, *English Literature in Our Time and the University* (Cambridge: CUP, 1969), 3.
[21] Ibid., 21.

English literature, magnificent and matchless in diversity and range, and so full and profound in its registration of changing life (which) gives us a continuity that is not yet dead. There is no other; no other access to anything approaching a full continuity of mind, spirit and sensibility—which is what we desperately need.[22]

But Leavis and Frye, and indeed the entire new critical tradition, are united in their anti-marxism, and this is still largely the basis for the critical pluralism avowed in India. The nostalgia, then, is not simply for the West, but for a particular kind of Western university—the kind Leavis often refers to and spent so much energy trying to create: 'Cambridge, then, figured for us civilisation's anti-Marxist recognition of its own nature and needs—recognition of that, the essential, which Marxian wisdom discredited, and the external and material drive of civilisation threatened, undoctrinally to eliminate'.[23] It is true that 'the oppositional' changes over time—in the last seventeen years of my association, feminism has replaced marxism as the pet bogey of many English departments. But the point is that avowed pluralism always excludes what it regards as subversive, and especially that which is seen to feed into an alternative pedagogy. For example, feminist criticism threatens because it connects academic critique and political practice within the academy. No doubt a variety of feminist criticism, purged of this insistence on the politics of theory and of reading practices is on its way, belatedly, to being accepted in our institutions, and is creating its own pedagogical tensions. Here I emphasize the selectivity which underlines the apparently pluralist invocation of the Western academy, and often of elements which may be passé in that academy itself; hence 'nostalgia' is a good word to describe the Western orientation of English departments. But it is perfectly possible to include, within such nostalgia, selective readings of Indian history and culture, themselves usually revivalist, and certainly essentialist and patriarchal. Hence, for example, the way in which Shakespeare and Kalidasa are compared sits easily with the premises of both liberal-humanist Western criticism and Hindu chauvinism.[24]

This combination of indigenous and foreign critical methods ties in with my earlier point about interaction. It also brings me to a crucial and neglected problem. The assumptions which we commonly attribute to

---

[22] Ibid., 60.
[23] Ibid., 18.
[24] Loomba, 146-8.

English literary education, in India and elsewhere—the transcendental text, literature as repository of truth, culture and value, the teacher of literature as cultural and moral guru, the writer as seer of the human condition, the great work of art as above politics and history—are not limited to the teaching of English literature alone. My own dialogues with students and teachers of literature in other languages reveal that some of our crises, our critical and pedagogical methods, are familiar there. Hindi and Sanskrit literature are taught, it seems to me, with similar ideas. My purpose is not to hark back to some undifferentiated notion of literature, but to insert assumptions about *literature* along with those about English as a crucial part of the history of this discipline in India, including its contemporary problems.[25]

To come back to my point about the overlaps between the 'high' and the 'low': the kunji displays both the selectivity and the pluralism I have identified. It too overlooks differences between, say, Bradley and Leavis, between Kalidasa and Shakespeare. But its shuttling is cruder, more displayed. It gathers together all the acceptable critics and squeezes them into ready-prepared answers; in this it is explicitly doing what our dominant pedagogy implicitly demands. Thus it really does obviate the need to go and read twenty unavailable books. The charm of the kunji, then, is shaped on the one hand by the critical and pedagogical require-ments of the academy and, on the other, by the underprivileged condi-tions in which these demands are made, i.e. the extremely poor library conditions, the inaccessible language of the texts, and the critical books, the inability of students to buy books, and above all the disjuncture between what is required of a 'good' student and the motivation of the average student who is really prepared to invest only a minimal amount of time and effort into the business of studying English literature.

The point was hammered home over the past two years. I took my second year English Honours class at Hindu College, Delhi University, as testing ground for many of the issues I explore here. Both times, the class was composed of both boys and girls from widely different class, social and linguistic backgrounds. I taught them practically the whole of the Renaissance Drama paper, meeting the class four times a week.[26] I

---

[25] See my 'Teaching the Bard', special issue of the CIEFL Journal (Hyderabad: forthcoming), for an elaboration of the problems besetting a superficial substitution of English literary texts by 'third world' or 'common-wealth' literature, or Indian literature in translation.

[26] Second year English (Honours) students in Delhi University are required to take two papers — this one currently consists of Marlowe's *Dr. Faustus*,

not only marked their tutorials but also had the entire class answer certain questions on the texts, which allowed me to monitor what happened to my efforts to teach the Renaissance differently. One of my colleagues asked the class of 1988, after they had graduated to the final year, how many of them consulted kunjis for the Renaissance paper. All of them put up their hands. I was shocked, since I had considered myself rather successful in leading them away from the usual sorts of criticism and had genuinely thought they had responded very well and had become interested, via the Renaissance, in a whole host of issues as well as in particular ways of seeing, in contesting received opinions, and so on. In this state of shock I asked them to write, anonymously if they wished, their responses to my efforts and their perceptions of studying English literature in Delhi University. I particularly asked them to spell out what made them go to kunjis, what they thought of exams, and so on. As students of a relatively privileged and up-market college, how-ever, their experiences cannot be taken as representative even of Delhi University; but their responses provide some insights.

They confirm that the power of institutional criticism indeed lies in the way in which its values and insights are institutionally rewarded. The student is the site of the battle between establishment and opposi-tional criticisms. As I said earlier, these criticisms, or their accompanying pedagogies, coexist with her other experiences, which (potentially) con-tradict and undermine the received 'truths' of existing English literary studies. The point is how to catalyse such contradictions and channelize them into a new way of being. This may sound rather grandiose—and it is certainly unfashionable, even naive, to assert the radical social consequences of alternative criticism. But to my mind the purpose of such criticism cannot be merely yet another interpretation of the text, though that is the point of entry into, and often the result of, teaching and learning differently. My student respondents unconsciously con-firm that they are aware of such connections between reading and living. That is precisely why they are what we may call 'resistant subjects'; resistant to both establishment and, unfortunately, opposition-al views. As many teachers in Delhi University find today, our average student is increasingly consonant with a growing commercial culture, so that alternative criticism finds it hard to precipitate a real conflict. In

---

Jonson's *Bartholomew Fair* (which is the least popular among students and teachers), and three plays by Shakespeare: *Much Ado About Nothing, Richard II* and *Macbeth*.

my experience, girls are more conflictual subjects to begin with, and more open to newer ways of existing. Their 'real lives' are harder, offer them fewer choices, and certainly fewer rewards than those of their male counterparts. But generally both male and female students in this situation are quick to realize the benefits of critical orthodoxy within the educational system. Secondly, their choice of English literatre as a college subject and their subsequent espousal of orthodox criticism are also largely a result of their perceptions about themselves and the world they live in.

All the more reason, then, that alternative pedagogy must explicitly address the ways in which particular criticisms are institutionalized. The teacher has to also negotiate within the situation—enter the domain of setting papers, examining papers, equip the student to manoeuvre her way within debilitating question papers, make alternative material accessible, and so on. But let me detail the responses I got.

Most of them frankly admitted that studying English literature would not get them the kind of jobs that other degrees would. Boys, in particular, continually referred to the belief that most girls in their class would get married after their degree. However, all of them talked about the great 'potential' of the subject—some in practical terms, but most in terms of the great human experience. One girl, for example, wrote:

It is supposed to be the great 'female' subject, where the majority of pupils are of the female sex, who are (supposed) to become school teachers, get married or if adventurous might become journalists. Not many consider this to be a stepping stone for a full time professional career. Which is sad, because we are exposed and capable of any of the options other graduates may be.

Another, disparaging the lack of intellectual curiosity in her classmates, put it down to 'uncultured Delhi', pointing out that her Calcutta counterparts were 'so aware, culturally alive, and consequently, more rounded people'. At the same time, she also reiterated that literature can create 'complete human beings'. My most articulate respondent was the classical Westernized Indian, except that he was self-critical and mocked his own alienation. He confessed that he expected to find, in his classmates, 'a certain intellectual elite'; instead he found people preparing to marry, take over their fathers' business, join the IAS (Indian Administrative Service) and in other ways 'chase after economic security'. Nearly all of them gestured both at the great humanizing potential of English literature and at the fact that its study would equip them for nothing. In this last context, as I said earlier, it is worth expanding the critique of English literary study to the study of literature in general, for I found similar attitudes among students of Hindi and Sanskrit literature who are required to study English as a subsidiary subject. That may be the reason why, whereas the Western text is used to foster a certain kind of alienation and neo-colonialism (one student wrote: 'When the last Englishman with thoughts of empire has perished, Enid Blyton will still be around converting a few more colonials, who will forever dream of potted meat sandwiches and buttered scones at four p.m. on Sundays, to the Christian universe'), the indigenous text as it is currently taught is the medium of reinforcing a most chauvinistic and reactionary interpretation of our culture. Thus literature teaching in foreign and native languages together may ensure the colonial dichotomies indicated variously by Franz Fanon, Rabindranath Tagore and Bipin Chandra Pal, among others.

In both cases, however, the perception that literary study is useless in market terms is related to the insistence on a value that is 'above' mere practical life; hence, again moral or cultural worth is today articulated from a position of devaluation. This itself leads to another peculiar aspect of literary education—the lack of motivation of both students and teachers and the lack of rigorous scholarship—which bolsters the mug-book syndrome. In our eagerness to chart out an alternative pedagogy we are often guilty of positing our own version of the 'ideal student' who is heavily mutilated by the teaching of English literature, but is latently radical. Elsewhere I have discussed the increasing feminization of the discipline, which ties in with its devaluation.[27] If the bulk of our Honours students are women being prepared for the marriage market, an overwhelming percentage of the rest cherish bureaucratic or managerial dreams, or are preparing to take over the family business, or at the very best are going to end up in secretarial jobs. Why do we expect them to be ripe for radicalization? The average student of English literature is obviously not prepared to undertake the Herculean task of locating the critical baggage, and yet is convinced that this baggage is actually far more important than the text itself.

This was borne out by my experience of teaching *Dr Faustus* and *Macbeth* to second year Honours students in 1988. I had spent a term and a half on *Faustus*, trying to introduce them to critical debates around the text as well as to recent work on Renaissance history and culture. I deliberately underemphasized the necessity of going to institutionalized readings, so that students would have a perspective on these

---

[27] Loomba, 23-8.

instead of following them uncritically. At that time we had only read *Macbeth* in class, and I had commented extensively on the text as we read it but had not yet begun to discuss it. At this point, departmental tests were held. On *Faustus* I set questions relating to the basic conflict in the play, Faustus as a Renaissance scholar, and whether the play was an inverted morality. On the other hand I asked them only for their personal responses to a first reading of *Macbeth*. The answers surprised, even shocked me. Nearly all the answers on *Faustus* were a badly assembled collage of traditional criticism; each of them had copied from the mug-book on the play: 'in trying to become God, Faustus becomes the not-God'. They all were confused about the conflict in Faustus, because all the material I had given them in class clashed with the easy collapsing of the play into an 'inverted' morality that one generally finds in traditional criticism. While writing about *Macbeth*, however, students felt free to express their own views, not just because of the question I asked them but because they knew that at this stage they were not expected to 'know' the play or attempt 'proper' answers. As a result they attempted, with varying success, to relate Macbeth's ambition to the context of Elizabethan politics, whereas Faustus was repeatedly seen in terms of absolute and essential paradigms of 'good' and 'evil'. My delight was short-lived. As soon as we had graduated to discussing *Macbeth* in greater detail, the students said they were 'confused'. I had introduced them to articles in John Russell Brown's *Focus on Macbeth* and given them a lot of material on Renaissance witchcraft and sexual politics. As examinations neared, they inevitably resorted to what they knew was acceptable, and finally confessed that every time they read Bradley they could 'think of nothing else'. Here we can locate one difference between the Indian and the British classroom. In India the bulk of the material is 'dated'; so that whereas I had to specially order one copy of Brown's book for our library and make sure it slowly circulated among the class, Bradley is abundantly available. I could talk about sexual politics for hours in the classroom, but the basic books necessary to back up such lectures, such as Lawrence Stone's *The Family, Sex and Marriage in England,* or Joan Kelly's article, 'Did Women have a Renaissance', or Lisa Jardine's and Simon Shepherd's books on the drama, are not available. The seductiveness of character criticism is unchallenged by the presence of newer and more unorthodox material, especially as the former is recirculated in even more digestable forms by kunjis. Given the anti-feminist stance of the majority of teachers in our university, my views could be reduced to the personal idiosyncracies of a crank feminist, rather than as deriving from a perspective and body of scholarship which is at least as valid and a lot more rigorously researched than a Tillyard's or a Bradley's. The point also is that I am asking the student to do a lot more than Bradley is. It is much easier to hold forth about character or intelligence than to research sixteenth-century notions of power or sexuality. It is much less work to read Renaissance politics in terms of our own conservative common-sense than to appropriate it through the specificities of two different cultures. Leavisite criticism creates meaning through the stance of assuming that there already is consensus. This should be considerably more strained in the Indian classroom, but paradoxically it isn't; the need to affirm that there is a shared culture smoothens the gaps between contexts. The schisms, then, need to be drawn out just as consciously as they have been sought to be erased. Interestingly, many students wrote that they got confused when they went to traditional criticism after my teaching. Clearly, I had not equipped them to hold their own against the authority of received scholarship.

I cannot resist quoting at length from one of my students, whose response was titled 'In Defence of Ramji Lal' (Ramji Lal being the most prolific and popular kunji writer). The significant thing is that this student, a boy, now about to appear for the final year BA (Honours) examination, was apparently one of the most interested in my Renaissance class of 1988; he participated in class, read the material I gave them, asked questions, made comments and, until I read this piece, I could have sworn he was not the kunji type; after that I started to really look—in the classroom and in buses—and found my brightest ones with kunjis in their hands. Although my cynical student remains convinced that this piece was written to 'annoy' me, and even wrote a response to it, the 'defence' ties together many of the issues discussed above—and more:

Earlier guides (kunjis) were used only as a last resort or by people who didn't pay attention in class. But now these aid-books are bought by us students right in the beginning of the term. The intelligent and the less intelligent, both use these guides. Ramji Lal is a star—a hero among students. Also climbing the ladder of success gradually is Raghukul Tilak. They are indispensable. Right on the first day of college, our seniors advise us to use Ramji Lal and company, because a thorough study of English literature is not possible without consulting Ramji . . . Moreover there is a dearth of good and relevant library books. If the books are there, they are issued—never to return. Just in case the book happens to be on the shelf, the relevant pages are torn. Also, you cannot always get the direct answers to our problems. So Ramji Lal comes to our rescue and saves us. Often enough there is a communication gap between the teacher and the student. Many a times, in an effort to impress the student, the teacher confuses him. Using high-sounding phrases and quoting a dozen critics is no help. Once again Ramji Lal fits the bill. His language is comprehensible and there is 100% communication between the two—the guide and the student . . . Ramji Lal helps class-bunkers also . . . The most important reason for using Ramji Lal is that the university examiners accept Ramji Lal's answers . . . Certain teachers have even announced in class that first he/she would give his/her own interpretations and at the end give those answers which are acceptable . . . If this is the state of affairs then why shouldn't we students use Ramji Lal? I can't find one plausible reason!

As is clear from this student's defence, the examination paper remains a major impediment to alternative teaching. The Renaissance paper of 1989 for second year undergraduates, for example, effectively mocked my efforts to lead students away from bardolatry. A question such as 'Macbeth is Shakespeare's most profound and mature vision of evil. Discuss', directly invites them to spill out all the usual eulogies of Shakespeare's special insights into 'human nature'. It would require considerable ingenuity for my students to squeeze my material on feudal power, witchcraft and sexual politics into this framework. At the undergraduate level we are not even speaking of students being penalized for alternative views but of a complete marginalization of huge chunks of classroom experience. At the postgraduate level, where students know who will be marking the papers, one sees a real fear of ideologically motivated penalities. In twelve years of teaching I have had one student who, by the time she reached the postgraduate level, was able to accommodate all the newer material into the stifling format of the question papers, and get marks without compromising her views. I put this down to her exceptional ability, and also to the fact that her perceptions were backed by her meticulous work. In other words a mediocre student with conventional views could get by, whereas an average student with unconventional ideas could not. Otherwise, and I'm sure my experience has been that of countless others, our brightest students do indifferently or even badly, or else learn to live a double life whereby a large part of the classroom experience—in those cases where this is trying to be different—becomes redundant to their examination preparation.

In our departments, actual teaching practices have remained static, though there may be the occasional formal deference to new critical stances. For example, whereas in the sixties, questions of 'form' became increasingly fashionable in our question papers, today there is the token question on 'women' of 'the third world'. In 1989, Paper VII for third year English Honours (Modern Literature I—*Fiction and Criticism*) carried the following compulsory question:

Write a note on one of the following topics:

1. Endings in the Modern Novel
2. Naturalism and the Modern Novel
3. Fictional Representation of the 'Colonies' and/or the 'Third World' in the Modern Novel
4. Fictional Representation of Women in the Modern Novel
5. Some Recent Theories of Fiction and Narrative
6. The Symbolist Novel

Questions 3, 4 and 5 certainly mark a welcome break from the usual. But they are at complete variance with the way texts are actually taught in class. Feminism, for example, is a dirty word among the English literature orthodoxy. Yet, in the same way as the Women's Development Cells threaten to co-opt and deradicalize growing female discontent in the university, or the official proposals for women's studies exist only to prevent any real demands for the same, we begin to have these questions as an oblique acknowledgement of—or is it a not so-oblique attempt to thwart? —the growing body of feminist studies in this country and abroad. There is no attempt to subject D.H. Lawrence, who is taught at undergraduate and postgraduate levels, to a feminist critique —I remember my half-hearted attempts to speak up in my MA class being silenced by the pronouncement that I could not understand Lawrence because I was not a married woman! Most likely, a feminist reading of *Sons and Lovers* would fetch no marks in the examination, nor indeed would a feminist response to question no. 4 above. The 1989 question: 'Trace Paul's relationship with Clara and, later, with Baxter Dawes in *Sons and Lovers*. Why does Paul reject Clara?', coupled with the dominant approach to Lawrence as the high priest of liberated sexuality, invites the student to reproduce the notion of Paul caught between two differently stifling women.

Again, how can a student answer question no. 3 when the 'third world' is represented on our courses by V.S. Naipaul alone—and a Naipaul who is tailored to fit mainstream notions of the novel—as Marwah argues elsewhere in this volume? I say Naipaul alone, even though Conrad and Forster are taught, not only because they are not themselves third worlders but also because both of them are even more thoroughly pruned of their significance to the colonial encounter, for obvious reasons. The liberal-humanist reading of Forster remains unchallenged in our classroom and in our question papers—'In *A Passage to India*, Aziz avers, "Nothing embraces the whole of India, nothing". Examine Aziz's statement in relation to the novel.' To insert the colonial dimension into Forster and Conrad could possibly lead to a questioning of the opinions and even the canonical status of these authors: therefore symbolism, form, evil and so on remain the focus of teaching.

The questions on women and the third world, then, are undercut by the weight of the entire approach so that they become almost meaningless concessions. This is one way in which examinations belie the classroom experience; but the reverse case, where the questions are traditional, so that unorthodox teaching is marginalized, is the more usual pattern. Again, the contradictions earlier referred to are worth keeping in mind, since college lecturers are themselves paper setters and examiners, though not all teachers are invited to be either; obviously, in students' minds, there is a huge gulf between the teachers they know and the impersonal 'examiners' they don't.

At a student seminar held in March 1990 at Hindu College, a four-hour session on Renaissance drama wound up with a long discussion among students on 'the system', including examinations. I was one of two teachers present. Some girls from Miranda House, Delhi University, had an interesting comment to make on the 'background' question which is a comparatively recent feature of Delhi University examination papers. They argued that this question, instead of directing the student to study the contexts of literature, clearly invited them to relegate these to 'background', and implicitly reinforced the existing removal of history or context from the main question. They felt that teachers too could then teach the Renaissance history/culture only for this background question and approach the plays in isolation from these. In their own presentations to the plays this had obviously not happened in their classroom—they were among the most informed students there and had moved far from traditional Shakespeare criticism. It was significant, then, that they were the ones to perceive the pitfalls of the current format.

F.R. Leavis believed 'that the undergraduate reading English . . . must inevitably be faced with more than he can get properly done, and that the profit of his education will involve his realizing this in a positive way'.[28] This saturation policy has been part of the early teaching of English literature in India, as that pioneering don of literature, Walter

---

[28] Leavis, 23.

Raleigh, testified.[29] Such a perspective was not at variance with our indigenous learning traditions, with their emphasis on memorizing and rote learning, and it is clear that it still informs our syllabus makers today.[30] But in Indian university English courses the material unleashed upon the student is also inappropriate, so that the Pass Course student can never get his/her work 'properly done' either, without the constructive advantage suggested by Leavis. If Leavis is desperately trying to create an audience for the culture imparted by English literature, in India it is assumed that it really exists. Clearly, it was a dissident reader who scribbled a note on the margins of the Delhi University library copy of Leavis's *English Literature in Our Time and the University* which I used: 'FRL always speaking to benighted academic spectres whom I cannot see'.

Like any other subject, English literature cannot exist as 'studies' without people wanting to learn it. Unlike some other disciplines, however, its pedagogic paradigms have been established on the basis of the inferiority of those it schools. These paradigms have required us to posit an uncultured recipient; at the same time the recipient is desperately needed. S/he has to be deemed capable of learning, otherwise there is no point in teaching, but s/he also has to be established as inferior. This is perhaps the final contradiction of English Studies. Mathew Arnold, Henry James, F.R. and Q.D. Leavis, as well as post-independence teachers of literature in India, have all deplored the effects of expanding education, which is seen to dilute quality. But in India this expansion intersects with an increase in the amount of 'forced' teaching of English literature, which disgusts our departments, who look down on the non-English literature wallahs. Yet, ironically, without Pass Course and Subsidiary teaching, the bulk of English teachers would lose their jobs. Those who are deemed incapable of imbibing the spiritual benefits of the text are the ones who ensure its propagation—this has been true of English literary education in Britain and is certainly one of the anomalies of our profession in contemporary India. This inclusion/exclusion principle is not just the ideological basis for the bulk of institutionalized criticism, it is the mould into which pedagogy has to be squeezed.

It is not my intention to paint a dismal picture for alternative teach-

[29] See Baldick, 76.

[30] See Rajeswari Sunder Rajan, 'After *Orientalism*: Colonialism and English Literary Studies in India', *Social Scientist 158*, July 1986, 23-55; and Loomba, 30.

ing: over the last twelve years, I have had students who responded passionately to, say, feminist criticism. But this response in many ways led them away from English literature; in some cases it produced astonishingly brilliant critiques of what they had to study. In both cases the majority of students did not go on to 'perform' well. In other words, the success of alternative pedagogy today may well be measured in terms other than 'academic'; perhaps the greatest success of 'radical' pedagogy is to produce alienated students. It is not within the scope of this paper to explore the possibilities for seizing the book; elsewhere I suggest these on the basis of certain texts and certain specific experiences of a majority section of our students, i.e. women.[31] Here I have tried to define the structural, ideological and pedagogic boundaries within which such exercises can be attempted—boundaries which are framed by the intersection of criticism and teaching in the Indian classroom. In as much as these are themselves unstable and wavering, the hope of a more conscious destabilization remains on the agenda.[32]

[31] Loomba, 1-158.
[32] I thank Rajeswari Sunder Rajan for her meticulous reading of several versions of this essay, and for her frank and detailed criticisms which helped shape it. I am grateful to Lola Chatterji for comments, and to my students at Hindu College (specially the third year class of 1989-90) for their responses, and for putting up with my eccentricities.

5

Mansfield Park in Miranda House

RUTH VANITA

The teaching of any literary text involves drawing upon whatever commonality may exist between the experiences portrayed in the text and the experiences of teacher and student. The more 'distant' the text in time or space, the more problematic—yet, paradoxically, the more unavoidable—this strategy becomes. Consequently, given the commonality of certain aspects of women's situations and their oppression, it is possible for an Indian middle-class woman student today to recognize aspects of her experience in the lives of Maggie Tulliver bullied by her brother and Cathy Earnshaw confined in her husband's home while yearning for her father's; or to locate aspects of her fantasies in Rosalind's or Portia's escapades. It is less possible for a male student, in the same context, to for a male recognize his experience in reflected in a Tom Tulliver, a Heathcliff or a Bassanio. This has also to do with the everyday nature of the female protagonist's dilemmas, and with the generally far more unreservedly sympathetic angle from which these dilemmas are represented by the authors. It is possible to argue that, in this sense, the struggles of an Antigone or a Medea have more of the 'universal' in them than do those of Oedipus—Freud notwithstanding.

Let us take the example of the nineteenth-century English novel, which provides the largest number of texts studied in Indian classrooms. The nineteenth-century English novel has a preponderance of literally or symbolically orphaned, neglected and maltreated protagonists. But while the male protagonist in such a situation is generally a symbol of the victimized sections of society—the labouring poor, urban or rural, the despised and wretched of the earth—the female protagonist is more usually a symbol of the specific predicament of woman within family and society. Frequently, her oppression is enclosed within a domestic space and is perpetrated in the interests of maintaining her respectability. It is not until the early years of this century that the repressiveness of the middle-class Victorian family, as it affected the *male* protagonist as son and heir, is explicitly critiqued in a sustained fashion—in *The Way of all Flesh* (1903).

Given this differing symbolic significance of the male and the female protagonist, and given also that most undergraduate students of Delhi University belong to some section of what may be termed, broadly, the middle classes, it is much more likely that women students' experiences will approximate to those of a female protagonist in the nineteenth-century English novel than is the case for men students *vis-à-vis* the male protagonist: for example, that girls would know what it is to be curbed and confined in the interests of being ladylike, as Maggie Tulliver or Cathy Earnshaw are, than that boys would have been starved like Oliver Twist, humiliated like Pip, or brutalized like David Copperfield or Heathcliff. This is true even when the woman protagonist belongs to the poorer classes. The punishment for pre-marital sexual experience is sufficiently similar across class to make the sufferings of poor heroines like Hardy's Tess or Mrs Gaskell's Ruth seem familiar, but few male students in a Delhi University classroom will have suffered anything like, say, Jude's struggle to survive or to acquire learning.

As a woman teaching women students, one often tends to assume that any expression of women's predicament or rebellion in a text will, first, be of special interest to these students, and, further, that it will arouse their special sympathy. While the first assumption has, by and large, been justified by my experience, the second cannot be made in any simple or straightforward fashion. The reactions of Miranda House (Delhi University) students to the only three texts by women writers in the English Honours course provide an interesting case study. These three texts (*Mansfield Park, The Mill on the Floss, Wuthering Heights*) represent worlds that no longer exist in a recognizable form anywhere. Many of the moral conflicts presented in these novels (for example, whether it is proper for a young woman to act in a play with young men not of her family) would in some ways be more alien to a woman student in England today than to her counterpart in India. In other social and cultural details, however, the texts are obviously more alien to an Indian reader. My students tended to deal with the latter problem by appropriating the text to their own experience, an approach which has both advantages and pitfalls.

I found that students tended to react most positively to Maggie

Tulliver, in a mixed way to Cathy Earnshaw (often preferring Cathy Linton to her), and with distaste or indifference to Fanny Price. This last reaction surprised me because, on my part, I had read Fanny's predicament and dilemma as in many ways the closest to those of the average middle-class young Indian woman today. Despite the differences in culture which emerge in almost every scene and detail—the horse riding, the dancing and other courtship rituals, the routine taking of a gentleman's arm while walking—it is surprising how the emotional component, easily isolated, in many of these situations, induces a shock of recognition in the woman reader. However, in the course of teaching the novel it began to seem to me that the shock is often a disconcerting rather than a pleasing one. This is something which I shall try to demonstrate.

In the analysis which follows I focus on the 1988-9 batch of English Honours first year students, because this class was unusual for its relatively large proportion of girls ready to speak their minds, engage in discussion, and uphold their opinions, even when these ran counter to mine. In other respects the batch was typical for Miranda House, in that most of the girls came from average middle-class backgrounds, many with fathers in various branches of government service, and with mothers who were, often, educated, and in some cases employed. Most regions of the country, and most communities, were represented, though the majority were Punjabis. The fact that they were studying in Miranda House, one of the elite colleges of the university, was important. This fact both indicated and shaped their aspirations, as emerged very startlingly in a confrontation that took place between them and some students of other colleges that I shall describe later.

WHAT PRICE FANNY PRICE?

Fanny Price, the heroine of *Mansfield Park*, is born into a poor family and adopted by her wealthy maternal aunt and uncle when she is ten years old. Overwhelmed by the transplanting this entails, and by the condescension of her new family, she grows into an excessively timid, self-deprecating and reserved young woman, yet is distinct from the others in the novel for her reliance on the resources of her own mind. Neglected and treated by most members of the family as a dependent poor relation, her childhood admiration for and gratitude to her cousin Edmund, induced by his kindness to her, develop into a romantic attachment, unperceived and unreciprocated by him. Henry and Mary Crawford, a vivacious brother and sister with independent fortunes, come from London to visit their sister in the neighbourhood. They win the hearts of Fanny's cousins, Maria and Julia, and of Edmund, respectively. Fanny suffers agonies in silence while Edmund confides to her the waxing and waning of his attachment to Mary.

After Maria's marriage to a wealthy but dull neighbour, Henry Crawford decides to flirt with Fanny but soon comes to perceive her sterling qualities and proposes marriage in earnest. The whole family, including Edmund, presses Fanny to accept. She, however, steadfastly refuses. Finally, Henry elopes with, and later abandons, Maria. Edmund, compelled by this event to break off his relations with Mary, realizes her unworthiness and turns instead to Fanny, who is recognized by the whole family as the true daughter and spiritual heir of Mansfield Park.

A major instance of the students' appropriation of the text to their experience was their assumption that the marriage system depicted in it is an arranged one —very similar to the system they confront in India today—and that Jane Austen's ironic comments on marriage are directed at this system. The question of marriage looms large over the lives of these young women students, in the form of an arrangement devised by their parents. While most of them plan to acquiesce in the arrangement, and some argue in favour of it, almost all betray, sometimes even openly confess, the desire for a 'love marriage'.

They simplified the dilemma of Fanny and the other young women in *Mansfield Park* to one of having to choose between a 'love marriage' and an 'arranged marriage', both defined in modern Indian terms. The specific confusions caused by the elaborate masquerade of what may be termed 'arranged love', conducted in and subscribed to by Mansfield Park society, eluded them until this was repeatedly pointed out by me in class.

Their reactions to Fanny and Maria fell into two categories. Some students, the more articulate, completely condemned of both women, Fanny for her 'hypocrisy' and lack of assertiveness, Maria for succumbing to the materialist lure of an 'arranged' and loveless marriage. Their reactions to Fanny were generally couched in indignant and derisory outbursts: 'Ma'am, she's so scared of everything! Why can't she say what she wants? She's so boring, Ma'am!'

Another set of girls took the 'Ma'am, what else can she do?' approach, arguing that women's actions were, after all, completely determined by their circumscribed situations, Fanny's that of a poor relation, Maria's that of the daughter of a tyrannical father. However, neither group spontaneously recalled Fanny's act of rebellion (her resistance to the pressure to marry Henry), although when they did recall it, after some encouragement from me, they agreed that it was indeed an act of rebellion.

THE UNWANTED GIRL CHILD

The portrayal of Fanny Price's situation seems to me one of the most true-to-life portrayals of the female predicament in English fiction. The device of displacing Fanny from her natural family (like that of making Mr Murdstone David's stepfather instead of his real father) allows a more heightened treatment of what is essentially a typical situation— where a girl child is unwanted, or less wanted, than a boy. The quiet bitterness of the portrayal arises precisely from its ordinariness. The forms which Fanny's oppression takes are far from dramatic. She is never harshly punished, as Jane Eyre is, only neglected and humiliated in the pettily cruel ways characteristic of the middle class. She is unfavourably contrasted with her prettier and more articulate cousins, deprived not of necessities but of comforts like the fire and the pony (equivalents of the cream in the milk or the motorbike that Indian girls are denied, but which their brothers get). Even when she resists family pressure to marry, she is not imprisoned or beaten, like Clarissa Harlowe, only made to feel guilty for her 'ingratitude' to her surrogate parents. The essence of the female child's situation (especially when she is the youngest and least wanted third girl in the house, as Fanny is) is summed up in Fanny's wistful remark: 'I can never be important to anyone.'

The psychological effects of this systematic neglect and putting-down are also easily traceable in Fanny's desire to be thought good, and to be valued for her goodness in a situation which does not allow goodness to be defined in any active, positive way, but only through service and self-sacrifice.

THE NON-HEROIC REBELLION

When it comes to the crunch, Fanny is as much, perhaps more, a rebel than the popular women rebels of nineteenth-century English fiction. When she refuses the really eligible match her family seeks to impose upon her, she is fully aware that she runs a much higher risk of remaining unmarried and unprovided for—an insulted dependant all her life—than does a woman of the likes of Elizabeth Bennet, who can trust to her beauty and wit to fetch her a better husband than Mr Collins. Fanny takes the risk of staying unmarried—this is precisely the risk many Indian middle-class girls fear to take when they agree to marriages arranged by their parents, even when they are unenthusiastic about the prospect. Since the social codes do not allow them to pursue, choose and propose to the men they prefer, refusing an offer entails a serious risk. This kind of rebellion is more difficult than the kind so common in literature, where a woman aligns herself with a man of whom her parents disapprove. By refusing an unacceptable offer which her family urges, a woman is forced to depend on herself alone.

The students recognized all this when we discussed the question in class, yet did not respond with wholehearted sympathy to Fanny's courage. An undercurrent of irritation, even hostility, to her persisted. This had much to do with her manner. Fanny weeps copiously even as she resists, she nearly faints with fright, she doubts and blames herself, she strikes no heroic poses and utters no proudly defiant speeches. Even a Dickens heroine would do better, not to speak of one in Bronte or Eliot. The depiction of Fanny frustrates the expectations we, as readers of fiction and viewers of films, have been led to build up.

The depiction of Fanny's love irritated the students similarly. When first mentioned, it is described as a 'fond attachment' and is so unstressed as to evade the reader: students had to search long and hard to detect this first mention of it. It is an assumption in the text that Fanny loves Edmund; we miss the elements of a grand passion that we, as readers of novels, have been led to expect. One might imagine that Fanny's love for a surrogate brother, shading by imperceptible degrees into romantic love, would strike a sympathetic chord in a culture like ours, where so many romances begin with the adoption of a brother's friend or a friend's brother as a *rakhi* brother.[1] Instead, it evoked rather negative, contemptuous reactions from students, one even going so far as to castigate it as 'unnatural' and 'immoral'.

The strong reactions of the students which led to passionate discussions in class (far more contentious between groups of students than those that arose around either *The Mill on the Floss* or *Wuthering Heights*) led me to confront my own mixed responses to Fanny. My initial

---

[1] For the information of Western readers, *rakhis* are ornate threads annually tied by sisters on their brothers' wrists, as a way of expressing affection, and a commitment to provide lifelong mutual support to one another.

analysis was that our reaction had something to do with our being women readers. Looking back today, however, I feel it also had something to do with being women with particular kinds of elitist aspirations.

In the process of teaching and classroom interaction, I began to feel that the identification we as readers seek with protagonists is, less often than we think, one that springs from recognition of our own compulsions or of the mixed motives from which we tend to act. More often, what we seek is a situation similar enough to our own to be recognized, but also a *reaction* sufficiently different to be flattering. Many girls might fantasize about cutting their hair without their parents' permission; few actually do it. Maggie Tulliver's defiant action thus allows the woman reader vicarious satisfaction of a vaguely self-congratulatory kind. When our own fantasies and unexpressed desires are acted out by the female protagonist, we can, in admiring her, feel we are equally, or almost equally, heroic and rebellious because we have the same desires, even though we may not have acted upon them.

Fanny knows what she wants but she goes about getting it in the ways available to the powerless. Her strategies (taking over a neglected room till she is acknowledged as its mistress; or making herself indispensable to her aunt and uncle by her quiet service, and to Edmund by being an ever-sympathetic listener), are much closer to the strategies available to, and relatively more successfully pursued by, women than the open defiance of a Maggie; but for that very reason they evoke less sympathy and respect. We would prefer not to be told that these are the strategies we adopt; our contempt for our own lives surfaces as contempt for Fanny Price's. Although a distaste for Fanny is by no means unique to women readers, as anyone familiar with criticism of the novel will know, it seems to me that in women readers an edge of self-contempt is added by our unwilling recognition in her of the 'feminine' traits cultivated in ourselves.

THE UNFASHIONABLE WOMAN

However, another and equally important aspect of this self-contempt was dramatically highlighted in an inter-college students' seminar organized at Miranda House in 1990. The articulate section of the cohort I have here used as a case study, now in the second year of the BA course, dominated the discussions at this seminar. They managed to silence, even terrify, students, both male and female, from other colleges, by their use of a deconstructionist terminology with which they had recently become acquainted, and which these other students did not understand. This terminology functioned at the seminar as a language of elitism, comprehensible only to a small set whose 'superiority' it established, much as, in other contexts, the English language functions as an indicator of superiority *vis-à-vis* non-English-speakers.

Interestingly, the only challenge posed to this domination came via *Mansfield Park*. In a paper entitled '*Mansfield Park* and the Indian Reader', a student of Gargi College, Delhi, analysed her own identification with Fanny Price as springing from her predicament as a student in a non-elite, off-campus college, one whom the jet-set would label a *behenji*,[2] but who sees herself as upholding older moral values that the jet-set is abandoning. She cited, among other things, a quality she identified with—Fanny's courage in remaining silent and passive even under pressure from her peer group to be articulate and active.

This paper was met with open hostility and derision from the Miranda House students, at least from those of them who habitually expressed their opinions (for there *is* a small section of students in Miranda House who are not confident enough to speak at seminars or in the classrooms, and are not too fluent in English either). But the paper-reader held her own, and the discussion rapidly shifted from the text to the reality of the differing aspirations of two sets of students. Most significant to me was the fact that there was no real difference in the 'class' origins—i.e the socio-economic background in terms of income level—of the two sets of students. The difference was cultural, involving self-perception and aspirations, and hence perception of a Fanny Price type of woman.

Fanny Price's manner and the values she stands for may well cast her, for the Indian reader, in the mould of the staple Hindi film heroine.[3] The Miranda House English Honours student, tending to identify the 'modern' with the 'Western', rejects with derision everything that this heroine represents—from her appearance and lifestyle (quiet, retiring, non-flirtatious, sensitive), to her manner (tears, shyness), to her kind of goodness (loyalty, self-sacrifice, modesty), to her mode of rebellion (firm but gentle). One aspect of the contempt for her may well be the contempt for the 'Indianness' in ourselves and in others, and a wholesale rejection of it in favour of that which is perceived and aspired to as modern—here represented by the fashionable, witty, aggressive, bold Mary Crawford, who is never at a loss for words and never sheds a tear.

---

[2] Literally 'sister', but colloquially an old-fashioned girl.
[3] I am indebted for the ideas in this paragraph to my colleague Prabha Dixit, who read an earlier draft of this paper.

AVOIDANCE AND ENDORSEMENT

That the students' rejection of Fanny was based more on her manner than on the substantive 'matter' of her character, that it was not a rejection of a 'conservative' in favour of a 'radical' position, was suggested to me by the fact that the *opposite* kind of heroine, the thoroughly self-assertive Cathy Earnshaw, tended to induce in them discomfort and a feeling that she was too 'extreme'. This was partly the result of their tendency uncritically to accept the narrator Nelly's viewpoint but, more importantly, of their unease with, as one student put it, Cathy's wanting to 'have her cake and eat it too'. Cathy's demand for 'more' than a woman is supposed to have would be seen as radical in any society, even today. She wants a relationship with two men simultaneously, on her own terms. The men's refusal peaceably to collude in this desire destroys her—hence her charge that it is they (Edgar and Heathcliff) who, between them, have killed her. Our culture, like most cultures, tends to romanticize (even while it may punish) youthful, marriage-directed love that flouts the wishes of elders and cuts across social barriers. While, therefore, in imaginative terms, for a woman to fall in love, even to elope, as Cathy Linton does, constitutes an 'acceptable rebellion' for the young woman reader, when the love breaks taboos (as distinct from conventions), when it hints, for example, at incest, polyandry or even adultery, acceptance becomes more equivocal.

The second disquieting feature of Cathy Earnshaw's behaviour is her sheer unconcern with being or appearing good. Students tended to characterize her as 'selfish'. Fanny Price they saw as the other extreme, an epitome of selflessness that they suspected as hypocritical. Maggie Tulliver they took to their hearts more unreservedly than they did either Cathy or Fanny since, lacking Cathy's arrogance, she is also free from Fanny's humility and, while wishing to please others, is also capable of acting impulsively to please herself.

What I am suggesting, then, is that the English text may either become a means for avoiding our own position as Indian women readers, or help us come to terms with and endorse it, depending on how we approach both in the Indian classroom.[4]

[4] I am grateful to Berny Horowitz, Harish Trivedi, Svati Joshi and Rajeswari Sunder Rajan for their helpful comments on earlier drafts of this paper. Also to the 1988-9 English Honours first year students whose lively responses helped me to many insights.

6

The Strange Case of Mohun Biswas[1]

ANURADHA MARWAH ROY

M y first assignment as a college lecturer was to teach V.S. Naipaul's *A House for Mr. Biswas* to third year BA English Honours students, a task that fittingly encapsulated for me the dilemma of a teacher of English in a post-colonial country. For some time, then, while dealing with the text, I was a neurotic, divided between the classroom and the examination hall, between my pleasure as a reader and my business as a teacher, between the politics of the text and its aesthetics.

My oscillations, I was aware, would not affect the larger machinery of which I was a part, nor persuade it to tick any differently. The teacher's position is, after all, defined by the system—the syllabus at one end and the examinations at the other. Buttressing the system and being buttressed by it in turn is literary criticism, as represented by the scores of secondary sources (explication, scholarship, interpretations and readings) provided by books and journal articles in the college library. The teacher is expected to harmonize the workings of the system. But here, unexpectedly, was a text that was preventing me from keeping time and making me empathize with an altogether different rhythm—the rhythm I shared with my students.

What was the context in which the text was lodged when it came to us? The university that had prescribed the syllabus had packaged V.S. Naipaul with D.H. Lawrence, E.M. Forster, Joseph Conrad and Ernest Hemingway in what was called simply Paper VIII of the English Honours course. The label read 'Modern Literature: Fiction and Criticism'.

---

[1] This paper arose out of detailed discussions with Zakia Pathak and Rajeswari Sunder Rajan (Miranda House, Delhi University). Their contribution to the argument is invaluable.

Whether these writers had been offered as representative voices in modern literature or as a random selection of major writers in the modern age—the intention of the syllabus-makers was accessible only by conjecture. V.S. Naipaul is neither safely dead nor yet canonized by the Nobel Prize; so 'pure merit', as we call it in India, could not have been a self-evident criterion for selection. Then was he included because a case can be made for him as a third-world writer—or because the case can be as easily annulled?

However, four of the five texts in this course described cross-cultural encounters. So, were *Biswas*, *Lord Jim*, *Passage to India* and even *A Farewell to Arms* to be read as colonial texts? (The fifth text prescribed in this course was *Sons and Lovers*). The intentionality of the system finds its most transparent expression in the examination papers. So I began to survey previous years' papers. I found no support for believing that *Biswas* was to be treated as a text of colonialism or a West Indian novel or even a novel any different from the ones the students had read earlier. Familiar (old) new critical terminology abounded in the formulations of questions: autobiographical genre, irony, bildungsroman, comic mode, the house as 'metaphor'. These questions, (except for incidental specificities) could have been framed for *David Copperfield*.

Criticism that is standard when discussing V.S. Naipaul, I found, is shrill in praise of his genius in a way that effectively deflects contextualizing. In Paul Theroux's breathless words:

Naipaul has disproved all the identifications that critics have attempted, the labels of 'West Indian writer' and 'Emergent Third-Worlder', 'Mandarin' and 'Transplanted Indian' . . . Wholly original, he may be the only writer today in whom there are no echoes of influence.[2]

This rather exuberant assessment is the extreme case, I found, of what is attempted elsewhere. Landeg White and his ilk prefer to see *Biswas* as a novel dealing with human problems of universal application.[3] On the one hand Naipaul is universal (and 'human') *in spite* of his West Indian origins; on the other he is universal *because* of his West Indian origins. In Michael Thorpe's words:

While Naipaul is by no means alone in coming from a makeshift colonial society

[2] Paul Theroux, *V.S. Naipaul: An Introduction to His Work* (London: Andre Deutsch, 1972), 7.
[3] Landeg White, *V.S. Naipaul: A Critical Introduction* (London: Macmillan Press, 1975).

and using the metropolitan language with a native surety, these origins have helped him more than any of his contemporaries from the Commonwealth to develop an inclusive view of many facets of the larger world—a view focussed by his intense sense of displacement from society, race or creed. He has gone beyond local conflicts to attempt something approaching a world view.[4]

This rather pathological urge for universalizing the subject matter of the novel that I saw all around me, in both the system and the criticism, made me uncomfortable. Gradually the so-called metaphor of the House began to assume an ironic, unintended significance. These efforts to read literature according to the prescriptions of the first world came to resemble an enterprise quite similar to that of Mr Biswas's. The hot, humid land had to provide inspiration for his paintings depicting cool, temperate landscapes. Samuel Smiles had to provide words to express a story which significantly remained unfinished through the course of the novel. 'At the age of thirty-three when he was already the father of four children . . . ',[5] began Biswas, time and again in the novel. Mr Biswas perceives his own situation as messy, undefined, and chaotic, and his own self as unaccommodated. The metaphor for his various efforts to impose an order on his environment is the doll's house he gifts to his daughter Savi. The acme of his ambition is to fulfil a dream of 'a house cosy in the rain with a polished floor, and an old lady who baked cakes in the kitchen' (p. 566)—undoubtedly the colonial legacy of a much-desired western lifestyle. As students and teachers of English literature aren't we also, I asked myself, trying to impose a similar synthetic structure upon our situation? Aren't we also looking for a comfortable house to live in—a house that transcends social structures, a house that is universal? And don't the specific conditions of our society doom us to only partial success, so that our house too lets the summer sun in and our doors too prove ineffectual against stormy winds.

Ironically, the author of this text who was making me review my own situation has the distinction of practising a rather dubious politics. Naipaul is undoubtedly aware of the difference that marks him off from the writers of the west. Speaking about his father's writing he attests:

The writing that has mattered most to me is that of my father. It taught me to look at things that had never been written about before. Other writers are aware

[4] Michael Thorpe, *V.S. Naipaul* (Harlow: Longman, 1976), 36.
[5] All quotations are from the Penguin edition of the novel (Harmondsworth: Penguin, 1978), 344.

that they are writing about rooted societies, his work showed me that one could write about another kind of society.[6]

But his awareness of difference has not led him to embrace an identity based on third world affiliations. His treatment of colonial and post-colonial societies in non-fictional works like *Among the Believers, The Middle Passage, The Loss of El Dorado,* and *India—A Wounded Civilisation,* is less than sympathetic, and has raised a furore not only among nationalistic sections but also among third world writers and critics.[7] His despairing view of the West Indies, his flight from what he called the Indian negation, his dismissal of protest literature as sterile and stereotypical posturing, create a picture of a complex post-colonial man who, while aware of his predicament, prefers to remain isolated in his *angst,* too suspicious to join hands with anyone.

I turned next to criticism that was more recent and which originated closer 'home'. A significant critical comparison provided a point of departure.[8] Comparing Bibhuti Bhushan Banerjee's *Pather Panchali* (a two-part Bengali novel published in 1929 and 1931) with Biswas, the author, Meenakshi Mukherjee, finds various differences—in their attitudes to life (inclusive *vs.* exclusive), their concepts of time (cyclic *vs.* linear), in their relations to tradition (rooted *vs.* alienated), and in the structures of their narratives (unselfconsciously meandering *vs.* consciously integrated). Though the attempt to historicize the third world novel by bringing out the complicity of language and form is interesting, her perception of *Biswas* as a mainstream realist novel raised many questions for me. Homi Bhabha holds a diametrically opposed view of the novel:

To demonstrate thematically how *House* resists its appropriation into the Great Tradition of literary realism would not be difficult. It would be possible to see the tropes of the text as metonymy and repetition instead of metaphor, and its

[6] V.S. Naipaul interviewed by David Bates, *Sunday Times,* 26 May 1963, quoted in Landeg White, 26.

[7] Nissim Ezekiel, for instance, labels Naipaul's perspective on India 'wholly subjective, wholly self-righteous'. Nissim Ezekiel, 'Naipaul's India and Mine', in *New Writing in India,* ed. Adil Jussawalla (Harmondsworth: Penguin, 1974), 74.

[8] See Meenakshi Mukherjee, 'The House and the Road: Two Modes of Autobiographical Fiction', in *Commonwealth Literature: Problems of Response,* ed. C.D. Narasimhaiah (Madras: Macmillan, 1981), 163.

mode of address as the 'uncanny' rather than irony. For the text abounds with reference to loss, circularity and the demoniacal.[9]

From Bhabha's reading of *Biswas* against its own grain, the resistant text that I sought began to emerge. If Mukherjee's comparative method helped me to see transcendent 'universal' and 'human' ways of writing not as a norm but as historically conditioned and culturally specific determinations, Bhabha's essay was the beginning of the theorization of the colonial text.

My final recourse was to the responses of my class of students. They do not of course come to the text innocent of expectation or training. Not only have they read the criticism and surveyed the questions, they have done courses in Fielding, Austen, Bronte, Dickens and Eliot. One such student is nineteen years old, apologetically bilingual. Her childhood and adolescent reading has comprised Enid Blyton, Sherlock Holmes and Mills and Boon romances. She has been to an English medium school, missionary-run or expensively 'public'. There she grew up writing essays in class about countryside holidays at a farm, perhaps called Green Meadows, where the air was fresh and healthy, the hay sweet-smelling, milk, cheese and butter plentiful. She has polished her English composition with Enid Blyton phrases. Like Anand Biswas she too is a victim of the 'daffodils in the tropics' phenomenon. She stands ready to daffodilize *A House For Mr. Biswas*.

And precisely this similarity between her and Anand Biswas became a point of identification in the classroom. Other recognitions occurred: of the Tulsi joint family, the caste-specificities and rigidities, the rituals and festivals of the expatriate Hindu society. Mohun Biswas, a rootless East Indian struggling between the tepid chaos of a decaying culture and the void of a colonial society, became a figure that elicited sympathy and not merely laughter from the reader. It is precisely this feeling of recognition of 'our' kind of society that I sought to encourage in my students—to convey to them that Anglo-American critical hegemony need not extend to their hearts and brains, that ways of perceiving literature need not be uniform. So our point of departure in class was the context of the West Indies. In the course of such a discussion we found that the novel deals with precisely its own genesis—arising out of

---

[9] Homi Bhabha, 'Representation and the Colonial Text: A Critical Exploration of Some Forms of Mimeticism', in Frank Gloversmith, ed., *The Theory of Reading* (New Jersey: Barnes and Noble; Sussex: Harvester, 1984), 115 and 123-46.

rootlessness, an alienating English education, escape to the West. It is autobiographical in more senses than one, not merely the story of an individual but of a community. The story led us again and again into drawing parallels with our own situation in India. The parallels were not only historical but also cultural. For example, to build and own a house is a cherished middle-class goal in Indian society, as it is for Mr Biswas—there is nothing symbolic about a house in that sense. Even the sexist biases of Biswas are those of our society.

At some deeper level Biswas appeared in all his splendour as a creation wrought in the image of a distorted reflection. His madness is symptomatic of the schizophrenia of his life. He is the self we are afraid of—his life a travesty of post-colonial ambition. Biswas could only die in small print because his type of death is inadmissible in headlines.

In all this I am aware that 'enthusiasm' and identification do not represent 'correct' critical positions. I am also aware that I run the greater danger of subsuming a specific account of East Indian acculturation in Trinidad forty years ago into a paradigmatic third world narrative of alienation, emergent modernity, comic cultural awkwardness. Nevertheless, while engaged in the dynamics of a classroom situation, where there is scope for dialogue and interaction, I believe that a process of identification between students and text is inevitably set in motion. In this particular case I treated it as a first step in the subsequent articulation of difference, cultural specificity and historical distance, though both the resistance to identification as well as the degree of identification were greater than usual.

I felt strangely saddened and exhilarated by this vision of literature that at last justified to me my own existence—somewhat like Billy Biswas must have felt when he left the civilized world to live with his tribal beloved Bilasia in Arun Joshi's memorable novel, *The Strange Case of Billy Biswas*.[10] Billy was hounded and killed by the stupidities of the bureaucracy and the police—the pillars of the establishment he had abandoned. I too was shot down in time by the examination system. My students, who had been so enthusiastic about attacking the established literary criticism world in class, retracted their heresies when called to order by the printed question paper. Out of thirty, only three attempted the question on the novel (exercising their choice of studying only four out of the five novels in detail)—and only one mentioned the West Indies while discussing it as a great comic novel!

[10] Arun Joshi, *The Strange Case of Billy Biswas* (Delhi: Orient Paperbacks, 1986).

7

Class in the Classroom: Pedagogical Encounters with *Nectar in a Sieve*

TAPAN KUMAR BASU

KAMALA Markandaya's novel, *Nectar in a Sieve*,[1] is without doubt the most over-prescribed text for study by English literature students of the University of Delhi: it is included in the syllabus for English as a core subject for students of the BA (Pass) course as well as in the syllabus for English as a subsidiary subject for students of BA (Honours) courses in the humanities, commerce, social sciences, physical sciences and natural sciences.[2]

The reason for this all-pervasive presence of what is, at best, a mediocre production by an Indo-Anglian author is not to be found within the guidelines preceding the syllabi for the different courses in which the text is included. Between the 'makers' of English literature syllabi and the 'takers' of English literature syllabi in the University of Delhi there is a 'natural' power/knowledge gulf which demands an unquestioning

---

[1] For all citations from *Nectar in a Sieve*, refer the Signet edition (New York: John Day Co., 1954).

[2] English Studies are conducted for three different categories of students in the University of Delhi at the undergraduate level (i) Honours students of English, i.e. those who wish to graduate with English as their major subject of study; (ii) Pass students of English, i.e. those who wish to graduate with English as one of several subjects (from the humanities, commerce, social sciences, physical sciences or natural sciences streams), but for whom English is nonetheless a compulsory subject; (iii) Subsidiary students of English, i.e. those who wish to graduate with any subject except English as their major subject of study, but for whom English is a compulsory additional subject.

acceptance of the standards of 'good taste' laid down by the former upon the latter. Teachers within undergraduate colleges in the University of Delhi have little more than recommendatory power in the selection of texts. A massive hierarchical edifice, consisting of the university's postgraduate Department of English, a Committee of Courses, the Arts Faculty, and the Academic Council, exists to authorize a syllabus revision. However, a fairly shrewd speculation would suggest that *Nectar in a Sieve* is a paradigmatic text for consumption by substream (as opposed to mainstream) students of English literature from the point of view of the guardians of English Studies in the University of Delhi, chiefly because it is a text of English literature written by a *woman*, and an *Indian woman* at that. From the point of view of the syllabi framers of English literature, the inclusion of *Nectar in a Sieve* in the substream (non-Honours) syllabus is a signifier of their 'democratic' credentials— in the matter of opening up an Anglo-American-oriented and phallocentric canon of English texts inherited from the colonial era—enabling them to studiously preserve inviolate the same canon for the mainstream (Honours) syllabus for English literature.

Needless to say, *Nectar in a Sieve* is neither a woman's text nor an Indian text, except in the very essentialist sense that Kamala Markandaya, its author, is an Indian woman (albeit a non-resident Indian woman). At a generic level, *Nectar in a Sieve* shares the sense of alienation necessarily attendant upon most realistic fictional representations of specific regional aspects of Indian reality through the medium of the cosmopolitan, global accents of the English language.[3] At an individual level, *Nectar in a Sieve* does not, in any sense, challenge the dominant constructs of 'India', of 'womanhood' or of 'womanhood in India' set up by a nationalist-humanist cultural consensus which forever protested but never contested a colonialist-patriarchal hangover.[4] Indeed, the

---

[3] For a well-argued thesis on the incongruity of the English realist novel set in Indian suburban or rural situations, see Amitav Ghosh's unpublished paper 'The Novel in a Multilingual Society'. Also P.K. Dutta, 'Studies in Heterogeneity: A reading of Two Recent Indo-Anglian Novels', *Social Scientist*, vol. 18, no.3, March 1990, 61-70, esp. 61-2.

[4] Homi Bhabha, in a persuasive article, 'Representation and the Colonial Text: A Critical Exploration of Some Forms of Mimeticism', in Frank Gloversmith, ed., *The Theory of Reading* (Sussex: The Harvester Press, 1984), suggests that there is a fundamental complicity of interests and ideas in colonialist and nationalist perspectives on representations of the colonial/ post-colonial subject.

novel seems to actually reinforce these hegemonic constructs. The representation of Rukmani, the central character and narratorial persona of *Nectar in a Sieve*, as a 'simple peasant woman in a primitive village in India whose whole life is a gallant and persistent battle to care for those she loved' (a descriptive note on the cover of the Signet edition) only strengthens the popular Occidental perception of 'Indian womanhood' as an embodiment of meek and long-suffering service to the cause of Indian society in general and Indian men in particular. These Orientalist perceptions of Indian womanhood, as recent investigations have convincingly shown, helped imperial authority in India define the larger text of 'Indian tradition' in such a way that disruptive questions about the exploitation of an oppressed indigenous population in the colony as well as the exploitation of an oppressed female population in the mother-country could be kept at bay.[5]

It is difficult to negotiate *Nectar in a Sieve* in a classroom if we adopt the perspectives of subaltern race or gender subjectivities. For though obstensibly a nationalist-humanist text, it is in reality a text constructed around 'derivative discourses' on Indian womanhood.[6] In view of this, I would argue that the subject-position of the *social class* (upwardly mobile, middle) of most students in an average Indian metropolitan classroom (undergraduate), as opposed to the subject-positions adopted on the basis of their gender and race, is the most strategically useful perspective for inviting empathy with, and enabling entry into, the world of *Nectar in a Sieve*. I am assuming that a critical method which encourages identification with the world of the text—rather than a critical method which encourages distancing from the world of the text—is the more efficacious in enthusing even mediocre students to study the text in their classrooms with interest.

Rather than read *Nectar in a Sieve* as a 'novel of rural India' (a descriptive note on the cover of the Jaico edition (Bombay: 1955), I suggest we read it as a story representing the inauguration of the moment of modernity in a simple rural community provoked out of its indigenous pace of life by the ruthless onslaught of a complex urban society. The advent of the urban in the world of *Nectar in a Sieve* is

[5] See Kumkum Sangari and Sudesh Vaid, ed., *Re-casting Women: Essays in Colonial Historiography* (New Delhi: Kali For Women, 1989), 1-26, 88-126.
[6] Partha Chatterjee argues in his book, *Nationalist Thought and the Colonial World: A Derivative Discourse?* (Delhi: OUP, 1986), that the discourse of nationalism itself did not preclude colonialist assumptions or antecedents.

signified by the establishment of a tannery, a massive industrial complex whose presence slowly but surely upsets the mores of a serene village existence. This shift in the modes and relations of production entails a corresponding shift in the modes and relations of living for the village folk—a dislocation that is more often than not fraught with pathos. Rukmani's family is only one of the numerous families who are afflicted by poverty and starvation in a changing economic and political environment. Already, the age-old institutions of political and economic authority in the village have been on the wane: village headmen find themselves in an increasingly disadvantageous competition for authority with district collectors. Against this backdrop of the disintegration of familiar structures of macrocosmic village organization, the microcosmic organization of Rukmani's family, among other families, soon begins to fall apart. On the one hand, the family is gradually forced to abdicate its ties to the land on which it has lived for years and through which Nathan, Rukmani's husband, who is a tenant farmer, has sustained their children through childhood and puberty. On the other hand the family is compelled to break up from within as, soon after the marriage of Irawaddy the daughter, the sons are driven by financial necessity to seek employment away from the soil which nurtured them. Arjun and Thambi, the eldest born, take up jobs as tanners, to begin with. Murugan, the third, is sent away by the parents themselves as a domestic help to a household in a distant city. Raja and Selvam, the youngest—with the exception of Kuti who dies a premature death—remain behind but do not take up Nathan's occupation as a farmer.

Yet even as the process of modernization uproots Rukmani's family emotionally and physically from their familiar norms of being, it brings some compensations for them too. Once Arjun and Thambi begin to earn wages as tanners, in defiance of all parental and social sanctions, the economic boom which the tannery brings to their village in general finally catches up with their particular household.

With their money we began once again to live well. In the granary, unused for so long, I stored away half a bag of rice, two measures of dhal and nearly a pound of chillies. Hitherto, almost all we grew had been sold to pay the rent of the land, now we were enabled to keep some of our own produce. I was especially pleased that I had not been forced to sell all the chillies, for these are useful to us; when the tongue rebels against plain boiled rice, desiring ghee and salt and spices which one cannot afford, the sharp bite of a chillie renders even plain rice palatable. I was able at last to thatch our hut again, substantially, with two or three bindings of leaves. For the first time in years I bought clothes for the older children, a sari for myself, and although he protested I bought for my husband a dhoti which he badly needed, since the other was in rags and barely covered his loins . . . (57)

Indeed, material prosperity is an important result of modernization for most of Rukmani's friends in the village. Kunthi and Janaki and Kali, in various degrees, learn to see modernization as progress: a 'clump of huts' becoming a 'small town', to use Kunthi's terms (33).

So they were reconciled and threw the past away with both hands that they might be the readier to grasp the present, while I stood by in pain envying such easy reconciliation and clutching in my own two hands the memory of the past, and accounting it a treasure (33)

Nevertheless, the rhetoric of counter-modernization in *Nectar in a Sieve* is not merely confined to Rukmani's nostalgic backward-looking glances towards a pre-industrial golden age. A critique of modernization from the perspective of the future is offered by Arjun and Thambi, Rukmani's eldest sons, who had once consciously rejected the past so as to be able to accept the present. As employees in the tannery, Arjun and Thambi soon discover that the social structures of industrial production within which they function can be as stifling and exploitative as the social structures of agrarian production within which Nathan, their father, had functioned, as long as the means of production are not in the ownership of those who produce. If Nathan exists at the mercy of an impersonal, absentee landlord, Arjun and Thambi exist at the mercy of an impersonal absentee industrialist-employer. Hence their involvement in the workers' movement in the tannery and their consequent dismissal from work in the tannery.

Arjun and Thambi prefigure a metropolitan middle-class aspiration for upward social mobility; they are typically 'modern' subjects for whom the dynamics of success (job opportunities as far as Ceylon) mean more than the failure of stagnation (a meagre settled income from their land in the village of their birth). 'There is nothing for us here', they explain to their parents before leaving their village for Ceylon, 'for we have neither the means to buy land nor to rent it. Would you have us wasting our youth chafing against things we cannot change?' (72) Arjun and Thambi are different from Rukmani and Nathan. While the older generation sees a fluid society as a hazard to a secure lifestyle, the younger generation perceives a fluid society as a challenge and a promise for more prosperous days to come. As modern subjects, Arjun and Thambi prefigure the hopes and fears of the average Indian metropolitan middle-class consumer-reader (of either sex) of *Nectar in a Sieve*, who too is trying to 'make it' in a social milieu only recently opened to the winds of change.

Yet it is significant that Arjun and Thambi's forward-looking vision represents a position of conviction rather than a position of compulsion. Unlike their sister Irawaddy, for instance, they do not, to use Nathan's memorable phrase, 'bend like the grass, lest they break'. They value upward mobility but not, as their role as trade-union leaders shows, at the cost of class solidarity. In other words, they are discerning subjects of a new-found modernity. Given the importance attached by Rukmani to reading and writing in what is an autobiographical narrative of her life (16), it would not be too far-fetched to attribute her sons' radical consciousness to their voracious appetite for learning (55, 56, 113, 114)— and for re-learning critically in the light of their lived experiences—the texts of literature and the text of life. Indeed Kali, the village gossip— whose chatter is more often than not an index of village sentiment—sees a direct link between Arjun and Thambi's erudition and their subversive activities (70). As readers/critics of Rukmani's experiences, Kamala Markandaya's Indian, metropolitan, middle-class consumer-readers (including men and women who have to study her novel as an university-prescribed text) need to adopt the subject-position of Arjun and Thambi as organic intellectuals of the restless working-class in the world of *Nectar in a Sieve* if they are to use their negotiation of this English text to transformatively/transmutatively renegotiate its Indian context.

However, I am not suggesting that the process of identification between the working-class, rural organic intellectuals in *Nectar in a Sieve* and the middle-class, urban, traditional intellectuals in our university classrooms can be a spontaneous process. Apart from their common ground as thinking people, these two categories of intellectuals have no shared identity. In fact, the gap between the middle-class, urban, traditional intellectual and the working-class, rural, organic intellectual is more than merely one of geographic and cultural background. The organic intellectual and the traditional intellectual differ in their essential function as intellectuals. For the traditional intellectual, on the one hand, 'the life of the mind' is an avenue for personal career-advancement. For the organic intellectual, on the other hand, 'the life of the mind' is an expression of the faith and the doubts of the class whose aspirations he represents and articulates. My own experience of almost a decade has been to lecture on *Nectar in a Sieve* to students of English from backgrounds as diverse as those opting for an Honours course in Economics or History (generally English-speaking, private-school-educated), to those opting for an Honours course in Hindi or Sanskrit (generally vernacular-speaking, state-school-educated); it clearly suggests that there is no monolithic Indian undergraduate student of English.

Classroom responses to *Nectar in a Sieve*, in my experience, have ranged from raving appreciation (for example: 'It is a statement of faith in the greatness of Mother India' from a student with Hindi major), to ranting deprecation (for example: 'It is merely an indigenous potboiler' from a student with History major). The agenda for a radical pedagogic intervention into *Nectar in a Sieve* is to make a virtue of this lack of consensus on the significance of the narrative by Rukmani. Thus, the undergraduate classroom can become a platform for discussion and dissension on the authority of Rukmani as chronicler of her own life (with the teacher instigating the taught to interrogate the primacy of her perspective), even as the chronicle itself is a platform for debate on the authority of Rukmani as parent (with Arjun and Thambi interrogating the primacy of her tutelage of them). In other words, Arjun and Thambi as organic intellectuals are model readers/critics of the text of which they themselves are a part. Their positionality is one which all traditional intellectuals who study *Nectar in a Sieve* in university classrooms must strive to occupy, in order to participate in a creative dialogue between the text and its context.

8

Master English, Native Publisher: A Publishing Perspective on English Studies in India[1]

RUKUN ADVANI

From the publisher's perspective the world of literary studies in India is a marketplace with its own political culture and economy, and it is by understanding the distinctive requirements and operations of this literature market that the Indian publisher hopes to exploit it. In the last instance, and usually in the first, second and every other instance as well, the reason for most publishers' existence is the profit to be made within the literary marketplace. The relationship between publishing and literary studies is also a reciprocal one, and, given the existence of particular varieties of publishing, particular varieties of literary activity are made possible.

This essay investigates the relationship between English literary studies in India and Indian publishing, and, more generally, argues for

[1] I am grateful to Rajeswari Sunder Rajan for posing a host of stimulating questions after reading an earlier version of this essay. Without her 'intervention', this essay would have approximated more closely to the standard dullness of academic prose. Detailed comments from Ravi Dayal, Manju Jain, Urvashi Butalia and Ahmer N. Anwar were extremely helpful. To Shahid Amin I am grateful for an approver's testimony, and to Ram Guha, Suvir Kaul and Brijraj Singh for reassuring approval. All these friends have thereby become 'implicated', 'imbricated', and 'complicit' in all faults that shall be found in this essay. For its general correctness, of course, I alone should be blamed.

the difficulty of establishing any specific 'ideology' of Indian publishing, if that word is distinguishable from a business ethic. It does this partly by discussing the relevant activities of Oxford University Press, where I work, as well as by looking at what frequently happens within the general publishing scenario in this country. The essay also uses what would earlier have been called digression, but which can now more reassuringly be called the deployment of digressive discursive strategies (a fine example of technical jargon coming to the rescue of a meandering mind) to execute its double purpose, which I hope is equally to entertain and inform. The master hegemony which has marginalized (if not booted out) casualness, irreverence and levity in favour of critical solemnity and undemocratic jargon within academic prose will thus be definitely and joyously transcended.[2] For this reason my essay also, whenever possible, satirizes the currently fashionable prose within which, in order to achieve academic credibility, Indian academics ape Western jargon when carrying out investigations of this sort; or, as a boa deconstructor might put it, this essay negates with needless negativity the need to subconsciously succumb to the Orientalist reversalism entailed in creating a discursive framework wherein comprehensibility is only accessed by initiated dissectors and discussants of deconstruction.

1. INDIAN PUBLISHING: THE BACKGROUND FOREGROUNDED

It is now customary, before embarking on such 'projects' and 'interventions', to emerge from clouds of 'mystification' by 'foregrounding' one's 'subject position' within the 'discourse', or, as might be said conversationally, introducing oneself. Born of partition refugees (father Sindhi, mother Punjabi) whose psyches were scarred enough by communalism to make them want to transcend it by making pots of secular money, this being a supposedly heritable trait, I was— to push to unnecessary limits an already long-winded Henry Jamesian sentence (he is, incidentally, a writer I loathe even more than did E.M. Forster, on whom I wrote a Ph.D. dissertation at Cambridge, a place I love and am sometimes nostalgic about to the point of soul-sickness)—educated in

---

[2] This represents a futile rearguard defence of the Bloomsbury common-reader tradition, as opposed to the high seriousness of the Leavises. Further knowledge of the difference between Bloomsbury and the Leavises would be best obtained by sampling the prose of the Woolfs and Forster, and then trying out the Leavises' turgidities.

an Indian public school which deeply scarred my own psyche in innumerable and unmentionable ways, until I escaped—like a barbarian entering decadent Rome—into the joyous hedonism of English literature in the gardens and ivory-towers of St Stephen's College and, subsequently, Cambridge. What followed is more mundane, though, I suppose, also more pertinent to the present essay: I joined the Indian branch of Oxford University Press in 1982 and have lived within the shadow of its hegemonic umbrella, though not in a very subject position, ever since. Given also that my favourite writers of English have for some time now been George Orwell (Conservative Left), E.M. Forster (Soft Liberal), and Auberon Waugh (Lunatic Right), I suppose my own ideological position should be described as tolerant scepticism or as radical aestheticism shading into a confused variety of left-leaning bourgeois anarchism. To put it plainly and, as my English teachers always said, in my own words, I am a person to whom music and prose matter much more than politics. I have no doubt that, in accordance with current critical logic, all this has a great deal of devious bearing on my perspective in this essay.

Writing as I am in a context within which people search zealously for post-colonial brown-skinned time-serving native informant-collaborators of white-skinned master-discursive multi-nationals, I suppose it is necessary also to further foreground what I would, by inclination, have normally backgrounded, namely the sort of organization within which my perspective (I forget the jargon word for 'perspective') was constituted. Fortunately, this foregrounding may be seen as a purposeful digressive strategy which enables the emergence of a broad picture wherein the OUP (and by implication other publishers not solely guided by business considerations) shows up by contrast its Other (a word which is, to quote Hamlet from another context, 'Horrible, horrible, oh most horrible') — i.e. much of the rest of Indian publishing. The broad character of Indian publishing, and some of the differences from it that define a publisher like the OUP, has quite a lot to do with the relationship between Indian publishing and English literary studies in the country.

On the face of it, the OUP in India is a multinational organization, for it is owned by Oxford University. But there are very many differences between multinationals and profiteering publishers on the one hand, and the OUP as well as a small handful of publishers on the other, which differences I shall take considerable pains to emphasize, operating as we do in a context that requires a careful distancing from people ever-ready to jump out of hidden corners in order to accuse the OUP of col-laborationist multinationality.[3] For one thing, the OUP in the UK is a non-profit and non-tax paying press closely tied to the University. 'Non-profit' does not mean that OUP's publishing activities are un-profitable—on the contrary, it makes loads of dough; it means, rather, that profits are ploughed back into further publishing activity. The press is governed by a committee of international academics and not by shareholders (there being none), no dividends are paid out, and profits made in India are not repatriated to our motherland (England, obvious-ly). The organization's acceptance of manuscripts worldwide is heavily determined by the dominant consensus on what constitutes educational rather than commercial literature. The OUP is currently one of the few significant publishers of academic literature operating in South Asia, publishing such literature primarily by and for South Asian readers and at prices determined by conditions in the indigenous market. In all these senses the OUP is distinct from both multinationals and the more nor-mal business sector of Indian publishing.

Perhaps all this reads like a self-serving brief for the OUP; it is actually a non-digressive discursive strategy which seeks to negotiate an imbricated path towards the sublime prose of Ultimate Incomprehen-sibility, by which alone may radical native academics become complicit with American salaries in excess of $ 100,000 p.a. Radical seekers of fifth-columnists would profit more by examining the British Council and the Ford Foundation, from which Indian government agencies draw substantial amounts of money, and from which in turn Indian academics, radicals included, draw funds for research trips abroad—when they aren't doing so more directly from these foreign bodies. They would also undoubtedly profit enormously by writing even more in-comprehensibly than they already do: in the Ivy League it literally doesn't pay to be understood.

The fact that OUP India's academic publications have found a recep-tive audience abroad is indicated both by library sales of these titles in the West, as well as by their use in university teaching and research work done there. It would have been very nice to have been able to argue that the same holds true of books published by lots of other houses in India,

[3] This phrase owes its existence to that master-phrase by Spivak, 'regulative psychobiography'—frequently deployed by that master master-critic in her lectures and writings—of which it is of course an unphenomenal epiphe-nomenon.

but several facts suggest otherwise. First, partly on account of the relatively low priority given to higher education within contemporary Indian culture (this being connected to low salaries and low funding by the government), the amount of high quality academic literature emanating from India is not voluminous enough to require more than the handful of committed academic publishers that there are. Second, after the demise in the sixties of the pioneering academic publisher Asia Publishing House, and the dilution of British capital invested in Indian publishing with the passing of the Foreign Exchange Regulation Act in the early seventies, the culture and interests of Indian publishing changed. There was a shift towards diversification of capital to non-publishing activities (e.g. hotels), as well as towards profit maximization within the orbit of traditional publishing. This latter meant a concentration upon areas other than academic publishing. Excluding OUP, the larger academic publishers—such as Macmillan, Orient Longman and Allied—moved visibly away from academic literature and towards school texts and college anthologies, these being areas within which, as I show later, the pickings are both easier and more substantial. Even today, well into the nineties, academic publishing is marginal to the activity of these houses, whereas this was not so before the seventies. Only very recently has there been a comforting glimmer of academic publishing becoming important for organizations like Sage and Kali.

The essential purpose of OUP's educational publishing being to promote ideas and learning rather than to make commercial profits, the organization is unusual in being exempt from an important pressure to which the ideologically uncommitted private sector of Indian publishing is subject, namely proprietors or shareholders for whom the return on investment is far more important than an undiluted publishing programme. 'Undiluted' is a word that people in hidden corners look for to pounce upon, and it needs to be clarified. The OUP has traditionally not posited an opposition between 'traditional scholarship' and 'interventionist politics', holding what is often denigrated as the liberal and eclectic view that merit, depth of analysis, richness of ideas, complexity of thought and other such nice things are independent of and regularly produced from varying and opposed ideological perspectives. This is a position to which the bulk of Indian publishers would also subscribe, though for different reasons: they are concerned not with ideological positions but with the marketability of their titles, not with politically committed perspectives but with politic alignments with the power hierarchies that will help to sell their goods and make recoveries on investment. Admittedly, the overt ideological positions of some Indian publishers are clearer than those of the bulk, but it is an unfortunate fact that these more committed publishers have seldom been significant in terms of a recognizable publishing programme, marketing ability and staying power; or alternatively, they have had to succumb to the pressures of an imperfect market to stay alive, whereby their distinctive character has begun to seem diluted. This is not to undermine the importance of small and committed publishers—on the contrary the heroism of such enterprises, and frequently the significance of their publishing, within a culture so fiercely oppositional is sometimes almost incredible—but to map a terrain within which such activities are unfortunately solitary, sporadically visible, and usually short-lived. In general it is less easy to determine the overall ideological position of most Indian publishers, including the OUP, than it is to determine the ideological position of an 'apolitical' Indian academic. A philosophy of quietism or aloofness from strikes among Indian academics seems to me a much more clearly definable political position than a publishing list within which Marxist, Conservative, Liberal and various nasty essentialist-humanist texts coexist to cause unacceptable ideological confusion. One way out of the confusion is, naturally, to deny that the Marxist portions of such a list are Marxist at all, there being now enough varieties of Marxism to make this an easy exercise. Besides, a publisher who allows such motley eclecticism to flourish unchecked can always be branded Fascist, or worse, Liberal, his ideology being thereby made satisfactorily clear. Reductionist labelling is as much the shallow Marxist's pastime as it is the Conservative's, and there is a very large number of both these sorts of people within Indian academia.

Unlike several other publishers the OUP does not determine its publishing either by the offer or the lack of subsidies. In India subventions are increasingly on offer, particularly for academic monographs, most often from second- or third-rate academics who spend their lives clambering into the bureaucratic power positions from which they can help themselves and, usually, their relatives. Such subventions are invariably turned down by the OUP if the organization's criteria of quality—whatever their limitations—are not met. This independence is very privileged and defines by its 'otherness' ('Horrible, horrible', etc.) the general context of non-governmental publishing in India. While it would be false to posit clear-cut distinctions between the OUP and other Indian publishers—several, such as Sage and Kali, seem equally committed to their own definitions of excellence—the differences are at present sufficiently clear for the Indian academic community, radicals included, to believe that the advantages of publishing with the OUP are considerable.

In general, as will I hope become clearer later in this essay, I am suggesting, within this prolonged business of foregrounding, that Indian publishing is in general ideologically uncommitted as well as difficult to position ideologically, given its willingness to publish more or less anything that has an acceptably large market within publishing horizons that are not renowned for their largeness. Or, to put it in prose that many now find satisfaction in digesting, Indian publishing exists in a spatio-temporal *localité* that might be deemed free of politico-ideological considerations. This needs to be qualified, I suppose, by adding (the sophisticated thought) that no economic activity can hold itself free of ideology. But there seems to me to be a distinction between business and financial profit on the one hand, and ideology on the other, even though the former implies some form of the latter. In other words, the distinction clearly exists between committed publishers and those who are 'ideologized' by having to operate within, and therefore who further extend, the general framework of capitalism and its often despicable nexuses. In this sense, Indian publishers are ideologized rather than ideological, i.e. they collaborate with and extend a dominant ideology; the number of Indian publishers ideologically committed to alternatives—and therefore relatively independent of the market—has never been significant enough to alter the overall character of the industry. This, I think, is what in other contexts has been termed 'the universalizing tendency of capital', though I wouldn't swear I've got it right.

I am also suggesting as a corollary a fact that might seem self-evident to everyone except hidden-corner academics—that Indian publishers are canny businessmen who publish whatever will make a decent profit, not ideologically motivated scoundrels intent on pushing a line that will subtly extend the hegemony of capital; or, to put it deconstructively, they are not people who carve out extended spatio-temporal locations (*pace localité*) wherein the frontiers of hegemonic capital and the penumbra of its corollorific ism may be more visibly discerned and less discernibly visible.

2. ENGLISH MASTERS AND NATIVE PUBLISHERS : THE ANTHOLOGY MARKET

Having suggested—by discussing the peculiar status of the OUP and the 'normality' of most other native publishers—the general politico-

economic context that defines Indian publishing, let us look more closely at how most Indian publishers operate in relation to English literary
studies. The publisher generally looks first at the dimensions of the
market. If the term 'literary activity' covers, for our purposes, everything
in the way of written material that is required by students and teachers
of English language and literature in the post-school stage, and if this
material, as commonly happens, is to be supplied by publishers operating in a free market, then the dimensions of this market from the
publisher's viewpoint are extremely large. The English language and
literature markets are seen as one and the same thing by publishers, for
at least in India language continues to be taught largely through literary
passages in what can loosely be termed the literary anthology. Even
with the current trend favouring a more vocationalized and job-oriented
approach to English teaching, the anthology itself is never dispensed
with, its contents merely reflecting the shift in emphasis from literary
passages to business letters, commercial conversation, etc. etc. The market for these is very much larger than, say, the markets for history,
economics and sociology textbooks. This is because every student in
every Indian university who enrolls for a BA or BSc studies English for a
year, and very often for two or three, so the potential market for English
at this level is vast, the stakes in it running to several crores of rupees.
This is the market that almost every Indian publisher is most interested
in, for this is where the bread is most thickly buttered. If a publisher can,
for instance, get the University of Delhi to allow him to publish an
anthology that is prescribed as a compulsory text for the First Year BA
Pass Course, or for Subsidiary English, he has, as Al Capone said after
eliminating one of his major rivals, made a killing in the market. One BA
Pass or Subsidiary anthology prescription means a sale of around 20,000
copies, each priced approximately Rs 15, with a recurring though slightly diminishing sale (on account of second-hand sales of first printings)
over let us say five years. Translated into money this means an annual
turnover from this one book of something just under three lakh rupees,
or nearly 15 lakhs over five years. If one also takes a conservative
average of three anthologies for each of our 150 universities, i.e. about
450 anthologies are prescribed at any one time in India, and multiplies
this by the 3 lakhs which is the turnover yield from one anthology, we
arrive at a figure of about 12 crores. This 12 crores is, roughly speaking,
the size of the anthology market; 12 crores may seem a small sum, but,
given the amount allocated to university education in India, it is far from
inconsiderable.

There are several hazards involved in this business of anthology publishing. First of all, the price of the anthology has to be just right, given the purchasing power as well as price expectations in this market. This means that the publisher will try to pressurize the prescribing authorities to prepare anthologies that are thin rather than fat, because a thin anthology means to the publisher less headache, less investment and a higher profit margin, given an optimal price that he knows is acceptable within his market. He will also prefer that the entire anthology be prescribed reading, because if only portions of it are prescribed, these prescribed portions will soon appear in a pirated edition which, because it involves the use of less paper, printing costs and overheads, will be cheaper than the complete anthology. The publisher will also usually prefer an anthology which includes notes and other spoon-feeding material, because the student is then more likely to stick to the anthology and not buy a *kunji* (colloquial Hindi for 'guide-book') instead. However, publishers can also be even more far-sighted, preferring an anthology without notes so that they themselves can also publish a kunji to go with the anthology. Such a kunji will appear a few months after the original anthology in order that the market has time to first buy up the anthology and then buy the kunji. All these market considerations are usually as well known to the prescribing authorities as they are to the publishers, so it may seem an insult to publishers to suggest that they need to exert something as primitive as 'pressure'. The nexus is normally subtler and smoother. Mutual requirements are mutually understood; public relations between academics in power and publishers might be described by both as satisfactory.

The pricing of an anthology is important for another reason as well. If the price is higher than market expectations, rival kunjis will sprout and the market will become an unweeded garden grown to seed, with things rank and gross in nature possessing it merely (cf. Hamlet on the state of Denmark). Pirated editions priced more cheaply than the original anthology will also appear, and Indian students, or merely about ninety per cent of them, buy what is cheapest, namely kunjis and pirated editions. In the Hindi belt, for example, kunjis sell many times more than the anthologies on which they are based; in other areas a kunji will sell only a few times more than the original anthology. However, if the price of the anthology is seen as being low, or at least reasonable, the kunji market suffers a little and pirates turn away. As regards pricing, therefore, the ideal price is one which, first, allows the publisher a decent profit margin, and second, keeps the pirates and kunjis at bay. In either case, however, it is more lucrative to be a kunji writer and a kunji publisher. The morality and interests of the majority of Indian publishers support such publishing, and it is no coincidence that the morality and interests of academics in positions of power are, in general, not markedly different. The frequent nexus between academics and publishers is only an aspect of what is routine within such economic relationships in the culture at large.

The profit margin on such anthologies, after taking into account the discounts given to the retail bookseller and the royalty paid to the author or editors, may not be very high—it is certainly considerably lower than the margins to be made on library hardbacks, which are priced much higher. But there are these crucial differences that make the anthology market so much more attractive and profitable—first, that the turnover is very large; second that the sales are assured on account of the book being prescribed; and third, that once the initial headache of editing and typesetting the book is over the publisher can sit back and rake in the rupees by the very simple operation of repeatedly reprinting the book year after year. Whereas he would have to sell a library hardback at his own risk, and spend money on warehousing it for several years, a prescribed anthology comes under the category of 'no-risk' publishing because he knows he cannot lose on his investment, and because he knows exactly how soon he will recover his investment. The Indian literary marketplace, in short, lacks none of the features that, on a larger scale, characterize other markets. This system, like many other economic systems, is well entrenched and reproduces itself regularly and with quiet efficiency. There are of course exceptions to this pattern. Several departments of English follow a sensible policy, by which the editors who prepare anthologies are nominated by a committee, and all royalties paid by the publisher are paid to the Department of English rather than to the individual editors. Such universities are also sensible in dealing with publishers who are more scrupulous than are those who bag anthologies elsewhere in the country, i.e. they favour publishers who will provide reasonable quality of production, a reasonable price, efficient distribution, reliable accounts of sale, editorial assistance, and so on.

3. CRITICAL EDITIONS AND FINANCIAL ADDITIONS

Like any other market, the Eng. Lit. market has its relatively clean areas. How does a publisher operate in the cleaner areas? Essentially by publishing not just anthologies but also worthwhile editions of literary texts as well as useful library hardbacks or academic monographs on literary subjects. These two areas, literary texts and academic monographs, are quite distinct from each other in the publisher's mind.

The bigger and therefore more attractive of these two is the market for editions of literary texts. Indian publishers like it when the dollar and sterling exchange rates are unfavourable to imports of foreign paperback classics, because their own rupee-priced editions are then much more likely to sell. A large number of Indian publishers produce editions of the widely prescribed out-of-copyright classics, such as the novels of Jane Austen, Thomas Hardy, Dickens, George Eliot, D.H. Lawrence and so on. The recent Indian copyright act has made it easier for Indian publishers to wrest permission from foreign publishers to reprint books that are still within copyright. However, the fact that very few copyright classics have in fact been reprinted reflects on the accepted literary canon in India, which is heavily weighted in favour of the Ancients. The archaic nature of the accepted literary canon in India is touched upon towards the end of this essay and is, of course, the epistemological *sine qua non* of the ontological status of the present volume.

Here again the 'softer' classics, i.e. those studied by the BA Pass rather than BA Honours and MA, are the plums in the pudding on account of the larger potential markets. In this area the Indian publisher can serve a more useful function. Whereas in the anthology market the publisher is handed over a monopoly for a certain consideration and seldom has any useful advisory role in determining the quality of the product, in the areas where he must compete to sell his wares the publisher can be of greater use to the literary community. This has in India been traditionally performed by the commissioning of editions of particular novels or plays that are part of the accepted literary canon. Macmillan, Orient Longman, Oxford University Press, Doaba House and various other publishers bring out texts that carry an introduction and detailed notes by reputed academics who have specialized in the academic area within which their texts are located. The introduction and notes cater to the needs of the Indian student, by which I mean that they are more exhaustive than those to be found in comparable texts abroad, where the level of knowledge assumed is often much higher. But it would be false to believe that the publisher can act as an important instrument of change, in the sense that he can bring about a revision of the literary canon by commissioning introductions and notes to texts that are not traditionally within the accepted canon. Publishers are, to reiterate, as uncommitted to the world of literary studies as they are generally to any particular ideology. Unless they're reasonably certain of a return on investment, they will not publish an unknown author or text, though they will certainly publish such authors or texts if their canonization seems imminent. The sort of change that radical idealists are looking for will I think have to emanate very largely from within the literary community, though some publishers may be more willing than others to aid that sort of change. Within the existing contexts, publishers are merely willing to help improve the nature of the annotations and introductory material currently available, though even this sort of work is mostly done because the publisher envisages a market for a better text rather than out of any political ideology or philanthropic motive. There has, to my knowledge, been no systematic attempt by Indian publishers to make foreign classics cheaply available, or to append prescribed canonical texts with material produced from a clearly distinguishable perspective, nor to propagate new writers and radical anthologies. (The availability of Russian classics in cheap editions is an honourable exception, though these emerge from the state-subsidized non-commercial sector—as do several important Indian texts from bodies such as the National Book Trust and the Children's Book Trust.) Such things have happened sporadically and at random, usually when a market is either envisaged by a publisher or assured by a prescribing authority. It is encouraging to find in India the equivalent of Western publishers like Virago or Zed or The Women's Press, but the history of such efforts in the country discourages the hope that they are here to stay without becoming, in several senses, diluted. At present it does seem that any breakthroughs in this direction can only occur if academic hierarchies actually prescribe the sorts of texts that are espoused by radical academics and radical presses, enabling the harmonious institutionalization of radicalism through the medium of pocket-gratifying profits. The general scenario certainly lends itself to such cynicism, though it is heartening to see the occasional committed publisher striving to first create an intellectual space instead of supinely squeezing into pre-canonized spaces. This happens by publishing a text for which the demand is apparently non-existent, and praying that such a text will be espoused by a prescribing authority. The occurrence has a Halley's Comet air about it, and the OUP's experience with such texts that it has published suggests that they will remain minor meteorites congratulated for being special only by the very few that yet see merit in such texts. Am I thereby cynically suggesting that commercial unsuccess and a minority audience render such efforts futile, and contradicting the claims to committed publishing made for the OUP? Not really; just that I might be less temperamentally wary of radical enthusiasm if the higher-education culture at large offered more space than it does for optimism *vis-à-vis* these most marvellous efforts to create new intellectual spaces. The more fervent radicals, I suppose, might argue—without necessarily reading them—that OUP's annotated texts ought to make anyone cynical. There being as many factions within radical camps as anywhere else, a publisher must often engage in a tight-rope act to keep several such factions happy at the same time, or at least prevent them uniting to throttle him.

But to move away from what might seem an excessive deployment of a deviant narratological narratology, most publishers' interest in this area of literary text publishing is likely to be proportionate with the size of the market, and to the size and ease with which profits can be made within it. By comparison with the anthology market, the literary text market is tiny. The combined all-India annual sale (i.e. turnover) from it is unlikely to exceed Rs 25 lakhs, as compared to roughly 12 crores obtainable in the anthology market. Furthermore, there are seldom monopolies in the literary text market, because specific editions of these literary texts are seldom prescribed, which means that publishers must compete to sell their editions of literary texts. This naturally restricts most publishers' interest in this market, particularly as they are seldom editorially equipped to ensure an adequate level of competition against editions that are already established sellers.

4. HARDBACKS AND THE LONG DURÉE

Finally, there is the smallest segment of the literary market, namely the market for library hardbacks. This is the smallest in terms of its turnover value to the publisher, but it is nevertheless of very considerable political or, more properly, strategic, importance. This is because, at one level, much publishing in this area ties up with anthology publishing. A publisher who can invest in the career of an academic by publishing a substandard monograph by him is that much more likely to receive patronage from such an academic whenever that academic is in a position to bestow patronage. Even publishers with reasonable reputations will often take on a substandard monograph as a sort of investment in the future, if the person who has written it either is in a position of power, or seems likely to be in such a position later on. And there is little denying the fact that most people who write substandard monographs are the very people who are either clambering up the power ladder, or have already clambered up into positions of power, or at the very least have the connections and ability to bestow patronage. State agencies, with the myopia and incomprehension that are to be expected from them, aid this nexus by handing out subventions or grants to practically every Ph.D. writer who can persuade a publisher to take on his thesis. The publisher's investment is thereby minimized, and there is less risk in publishing such books if the publisher has built up his contacts with purchasing librarians and the library network well enough. This is what partly accounts for the fairly large numbers of bad hardbacks that appear regularly on literary as well as other subjects; it is also one of the reasons for the OUP's relative abstinence within this area of publishing for English Studies. The point is that such monographs would not appear if they were not economically viable, or in other words they would not appear if the corrupt preconditions for their economic viability did not exist. Strategic considerations rather than the economics of publishing have in the past been the dominant factor in this market, because the turnover yield from Indian monographs in English Studies has been low even in relation to the literary text market. However, as we shall see later, lower costs of production on account of superior technology have now made the economics of this operation as important as strategic considerations.

The lack of good quality research monographs in English literary studies from Indian publishing houses is due to the somewhat peculiar status of English Studies in India. A specialized undergraduate course in English is for most school-leavers a third or fourth option, especially among male students who are traditionally under greater pressure to find high-income jobs than are Indian women students. The quality of intake into English Studies is thus poor in relation to the intake in science subjects, or economics and commerce, the prospects of a high-income job after studying English being seen as much dimmer than after studying practically anything else (except perhaps Sanskrit and Hindi). At the same time, a reasonably large number of the mainly mediocre students who do end up studying English also end up teaching it to undergraduates, there being many middle-income jobs available in this area on account of the huge numbers of university students, all of whom have to be taught English (out of anthologies) for at least one academic year. The result is that such teachers, under increasing pressure to publish for career mobility, produce, irrespective of ideology, poor-quality Ph.D.s or collections of essays. These are rewritten for publication. Advances in publication technology make it much easier now to publish 300-400 copies of such books, at a unit cost that would, even five years ago—when typesetting costs were much higher—have been achieved only with a minimum printrun of 1000 copies. These copies are then off-loaded, usually via wholesalers and retailers, to the happy nexus that ensures sufficient sales to underwrite the costs of production plus the minimum level of profit that the publisher expects. The proportion of monographs that really merits an audience is small in relation to the overall number of titles that is published. Within the publishing world, therefore, there is a definite shift from generating turnover via large-volume sales of a limited number of 'good' titles towards low-volume sales of large numbers of a mix of good, bad and indifferent titles. The situation in English Studies, where large numbers of poor-quality academics are crying out to get their mostly indifferent work published, therefore suits the present techno-economic situation of Indian publishing. Given the need for what has been described earlier as 'strategic' publishing, the economic viability of titles with low printruns has proved a boon as well as a boom-area for, especially, small publishers.

Another important factor responsible for the poor quality of Indian monographs in English Studies is that the literature studied here is that of England and America. By and large, the significant Indian critical contributions to the study of this literature have been made by those who have studied it abroad, in England and the USA, rather than in the periphery, India. Research materials and facilities for sound scholarship as well as sufficiently high-powered theoretical training in this sphere are unavailable in India, or at least, like many commodities, scarcer and less easily accessed than in the Anglo-Saxon world, which has for English Studies more scholars, more funds, more libraries, more primary and secondary literature, etc. These collectively constitute the surely honourable reason for Indian academics wanting to rush off to shop around there—for research materials, of course—whenever the all-too-rare opportunity arises. Furthermore, the base market for books in this sphere is in the metropolis rather than in the periphery, there rather than here. Most scholars worth their salt in English Studies will therefore want their monographs published in England or the USA, because their largest—though not always most receptive—audience is located there. Indian publishers are and I think should be a second choice for worthwhile Indian academics in English Studies, as they should for instance in European history, particularly given the fact that if a good book is published by an undiscriminating Indian publisher it is likely to get swamped by all the bad books that are simultaneously being promoted by such a publisher.[4] For the very same reasons, the sensible Indian publisher is far more interested in acquisitioning monographs from departments of history, economics, sociology, management, etc., where the standards of indigenous research are higher, rather than from departments of English Studies. I do not wish to suggest that good monographs in English Studies by Indian scholars are axiomatically those that have been produced or published abroad; but to my mind the frequency with which this is actually the case, both in the interventionist and conservative traditions, is high enough to tempt one towards what any self-respecting deconstructionist would term 'axiomatism'.

It seems to me that the space for high-standard monograph publication in English Studies in India will only be created if and when the dominant ideology, which has an outdated and derivative but firmly entrenched notion of what English Studies means, is replaced by newer thinking wherein the conception of English Studies is broadened to mean literature in English and includes, for instance, fine English translations of regional Indian classics. At present we are quite prepared to teach the Greek classics and, more recently, English translations of Brecht, but have neither sponsored fine English translations of our own fictional classics nor are prepared to look seriously at the few such translations that do exist. The reason for the perpetuation of this dominant ideology is not difficult to understand if one looks, as this essay attempts, at the financial stakes that are involved. The people in power in English literary studies today are in this sense like the Indian state— the faces may change but the Leviathan itself lies unmoved and unmoving, watching the few idealists around it who will either shout themselves into the ground or fall silent when they have exhausted themselves.

This scenario is a generally dim one. At the same time, there are very large sectors of Indian life as a whole that look exactly like this, so I don't wish to suggest that things are more dismal in English literary studies than they are elsewhere. But from the publisher's perspective English Studies in India seems dominated less by talent and ideas than by the

---

[4] I hope my own definition of 'good' and 'bad' can be inferred from this essay generally. If not, too bad.

racketeering of a powerful and well-entrenched orthodoxy. Even among the better people who inhabit the world of literary studies there has in the past been less vibrancy and less concerted or articulate effort towards radical thinking and radical change than there has been in departments of history, economics and sociology. Not so long ago, the discourses generated by these departments in India were also derivative and Eurocentric. But whereas these departments have successfully created a native space for themselves within the country—theoretically, empirically and from a variety of perspectives that are internationally respected (thanks at least in some tiny measure to collaborationist multinationality in publishing)—departments of English have remained strikingly stuck in what delectable phraseologists might call the Otherness of a newly forged nativity. Without this talent, vibrancy, continuous rethinking and search for alternatives to an orthodoxy that is itself intellectually stagnant, the academic scenario in literary studies is unlikely to alter, and publishing, at least in its relation to this area, will continue with its traditional subservience to the orthodoxy in power. This should not, of course, be presumed to mean that publishers are likely to be less subservient to radicals in power. Subservience, like literary merit, has much more to do with power than with ideology.

5. PRESCRIBING A TEXT : ELITES AND SUBALTERNS

One desirable change that emerges by implication from this essay is a more careful focus on texts for the BA Pass and Subsidiary English, for this is in economic terms by far the biggest segment of English Studies in India, and also affects the lives and thinking of the largest number of people who exist in this domain. It seems perverse to a publisher that an area of English Studies that is so central to his vision, and which constitutes 90 per cent of the English market, should be so peripheral to the best Indian teachers of English. Most good teachers of English are generally fairly exclusively concerned, not always for good or understandable reasons, with academic research, critical theory, and the elite end of their academic world. A corrective focus on the subalterns of BA Pass might occur by their occasionally dismounting from the high horses of critical theory; this would help ensure better standards and better publishing in what ought to be seen as a very crucial and important area of English Studies in India. The fact that publishers have no very clear conception of what sorts of alternative teaching materials are desirable for BA Pass and Subsidiary English is less significant than the fact that, within the teaching community itself, there is neither such a conception, nor as much effort to arrive at one as may be believed by radical idealists. Even the radical section within the English teaching community, by marginalizing the BA Pass and concentrating on their own new and radical interpretations of literary texts that have very little relation to what is taught to the BA Pass, may be implicated at one level within an elitism which they, at another level, seek to repudiate.

In a more general sense it also seems to me, from the margins of the Lit. Crit. world in India, that things may be poised for some sort of change. In the last five or six years there seems to have built up a group of people that, though not politically united, is significant enough even in terms of individuals thinking in isolation but along similar lines, to mount a challenge to an orthodoxy that is quite visibly, in several centres, beginning to dig in its heels. The organization of seminars that focus not formalistically on literary texts but on the historical, political and sociological links of the discipline within a specific context, are undoubted indications of a strong intellectual, even if not politically unified, alternative to the status quo. Any publisher who sympathizes with this search for alternative perspectives will watch with interest and some excitement from the wings to see if the potential revolution matures, but his interest as a person with friends in the Jacobin camp will be tempered by his scepticism as a publisher. This is because, even in the unlikely event that the Indian Eng. Lit. world gets turned upside down, the publisher will merely have to collaborate with a new set of people who will, sooner or later, have to produce their own BA Pass anthologies. The BA Pass anthology thus more or less sums up the publisher's ontological status; it is the Given Thing that cannot be done away with, even if its format and contents are radically rethought. This being the case, publishers must hope that they have enough friends in the new power hierarchy, if there is ever one, to ensure that their organizations are given the enviable task of publishing an unending series of BA Pass anthologies. Or, as one might say in order not to end with a whimper, publishers must aim at constructing a spatio-temporal *localité* within which is operationalized a discursive paradigm that is simultaneously enabled by and enabling of the paramountcy of an essentialist-universalist commodity-fetishized anthologization of a semi-feudal, semi-colonial, quasi-hegemonized and bourgeois-imperialist discipline.

9

Brokering English Studies: The British Council in India

RAJESWARI SUNDER RAJAN

O ne of the avowed purposes of the British Council is to extend 'specialist support for English Studies' in the host country.[1] The Council gains a major part of its influence from the widespread perception that it is a repository of authentic English-language use as well as a natural source of authoritative information on the literature of Britain. Therefore any investigation of English literary studies in India must take this role into account.

The presence of the British Council in our midst necessarily poses the question: can English literature be taught in India independently of its institutional apparatus in the country of its origin—the universities, the critical and scholarly texts, the professional critics and teachers, the libraries, 'out there'? It would appear not, in its present form; hence the mediating function of the British Council must seem inevitable. For people for whom the present situation of English Studies in India is a cause for some unease, an extended genealogical investigation seems called for. In such an exercise the British Council is a necessary text for scrutiny.

It is this that prompts me to begin with a brief analysis of a British Council-sponsored workshop in an Indian university. The issues that

---

[1] British Council Information Brochure. (Hereafter BCIB.) This also gives other 'facts and figures': there are 976 Technical Co-operation Training Awards; 80 Commonwealth scholarships by Britain to India; 72 Academic Link visits; 2.25 million issues from libraries; 81,000 library members; 5000 library users.

emerge will, I believe, serve as a first step in understanding how a conduit between the British university and the Indian is set up under the British Council's aegis, and the implications this has for teaching English literature in India.

An eight-day faculty workshop titled 'The Teaching of Literature' (3 April–12 April 1989) was offered by Alan Durant of the University of Strathclyde, Glasgow, at the Department of English in Rajasthan University, Jaipur. Durant was exploring 'alternative' ways of teaching English literature.

In view of a crisis that might eventually prove severe enough to destabilize the traditional role and function of English literature in the Indian university, the urgency with which the British Council sought to discover and offer a rationale for its continued study was not difficult to understand. Alan Durant, whose involvement with English Studies in India through the British Council has been of long standing, had earlier contributed an essay, 'English Literature Teaching in India' (in four parts) to *Focus on English*, which is the British Council's local, mimeographed journal for the teaching of English, circulated to English teachers in Indian universities. In it he made a persuasive plea for a synthesizing strategy through which English literary texts may be used 'as a language teaching aid in the early stages', thereby recovering for traditional English literature a role within a situation where its uses are being increasingly questioned. In this context, it can be assumed that English teachers in India have a similarly vested interest—for professional reasons—in the continuation of English as a university subject.

The BC workshop could therefore be seen as addressing a problem—how to make English texts *useful*—which was of concern to both British instructor and Indian participants. Accordingly, the approach was suitably low-keyed, pragmatic, and flexible, with an emphasis on the feasible rather than the grandiose, on the immediate situation rather than the larger context. Though Durant did work his way through the history and ideology of English Studies (both in his article and in his opening lectures), these did not impinge in any perceptible way upon the situation of English literature in the classroom.

Instead, the intervention of contemporary critical theory, linguistics, stylistics, discourse analysis, film and media theory was sought, to clear a space for the more efficient, and certainly culturally untainted, study of English literature. Methodology, in this context, has somewhat the air of technology, and is offered, like the latter, as a modern, progressive, efficient, and ideologically neutral product of the west. Like western technology, it was understood that western pedagogic methods will have to be adapted and indigenized for use under local circumstances, but that, overall, it travelled well. What was strikingly absent in the actual demonstrations of activities involving the use of the literary text for linguistic, stylistic and structural analysis was any sense of the texts' historical, cultural or political dimensions—except as these posed difficulties for second-language users and necessitated negotiation in the pedagogic process.

Durant advocated a 'learner-centred' pedagogy in place of the knowledge-centred practices of the past: this, in his view, is achieved by engaging students in a variety of activities. The activities—if they are not to be totally vacuous—clearly have to be designed with considerable skill, as in a computer software. The question of who designs these activities did not come up at the workshop; logically, the actual teacher would be the person best fitted. But judging from the number of activities that Durant reproduced from his own published work, it is likely that the Indian teacher is expected to rely on 'experts' to produce a package for his/her use; this will then serve, as the equivalent of the old critical texts, as a pedagogical crutch. Like several ESL programmes, these learner-centred activities for literature courses appear to have been designed for experiment and eventual use in the *Indian* classroom. It is probable, however, that similar programmes exist for use in British schools, where they address problems of linguistic inadequacy in students from working-class and racially-mixed communities.

The major aspects of Durant's workshop can be summed up: first, that the emphasis for English Studies in India is on *function* (the uses of the literary text), and *method* (learner-centred activities). This contrasts with the increasing emphasis in the British academy on literary studies as *cultural politics*. Second, the audience Durant addressed—college and university teachers—has a very limited influence in bringing about syllabus reforms within existing teaching systems. Therefore the actual effect of Durant's proposals, regardless of the responsiveness of the participants, is unlikely to be significant. It should be added here that, during his stay, Durant was also consulted at higher levels about syllabus changes in the M.Phil. courses, a privilege rarely extended to Indian college teachers. Given this access to several levels of influence, the *actual* effectiveness of a British academic's proposals is vastly enhanced, though this is likely to be a direct rather than a mediated impact. Third, Durant's suggestions for the teaching of literature in India envisage the continuing reliance of Indian teachers upon the British academic 'expert', rather than a severing of dependency ties—this in spite of a proposed parting of the ways in the purposes and methods of literary studies in the two countries. Finally, the nature of the instruction itself (learner-centred), the mode of interaction (the workshop), the bearing of the instructor (self-effacing, mediating), all reinforce the BC's own brochured self-representation as an organization *responsive* to articulated local needs rather than gratuitously interventionary.

This brief analysis allows me to point to some of the issues at stake in the BC's association with English Studies in India. A faculty workshop should have been, ideally, an intellectual and cultural exchange in which, as Colin MacCabe has put it, teacher and taught 'should all be learning'. If, however, the instruction ends—as it did at Durant's workshop—by being largely a one-way flow, it is not enough to attribute this process to the asymmetry of power inherent in the *teaching situation* alone, as MacCabe does.[2] What is also relevant is the *institutional context* within which this transmission takes place (the British cultural agency, the British and Indian universities); the *historical context* within which it is located (the neo-colonial situation, where questions of 'knowledge' become associated with question of foreign aid and propaganda, and hence become fraught issues); and the *object of knowledge* that is sought to be transmitted ('English', both Britain's national language / literature, and an international counter of exchange). It is the interactions among these different aspects that produce specific kinds of 'results'.

But none of these entities—the Indian university, the BC itself, 'English', or the British university (represented here by its academics)— is monolithic, identically constituted everywhere and at all times. On the contrary, they are heterogeneous, varied, and susceptible to change, as the ensuing arguments will try to show, and therefore produce different kinds of totalizing effects.

THE BRITISH COUNCIL IN INDIA

As an organization the BC is neither distinctively fish nor fowl. It is described as 'an independent body which promotes Britain abroad', and, as such, has its own chairman and board of members, with a director-general as executive head. It is covered by a royal charter, with the queen as its patron. Nevertheless, it is heavily dependent for many

---

[2] Colin MacCabe, 'English Literature in a Global Context', in R. Quirk and H. G. Widdowson, eds, *English in the World: Teaching and Learning the Language and Literature* (Cambridge: Cambridge University Press, 1985), 46.

of its activities on grants from the British government, and is therefore constrained by the latter's foreign-policy decisions. In India, the BC is the division of the British High Commission in charge of 'cultural affairs and technical co-operation', and it runs 'Britain's largest network of libraries abroad'.[3] It pursues 'cultural diplomacy' as a wing of Britain's foreign relations policy.[4]

The BC's spending in India (£ 18,598,000 in 1988) is its largest overseas budget. Fifteen per cent of these funds are spent on English Studies, the rest on science and technology (50 per cent), Education and Social Studies (14 per cent), and Information Services and Media (5 per cent).

The BC began operations in India in 1948. When Independence began to seem imminent, India came to assume strategic importance for British interests. T.W. Murray, an official of the BC had argued after a preliminary visit to India in 1944:

Indians still look instinctively to England: the extent to which we have anglicized the Indian public mind is often under-rated and is one of the most extraordinary achievements of the British connection. But India is looking to other countries, notably America, and unless steps are taken in a systematic way to maintain the intellectual communion of the past, our best asset may be lost or cheapened.[5]

Nehru himself, the BC information brochure does not fail to tell us, formally invited the BC to set up office in India. The ministry of education, in spite of a decision to make Hindi the national language, 'welcomed the Council's assistance and advice in introducing the most modern and effective methods of teaching English as a foreign language'.[6]

The BC's India policy was part of a larger colonial policy dictated by the British government's colonial office, which took over all the Council's activities in the colonies from the foreign office in 1948. The BC

[3] BCIB.

[4] John Burgh, director-general, the British Council, is quoted in 'The British Council Report, 1986-7': 'Britain is fortunate: our way of life, our excellence in the arts and education are widely admired overseas. It is the Council's task, in collaboration with our partner countries, to ensure that our cultural achievements are used to benefit Britain. Our values, our language and our culture are the three most enduring of Britain's invisible exports.'

[5] Frances Donaldson, *The British Council: The First Fifty Years* (London: Cape, 1984), 157.

[6] Ibid., 150.

is described by the colonial office as 'not only a possible instrument . . . but perhaps the only possible instrument in multi-racial communities.' Further,

> In present world conditions, the first priority should be to consolidate the Commonwealth and in particular to strengthen the cultural links with those parts of the Commonwealth (i.e. India, Pakistan, Ceylon and most of the Colonies) where the link of blood-relationship with us is absent ... It is, I imagine, fair to say that one way of looking at the present world picture is as a struggle for the soul of vast 'backward' populations of Africa and South Asia. In that struggle the Council can be a potent weapon . . .[7]

A colonial office circular of 1949 formulated these sentiments into policy:

> In the long term we want to strengthen the ties between Britain and the colonial peoples so that the latter, as they obtain greater control over their own affairs, will still value the British connection . . . We feel the Council can do valuable positive work in countering Communist propaganda by showing that Britain and the Western tradition for which Britain stands has something better to offer than the Communist way of life.[8]

The Drogheda Committee of 1953, set up to determine the impact of the BC's work on the people of the different countries in which it operated, also demanded the need for 'a fundamental re-orientation of the work of the Council—a change of emphasis from cultural to educational work and from the more developed to the less developed parts of the world.'[9] The Committee especially urged the necessity to develop the Council in the Indian subcontinent, 'and to increase its range to that it would be in touch with all the principal university towns.'

[7] Ibid., 165.

[8] Ibid., 155.

[9] The Drogheda Committee identified the following factors to determine the nature and value of the British Council's work in the host countries: (i) the nature and extent of British political and commercial interests; (ii) the attitude of the educated classes in these countries towards the United Kingdom; (iii) the extent to which the educational and cultural leaders and university graduates were likely to have political influence; (iv) the extent of the danger of communism, especially in universities and among intellectuals and the degree to which the work of the Council was likely to lessen this danger; (v) the demand for cultural and educational contacts with the United Kingdom (including the desire to learn English); and the extent to which this demand could be filled by private enterprise or required official assistance. See Donaldson, 183.

Given this background to its functioning, and the explicit connection to Britain's earlier colonial rule, the BC might have been expected to be far more aggressive in pursuing its goals in India than it has actually been. This low-keyed approach is adopted in part because its activities are subject to Indian government controls and scrutiny despite the generally favourable climate in which it operates in the country. All British aid to India is given in response to specific requests from the Indian government: 'The general principle is that nothing happens without a formal request from the Indian government.'[10] The English Studies office of the BC similarly asserts that every visitor, every film, every programme handled by the Council is vetted and cleared by the Indian Council for Cultural Relations before it is passed. Most language programmes—seminars, workshops, summer institutes, and visiting professorships—are initiated following requests from Indian colleges and university departments. Therefore any concept of unidirectional aid—single-minded and clearly-defined in its scope and targets, and put over an unsuspecting Indian population—would be oversimplified, even distorted.

The BC's *modus operandi* in English Studies in India, as in other educational spheres, requires specific attention. Chiefly, this consists of: (i) arranging scholarships and short-term visits to British universities for Indians; (ii) providing research and loan facilities, as well as information services, at its libraries; (iii) exhibiting British cultural products in the performing arts, cinema, painting, etc.; (iv) organizing lecture tours or visiting professorships in India for British academics and technical experts; and (v) conducting workshops and summer institutes for Indian teachers in local BCs or universities. The issues involved in the functioning of these schemes require examination.

First, how the BC hopes to be effective with a relatively modest budget and a limited sphere of activities in a large third world country is explained in part by the employment of what is called *scholarship diplomacy*, the term used for wooing native elites by offers of scholarships in British universities. This concept has been spelt out:

[it is] the offering of special university places to students likely to play a central role in a target country's administrative and commercial life. Studies conducted . . . show the benefit of having a large stock of influential leaders around the world to whose education one has contributed. This is a field in which Britain, partly through empire, partly through the English language, has always

<hr/>

[10] BCIB.

been pre-eminent. As recently as 1985, of the 70 countries whose leaders had been educated abroad, 27 have been taught in Britain, 14 in France, 13 in America, and 4 in Russia.[11]

It is the Council's work of selecting people for its prestigious fellowship and visitors' programmes, a director-general points out, that 'enables us to select the leaders of tomorrow'.[12] In the areas of teaching, research, industry and administration, those taught and trained abroad may be expected to pass on their own knowledge and training to substantially larger numbers in their countries, and in this way propagate the host country's ways. The success of this filtration system was strikingly evident in colonial education policy as well.

The Colombo Plan Scholarship and the Commonwealth Scholarship and Fellowship Scheme have ensured that a steady stream of the best administrators and teachers in India proceed to the United Kingdom (and Canada) for higher education.[13] The BC is closely involved in the selection processes of both these programmes. Of the eighty or so Commonwealth scholars selected every year, three or four continue to represent the discipline of English literature. Thus, if the teaching of English literature in India continues to be in the tradition of the mainstream British university, some part of the reason is to be sought in the number of Commonwealth scholars occupying key positions in the English departments of Indian universities. The BC also offers visitors grants for short-term language courses, as well as research fellowships in British universities to Indian academics.

I do not wish to offer a scenario of the sinister foreign hand in all this. Scholarship diplomacy is an open enough practice, and the co-operation of educated 'native' elites is essential to its success. The competition for the Commonwealth and other BC scholarships shows beyond doubt that such co-operation exists in India. But the dismay of the Council over budgetary cuts that have led to Britain losing 'its share in the market' of overseas students to other advanced countries is sufficient evidence of

---

[11] Simon Jenkins, 'The British Council—A Case for Treatment', *The Times Literary Supplement*, 6-12 November 1987, 1222.

[12] 'British Council Report 1986-7'.

[13] The Colombo Plan scholarships were instituted at a Commonwealth foreign ministers' meeting in 1950, and were designed 'to promote economic and social development and political stability in South and South East Asia'; the Commonwealth Scholarship and Fellowship Scheme was decided upon at the 1959 Commonwealth Educational Conference.

the substantial benefits of scholarship diplomacy to the host country as well.[14]

Second, the institution of English literature in India receives more systematic and influential support from the BC by way of its *library services*. The number of libraries is small (thirteen, all in the major Indian cities), but library membership—though a fairly steep fee is charged—shows annual increases. About twenty per cent of the total number of books in the library is devoted to English literature, and there are at least twenty literary journals available.[15] The texts that make up the prevailing metropolitan canon, and the standard secondary sources, are stocked. But, in addition, the drama and fiction sections emphasize contemporary writing, so that, like its house journal *Literature Alive*, BC libraries would appear to want to counter the notion that English literature is a collection of sacred texts written by dead writers. Finally, it is not the size or the selection of books that makes BC libraries popular—they are clearly inadequate for academic or research purposes—but rather the efficiency of their services. In a country where public libraries are scarce, and college and university libraries musty, ill-ventilated, and badly lit, the existence of a clean, well-lit place is sufficient appeal. In this area the BC renders a public service.

Third, in terms of image building, *literary and cultural programmes* are undoubtedly the most highly visible and prestigious among the BC's activities. However, since the funds for these come from the principal government grant, they form a relatively small part of its budget. The cultural exports that find their way to the third world may sound sublimely irrelevant: the Bolton Octagon Co.'s *Hobson's Choice* to Pakistan, the Sherman Theatre's *A Midsummer Night's Dream* to Africa, planeloads of Henry Moore statutaries to India (all between 1986 and 1987). But these are by no means misdirected ventures. In all these countries small but significant populations exist to whom the appeal of British culture is addressed, and who respond in full measure. In particular, a thirst for the English 'book', diffuse but pervasive, continues to charac-

---

[14] The 1987-88 Annual Report offers a modest instance of dividends yielded by the scholarship scheme: a professor of English in Japan, to whom the British Council had given a scholarship in 1962, recommended the construction of a replica of Shakespeare's Globe Theatre in Tokyo in 1986 in what is described as 'a major property development'.

[15] K. Sankaraiah, 'English Literature and the British Council Library', *Literature Alive*, 1, 4 (1988), 60-2.

terize sections of the educated Indian middle class which the BC serves. One library member explained the widespread preference for English fiction over technical books: 'English literature is the only real British heritage; technology comes from all over the world'.[16]

Fourth, the number of *British visitors* to India that the BC sponsors is only a small fraction of the number of Indian visitors who go the other way. The main purpose of visits by literary figures seems served when good public relations are achieved. The Council also supports large-scale seminars in Indian universities by funding the visits of British participants to them. In all this the BC claims to act only as a broker in the transactions between British academics and Indian universities, merely responding to the interest they mutually evince in each other; it denies that the selection of visitors reflects any ideological preference on its part. But in reality it is the 'establishment' figures and institutions that are privileged in these exchanges—as we might expect of any official sponsorship scheme.[17]

Fifth, the large-scale operation and the major interventionist thrust of the BC's educational activities in India is found in its *language programmes*: its part in training staff at the CIEFL (Central Institute of English and Foreign Languages) in Hyderabad, the Language Teaching Institute at Allahabad, and in training programmes for schoolteachers in Madras. The pattern in these cases is to train people to train people. This in fact became an articulated policy of language teaching, defined as 'co-opera-

[16] Donaldson, 359. There is other evidence of popular—in contrast to specialist and academic—demand for English literature programmes. The BBC Shakespeare video cassettes are screened at Council libraries for group viewing two or three times a week. Visiting British writers are feted (the 1986-7 Annual Report expresses amazement at Golding's reception in Calcutta). The Council now issues a journal, *Literature Alive*, which carries reviews of current books and interviews with writers; it also supports Dhvanyaloka, the Literary Criterion Centre for English Studies and Indigenous Arts in Mysore, and sponsors an annual short story and poetry competition in English, and translations into English.

[17] Certainly from the Indian end the magnitude of the academic event—its duration, scope, number of participants, other funding agencies—as well as the perceived importance of the seminar's theme, are factors that influence the Council's sponsorship. Two recent seminars co-sponsored by it were an 'international' seminar on Shakespeare organized by Delhi University, and an all-India seminar on English in India at Jawaharlal Nehru University.

tive work within the academic institutions of the receiving countries'. While such participation can be influential, it is relatively limited in its interventionist scope when contrasted with the kind of work the BC has been called upon to do in smaller countries like Nepal.[18]

Still, British language experts (and occasionally literature teachers as well) are in a position to influence English teaching in India in significant ways, since they continue to be consulted by Indian universities wherever the need for revising or framing syllabi is felt. Though they generally work in collaboration with Indian college teachers, reports on such revision exercises leave us in no doubt that the leadership, and the greater initiative and influence, come from the British 'expert'.[19]

Language teaching by direct means is also occasionally undertaken under BC auspices, although generally for experimental purposes. In such situations the mutual reinforcement of the ESP/EFL 'theory' and actual practice 'in the field' takes place. That experiments might be viewed with scepticism, if not outright hostility, by English teachers in India engaged in the daily teaching of the language in their classrooms, is to be expected—even if such an attitude stands in opposition to the tacit approval extended by Indian university authorities to the schemes.[20]

[18] In 1986 two British ELT specialists were asked to conduct a survey among the Nepalese and advise the ministry of education of the Nepal government on ways of wooing back large segments of the local population whose children had been moved to Indian schools in search of education in English. The specialists describe the outcome as a case of 'professional advice' conflicting with 'political constraints'—and, in the event, political constraints won the day. The project nevertheless reveals how a small nation's reliance on the expertise of the British language expert allows the latter to intervene in a sensitive socio-political situation and significantly influence it. See Alan Davies, 'When Political Constraints and Professional Advice in ELT Conflict: The Case of Nepal', *Focus on English*, 3, 3 (1987), 59, 66.

[19] See, for instance, reports in *Focus on English* on Eric Glendinning's restructuring of the English Programme at the Indian Institute of Science, Bangalore, and Kenneth James' revision of the Functional English Course at Padmavathi Women's University, Tirupathi.

[20] See, for instance, the criticism mounted by Rajul Bhargava (University of Rajasthan) against the much-lauded Communications Teaching Project (CTP) led by N.S. Prabhu of the BC, in Bangalore. Bhargava argues that not only has there been no authoritative evaluation of Prabhu's methods, but

This leads us to pose the necessary questions about the *reception* of the BC's activities in India, especially as these relate to English Studies. Given the number and variety of Indian institutions in question, we cannot expect a definitive evaluation of the degrees of acceptance or resistance with which the BS's different offerings are actually received. It would appear, for instance, that the Council's services, especially in language teaching, are in greater demand in south Indian cities than in the north. This may be due to the greater support for English in these states, and to the greater dependence of the smaller southern universities on external assistance. But it seems to me that the *politics* of this interaction will have to be judged on the basis of certain broad realities:

(i) The BC's mediating role between Indian and British universities in the disciplinary formation and teaching of English can be politically fraught because of the larger, unresolved debate in Indian education between the proponents of indigenization and self-reliance on the one hand, and those who fear self-marginalization and isolation by such a move on the other. The connection between higher education in India and the western academy undeniably exists—it is not only historical and paradigmatic but is also a *continuing* relation of dependence and support in matters of scholarship and expertise, material aid, the training of personnel, the framing of syllabi, and pedagogical methods. The most prestigious and advanced centres of study in India—the institutes of technology and management —have explicit partnerships with foreign governments and educational institutions. In the case of English language, literature, and culture, however, while the British university (and the BC as its surrogate presence here) can seem to be a 'natural' authority—and hence be influential—these are also ideologically sensitive areas where intervention can encounter extreme resistance.

(ii) The BC's historical connection with colonial British rule has been pointed out. In the *post-colonial situation* that connection both empowers and haunts its image. As Colin MacCabe has pointed out, a country's

---

that the project reflects the 'insidious practice of having "client experts" in developing countries mouth propaganda on behalf of the professional overseas masters.' Such projects only end in 'giving [the masters] extensive markets for selling their wares and . . . bring untold patronage and rich rewards to the client spokesmen.' Rajul Bhargava, 'Communicative Language Teaching: A Case of Much Ado About Nothing', *Rajasthan University Studies in English*, XVIII (1986), 86.

political independence does not lead to its immediate access to power; and in the interregnum an organization like the BC is bound to 'wield considerable patronage and power.'[21] At the same time, an institution such as this is required to obliterate that connection, so that a new and more 'equal' diplomacy is established between the two countries, and therefore it moves with circumspection. Further, just as the colonial beginnings of English Studies were themselves by no means single-minded and unambiguous,[22] so also the BC's policy on English has been beset by its own changes in direction and by other limitations, as my later discussion shows.[23]

(iii) The fact that the BC is a *propaganda* wing of the foreign office, and an *aid* agency, creates conflicting responses to it. In any developing country the response to foreign aid (in whatever form) tends to be divided between pragmatic acquiescence and ideological resistance. The realization that a foreign aid agency is motivated as much by self-interest as philanathropy in directing its aid programmes can arouse cynicism and hostility in its would-be beneficiaries. At the same time, precisely in this country's context of lack of opportunities, funding, and other amenities, there are many who are prepared to ingratiate themselves with the perceived dispensers of such good things.

If, therefore, the BC's scholarships, its supply of 'knowledge' in the form of visiting experts, computer programmes, exhibitions, books and films, its support and sponsorship of English language programmes and literary seminars—if these offerings to Indian universities get a mixed reception, the reasons must take into account both the inherent politics of such assistance and the heterogeneity of the recipients.

Shifting our perspective to the *donor* agency, we may now see how the BC's own functioning has been marked by ambiguities and contradictions, with consequences that affect the success of its ventures.

---

[21] MacCabe, 44.

[22] Gauri Viswanathan, 'The Beginnings of English Literary Study in British India', *Oxford Literary Review*, 9, 182 (1987), 2-26.

[23] There are other interesting parallels between the BC's role in the perpetuation and continuation of English Studies in India and the colonial beginnings of English Studies. In the light of Viswanathan's essay it is possible to read the BC as a vastly-reduced machinery—in no way comparable, of course, to the size and influence of the colonial state—for ensuring a certain form of client relationship with a former colony.

THE BRITISH COUNCIL: HISTORY AND POLICY

The BC's as even a quick review of the record of its first fifty years will show, is an embattled institution.[24] It has been subjected to as many as twenty-one reviews and enquiries, it has had to define its goals, defend its expenditures, and justify its *raison d'etre* over and over again. It has on occasion had to curtail or abandon operations in some countries, on account of unfavourable political conditions or financial problems. There are other constraints: a three-way funding structure; changes in policy or direction in accordance with political developments; dislocations within the larger homogeneous and central policy because of the problematic division of non-English-speaking areas of the globe into different sectors; the problem of arriving at a politically viable definition of 'culture', envisaged both as humanistic 'value' and as commodity; and, finally, the disparity between a growing empire of English and a shrinking British empire which has made English itself a problematic entity, as much as an asset.

There is, first, the question of funding. As already pointed out, the BC's dependence on government grants implies that it is the government's foreign policy which will call the tune for its activities. In certain countries, as in India, the Council's 'autonomous' status is not even nominally in force: it is reduced to a division of the diplomatic establishment. The Council also administers British government programmes, chiefly in developing countries, under the Overseas Development Administration (ODA) scheme. Another major source of the Council's income is its earnings from educational services (predominantly English language teaching programmes). The income-generating potential of the BC has led to intermittent demands that the Council be privatized and turned into a consultancy organization which is cost-effective. But it is the government grant (less than 30 per cent of the total budget, or about £ 75 million) that funds the most highly visible of the Council's activities—the libraries, the theatre, dance and music tours, the fellowships, scholarships and visitors' programmes. The privatization argument, in line with Thatcherite policy, would have these administered by Britain's diplomatic missions with more clear-cut political (as opposed to merely cultural) goals.

---

[24] The official biography, commissioned by the British Council, is Frances Donaldson's, and much of the historical information provided in this paper relies upon this invaluable account.

The problem of balancing its budget by juggling these activities is trenchantly formulated by the BC's director-general in the 1986-7 Annual Report: 'We set out to run our business to achieve cultural relations objectives, not to earn dividends for shareholders.' Clearly the pressure to be more self-supporting (if not to earn dividends) is bound to, and does, conflict with the cultural relations objectives.

A brief narrative of the beginnings and development of the BC reveals another of the handicaps from which it has suffered—a historical fluctuation, reflecting the predicament of Britain itself, between an engagement with Europe on the one hand, and continued presence and involvement in the rest of the world on the other—with differently defined roles in each case.

The BC was set up in 1934, in response to the fraught pre-war political situation in Europe. The need for a propaganda organization to capitalize on the demand for English language classes, on the good will towards the English people, and on the admiration for British culture to be found in some countries of Europe served as a modest start, the annual initial outlay being £ 5,000. The BC's major engagement with colonial countries began only after the war ended and when many of its European activities had to be curtailed. In the past ten years, however, Britain's flirtation with the European Economic Community has reactivated the Council's role as its country's cultural propaganda wing in Europe.

The Council's funding structure reflects these different emphases. Government grants subsidize most of the Council's cultural and arts work in Europe, but at the same time Europe also provides earnings through the success of the BC's English language centres there. Developing countries, chiefly Britain's former colonies, are the recipients of aid, channelized through the BC by the ODA. The spread of the BC into new areas, Japan and West Asia, has been motivated chiefly by the earning potential of the English language centres in these countries.

A fourth area of contradiction can be located in the sphere of culture. In its early years the BC had to struggle to define its role as being distinct from that of the British foreign office, in the war years its sphere of activity needed to be defined as separate from the ministry of information. In other words, it had to argue that its work as a cultural mission was both more and better than diplomacy or propaganda in order to justify its independent existence. But the concept of culture—in a country described as 'deeply philistine, with paradoxically one of the great cultures of the world,'[25]—had to be negotiated carefully. While Italy, Germany and France frankly and openly promoted their cultural goods through organizations like the Dante Alighieri Institute, the Goethe Institute, and the Alliance Française, the BC was half embarrassed about showcasing Britain's wares. The most recent distinguished supporter of the BC, Richard Hoggart, laments that 'British perversity' does not adequately respond to the admiration and appetite for the British arts in the rest of the world.[26]

Therefore, first the concept of cultural propaganda, and then what came to be explicitly called 'the commercial importance of cultural influence',[27] had to be spelt out as the 'real' and pressing justification for the BC's cultural activities.

The question, in other words, as one correspondent to the *TLS* put it, is: 'how do you convert Britain's cultural goods into a set of packages suitable for export?'[28]

In the face of such a demand the BC is forced to explicitly spell out the pragmatic political and economic grounds for its more intangible cultural and educational schemes. The 1986-7 Annual Report, for instance, points to the British Invisible Export Council's endorsement of BC activities in terms of tangible returns in trade and commerce.[29]

---

[25] Richard Auty of the BC, quoted by Donaldson, 65.

[26] Quoted by Simon Jenkins, 1222. Jenkins points out that the BC's paranoia is not unique. Other culture organizations and scholarship offices beset by Thatcherite economy and similarly beleagured are the Royal Society, the BBC, the Arts Council, the National Book League, the Commonwealth Institute, and the Central Bureau of Education Exchange. Jenkins, 1223.

[27] This is the title of the final chapter of the D'Abernon Report on British trade missions to South America, 1929. The Report strongly urged a 'more deliberate inculcation of British culture' and guaranteed that 'the reaction of trade . . . is definitely certain and will be swift'. Donaldson, 17-18. Similarly, in 1950 the Shell Company offered to take on the Council's wound-up operations in Venezuela—so productive in commercial terms had the Council's educational and cultural activities been. Donaldson, 166.

[28] John Mitchel, Letter to the *TLS*, 20-26 November 1987.

[29] It is revealing that though the director-general in his Annual Report (1987-8) concludes with the rhetoric of a universal culture—'our purpose must be to share with those who are likely to be influential in other societies a culture which enriches the human spirit, enhances international understanding and expands the horizons of men and women throughout the world'—he has also been careful to provide, earlier in the same report,

I wish to make clear that the double stance is not being read here as an indication of duplicity. It is part of the necessary double-ness of the Council's operation that it should have to justify itself to two constituencies, at home and abroad, and on different grounds. If the mode of justification seems to be inherited from an enterprise that combined trading activities with the civilizing mission for over two centuries, that would only appear to be historically inevitable.

'Culture' therefore works with different connotations and functions in the Council's discourse: a blandishment aimed at Europe, a big stick waved at the former colonies to impress and overawe, and, increasingly, a somewhat aesthetic indulgence to be replaced wherever possible by the more utilitarian tasks of education and technology transfer.

Finally, the BC must contend with the question of 'English'. The development of English into an international language, even as Britain itself diminished as a world power, has meant, first, that the council's commitment to the teaching of the English language has had to take precedence over its cultural allegiance to the literature of England; and, second, that 'English literature' is now more accurately defined as 'literature(s) in English' than as the 'literature of England'. The BC has to straddle both definitions in attempting to fulfil its dual role as an international cultural organization and a national agency.

My analysis of the Council's status, history, policy and functioning is an attempt to point out the contradictions and difficulties that beset the organization, with a view to arguing the scope and limits of its operations in the sphere of English Studies, in India and elsewhere. It would be misleading to suggest, however, that contradictions and changes of policy are *always* limiting factors: they are, equally, signs of adaptation and tactics for survival. In spite of its problems, the Council has grown in size, if not in influence, over the years. Its detractors at home are opposed by its champions, its Leavises by the Hoggarts, and the hostility it occasionally evokes in host countries is more than compensated for by the hospitality with which it is welcomed. The many faces of English that the BC projects have been dictated by choice as well as necessity. My analysis seeks to advance the argument that an institution is not monolithic and unchanging, but is susceptible to divisions and historical shifts. Any discussion of the construction of a discipline must be informed by an awareness of this aspect of its institutionalization.

---

examples of 'the multiplier effects' of the Council's educational activities— such as a contract from Indonesia for the production of British textbooks.

'ENGLISH'

The Council's association with English language and literature is its core activity. As one foreign teacher of English put it: 'To me the first task of the British Council is simply to be present in the countries of the world, irrespective of the attainment in the English language, representing English language and culture in an authentic way and making its living context accessible'.[30]

This connection is, at one level, unproblematic and productive; at another level it is complicated. In its early years the Council's very survival was tied up with the formation of English teaching institutes all over the world, particularly in the major European cities; in many cases the newly created BCs simply took over existing British institutes that were already teaching the English language.

In the post-war decades the growing status of the USA and the consequent acceptance of English as the language of international commerce and technology made the Council's association with English teaching a strategically useful one. In 1987-8, fees earned from language teaching classes were £ 24.6 million, or forty per cent of the Council's total earnings.[31]

The double status of English, as England's national language as well as a new international language, produces an interesting doubleness in the BC official's attitude towards it: a disavowal of any special rights over what has become a global language alongside a sense of original

[30] Christoph Edelhoff, 'A View from Teacher In-Service Education and Training', in Quirk and Widdowson, 135.

[31] 'Annual Report, 1987-8'; see also *The Times of India*, 30 January 1989. A news item headlined 'Value of English', quotes a study, 'English: A World Commodity,' conducted by *The Economist*. According to this study, the 'market value' of English is £ 6 billion a year, of which £ 1 billion is generated by the English as a foreign language industry in the UK alone. English language courses account for £ 630 million of that, with £ 170 million generated by textbooks. In a nice mix of metaphors, the director-general of the Council claims that what has 'long been the root of our culture', viz. the English language, is now 'Britain's real black gold.' Annual Report, 1987-88. Other metaphors such as 'milch cow' (Jenkings 1233), and golden egg (Donaldson, 35), similarly suggest the profitability of English. But the missionary/colonial aspect of propagating English is not wholly absent either: 'the first British Council English language office officer' has been compared to Robinson Crusoe! See the essay by Jena Politi in Quirk and Widdowson, 195.

proprietorship: 'the development of "Englishes" world-wide' has no doubt begun to mean that second language users 'look less and less to countries in which English is spoken as the native language for the setting of linguistic norms'; nevertheless, 'the BC has no intention of reducing its involvement in the promotion of English studies. It will continue to do all it can to help those who wish to acquire a knowledge of the English language for a variety of purposes', among them, 'to get to know us, our language, culture and literature'.[32]

The vested interest in English as a *commodity* is occasionally qualified by the realization that language use is also a *political* issue. This worried note is struck by David Crystal:

We must not forget those areas where the spread of English is bad news, and where people are antagonistic towards the language, for a variety of social, economic or political reasons . . . The question is not so much *do* people use English internationally, but in what state of mind, with what attitude, do they use it? Are they proud of it, or ashamed of it? . . . should not the quantitative view of English in the world be supplemented by a rigorous qualitative view— a pragmatic or ergonomic view—in which we recognize levels of acceptance, acquiescence and antipathy amongst those who have come to use the language; and in the end is not this view of far greater importance for those involved in world English teaching and research than a simple awareness of the unity and spread of the standard language?[33]

Unlike the direct commercial function of the BC's English-language teaching institutes in the advanced non-English-speaking countries, in developing countries language must be treated as a matter of political and diplomatic urgency. Historically also, the real political thrust in BC teaching programmes came only in the wake of its involvement in the former colonies. The Drogheda Report's concerns were repeated in the Teaching of English Overseas Report (1956): 'Unless present opportunities are seized and the spread of English reinforced by more co-ordinated effort and more generous financial support, it might be supplanted as a lingua franca, either by regional languages such as Hindi or Arabic, or by some other European languages'.[34] The Council's brief was to watch and protect the interests of continuing English use, and

[32] Quirk and Widdowson, vii; see also the foreword by the director-general, BC, to a collection of seminar papers titled *English in the World*, edited by Quirk and Widdowson, viii.

[33] David Crystal, ibid., 9-10.

[34] Donaldson, 201.

also to see that it was not used for 'politically biased purposes, as in communist countries'.[35]

The distinctions between the profit motive and the political motive in English language interests does frequently blur. The benefits, commercial as much as political, of English teaching even in developing countries are clear enough:

English is an export which is very likely to attract other exports—British advisers and technicians, British technological or university education, British plant and equipment and British capital investment. There are clear commercial advantages to be gained from increasing the number of potential customers who can read technical and trade publicity material written in English.[36]

In the 1960s, when the emphasis on English language programmes worldwide led to the more highly professionalized teaching of English, the BC was in a specially privileged position to initiate and sponsor the development of language studies into specialized areas like EFL, ESL and ESP. These are now institutionalized and refined in British universities and polytechnics in ways that recall the disciplinarization of English literature in the last century, following its introduction in the colonies.[37]

Under the circumstances, language experts were bound to question the relevance of English *literature* to language acquisition. One BC official declared in the 1960s that it was a mistake to carry the luggage of literature into the sphere of language teaching. Shakespeare does not help one to write minutes. He goes on to argue, 'What I tried to do during my years on the subject was to bring reality into it by refusing to admit literary targets where literary targets were not possible because linguistic targets were not fulfilled'.[38] Consequently, in the next two decades, the emphasis on purely literary activities was reduced and more functional language programmes were pursued.

Nevertheless, literature continues to have a value as a component of

---

[35] Ibid.

[36] The TEO report, quoted in ibid., 201.

[37] In the late 1970s the surge in language teaching activity led to large sales of British textbooks. Bhargava refers us to A.P.R. Howatt's *A History of English Language Teaching* (Clarendon: Oxford University Press, 1984), for 'a good account of the profit-motive' behind such activity. See Bhargava, 84.

[38] Donaldson, 25.

the package of British culture,[39] even as it is reconciled with the reality of other national literatures in English. The spread of English has meant the emergence of substantial and significant bodies of creative writing in English in India, Pakistan, Sri Lanka, some African nations, and in the Caribbean, as well as by immigrant writers in Britain. The Council, like the British literary establishment as a whole, is able to assimilate these writings under the rubric 'Commonwealth' literature,[40]—a designation increasingly regarded in these countries as having lost its political and cultural usefulness.

Apart from *what* is offered in the package 'literature' by an institution like the BC—whose commitment to an undiluted 'culture' must come second to other issues of economic, political and diplomatic expediency—there is also the question of *how* it is packaged—primarily in terms of standardization, popularization, and the assimilation and inclusion of a variety of texts. The most well-known opposition from the literary academic establishment to the implications of the Council's patronage of English literature came from F.R. Leavis. Leavis saw the Council as a bureaucratic organization for administering state-associated values:

Such a system works not only against the critic but against the creator . . . an organization financed by the state for the promotion of British culture will inevitably work to impose the social person and currency values of metropolitan literary society and the associated University milieux as the distinctions and achievements of contemporary England, and so to repress the stir of genuine life. Of this truth, I have pointed out, those British Council 'Surveys' present unanswerable and readily accessible evidence.[41]

[39] The Annual Report for 1987-8 lists the year's activities in this field: seminars on teaching in Oxford and on creative writing in Cambridge, a Sherlock Holmes poster exhibition, festivals of 'Fantasy and Science Fiction' and 'Spy Fiction' in Germany. More recently an exhibition of illustrated panels on sixty-six contemporary British novelists was sent to the Council's offices worldwide. The exphasis in this representation of British literature is on popular and contemporary productions rather than on the traditional canon.

[40] The Council's Indian journal, *Literature Alive*, and its literature department's newsletter, *Literature Matters*, give considerable coverage to 'Commonwealth' writers.

[41] Leavis's ideological opposition to the Council, it must be added, was buttressed by hostility caused by the neglect of *Scrutiny* by official organs like the BC, the BBC, and the *Times Literary Supplement*. See William Walsh, *F.R. Leavis* (London: Chatto and Windus, 1980), 94, 27, 83.

What are the implications of these different aspects of English for the Council's functioning in India? Its involvement with language teaching is of course more profound and substantial than its admittedly superficial interest in promoting British literature. On the other hand, English language teaching in India is such a vast enterprise, carried out in so many thousands of English-medium schools, local bazaar institutes, colleges and universities, that the Council cannot be said to be a specially privileged participant in this activity. It is at least significant that in the current anti-English movement in the northern Indian states the Council has not been targeted for any special attacks (the bulk of these being borne by missionary and elite public schools). And, paradoxically, in spite of the minority elite and academic clientele for English literature, as also the Council's own lukewarm support for it, the BC's influence in this field is arguably greater. This is partly because of its library services, partly because of its excellent liaison with English departments in the major cities, but above all because English literary study in India, in spite of its extent and spread, does not have an authorizing and central apex body like most other disciplines do. In the absence of such a body the Council has come to be regarded as a kind of authority.

THE ENGLISH ENGLISH TEACHER

Visiting British writers-scholars-teachers-critics provide few accounts of India beyond the superficial tourists' impressions and the invariable collection of howlers perpetrated by foreign students; interviews in the press and in Council newsletters rarely proceed beyond politenesses. Therefore no real sense of any meaningful cultural exchange seems to come out of such encounters.[42] However, given the constraints of most of these visits—the institutional context, the rigid schedules, and the brevity, they cannot be expected to be passages to India.[43]

---

[42] Some of D.J. Enright's poetry, however, reflects upon his years in the East. A writer and critic, Enright served for some years as a Council-sponsored Professor of English in Singapore. He has an acute sense of the post-imperial Englishman's awkward presence in the former colony, as seen in this poem ('Entrance Visa'): 'We were the Descendancy/Hurt but not surprised. Atoning for our predecessors' every oath and sneer/We paid in poverty the rich man's debt.' See William Walsh, *D.J. Enright: Poet of Humanism* (Cambridge: CUP, 1974), 22.

[43] While the Council is careful to avoid giving the impression that the

These superficial and impressionistic observations of mine must be balanced, and checked, by Colin MacCabe's movingly introspective and richly speculative essay, 'English Literature in a Global Context'. Conceding, in an abstract sense, that the British academic addressing the ('third?') 'world' on his literature is doomed to 'ethnocentrism', he turns to the bearer of this enthnocentrism, himself. He discovers there not a unitary racial identity, but one riven by contradictions:

Given my own racial background, one of the most persistent contradictions for me is that the greatest poet, novelist and dramatist of this century of English literature have been Irish—Yeats, Joyce and Beckett. In their writings one can read all the strains and contradictions of working within a tradition which is both alien and their own.[44]

English literature, he points out, is itself a parochial affair, a body of texts that leaves out the 'other' literatures of Britain; but it is also one that in the recent past has become 'a literature of decolonization from Joyce and Yeats to Rushdie and Lessing'. Therefore, he concludes, ethnocentrism cannot be sustained because of 'the contradictions historically present within the culture'.[45]

MacCabe's reflections are addressed monitorily to participants in a Council seminar, many of them British academics like himself. But it is salutary for us to realize that divisions—racial, political, gendered, class—exist within the identity 'British'. At the same time, perhaps, we could also suggest that just as a British *national* identity was precisely formed—or assembled—under the pressures of British colonialism, so too it has a tendency to be reactivated as ethnocentrism in situations of 'teaching [English] in and to another culture'.[46] But self-consciousness

---

visitors it sponsors are anything less than totally free in their activities, there is always the subtle pressure of institutional hospitality (schedules, escorts, etc.) that directs the guest's behaviour. The Council's past record also carries the blot of the Enright episode. After having done two short contracts for the Council, Enright wrote a novel mildly critical of the British abroad. He was asked to withdraw the novel, or never expect another contract. Enright offers this story more as an example of official stupidity than real censorship. See D.J. Enright 'Flying the Cultural Flag,' *TLS*, 7 December 1984, 1407.

[44] MacCabe, 44.

[45] Ibid., 38, 45.

[46] See, for instance, and by way of contrast, Michael Thorpe's essay 'Calling the Kettle Black: Some Thoughts on "Cultural Imperialism"'. Thorpe describes an international conference on New Literatures in English, in which

of the kind MacCabe displays and recommends in such situations will undoubtedly help to bring about the more transformative models he envisages.

CONCLUSION

In the end, an evaluation of the BC's influence needs to be attempted. The limitations and strengths of its operations, as I have tried to show, are more or less evenly matched. The reasons for the limitations are not far to seek: Britain's diminished world position, the shadow cast by the United States in global affairs, and a disinclination for the more overt forms of propaganda (particularly in its former colonies) make Britain's overseas operations generally modest. The BC enterprise is also limited by meagre resources, and by its generally embattled position within Britain itself. An overall sense of insecurity and uncertainty of policies, and an over-centralized administrative structure, are the consequences. The confinement of the BC's educational activities to the higher spheres of education is another limitation. The constraints upon and general supervision of the programmes of the BC by the Indian government circumscribe its freedom further.

The functioning of the USIA stands in contrast to the BC in these areas. Its tasks are better funded and more aggressively propagandistic than the BC's on account of the very different political imperatives of the two parent countries with regard to India. Further, the American organization is able to exploit the global appeal, in the post-war era, of the United States as the promised land. Typically, the USIA offers American culture, along with American science, technology and political systems, as part of a packaged American way of life. (This glossy and bland homogeneity is best reflected in its publication, the magazine *Span*.) The brain-drain from India, consequently, conspicuously collects in the USA. The number and affluence of American universities have led to a much larger number of Indian students seeking advanced degrees there than in the UK. Even among teachers of English literature in India, the proportion of those who have been students in American universities is, currently, significantly higher than those who have studied in Britain.

---

he tried to retrieve 'universal' values from the charge of ethnocentrism. He concludes by calling for a recognition (by whites) that the 'colonial legacy' is 'more than a guilty burden', and for an acknowledgement (by blacks) that it is a 'shared inheritance', in *Encounter*, December 1989, Thorpe, 40-4.

The impact of this on the educational system, syllabus, and pedagogical methods in English departments, though as yet not marked, is beginning to be noticeable, especially in advanced programmes. Here the American Studies Research Center, in Hyderabad, is able to make a contribution to the research interests of Indian scholars.

But the same factors that, in one sense, serve as constraints also translate in other ways into the strengths of the BC's work. Certainly, the continuing prestige of British culture established by the historical colonial connection and preserved by India's Commonwealth affiliation cannot be gainsaid. Where the BC has been able to take advantage of the fairly stable political relationship of Britain with India, the nature and scope of the USIA's activities have had to be adjusted to the more fluctuating relationship of the USA with India. The BC's low-key approach in cultural diplomacy, less strident than propaganda, succeeds to a great extent in establishing goodwill and winning acceptance among Indians. The limiting of the BC's educational activities to target groups at the higher levels of academy, industry and administration also succeeds by the logic of the 'key figures' scheme. Above all, the BC's commitment to English language propaganda ensures its entry into many spheres of Indian life, its interaction with government policy in language issues, as well as a modest influence on teaching in schools, colleges, and training institutions.[47]

The BC's role is linked with the spread and the shape of English Studies in India rather than with the basic fact of its existence. As ideological state apparatus the institution works as a subtle and mediating mechanism whose exact impact would be hard to measure in quantitative terms. The inevitable—but necessarily speculative—question of determining how literary studies in India might look in its absence has not been engaged here (though undoubtedly, in such a case the British diplomatic organization would support some sort of cultural or area studies in a more limited and specialist sphere, as do the embassiers of other countries). The BC has been viewed here as an aspect—significant, but not crucially determining—of the diffuse phenomenon of English in India. Such a view is based on the premise that the texts of English literature, which have dominated literary studies even in the very alien

[47] As early as 1956, the Teaching of English Overseas Report had noted that the USIA had not made any major commitment to 'extensive English teaching overseas until it compared notes with the British Council'. Donaldson, 203. In India there is no competition in the field between the two organizations.

context of the colony and the third world, must be grounded in what Vincent Leitch has called its 'sociology' and political practice.[48] The BC is offered as part of the social text in which the study of English in India is enmeshed.[49]

[48] Leith, outlining a tentative 'theory of institutions', emphasizes the need to identify the *material* and *ideological* forces and factors that determine institutional discourse, the linkages between these and the 'localized subtle mechanisms of knowledge and power—grounds of authority', and the *context* of the institution within other cultural and social institutions which would both enable and inhibit its many functions. See Vincent Leitch, 'Institutional History and Cultural Hermeneutics', *Critical* Texts, II, 1 (1984), 9.

[49] I am grateful to Alok Rai, Ania Loomba and Sudesh Vaid for comments on earlier drafts of this essay.

10

Attitudinal Orientation Towards Studying English Literature in India

YASMEEN LUKMANI

I

When examining a course of study, three basic factors have to be borne in mind: student motivation and need; social desirability; and feasibility in practical terms. The first, student motivation, is itself a broad area, within which attitudinal orientation is a significant component. This is the subject of the present investigation.

Numerous attitudinal studies have been conducted on learning languages, particularly English. The spate of such studies in the last few decades was set off by Gardner and Lambert (1959) in connection with the learning of English and French in Canada.[1] The attitudinal orientation for studying language rather than literature has been focused upon, it seems, partly in order to justify the large-scale expense in teaching languages, and partly because of the sensitive nature of specific languages in certain regions. The motivation for studying literature has seemed less controversial, perhaps because literature courses are comparatively well-entrenched in the educational system. Nevertheless, in view of the fact that student motivation seems to be low for studying any of the arts (humanities) subjects in India, including English literature, it

---

[1] R.C. Gardner and W.E. Lambert, 'Motivational Variables in Second Language Learning',. *Canadian Journal of Psychology*, 13, 266-73.

is necessary to try and examine the reasons why, thus allowing for the possibility of changing priorities in teaching and for the development of more need-based courses. The present study, which sets out to determine the nature of the attitudinal orientation for studying English literature, is one attempt in this direction.

Attitudes are considered to have cognitive, affective and conative components.[2] The cognitive component is related to the individual's belief structures, the affective to her emotional reactions, and the conative to the tendency to behave in a particular way towards the object of the attitude. However, when social scientists attempt to measure an attitude they typically infer it on the basis of reactions to value-loaded statements of belief.[3] It is also useful to distinguish 'motivation' from 'orientation'. 'Motivation', following Gardner, is taken to include effort, the desire to achieve the goal of learning the target language, as well as a favourable attitude or a positive orientation towards the language.

One of the important parameters which emerges from attitudinal studies on language learning is the distinction between integrative and instrumental orientation.[4] 'Integrative orientation' relates to the desire to integrate oneself into the culture of the community associated with, say, English, while 'instrumental orientation' relates to the purpose of studying it only in order to achieve certain specific goals—such as furthering one's career—while remaining culturally aligned to one's own community. The major findings, when the studies were conducted in Canada or the USA,[5] were that integrative orientation was strongly linked to proficiency in the language. However, studies done in the third world, e.g. India,[6] or the Phillipines,[7] revealed the opposite finding,

[2] J. Harding, B. Kutner, H. Proshansky and I. Chien, 'Prejudice and Ethnic Relations', in G. Lindzey, ed., *Handbook of Social Psychology* (Cambridge, Mass.: Addison Wesley, 1954).

[3] R.C. Gardner, *Social Psychology and Second Language Learning : The Role of Attitudes and Motivation* (London : Edward Arnold, 1985).

[4] See Gardner and Lambert (1959).

[5] See ibid.; W.E. Lambert, R.C. Gardner, H.C. Barik and K. Tunstall, 'Attitudinal and Cognitive Aspects of Intensive Study of a Second Language', *Journal of Abnormal and Social Psychology* (1963), 66, 358-69; B. Spolsky, 'Attitudinal Aspects of Second Language Learning', *Language Learning* (1969), 19, 272-83.

[6] See my 'Motivation to Learn and Language Proficiency', *Language Learning* (1972), 22, 2, 261-73.

[7] R.C. Gardner and W.E. Lambert, *Attitudes and Motivation in Second Language Learning* (Rowley, Mass.: Newbury House, 1972).

namely that students who were instrumentally oriented performed better in the language.

Subsequently, Gardner *et al.* found no links between integrative/instrumental orientation and language learning in their study of an intensive course in French as a second language in Ontario, Canada.[8] Nevertheless, at the end of the course there was a marked improvement in lecturers' attitudes to French-Canadians. Then Oller and Perkins tried to demolish the value of affective factors in relation to language learning by claiming that what was in fact being measured on the attitude test were 'surreptitious measures of verbal intelligence and/or language proficiency'.[9] Gardner attacks their findings on statistical, contextual and conceptual grounds, showing that for 29 samples there were high correlations on the Attitude Motivation Index with a standard French test, and grades received on French in the course.[10] He found that 14 per cent of the variance in the second language grades could be accounted for by affective variables. This is considered remarkably strong, considering the nature of the variables involved.

Following in the tradition of these studies, and partly in order to compare my previous work on the motivation for studying the English language in India (more specifically in Bombay), one of the main dimensions of the present study is the integrative-instrumental orientation dichotomy. The basic concern will be to explore the relationship of integrative and instrumental orientations with the following parameters: academic performance, performance in English literature, exposure to the English language, and level of income.

[8] R.C. Gardner, P.C. Smythe and G.R. Brunet, 'Intensive Second Language Study : Effects on Attitudes, Motivation and French Achievement,' *Language Learning* (1977), 27, 243-61.

[9] J.W. Oller and K. Perkins, 'Intelligence and Language Proficiency as Sources of Variance in Self-Reported Affective Variables', *Language Learning* (1978), 28, i, 85-97; idem, 'A Further Comment on Language Proficiency as a Source of Variance in Certain Affective Measures', *Language Learning* (1978), 28, 2, 417-23.

[10] R.C. Gardner, 'On the Validity of Affective Variables in Second Language Acquisition : Conceptual, Contextual, and Statistical Considerations', *Language Learning* (1980), 30, 2, 255-70; R.C. Gardner, R. Clement, P.C. Smythe and C.L. Smythe, 'The Attitude/Motivation Test Battery— Revised Manual', *Research, Bulletin 15* (London, Canada: Research Group, University of Western Ontario, 1979).

While a direct questionnaire has been employed to tap these dimensions, it was felt that an indirect measure of integrative and instrumental orientation was also necessary to tap less consciously perceived and therefore less edited responses to the subject. One of the indirect measures used by Spolsky—and by others in his wake, including myself—taps the subjects' attitudes to their own culture, themselves, their ideal selves, and the new culture to which they are being exposed through the language or literature being studied.

In my earlier study, I found that average non-westernized Marathi-speaking school-leaving female students were instrumentally oriented to study the English language, i.e. they wished to use it to further their careers and achieve success in their lives. They were also in tune with both cultures, their own mother-tongue community as well as that of the English-speaking Indians (taken as the relevant group, as the experimental subjects were unlikely to have had much contact with British or American speakers of English). They appeared to see themselves as poised between the two, with leanings towards both. There was a slight preference for the English-speaking group, which was explained by the much higher scores it received for characteristics relating to material success and a bright future, in comparison with the Marathi group. The ratings showed that the students had a maturity and balance which seemed to belie, on the one hand the jingoistic parochialism that seems so much in the air, and, on the other, a supine emulation of the West. In addition, since their instrumental orientation scores correlated so highly with their proficiency in English, it seemed that they were oriented towards courses of study in English which satisfied their instrumental leanings, i.e. the use of the English language for a variety of purposes, rather than a knowledge of English literature. An integrative orientation towards the language would have led them into its literature, as literature would tend to draw them further into the culture of the English-speaking world and increase their identification with it. So it was felt that a further investigation was needed to ascertain the kind of orientation among students who opted to specialize in English literature at college.

Consequently, a study was designed to tap the attitudinal orientation of final year BA English literature students studying in Bombay, as well as the relationship of their orientation to other variables, such as academic success, an exposure to the English language, and income. Their attitudes towards their own community and the English-speaking community of Indians were also ascertained as an indirect measure of their cultural leanings. In addition, their self-concept and ideal self-concept were tested in order to place them in relation to the two communities. Their attitudes towards these four groups were next subdivided under three categories of traits for each group. These categories related to (i) personal characteristics; (ii) material success; and (iii) two culturally divergent characteristics, namely modernity and independence. These categories were tested in order to determine their effect on the composite picture the subjects formed of the four groups, namely the two communities, their self-concept and ideal self-concept, as well as the relationship of these sets of traits with the other variables.

The parameters for the indirect questionnaire in the present study are identical to the ones used in the previous study. They follow in the tradition of the types of attributes selected for use in other semantic differential tests used in orientation studies by Gardner and Lambert and others. The attributes chosen then were selected on the basis of a pilot test conducted on Indians in the USA (the most accessible group at that time). Respondents were asked to write their reasons for studying English, as well as the attributes they considered characteristic of the Indian and the English/American communities. Those attributes which recurred in their responses, and which thus seemed meaningful to them, were selected. (Interestingly, reliability was a trait that was very important for all Marathi-speaking respondents.)

In the present study, the same traits have been retained, partly for easy comparability, but more importantly because they seemed to be relevant in capturing stereotypes about Indian communities *vis-à-vis* their westernized counterparts. Any such list of traits would have to include personal characteristics as well as the two major variables in determining the need to study English, namely (i) affluence (material success); and (ii) westernization, exemplified in the traits modernity and independence.

II. METHOD

Subjects. Fifty students specializing in English literature at final year (or third year) BA from six colleges within the University of Bombay, falling within Greater Bombay, served as the subjects The total number of colleges offering English literature honours courses at final year BA within Greater Bombay is 23, so the sample consisted of students from 25 per cent of the relevant colleges. The colleges fell into the range of good to average to relatively poor (the really mediocre colleges being outside Greater Bombay), as judged by reputation and general student performance at university examinations in English. They also covered a range of 'westernization'—in terms of student lifestyles and behaviour patterns—from being very westernized through average westernization to being relatively unwesternized. The subjects were all students who had offered eight courses in English literature, five of which were being studied in their final year. The attempt was to test all the relevant students from each of the colleges under consideration. Only those who remained absent or were otherwise unavailable were not covered. The subjects fell into a number of different linguistic and religious/caste-based communities, Bombay being a highly cosmopolitan city. In the sample, there were only, four males, which is not an unnaturally low figure. All the subjects were in their late teens.

Experimenters. The regular teachers of the students concerned conducted the experiment during regular class periods and ensured that the students attempted the task seriously.

Materials and Procedures. The test was conducted at the end of the first term, so that the students had had enough exposure to literature to be able to express their attitudes to it.

Three instruments were used in the experiment. In order of presentation, these were: (i) Demographic Information Questionnaire; (ii) Indirect Questionnaire; and (iii) Direct Questionnaire.

The Demographic Information Questionnaire sought information on the following parameters:

1. Academic performance as judged by the average of the aggregate percentages at three examinations, namely Higher Secondary Certificate or HSC (board exam), first year BA (FYBA), and second year BA (SYBA) (both college exams) (TOTPER).

2. Performance in English literature as judged by the average of the percentage of marks on the English course at the HSC (which consists of prose and poetry selections with essay-type answers) and the English literature courses at FYBA and SYBA (ENGPER).

3. Exposure to English as judged by the subjects' medium of instruction at school and the HSC (the subjects all being from the English-medium stream at the three-year degree course), the degree of proficiency in English of the members of the family and whether they spoke to their families in English (EXPOS).

4. Family income per month (INCOME).

In computing the data, the average of the aggregate percentages at the three examinations as well as the average of the English percentages at the same three examinations were calculated. Ratings were given to the different aspects of exposure to English, and these were then coded into four categories. Family income was also coded into four categories.

The Indirect Questionnaire had four parts, namely ratings on (i) self-concept (SELF); (ii) ideal self-concept (IDEAL); (iii) subjects' own community (OWNCOMM), which was to be determined as they chose on the basis of religion/caste, region or social class; and (iv) the English-speaking community of Indians (ENG). The questionnaire was administered in the order of the parts given above. Each part had the same set of sixteen traits on a semantic differential scale.[11] These traits were selected for their relevance to the subjects in determining what they considered to be a desirable reference group image and for assessing the level of their self-satisfaction. Subjects were asked to mark the polarized traits on a 6-point scale. A 6-point scale was chosen because it does not permit neutrality: subjects have to take a position in one of the two directions, but at the same time it allows them enough flexibility to express their views. In order to prevent order effects, the traits were randomly ordered on the page, with a different order for each of the parts, so that the subjects would be forced to respond to each of the parts separately. Negative and positive traits were also counterbalanced in the two columns.

The traits on each of the groups were also divided into three categories: (i) personal characteristics (CHR); (ii) material success (SUC); and (iii) modernity and independence (MOD). Personal characteristics consisted of the following traits: interesting, happy, open (frank), intelligent, cultured, reliable, attractive, impressive, have social graces, and self-confidence (10 traits); material success consisted of: educated, successful/have high-ranking jobs, high standard of living, bright future (4 traits); modernity and independence (2 traits).

The Direct Questionnaire, testing attitudinal orientation (ORIENT) directly, consisted of five instrumental (INSTR) and five integrative (INTEG) reasons for studying English literature, and the subjects had to check one of five possible reactions to the reasons, ranging from 'very important for me' to 'absolutely not important for me'. The reasons were selected for their relevance and applicability to the subjects, and the two kinds of reasons were randomly ordered on the page. The possible reactions were also given in a jumbled order to ensure careful marking.

This order of presentation was chosen in order to get responses to

[11] See C.E. Osgood, G.J. Suci, and P.H. Tannenbaum, *The Measurement of Meaning* (Urbana : University of Illinois Press, 1957).

traits (on the Indirect Questionnaire) which would not be biased by reasons for studying English literature (on the Direct Questionnaire). All three questionnaires are reproduced in Annexure I.

III. HYPOTHESES AND RESULTS : ANALYSIS OF CORRESPONDENCES

I began with certain hypotheses which were not always confirmed by the results of the study. (The detailed results of the study, with tables, are given in Annexure II.) I analyse the correspondences below:

1. Hypothesis 1 was that attitudinal orientation would be linked with (i) general academic performance; (ii) performance in English literature; (iii) exposure to the English language; and (iv) level of family income. The study, however, indicates no significant correlations between attitudinal orientation and the other variables. In other words, attitudinal orientation seems to exist in all the experiment's subjects, regardless of whether or not they are academically superior, do well in English literature, have exposure to the language, or come from affluent families. The desire to study English literature is so great that it overrides these considerations, and applies to all the experimental subjects.

2. Hypothesis 2 was that integrative orientation would be associated with (i) exposure to the English language; and (ii) level of family income. While significant correlations are in fact established, there is a trend to indicate that integrative orientation (or a desire to identify with the English-speaking community) is linked with the extent of the subjects' exposure to the English language. There is, however, no connection at all between affluence and the desire to identify with the English group.

3. Hypothesis 3 stated that instrumental orientation would be associated with (i) general academic performance and; (ii) performance in English literature; but this prediction is not borne out. The brighter and more hardworking students are not necessarily instrumentally oriented to study English literature (nor, for that matter, are they necessarily integratively oriented).

4. Hypothesis 4 held that integrative orientation would correlate with scores on the English-speaking community of Indians, while instrumental orientation would correlate with scores on the subjects' own community. The results, in fact, indicate the opposite: (i) instrumental orientation to study English literature is significantly linked with the subjects' concept of English-speaking Indians. (It is also significantly linked to their own ideal self-concept.) Coupled with other findings, such as the

fact that traits of the English-speaking community relating to their personal characteristics and material success correlate with instrumental orientation, it appears that for the subjects material success and other personal characteristics associated with English-speaking Indians are linked with a desire to study English literature in order to do well in life; (ii) there is a trend to indicate that integrative orientation is linked with the subjects' concept of their own community, indicating that they do not perceive any need to give up the characteristics of their own community even if they wish to identify with the norms of behaviour connected with English-speakers (i.e. integrative reasons). In fact their composite picture of the two communities, their own and that of English-speaking Indians, is not very different.

What also emerges importantly is that attitudinal orientation to study English literature is linked in some way with the subjects' concept of the two relevant communities, thus ratifying the experimental design.

5. Hypothesis 5 was that scores on the subjects' self-concept and ideal self-concept would correlate. Additionally, scores on self-concept and ideal self-concept would correlate both with the English-speaking community of Indians and the subjects' own community. This hypothesis is borne out to the extent that (i) self-concept and ideal self-concept correlate, indicating that the subjects have a healthy view of themselves; (ii) the subjects' self-concept is linked with both their own community and the community of English speakers, indicating that they see themselves as a part of both, with a balanced approach towards tradition and modernity (note, in this context, the rank order of mean scores on these groups: the highest scores are given to ideal self-concept, next to English-speaking Indians, next to their own self-concept and lastly to their own community, which supports the above interpretation); (iii) the subjects' ideal self-concept is only linked with their view of the English speakers. The hypothesis regarding the connection between ideal self-concept and the subjects' own community does not hold.

6. Hypothesis 6 stated that (i) scores on the material success of the English speakers would correlate with instrumental orientation, and scores on their personal characteristics and modernity and independence would correlate with integrative orientation; (ii) scores on their own community relating to material success and personal characteristics would correlate with instrumental orientation and those on their modernity and independence would correlate with integrative orientation; (iii) scores on their own self-concept relating to personal characteristics and modernity and independence would correlate with integrative orientation, and those on their own material success with

instrumental orientation; (iv) scores on their ideal self-concept relating to personal characteristics and modernity and independence would correlate with integrative orientation, and those on material success would correlate with instrumental orientation. The hypotheses are only partially borne out. The results indicate that: (i) for the English-speaking community, both personal characteristics and material success are linked with instrumental orientation, while the traits of modernity and independence are not linked with either type of orientation; (ii) for their own community, modernity and independence show a trend towards association with integrative orientation, while the other two categories of traits are not linked with either type of orientation; (iii) the categorized traits on self-concept are not linked with either type of orientation; (iv) for their ideal self-concept, it is found that personal characteristics and material success are linked with instrumental orientation, while modernity and independence are not linked with either type of orientation. These results support the findings reported above under Hypothesis 4.

IV. DISCUSSION

1. *Problem.* The Indirect Questionnaire was intended to measure the same attitudinal area as the Direct Questionnaire. It was felt that instrumental orientation scores would correspond to ratings on the subjects' own community, while integrative orientation scores would correspond to ratings on the English-speaking community of Indians. It was considered that the results would be more reliable if two independent measures yielded the same information. Did the information from the two questionnaires in fact correspond?

Findings. The t-tests reveal that: (i) the English group and subjects' own community are not significantly different from each other; (ii) ratings on the English group differ as significantly from integrative orientation scores as from instrumental orientation scores ($p<.001$; (iii) ratings on the subjects' own community differ from integrative orientation scores, ($p<.001$) and from instrumental orientation scores ($p<.05$).

Contrary to expectation (i) ratings on the English group correlate with instrumental orientation scores ($p<.025$); (ii) ratings on the subjects' ideal self-concept also correlate with instrumental orientation scores ($p<.025$). On the other hand (iii) there is a trend indicating that ratings on the subjects' own community correlate with integrative orientation scores.

Interpretation. The nature of the relationship between the Direct and Indirect Questionnaires is seen to be reversed to a certain extent, with the English group being linked with instrumental orientation, and the subjects' own community being somewhat linked with integrative orientation. However, orientation scores, while being distinct from ratings on the two communities, do relate to the attitudinal areas connected with the two communities.

2. *Problem.* The link between instrumental orientation and the English-speaking community had to be analysed further in order to get a better understanding of the subjects' position on instrumental orientation *vis-à-vis* English speakers and their own community, as well as their own self-concept and their ideal self-concept. This was done in terms of an analysis of the three categories of traits for each group, namely personal characteristics, material success, modernity and independence.

Findings. (i) Instrumental orientation scores were found to correlate with the personal characteristics and material success of both the English community and their own ideal self-concept; (ii) instrumental orientation was, however, not associated with modernity and independence in the English speakers; (iii) modernity and independence stood out as the only category of traits in which the subjects' ideal self-concept was linked with their own community and was markedly not linked with English speakers; (iv) the subjects' self-concept was linked to their perception of both their own community and the English speakers (p<.005); (v) their self-concept was also linked to their ideal concept of themselves (p<.005).

Interpretation. The results indicate that the subjects are closely allied both to their own community and to English speakers, with a healthy self-concept which is closely linked with their ideal self-concept. They also showed that they did not wish to be as modern or independent as they perceived the English speakers to be. They thus indicated a balanced and mature attitude to the two communities, an attitude which seems free both from parochialism and an uncritical emulation of westernized norms.

3. *Problem.* What was the relationship between the students' attitudinal orientation and academic success, performance in English, exposure to the language and family income?

Findings. Attitudinal orientation as such (inclusive of both instrumental and integrative types) was not found to be linked with the subjects' aggregate percentage, their marks in English literature, exposure to English or their level of income; (ii) instrumental orientation was not related to these either; (iii) it is only integrative orientation which, in any case, does not appear as being important in this study, which showed a trend towards correlation with exposure to the English language, but not a strong trend. Additionally, income was found to be linked with academic success, English marks, exposure to the language and self-concept.

Interpretation. (i) It appears that the subjects are oriented to study English literature irrespective of background or ability. The need for English is so overwhelming that, regardless of socio-economic status, exposure to English in their homes, or the marks they get in their total academic or English performance, they are oriented to study English; (ii) students from more affluent families are found to have greater academic success, better marks in English, and also have a higher exposure to the English language. Moreover, the higher the income, it appears, the higher the self-concept.

4. *Problem.* Instrumental orientation to study English literature has been found to be linked to the English-speaking community. What support do we find in the rest of the data for the predominance of instrumental orientation?

Findings. (i) It is instructive to look at the reasons which are considered important for studying English literature. The mean scores on the reason, 'The study of English literature will improve my competence in the English language', are considerably higher than on the other reasons, indicating the strength of the need to learn the language and suggesting that this is the students' major reason for pursuing English literary studies. This testifies to the instrumental nature of their study of English literature; (ii) the students identify with traits relating to the material success of their own community. (As there is a similarity in the way they perceive their own community and the English-speaking community on personal characteristics, this aspect cannot help us in explaining the importance of the instrumental orientation to study English literature.) However, as the material success of their own community is not linked with any attitudinal orientation to study English literature, this is not of importance. Instead, the material success of their own community is linked with modernity and independence in the English group, traits which, even ideally, the students do not wish to possess. Note that modernity in the English group is related to income. The material success of their own community is also linked with exposure to the English language. Additionally, their own material success (SELSUC) is perceived as being linked to some extent to the personal characteristics of the English community, but not to the personal characteristics of their own community.

Interpretation. The overall picture that emerges is that while the students are instrumentally oriented to study English literature, their own material success (instrumental orientation) is linked with the personal characteristics (integrative orientation) of the English group, which makes for an interesting mix of instrumental and integrative orientations towards that group.

Comparison with the previous (1972) study. My previous study looked at the attitudinal orientation of Marathi-medium school-leaving students for learning English as a language. As the parameters used in that study were almost identical to the ones used here, it is possible to compare the findings of the two. Even though the present study is concerned with final year BA students studying English literature, the parallels in the findings are quite remarkable. This has the effect of making the results of both the studies more reliable. The comparison also provides new information. It indicates that the more mature perceptions of final year BA students are on the same continuum as those expressed by school-leaving students. It also indicates the fact that the sample of school-leaving students which was drawn from a Marathi-medium school— while the BA students were predominantly from English-medium backgrounds—made little difference to the similarities in attitudes they displayed. This highlights the irrelevance of language background in determining students' orientation to learn English.

In the previous study as well, instrumental orientation for learning English emerged as being more important than integrative orientation. It was found that (i) integrative orientation scores correlated significantly with ratings on the Marathi community; but (ii) provided only a trend towards correlation with ratings on the English community; (iii) neither the Marathi nor the English community ratings correlated with instrumental orientation; and (iv) factors dealing with material success made the English group correlate much better with the ideal self-concept of the subjects than the Marathi group.

In the present study, as reported earlier, instrumental orientation correlates significantly with the English-speaking group and is also closely linked with the ideal self-concept of the subjects, while there is a trend indicating a link between integrative orientation and the subjects' own community. Aspects of material success, in this study as in the earlier one, are very important in making the English-speaking community more valued than their own community. The fact that final year

BA students are even more inclined than school students to study English (in this case, English literature) for instrumental reasons, in spite of their much greater exposure to the language, in spite of the fact that they have opted to specialize in it, and in spite of their greater exposure to/assimilation of westernization, is remarkable. This indicates beyond any doubt the strength of their instrumental orientation towards English.

V. CONCLUSION

English literature courses in British and Indian universities may appear identical (except perhaps in terms of overall weight, i.e. the number of texts in the syllabus for required study, which is likely to be smaller in universities in India). It is in view of this apparent sameness that the attitudinal orientation of Indian students, as revealed in this study, is likely to take on significance.

While curriculum-developers think (or like to think), that students of English literature (Honours) programmes are already proficient in English, and that their proficiency may be assumed in classroom pedagogy and testing, teachers in the classroom know differently: their task is often that of explication, gloss, and even translation. Conversely, where English is taught primarily as a language skill (as in compulsory undergraduate courses in the sciences, commerce, or social sciences), it is often still through the medium of the literary text, invariably the literary 'classic'.

Some separation of pedagogic aims and methods, in conformity with students' English-language proficiency, is already recognized as an urgent need. The University of Bombay, for instance, has responded by introducing three language-oriented courses at different levels in the curriculum. At the first year BA level, 'Communication Skills in English' is a compulsory course that engages students in active analysis of texts—both literary and non-literary—and in the production of texts for various purposes: such as concise, schematic writing (précis), the writing of reports and speeches, creative writing, etc. At the third year BA the course 'The Art of Writing', is part of the English literature programme. It trains students in the analysis of those features of texts which make them 'effective' or otherwise, with a view to helping them write better themselves. At the MA in English, a course called 'The Structure of English'— traditionally a purely linguistic course—has been reoriented so as to integrate linguistic with stylistic analysis.

However, curriculum-developers at most other Indian universities have largely ignored the chief motivation of English literature students in studying their subject—that of acquiring better language skills. They have continued to treat English literature as a component of a humanities programme, ideally leading to students' cultural enrichment, adding to their knowledge of life, and inculcating in them the 'right' values—which are its professed functions in the university in the West. But Indian students, as this study shows, tend to remain aloof from involvement in the representation of life in English texts. Their interest is in the medium rather than the message, the language rather than the culture, and the benefit they hope to attain is proficiency in English rather than integration into a western cultural ethos.

Such a dichotomy may not always hold in actual practice, but certain popular educational assumptions are problematized by this broad attitudinal difference. Ascertaining student motivation in studying the subject is a necessary preliminary step in bringing about changes in the system.

ANNEXURE I

Questionnaire I

(Demographic Information Questionnaire)

1. Name:
2. Address:
3. Date of Birth: 4. Male/Female
5. College:
6. Educational background:
   (a) (i) Division and percentage of marks obtained at HSC/equivalent examination.
       (ii) Marks in English at HSC/equivalent examination
   (b) (i) Division and percentage of marks obtained at FYBA:
       (ii) Marks in English literature at FYBA:
   (c) (i) Division and percentage of marks obtained at SYBA:
       (ii) Marks in English literature at SYBA:
7. Medium of instruction
   (a) Upto Std X:
   (b) Std XI - XII:
8. Do you speak to your family in English?
   A: always   B. sometimes   C. never
9. How well does your family speak English?

	Very well	Satisfactorily	Unsatisfactorily	Badly
Father				
Mother				
Brothers				
Sisters				

10. Family income per month
    (i)   Below Rs 1000
    (ii) Between Rs 1000 and Rs 3000
    (iii) Between Rs 3000 and Rs 5000
    (iv) Above Rs 5000
11. Community to which you belong:
Coding System for Exposure and Income
    Exposure to English: Items 7, 8, 9
    Item 7: Regional language: 0; English:1 (Total: 2 points)
    Item 8: Always: 2; Sometimes: 1; Never: 0.
    Item 9:

	Very well	Satisfactorily	Unsatisfactorily	Badly
Father	3	2	1	0
Mother	4	3	2	1
Brothers	3	2	1	0
Sisters	3	2	1	0

Family income: Item 10
(i) 1 point; (ii) 2 points; (iii) 3 points; (iv) 4 points.

Questionnaire II

(Indirect Questionnaire)

A: This is how I'd rank myself on the following scale:

boring	interesting
happy	depressed
traditional	modern
have social graces	lack social graces
uneducated	well-educated
successful	a failure
have self-confidence	lack self-confidence
deceitful	open (frank)
stupid	intelligent
independent	lack freedom

uncultured	cultured
reliable	unreliable
have a high standard of living	have a low standard of living
unattractive	attractive
impressive	make a poor impression
have a bleak future	have a bright future

B : This is my ideal self-concept on the following scale:

successful	unsuccessful
stupid	intelligent
attractive	unattractive
make a poor impression	impressive
independent	lack freedom
deceitful	open (frank)
have a low standard of living	have a high standard of living
happy	depressed
have self-confidence	lack self-confidence
modern	traditional
uneducated	well-educated
reliable	unreliable
have social graces	lack social graces
have a bright future	have a bleak future
boring	interesting
uncultured	cultured

C : This is how I'd rank my own community on the following scale:

well-educated	uneducated
unreliable	reliable
happy	depressed
independent	lack freedom
have a low standard of living	have a high standard of living
interesting	boring
stupid	intelligent
impressive	make a poor impression
traditional	modern
have low-ranking jobs	have good jobs
attractive	unattractive
have self-confidence	lack self-confidence
open (frank)	deceitful
lack social graces	have social graces
have a bright future	have a bleak future

uncultured   cultured

D: This is how I'd rank English-speakers on the following scale:

impressive	make a poor impression
traditional	modern
have social graces	lack social graces
interesting	boring
uneducated	well-educated
have good jobs	have low-ranking jobs
uncultured	cultured
reliable	unreliable
stupid	intelligent
open (frank)	deceitful
have self-confidence	lack self-confidence
have a high standard of living	have a low standard of living
unattractive	attractive
have a bleak future	have a bright future
independent	lack freedom
depressed	happy

Questionnaire III

(Direct Questionnaire)

Below are ten reasons which might be given for studying English literature. Please read each reason carefully and rate it according to the extent to which it describes you. Circle the letter in front of the answer that best represents your feeling. Your responses will be treated as confidential. The study of English literature is important because:

1. The study of English literature will improve my competence in the English language.
    (a) definitely important for me
    (b) important for me
    (c) slightly important for me
    (d) not very important for me
    (e) definitely not important for me
2. A knowledge of English literature can help me mix freely with people who are in touch with the latest trends in thought and behaviour in the West.
    (a) slightly important for me
    (b) definitely not important for me
    (c) definitely important for me
    (d) important for me

(e) not very important for me

3.   A knowledge of English will improve my social status.
(a) important for me
(b) slightly important for me
(c) definitely not important for me
(d) not very important for me
(e) definitely important for me

4.   A knowledge of English/a degree in English is necessary in order to get a good job in the professions or in industry/secure a good marriage.
(a) definitely not important for me
(b) important for me
(c) slightly important for me
(d) not very important for me
(e) definitely important for me

5.   A knowledge of English literature will enable me to learn appropriate forms of behaviour in public life.
(a) not very important for me
(b) definitely important for me
(c) slightly important for me
(d) definitely not important for me
(e) important for me

6.   The study of English literature will put me in touch with the great minds of the world and enable me to acquire the right values in life.
(a) slightly important for me
(b) definitely not important for me
(c) definitely important for me
(d) important for me
(e) not very important for me

7.   A study of English literature will give me a broader perspective on regional literatures/other world literatures.
(a) definitely not important for me
(b) important for me
(c) definitely important for me
(d) slightly important for me
(e) not very important for me

8.   English literature is an easy option in comparison with other subjects.
(a) important reason for me
(b) slightly important for me
(c) definitely not important for me

(d) not very important for me
(e) definitely important for me
9. A knowledge of English will help me write creatively in English (e.g. write poems).
    (a) definitely important for me
    (b) important for me
    (c) slightly important for me
    (d) not very important for me
    (e) definitely not important for me
10. A knowledge of English will help to sharpen my mental faculties and enable me to come to grips with the pressures of modern life.
    (a) not very important for me
    (b) definitely important for me
    (c) slightly important for me
    (d) definitely not important for me
    (e) important for me.

ANNEXURE II

Results

Table 1 : Mean scores on attitudinal orientation

Groups	Mean Scores	Standard Deviation (S.D.)
ORIENT	63.85	12.48
INSTR	13.32	3.27
INTEG	12.22	3.80

Table 2 : Mean scores on instrumental-integrative reasons

Item	Instrumental Mean	S.D.	Item	Integrative Mean	S.D.
1*	3.46	0.58	2	2.16	1.20
3	2.50	1.18	5	1.68	1.44
4	2.74	1.31	6	2.54	1.13
7	2.60	1.11	9	2.84	0.96
8	2.02	1.61	10	3.00	0.99
Total	13.32	5.79	Total	12.22	5.72

* Numbers refer to the order of questions in the Direct Questionnaire

Rank ordering of the reasons in order of importance:

  1. The study of English literature will improve my competence in the English language.
 10. A knowledge of English will help to sharpen my mental faculties and enable me to come to grips with the pressures of modern life.
  9. A knowledge of English will help me write creatively in English (e.g. write poems).
  4. A knowledge of English/a degree in English is necessary in order to get a good job in the professions or in industry/secure a good marriage.
  7. A study of English literature will give me a broader perspective on regional literatures/other world literatures.
  6. The study of English literature will put me in touch with the great minds of the world and enable me to acquire the right values in life.
  3. A knowledge of English will improve my social status.
  2. A knowledge of English literature can help me mix freely with people who are in touch with the latest trends in thought and behaviour in the West.
  8. English literature is an easy option in comparison with other subjects.
  5. A knowledge of English literature will enable me to learn appropriate forms of behaviour in public life.

The table indicates that the items ranked first, second and third in terms of mean scores also have a low standard deviation, that is the ratings of the whole group cluster together on these items.

Table 3 : Mean scores on academic performance (TOTPER)and English performance (ENGPER)

Groups	Mean Scores	Standard Deviation
TOTPER	56.06	7.38
ENGPER	57.50	7.45

(The mean scores of exposure to English language and income level cannot be given as these were coded categories.)

Table 4 : Mean scores on groups in the Indirect Questionnaire

Groups	Mean Scores	Standard Deviation
SELF	60.64	9.70
IDEAL	69.48	8.61

Groups	Mean Scores	Standard Deviation
OWNCOMM	58.32	2.47
ENG	60.50	9.14

(In order of rank, ideal self-concept was marked highest, next self-concept, then concept of English-speaking community, and last, concept of their own community.)

Table 5 : Mean scores on categorized traits in the Indirect Questionnaire

Category of traits	OWN COMM		ENG		SELF		IDEAL	
	Mean	S.D	Mean	S.D	Mean	S.D.	Mean	S.D.
CHR*	37.08	8.00	37.48	5.62	38.38	6.54	44.06	5.48
SUC*	15.58	2.93	15.48	2.77	15.42	2.48	17.70	2.25
MOD*	5.66	2.83	7.54	1.46	6.84	1.94	7.72	1.90

* Traits were categorized into personal characteristics (CHR) (10 traits), material success (SUC) (4 traits), and modernity and independence (MOD) (2 traits).

(The data were then analysed in terms of certain tests. One-tailed tests of significance were chosen for all intercorrelations (but not for t-tests) as the direction of the hypothesized link was specified in advance. First, t-tests were run on the following groups, each with each: Instrumental orientation, integrated orientation, OWNCOMM and ENG; SELF, IDEAL, OWNCOMM, ENG; and OWNCOMM and ENG in terms of CHR, SUC and MOD in order to test whether there was any significant difference between them.)

Table 6 : t-tests on groups in Direct and Indirect Questionnaires

Groups	t value	Table value	Significance
INSTR with INTEG	1.54	1.30	.20
OWNCOMM with INSTR	1.94	1.67	.10
OWNCOMM with INTEG	3.86	3.55	.001
OWNCOMM with ENG	–1.16	1.30	n.s.
ENG with INSTR	3.82	3.55	.001
ENG with INTEG	4.98	3.55	.001
SELF with IDEAL	–8.18	3.55	.001

Groups	t value	Table value	Significance
IDEAL with OWNCOMM	5.80	3.55	.001
IDEAL with ENG	6.33	3.55	.001
SELF with OWNCOMM	1.28	1.30	n.s.
SELF with ENG	−0.09	1.30	n.s.
OWNCHR with ENGCHR	−0.34	1.30	n.s.
OWNSUC with ENGSUC	0.20	1.30	n.s.
OWNMOD with ENGMOD	−4.35	3.55	.001

Note :   Degrees of freedom in all cases = 49

The tests revealed that the concept of the English-speaking community (ENG) was considered to be significantly different from both instrumental orientation (INSTR) and integrative orientation (INTEG) taken separately, while concept of own community (OWNCOMM), was significantly different only from integrative orientation (INTEG). Ideal self-concept (IDEAL) and concept of own community (OWNCOMM), ideal self-concept (IDEAL), and concept of English-speaking community (ENG), were significantly different from each other. In addition, self-concept (SELF) was distinct from ideal self-concept (IDEAL), with ideal self-concept (IDEAL) being rated considerably higher than self-concept (SELF). The following pairs were not distinct from each other: instrumental orientation (INSTR) and integrative orientation (INTEG); concept of own community (OWNCOMM) and instrumental orientation (INSTR); concept of own community (OWNCOMM) and concept of English-speaking community (ENG); self concept and concept of own community (SELF and OWNCOMM); self-concept and concept of English-speaking community (SELF and ENG); that is, they were perceived in much the same ways. On the categorized traits, it was found that only own-modernity (OWNMOD) was significantly different from modernity of English-speaking community (ENGMOD), with ENGMOD being much higher.

A Pearson Product-Moment correlation was performed to test the correlation of attitudinal orientation (ORIENT) and next, INSTR and INTEG individually with each of the following: total performance (TOTPER), performance in English (ENGPER), exposure to English (EXPOS) and family income (INCOME).

Table 7 : Intercorrelations of orientation, academic performance,
exposure and income

	ORIENT	INTEG	INSTR	TOTPER	ENGPER	EXPOS	INCOME
	1	2	3	4	5	6	7
ORIENT	1.00	0.76	0.65	–0.10	–0.01	0.04	0.04
INTEG	0.76	1.00	–0.01	–0.11	–0.15	0.23	0.04
INSTR	0.65	–0.01	1.00	0.02	0.15	–0.21	0.01
TOTPER	–0.10	–0.11	–0.02	1.00	0.78	0.18	0.47
ENGPER	–0.01	–0.15	0.15	0.78	1.00	–0.02	0.28
EXPOS	0.04	0.23	–0.21	0.18	–0.02	1.00	0.24
INCOME	0.04	0.04	0.01	0.47	0.28	0.24	1.00

The results indicate that attitudinal orientation (ORIENT) correlates significantly with integrative orientation (INTEG) ($p<.0005$) and with instrumental orientation (INSTR) ($p.0005$). Total performance (TOTPER) is significantly linked with English performance (ENGPER) ($p<.0005$) and also with family income (INCOME) ($p<.0005$). INCOME, interestingly enough, is linked with total performance (TOTPER) ($p<.0005$), performance in English (ENGPER) ($p<.025$), exposure to English (EXPOS) ($p<.05$), and self-concept (SELF) ($p<.05$). Better advantaged homes, it would seem, give rise to better overall academic performance and better performance in English literature, and also provide a greater exposure to English. Moreover, it emerges that the higher the income the higher the subject's self-concept. However, attitudinal orientation as such or INSTR and INTEG separately are not significantly linked with total performances, performance in English, exposure to English, or income, though there is a trend to indicate that integrative orientation is linked with exposure to English ($p<.05$). It seems that there is an orientation to study English literature regardless of academic success, or performance in the field, or exposure to the language or level of income. So, whether the experimental subjects are placed high on the socio-economic scale or not, whether they are academically good or otherwise, are exposed to English or not, they all wish to study English.

A Pearson Product-Moment correlation was also conducted to test the correlation of the four demographic variables (TOTPER, ENG PER, EXPOS and INCOME) with the groups on the Indirect Questionnaire (SELF, IDEAL, OWNCOMM and ENG).

Table 8 : Intercorrelations of scores on the demographic variables with those on the Indirect Questionnaire

	TOTPER	ENGPER	EXPOS	INCOME	OWNCOMM	ENG	SELF
	1	2	3	4	5	6	7
TOTPER	1.00	0.78	0.18	0.47	0.01	0.13	0.20
ENGPER	0.78	1.00	0.02	.0.28	–0.10	–0.08	0.17
EXPOS	0.18	–0.02	1.00	0.24	0.21	0.12	0.18
INCOME	0.47	0.28	0.24	1.00	0.02	–0.18	0.24
OWNCOMM	0.01	–0.10	0.21	0.02	1.00	0.28	0.36
ENG	0.13	0.08	0.11	–0.18	0.28	1.00	0.36
SELF	0.20	0.17	0.18	0.24	0.36	0.36	1.00
IDEAL	0.25	0.30	0.08	0.18	0.21	0.36	0.66

The table indicates that total performance (TOTPER) and performance in English (ENGPER) correlated to some extent ($p < .025$) with ideal self-concept (IDEAL). These variables, however, do not correlate with self-concept (SELF), concept of own community (OWNCOMM) or concept of English-speaking community (ENG). This means that except in their ideal self-image, there is no relationship between academic/English performance and subjects' perceptions of themselves, their own community or English-speakers. Again, exposure to English (EXPOS) does not correlate with any of the four groups on the Indirect Questionnaire, not even with concept of English-speaking community (ENG), which is surprising. Family income (INCOME) does not correlate significantly, either, with any of the groups on the Indirect Questionnaire, though there is a trend towards correlation with self-concept (SELF) ($p < .05$). So, subjects do not view their family income as being representative of their own community, or of the English group, nor is it in line with their ideal leanings.

Self-concept (SELF) correlates significantly with ideal self-concept (IDEAL) ($p < .0005$), with concept of own community (OWNCOMM) ($p < .005$), and with concept of English-speaking community ($p < .005$), indicating that the subjects had a good self-concept and, in addition, saw themselves as poised between their own community and the English-speaking community of Indians. Ideal self-concept (IDEAL), on the other hand, correlates significantly only with concept of English-speaking community (ENG) and not with concept of own community (OWNCOMM), indicating that ideally they would like to have the characteristics of the English-speaking community. The concept of English-speaking community (ENG) also shows a trend towards correlation with concept of own community (OWNCOMM) (p<.025), indicating that there was a similarity in the way the two communities were perceived by the subjects.

A Pearson Product-Moment correlation was also performed on the groups on the Indirect Questionnaire (SELF, IDEAL, OWNCOMM, ENG) with ORIENT, INSTR and INTEG, in order to ascertain whether the variables on the two questionnaires tested the same phenomena.

Table 9 : Intercorrelations of the scores on the variables on Direct and Indirect Questionnaires

	ORIENT	INTEG	INSTR	OWNCOMM	ENG	SELF	IDEAL
ORIENT	1.00	0.76	0.65	0.15	0.32	0.06	0.23 (.2256)
INTEG	0.76	1.00	−0.01	0.23	0.15	−0.00	0.05
INSTR	0.65	−0.01	1.00	−0.03	0.32	0.10	0.29
OWNCOMM	0.15	0.23	−0.03	1.00	0.28	0.36	0.21
ENG	0.32	0.15	0.32	0.28	1.00	0.36	0.36
SELF	0.06	−0.00	0.10	0.36	0.36	1.00	0.66
IDEAL	0.23	0.05	0.29	0.21	0.36	0.66	1.00

The results indicate, as stated before, that both the aspects of attitudinal orientation under consideration here, integrative orientation and instrumental orientation, correlate highly significantly with attitudinal orientation (ORIENT). The t-tests (Table 6) had however indicated that though INSTR and INTEG were not significantly different from each other, INSTR was to some extent higher than INTEG, though this value did not reach any level of significance (t=.54). Self-concept, ideal self-concept and concept of own community did not correlate with attitudinal orientation, while concept of English-speaking community correlated significantly with attitudinal orientation. When INTEG and INSTR were looked at separately, self-concept did not correlate with either of these, while ideal self-concept correlated to some extent with INSTR (p<.025). While concept of English-speaking community (ENG) correlated significantly with INSTR (p<.01), OWNCOMM showed a trend towards correlation with INTEG (p<.05), thus indicating the opposite of what was expected, namely that concept of English-speaking community and INTEG on the one hand, and concept of own community and INSTR on the other would tap the same kind of response. This did not happen.

Table 10 : Intercorrelations of the categorized traits on OWNCOMM and ENG with the demographic variables, and INTEG, INSTR, ENGCHR, ENGSUC, ENGMOD, OWNCHR, OWNSUC, OWNMOD

TOTPER	0.11	−0.08	−0.22	−0.05	0.11	0.08
ENGPER	−0.07	−0.01	−0.20	−0.16	0.08	−0.08
EXPOS	0.07	0.09	0.22	0.20	0.23	0.11
INCOME	−0.15	−0.13	−0.26	0.02	0.07	−0.04
ENGCHR	1.00	0.81	0.67	0.31	0.37	0.20
ENGSUC	0.81	1.00	0.71	0.14	0.25	0.02
ENGMOD	0.67	0.71	1.00	0.15	0.27	0.09
OWNCHR	0.31	0.14	0.15	1.00	0.80	0.62
OWNSUC	0.37	0.25	0.27	0.80	1.00	0.56
OWNMOD	0.20	0.02	0.09	0.62	0.56	1.00
INTEG	0.16	0.14	0.08	0.20	0.18	0.25
INSTR	0.35	0.33	0.02	0.02	-0.07	−0.13

The table shows (apart from significant correlations of all categorized traits on their concept of the English group with each other and of all categorized traits on their concept of their own community with each other), that instrumental orientation correlates significantly with both their concept of the personal characteristics of the English group and their material success (p<.01), but not with any of the categorized traits on their concept of their own community. On the contrary, there is a trend towards showing that their concept of modernity and independence in their own community correlates with integrative orientation (p<.05), suggesting that these traits of modernity and independence in the subjects' own community are considered to be linked with a desire to integrate with the English group. However, as their ratings on these traits in their own community, in themselves and their ideal selves, are low, it appears that they do not wish to emulate English speakers on these. The expected match in responses to at least some of the categorized traits in the English speakers with integrative orientation on the one hand, and to some of the categorized traits in the subjects' own community with instrumental orientation on the other, therefore, is not borne out. Instead, the data clearly suggest that any association the subjects might have with the personal characteristics or with traits relating to the material success of the English-speaking community of Indians is linked with an instrumental motivation to study English literature.

Of course, own personal characteristics (OWN CHR) does correlate to some extent with personal characteristics of the English-speaking community (ENG CHR) (p<.025), though not at the desired level of significance, indicating that the subjects do not view the personal characteristics of the two communities as being too different. The t-tests (Table 6) had also revealed that the modernity of own community was significantly different from the modernity of the English-speaking community (p<.001), and this was the only category to emerge on which the concept of own community was significantly different from the concept of English-speaking community. The above table indicates that there is a trend towards modernity of the English-speaking community (ENG MOD) being correlated with family income (p<.05). This is interesting because apart from SELF (their view of themselves) no other group or category of traits on the Direct or Indirect Questionnaires shows any relationship with income. Given the relationship that has been established between material success and instrumental orientation, it would have been reasonable to expect that the material success of the English-speaking community would be related to income. But this does not happen.

Table 11 : Intercorrelations of the categorized traits in SELF and IDEAL with the demographic variables, and INTEG, INSTR, SELCHR, SELSUC, SELMOD, IDLCHR, IDLSUC, IDLMOD

TOTPER	0.18	0.17	0.20	0.22	0.30	0.16
ENGPER	0.15	0.14	0.17	0.25	0.42	0.15
EXPOS	0.21	0.13	0.01	0.09	0.05	0.03
INCOME	0.24	0.24	0.10	0.18	0.21	0.05
SELCHR	1.00	0.70	0.55	0.60	0.47	0.47
SELSUC	0.70	1.00	0.55	0.51	0.50	0.36
SELMOD	0.55	0.49	1.00	0.42	0.43	0.80
IDLCHR	0.60	0.51	0.42	1.00	0.84	0.50

IDLSUC	0.47	0.50	0.43	0.84	1.00	0.50
IDLMOD	0.47	0.36	0.80	0.50	0.50	1.00
INTEG	−0.03	0.08	−0.01	0.11	−0.06	−0.04
INSTR	0.11	0.01	0.11	0.26	0.38	0.12

The results indicate that all categorized traits of self-concept correlate significantly with those of ideal self-concept (p<.0005), with IDLMOD correlating only slightly less significantly with self's material success (SELSUC) (p<.005). Ideal material success (IDLSUC) correlates significantly with instrumental orientation (p<.005) and there is a trend showing that ideal personal characteristics correlates with instrumental orientation (p<.05). Both ideal material success and ideal personal characteristics (IDLCHR) correlate with performance in English (p<.005 and <.05 respectively) which reinforces the connection of ideal self-concept (IDEAL) with INSTR. Also, valuation of self-characteristics (SELCHR) and self-success (SELSUC) show a trend towards correlation with income (p<.05).

As instrumental orientation (INSTR) is the only type of attitudinal orientation which seems to be of importance, it is useful to analyse its relationship with the groups in the Indirect Questionnaire. The relationship of the categorized traits of ideal self-concept (IDEAL) match those of the concept of the English-speaking community (ENG); INSTR correlates sig- nificantly with both personal characteristics of the English-speaking community (ENGCHR) and the success of the English-speaking community (ENGSUC) (p<.01) (see Table 10); and, similarly, as seen above, INSTR ap- pears to correlate with ideal personal characteristics (IDLCHR) (p<.05) and ideal success (IDLSUC) (p<.005). Also, self-concept (SELF) correlates significantly both with the concept of own and the English-speaking communities (OWNCOMM and ENG) (p<.01); but ideal self-concept (IDEAL) correlates only with the latter (p<.01) (see Table 8). Ideal characteristics (IDLCHR) and ideal success (IDLSUC) correlate significantly with characteristics of the English-speaking community (ENGCHR) (p<.01), but not with the categorized traits of subjects, own community (OWNCOMM) (see Table 11). So, ideally, the experimental subjects are linked with the concept of English-speaking community on all traits except modernity and independence, which is the only category on which they are ideally linked with the concept of their own community (OWNCOMM). It appears from the above discussion and the emerging relationship between ideal self-concept (IDEAL), the concept of English-speaking community (ENG), and instrumental orientation (INSTR) that in order to achieve the personal characteristics and the material success of the English-speaking community, subjects are instrumentally oriented to study English literature.

Table 12 : Intercorrelations of the categorized traits on SELF and IDEAL with ENG and OWNCOMM, SELCHR, SELSUC, SELMOD, IDLCHR, IDLSUC, IDLMOD

OWNCHR	0.37	0.19	0.17	0.22	0.05	0.16
OWNSUC	0.35	0.30	0.21	0.28	0.20	0.22
OWNMOD	0.20	0.19	0.37	0.06	-0.02	0.32
ENGCHR	0.35	0.24	0.23	0.41	0.33	0.33
ENGSUC	0.40	0.38	0.08	0.36	0.25	0.15
ENGMOD	0.19	0.18	0.00	0.05	-0.07	0.04

The results indicate that the valuation of self-characteristics (SELCHR) is significantly associated with the characteristics of own community (OWNCHR), the success of own community (OWNSUC) and the characteristics of the English-speaking community (ENGCHR) (p<.01) and a little more strongly with the success of the English-speaking community (ENGSUC) (p<.005). The concept of self-success (SELSUC) correlates significantly only with the success of the English-speaking community (ENGSUC) (p<.005), though it shows a trend towards association with the success of own community (OWNSUC) (p<.025) and the characteristics of the English-speaking community (ENGCHR) (p<.05). Valuation of self-modernity (SELMOD) however, correlates significantly only with the modernity of own community (OWNMOD) (p<.005) and not with the modernity of the English-speaking community (ENGMOD). The results show that subjects consider themselves radically different from the English-speaking community on the traits of modernity and independence, but in other respects there is little difference between their perception of their relationship with their own community and with the English-speaking community of Indians. In fact, they see themselves as very closely related to the material success of the English-speakers. The picture of the subjects which emerges is one which shows them to be culturally aligned to both communities but, in crucial matters like modernity, they abide by their own community norms, going beyond their own community chiefly in terms of material success (both present and projected) to what is perceived as the greater success of English-speakers.

Ideal personal characteristics (IDLCHR) correlate significantly with the characteristics of the English-speaking community (ENGCHR) and with the success of the English-speaking community (ENGSUC) (p<.005), ideal success (IDLSUC) with the characteristics of the English-speaking community (ENGCHR) (p<.01) and ideal modernity (IDLMOD) with the characteristics of the English-speaking community (ENGCHR) (p<.01). There is even a trend indicating a relationship between ideal success (IDLSUC) and the success of the English-speaking community (ENGSUC) (p<.05). On the other hand, the only category on which ideal self-concept (IDEAL) is linked with the concept of own community (OWNCOMM) is modernity and independence: ideal modernity (IDLMOD) correlates significantly with the modernity of own community (OWNMOD) (p<.01) and does not correlate at all with the modernity of the English-speaking community (ENGMOD). Thus, the ideal self-concept of the subjects is seen to be closely linked with the English- speaking community in terms of both personal characteristics and material success, but not in terms of modernity and independence. With regard to these two features they see themselves, not only in their present circumstances, but even ideally, as linked with their own community.[12]

[12] I wish to acknowledge my gratitude to Mr K. Murdeshwar, Department of Statistics, University of Bombay, for extensive help given in statistical analysis and the computerization of data for this study. I also wish to express my indebtedness to Dr Rahul Roy of the Indian Statistical Institute, New Delhi, and to all the teachers and students in Bombay who so willingly participated in the experiment.

11

Siting the Teacher

RIMLI BHATTACHARYA

The privileging of English literature in India has, ironically, made it the most vulnerable of academic disciplines today. For too long, 'literature' has been synonymous with English literature, and that too with a certified list of classics recognized by the Anglo-Saxon world. Mercifully, the study of 'pure' literature is an endangered activity the world over, and literary studies appear to be increasingly interdisciplinary, intertextual, historically and socially informed, and to some extent politically conscious. Leaving aside, for the moment, the complex of reasons behind this opening up,[1] we could in India welcome the breakdown of hitherto hermetic compartments of disciplines and texts and assume a 'natural' change in our study of and participation in English literature. But such changes, or possible changes, will take place within existing conditions, which I shall outline briefly, choosing to foreground the teacher as a mediating agent within the system.

The unique features of English, as it is operative in neo-colonial India, in tandem with the conditioning processes prevalent in academia, doubly burden the teaching of English literature. I argue that although the English teacher is herself thus doubly determined, she is paradoxically in a position most suited to make visible the scars and the continuing wounds of colonialism. English Studies can be potentially liberating only if the teacher is willing to confront the comfortable conventions of

---

[1] For a succinct account of how 'a whole range of people' [in the West] have had to 'open up this buried continent of Literature to the scrutinizing gaze of history and politics . . . as a response to nationalist pressures', see Aijaz Ahmad '"Third World" Literature and the Nationalist Ideology', *The Journal of Arts and Ideas*, 17 & 18, June 1989, 118-25.

academia in direct response to unsettling questions about language and ethnicity, class and gender, education and employment—questions that loom large in our daily lives forty-five years after Independence.

IS THE SYSTEM CHANGING?

I shall begin with an attempt to sketch some of the features of the educational framework within which the process of teaching and evaluation takes place. For the most part, the 'system' (a convenient term that captures perfectly the elusive but omniscient qualities of 'something' we would like to believe as a force outside), affords little flexibility to the individual teacher who has to work within formulaic courses, usually known by the ubiquitous terminology of Papers (I, II, etc.), geared towards equally formulaic examinations. There are large numbers of students, many of whom may lack even basic competence in English, a limited number of primary texts and other resources, and a fixed quota of classes to be taught which have little reference to the teacher's own interests or competence. Until recently, therefore, the stock figure of the teacher was that of a drudge waging a heroic (and unrewarded) battle against, or giving into the deadening powers of, these formulae. As the English teacher in R.K. Narayan's novel of the same name disarmingly informs the college principal, 'Sir, what I'm doing in the college hardly seems to me work. I mug up and repeat and they [the students] mug up and repeat in examinations . . . it doesn't please my innermost self.'[2]

The teacher of English literature was a respectable and perhaps respected, but ultimately marginalized and even comical, figure. There is, in literature, a long line of such 'types' who are at home in the unreal world created primarily out of the books of a foreign literature. In a recent short story called 'Buried Alive', Bharati Mukherjee makes clever use of all the stereotypes of the erudite but somewhat ridiculous figure of an English teacher in war-torn Sri Lanka, who is suddenly yanked out from the comfortable world of books and finds himself eventually in an illegal boarding house in Germany.[3] The story, in its violent juxtaposition of alien books and homespun bombs, says as much about the times

[2] All references to this novel are to the 1953 edition, entitled *Grateful to Life and Death* (Michigan: Michigan State Press, 1954).

[3] Bharati Mukherjee, 'Buried Lives', in *The Middleman and Other Stories* (New York : Fawcett Crest, 1988).

we live in as it does about the 'material' and the way in which it is processed in Mukerjee's narrative technique. A few excerpts, which bring out her caustic treatment of the figure and of the familiar theme of incompatible worlds, suggest that she has not really moved very far from Kipling's treatment of the pathetic 'English educated' Bengali 'baboo':

if the monks hadn't chased his sister . . . Mr. Venkatesan would have stayed on, in Trinco, in St. Joe's teaching the same poems, year after year, a permanent prisoner.

Or consider the reference to

A Treasury of The Most Dulcet Verses Written in the English Language, which he had helped the headmaster to edit though only the headmaster's name appeared on the book.

Of the application letters he writes to eight American universities in his efforts 'to get out', Mukherjee observes:

He took great care with cover letters, which always began with 'Dear Respected Sir' and ended with 'Humbly and eagerly waiting your response'. He tried to put down in the allotted blanks what it felt like to be born so heartbreakingly far away from New York or London.

Mukherjee's parody is finally used for an overkill, when we are told of Mr Venkatesan in Germany:

Now he wanted to walk where Shelley had walked, to lie down where consumptive Keats had lain and listened to his nightingale sing of truth and beauty.

Even allowing for the parodic licence exemplified in 'Buried Lives', Bharati Mukherjee's schoolteacher is a close cousin of the university teacher, whose sole academic function was to teach, or more precisely to lecture, in the classroom. The absence of a 'publish or perish' edict, or of a high-profile conference circuit, meant that of the overlapping roles (or selves) of scholar, critic, intellectual and teacher, the last was the one most operative both for the individual teacher as well as for the students and other members in the same field. An older colleague once told me that what struck her most when she first went to study abroad was that the library was full of books written by the very people who taught her in class. My colleague's surprise at this phenomenon was perhaps inevitable, given the general lack of pressure to publish in India, and, more pertinent to the case of English literature, the unhesitating valorization of critical texts from 'there' (the place of origin) over those written 'here'. Indigenous notes and guides (otherwise referred to as kunjis in north

India), produced by both well-known and not-so-well-known teachers are, of course, quite another matter, requiring separate discussion.

The situation has changed somewhat in all respects, although the academic's preference for a foreign publisher over an Indian one, or a metropolitan journal over an Indian one, still continues for reasons too disparate to be adequately discussed here. There are now a good many departments where there is more autonomy in choosing and designing courses, and more systems of internal assessment alongside a conscious attempt at organizing interdisciplinary seminars. Most important, conferencing or seminaring and publishing (extensively) are now the approved *modus operandi* in Indian academic circles. These have taken over unquestioningly all the performative aspects of first world academia, without demanding or necessarily demonstrating the kind of intellectual rigour which accompanies professionalism. In addition, there has been a substantial increase in funds for organizing seminars as well as for sponsoring the individual scholar's trips abroad. This has meant that the business of teaching has become a less urgent matter for discussion, precisely at a time when the system as a whole appears to be in a state of transition and is therefore in urgent need of reorientation.

There is no question that, because of revised pay scales, teachers—certainly at the college and university levels—have 'emerged as one of the more privileged sections of the community'.[4] An earlier state of genteel poverty often pushed a teacher into producing guide books or holding huge tutorial classes outside the college/university premises, simply in order to supplement a low salary. Such practices continue, despite the vastly improved economic status of teachers today. They have in fact strengthened in response to the pressures of upward mobility, most explicitly visible in the Indian middle class since the eighties. Considering that a bulk of English literature teachers are from the various levels of the middle class, it is understandable that the whole problematic arena of classroom teaching is left largely unexplored, other than in isolated and partial forays into teaching strategies.

There are other changes too, which, potentially, could help clean up the cobwebs of the mind or of the system, but which fail to do so: the waves of theory which challenge many established and often deadly ways of seeing; the increased flow of visiting teachers and speakers; the

---

[4] Amrik Singh, 'Vested Interests of College Teachers', in *The Times of India*, 24 March 1990.

return to important (elite) institutions of fresh teachers with foreign degrees; and the inclusion under the rubric of English literature texts from Africa, Australia, the Caribbean, not to mention our very own 'Indian literature in English'. One would assume then that the time was ripe to deconstruct the ghosts of the Colony and the Canon and re-construct an (or several) version of English Studies.

Jeremiah-like, I'm obliged to maintain that the decolonizing and decanonizing will have to be worked out *first* in our own persons as teachers who are very much a part of what we choose to call the system. It is not as if we stand outside its pale and do not have a stake or share in its distribution of power and privileges. The re-siting of English literature is less a matter of overnight revolution than an arduous pro-cess not only of rethinking course content but of dismantling and re-structuring the existing structures of departments, specializations and interests. Re-locations may often mean dis-locations and shifts of exist-ing 'balances of power', since English Studies cannot and should not have a uniform character all over the country. Teachers will not only have to discard as 'prejudices' much of what was held to be sacrosanct, but may have to engage in a substantial programme of learning (a little different from the kind of learning that is ostensibly a life-long process) before they can teach. Consequently, their resistance to any radical reorganization of the discipline may well emerge stronger than ever, both within and without the classroom. One set of canonized readings will be easily replaced by a new set, and old gods by new ones, unless we are prepared to examine ourselves in that configuration of The World: The Student: The Text: The Teacher.

In this ideally open-ended and free-flowing combination, 'the World' is quite reductively read to mean the operative checks and flows in the curricula and the examination system which lead to job opportunities and determine social position. 'The Teacher' is used, consciously and unconsciously, to plumb this world. This is possible primarily because —despite the changes noted above—ours is still a system where the presence of the teacher (however irregular or infrequent this may be) is the chief constitutive factor in the student's attitude to her discipline and, by extension, to her notion of education. The faceless conglomerate of an university body, with its system of mass annual examinations, ensures syllabus-oriented study, which often involves, quite literally, a study of question papers and prepared answers against the received lore of what is bound to succeed. The student perceives/evaluates the teach-er in terms of her efficacy in dealing with the monolith.

Paradoxically, the hazards of intellectual straitjacketing are greater in institutions which function with more autonomy and follow a semester system with a continuous process of internal assessment. 'Freedom' from the vagaries of an invisible regulatory body is not necessarily freedom to think in ways that might challenge the more visible bodies who teach and evaluate in the autonomous institution. Conditioned throughout her early years of education not to think, or to think in prescribed channels for specific objectives (examinations and jobs), most students regard teachers as 'insiders' possessing information about examination questions or actually setting and evaluating papers, and as superior beings in command over the 'real' meaning of the text(s) in question.

So strong is this conditioning that the introduction of theory intended to question the notion of 'a real meaning' can unfortunately result in the transfer of an uncritical, deferential, if not reverential, attitude to theory and to the teacher who brings or translates for the uninitiated newer versions of power from the academic metropoles of the West. While most disciplines in Indian academia depend greatly on imported theory, in recent years English literature teachers, particularly younger teachers, appear to be more interested in and more receptive to theory—both of the strictly literary and the non-literary kind. English literature departments, in fact, often act unofficially, but not unconsciously, as a clearing house for theory (Western theory) for other departments. Viewed thus, 'receptivity' is all too often a prelude to a 'third world dumping' rather than an indication of a genuine critical process. English departments offer (in both senses of the word) an ideal dump site because the universal urge (and now, an academic compulsion) to be *au courant* is at work in an already beleagured zone.

The student thus sees in the teacher a visible link between transatlantic Eurocentred master discourses and their somewhat removed 'third world' (inferior) selves, and rarely if ever considers critically the several layers of mediation involved in this interpretive process. The process of reification within the classroom may continue, albeit in a new guise. This observation is certainly not an attack on theory; it is merely a cautionary note on the modalities at work in the classroom. Questions about the relevance of theory (currently a subject of intense debate) are actually quite irrelevant; what needs to be discussed is how theory may be used/taught, and in what context, against the larger frame of teacher-student relationships as they exist today. A basic requirement for the success of theory is space for discussion—the possibility of dialogue, interventions and even interruptions during and through teaching.

SEPARATE SPHERES

The primary sense of the distance of English literature in India is magnified by the actual teaching conditions. However, even in those cases where the teacher is not under the constraints of a fixed curriculum and a predetermined examination system, there is a certain separation of the spheres of 'life' and 'literature'. Meenakshi Mukherjee has diagnosed this gap as one arising from the 'enforced monolingualism' of the 'English-medium student' situated in a 'naturally multi-lingual situation'.[5] I would like to argue that this gap between the verbal and the extensional world of the individual is not experienced by the English-medium urban elite student alone, in whom it may be manifested—or who may actually flaunt it—more starkly than others, but is *symptomatic of English literature studies in general in India*. Both the person of the teacher and the teaching process itself continuously reaffirm and perpetuate the schism between the two worlds.

English literature is taught primarily through what we may call frozen transactions in the form of lecture notes which, once written, are never discarded, and the educational process is travestied in the reproduction of these notes. This is essentially a time-saving approach adopted by the teacher, who is often obliged to teach a gut course to a huge and mostly indifferent class. Ultimately, it matters little whether these notes comprise a traditional assortment of dates, biographical details and (the usually unacknowledged) 'sayings' of a limited number of well-worn critics, or, as in the more sophisticated versions, are a pastiche of ill-digested, unformulated theories from different disciplines. Both versions are equally removed from the teacher's own extensional world. This has grave consequences not only for the next set of scholars/teachers being produced in such an environment, but also for the bulk of the students, who go on to professions as diverse as advertising, journalism, the civil services or the police, and who form *a large proportion* of what one would call the Indian intelligentsia. The people who make up this fairly wide spectrum of professions have in

[5] Meenakshi Mukherjee, 'The Unhoused Sensibility: Responding to English Literature', in *Modern Thought and Contemporary Literary Trends*, edited by B. Narsing Rao and Kadir Zaman (Hyderabad: 1983), 184. Mukherjee cites Hayakawa (*Language, Thought and Action*, 1952, 32) to explain her use of the terms: 'Let us call this world that comes to us through the word the Verbal world, as opposed to the world we know or are capable of knowing through our own experience, which we shall call the Extensional world'.

common the important positions they occupy in a society where power is concentrated in the hands of the few.[6] I therefore focus here on the nexus between pedagogy and language skills, and attitudes to language and the individual teacher's personal 'interests', which reflect so clearly the alienating phenomenon of English literature in India.

'Separateness' is most evident in the material taught. The isolation of the text is not peculiar to the Indian situation and recent studies have linked it to the pedagogy derived from, or at least influenced by, New Criticism.[7] In India the teacher—working within the confines of a syllabus which segregates The History of English Literature (more often than not a list of dates, periods, biographical sketches and major 'events') as Paper I, Romantic Poetry as Paper IV, and so on, and usually teaching one discrete section of any one of these papers—does not need to be a conscious practitioner of New Criticism to practise it nevertheless.

Even when there is a conscious attempt to relate texts with social, political and cultural changes, i.e. to situate the text in the world, it is without question the world of England. The immediate world around, and of, the teacher is kept exiled, or at least temporarily banished, as if the process of transmission has to be kept sacred, uncontaminated by non-English elements. (One wonders, in the case of teachers of English literature who are also writers of regional literatures—a fairly significant number—whether the influence or interflow of English literature into their writings is matched by a similar overflow of the world of their writings into the teaching of English literature.) Given the artifically maintained privileged status of English literature on the one hand, and the poor-relation status of regional literatures in academia on the other, the lack of formal interaction between the two 'classes', and the extremely small group of readers/writers who are equally comfortable in both literatures, the sacralized teaching of English literature seems inevitable. This was particularly true of a generation which, in U.R. Anantha-

---

[6] August, the young IAS officer with an English literature background placed in rural India, epitomizes in Upamanyu Chatterjee's novel the misalliance between education and life in contemporary India. It is a tribute to the resistance within the system that this work, which attempts to question the descriptive space accorded to 'English', should itself become a catchy and ultimately de-barbed literary reference to be circulated in the academic channels of seminars and term papers. See *English, August* (London : Faber, 1988).

[7] See for example, Ahmad, 120.

murthy's pithy phrase, was unable to 'domesticate English' with the *conscious use* of separate spheres.[8]

As a result of these (and possibly other) causes, there are innumerable English literature teachers who have other, often passionate, 'interests' which are perceived as being marginal or quite unrelated to their professional discipline. There is rarely an attempt on their part to integrate the two, or see one in terms of the other, although such integration would most certainly be enriching, even if confusing in the early stages. Such interests may include theatre work, creative writing, and small-time journalism, and may even extend to activism of an explicitly political nature around issues that may appear unrelated at first sight to English literature. R.K. Narayan's novel again provides a deft representation of the problematic issue of reconciling livelihood or career with interest— the merging of the professional and the personal. The protagonist tries to 'explain' why he wishes to resign from what seems to be a perfectly satisfying job as an English teacher in a prestigious college. To Brown's (the principal's) query, 'Any special reason?' we have the following revelation:

I remained silent. I didn't know what to say. I replied: 'I am taking up work in a children's school'. 'Oh' he said ... 'But I didn't know you had primary school training ...' he replied. I looked at him in despair: his western mind, classifying, labelling, departmentalizing ... I merely replied: 'I am beginning a new experiment in education, with a friend.' 'Oh, that is interesting,' he replied. 'But look, here, must you resign? Couldn't you keep it on as *an extra interest* ... We do want a lot of experimenting in education, but you could always ...' He went on, suggesting it as a *hobby*. (207; italics mine)

As the first person narrator attempts to establish, such interests are quite different from hobbies in other contexts; they suggest a powerful need in this group of people for some direct relational contact with the everyday world in which they actually live. Papers on teaching strategy often underline and acknowledge this primary need, which remains undeniable even if we argue about the ways in which such needs may be fulfilled, or if the ideological position we may ascribe to this or that way is debatable.

However, the desirability of merging the two worlds has to be

---

[8] Inaugural address in a seminar on 'Perspectives on the Teaching of English Literature in India' (hereafter 'Perspectives', 1990), jointly organized by The Centre for Linguistics and English, Jawaharlal Nehru University, and the British Council Division (30 March–3 April 1990, New Delhi).

balanced/weighed against the very real danger of yoking together the spheres. It is often the case that the remedies prove a greater evil: connecting in superficial and facile ways the text with the everyday world; uncritically drawing upon Indian sources with which the teacher is not familiar (or worse, which have been assimilated under western eyes); and teaching a pastiche course which is grounded only on eclecticism and hybridity—these are all possible dangers.

As damaging or restrictive as this separation of profession versus interest is to the individual teacher, its effect on the *teaching process* is of greater consequence since it ensures the preservation of the status quo— the systematic and unquestioning continuation of practically the same texts, the same examination system and the same teaching methods.

Despite the preservation of sameness in the discipline, there *are* certain aspects of academia today which suggest that, like any other institution, it is not immune or unresponsive to changes of power structure in other state apparatuses. Besides overt instances of political appointments, the increasing control of government bodies (such as the University Grants Commission) over admission politics, curriculum changes, examination guidelines and the bureaucratization of almost every step in the day-to-day running of a department, have all meant that the educational system works on a similar framework of plans, proposals, amendments and cancellations as other state apparatuses. The immediate and urgent needs of a department are shelved or reworked to suit the elaborate but usually ineffectual 'operating instructions' of that unwieldy juggernaut, Education Policy. Deliberate care is taken to ensure that by-laws and sub-clauses are duly followed or flouted within 'legal limits', while any attempt at radical experimenting is perceived as a threat and treated accordingly.

Over the years the teacher–student relationship has acquired characteristics that both mirror these larger social processes and are also specific to the discipline under discussion. I will later examine the vexed question of authority as an example of the academia–society interface.

THE TEACHER AS TEXT

However isolated or alienated she may be from the world outside academia, the teacher is the *other* text in the classroom who is constantly being read by the students *vis-à-vis* the pre-texts of academia, social symbols of power and various other ideologies that are connected to systems of mobility in our present infrastructure. For young aspirants planning to make a living in academia, the 'insider' status of the teacher is not just the key to more inside information about texts and examinations, but is also a visible indicator of survival tactics within the system. The lessons learnt constitute a strategy of contentment/containment aimed not to threaten in any serious way the conceptual and institutional parameters of pedagogic practice, but to ensure the continuation of system-conforming benefits.

The standard response to this initial recognition that the teacher is indeed the other text is to propose a certain 'wholeness'— a confident and a certain clearly definable self. In short, the teacher must project an integrated self, which in the context of the reality of our historical situation is perhaps a project in which we would all like to participate, but which as yet remains just that— a projection into the future. I am not advocating a relapse into a postmodern celebration of a doubt-ridden, fragmented self (or selves), and hence eliding or deferring endlessly the possibility of a reconstituted self.[9] The negative impact on students of what I would call a narcissistic enactment of the self is too evident to be spelt out. Neither is the recognition of our fractured position an invitation to anarchy, as many believe. Awareness of the cracks on the ground on which we stand, and conscious use of our unstable position, are perhaps crucial steps towards a positive 'refunctioning' of English literature teaching.

No amount of innovative teaching techniques alone (whether of indigenous or of foreign origin) will serve as a substitute for an 'effective community of experience' if we do not first deal with what Suvir Kaul has called 'the lie of English in our land'. Our classrooms, our texts, and the very process of teaching offer in fact the ideal site for a confrontation of and an engagement with the problematic status of English literature in a post-colonial situation. Addressing our inner uncertainties in the

---

[9] Many of the essays on New Historicism in a recent anthology offer a fascinating example of the extent to which academia (in the USA specifically) is a victim of what it seeks to exorcise. See *The New Historicism*, ed. H.A. Veeser (London: Routledge, 1989). Self-analysis as part of one's intellectual honesty entails a certain performance which often overwrites that which it seeks to problematize. In this regard, the 'third world' critic who is situated in the West is perhaps necessarily in a far more vulnerable position than his/her Western counterpart, as is suggested for example in Gayatri Chakravorty Spivak's position in 'The New Historicism: Political Commitment and the Postmodern Critic'.

(enclaved) public space of the classroom and in seminars would be one way of reconstructing, in a participatory fashion, a drastically revised programme which will be both relevant to, as well as engender, responses to the living world.[10] At present we only train students to cite and recite the 'objects of knowledge' that are thus recycled and which, despite considerable mutation and mutilation, function effectively in warding off or deflecting possible resistance and uncomfortable questions.

In the best of all possible worlds, teaching is a mode of interaction rather than one of transaction. A transaction, or the handing over of a commodity to a recipient, makes the teacher an actor (someone with exclusive access to a particular reservoir of knowledge or script) and the student a passive beneficiary.[11] Much like development programmes meant for the poor/underprivileged/backward, such a model assumes that there is a desired goal or target, that the potential recipients are assured of success if they surrender completely to the demands of the programme, and the development implementor/teacher is in the possession of the necessary knowhow to make this possible. In contrast to this, teaching as an interactive mode makes the teacher and student look upon the learning/teaching process as one based on a kind of shared experience deriving from and in turn feeding into the world in which both live.[12]

Unfortunately, our present situation only allows us— Frankensteins

[10] Speaking of the relevance of literature to all sections of society, Raymond Williams concedes that while 'a large part of the literature, carrying as it does a body of vital common experience, will be attracted to the dominant language mode . . . at the same time, a *national literature*, as English has never ceased to be, will while containing this relation, contain also elements of *the whole culture and language*'. Raymond Williams, *Culture and Society 1780 –1950* (London : Chatto and Windus, 1967), 233. There is for us, however, the question of diverse cultures and many languages, which I would categorize as the differences we have to find a place for, in our current movement towards national disintegration.

[11] See Halliday's model of teaching literature cited in David Birch, *Language, Literature and Critical Practice : Ways of Analysing Texts* (London: Routledge, 1989), 27-8.

[12] Williams's concluding section in *Culture and Society*, although dealing specifically with the question of 'mass communication', offers an additional insight. He warns: 'We fail to realize that much of what we call communication is necessarily no more in itself than transmission; that is to say, a one-way

—to put together or assemble more creatures (known subsequently by the name of Frankenstein). We then spend the rest of our resources and lives trying to turn monsters into wo/men. Lest this paper read like 'The Diary of a Mad Woman' or even 'The Mad Woman in the Classroom', let me refer in passing to another term— 'cannibalism'— used in the course of a recent seminar, by the handful of others who must have felt a similar terror in looking at what we perpetrate/perpetuate in the name of teaching. In my view the horror lies in the reproduction, in more and more grotesque forms, of the original sin that was visited on us.

QUESTIONING AUTHORITY OR THE GREAT TRADITION

The perpetuation of the project outlined above is possible because of our stress on conformity and respect to authority, or on lip service to authority. This attitude is not confined to the classroom alone, but infects our entire social system today. I shall not here attempt to trace the historical reasons behind this classic combination of servility and arrogance, or go to the other easier extreme and posit a typical *Indian* mentality as some kind of a given which is then used to read and construct the history of India.

I will consider briefly, and perhaps unfairly in attempting to be brief, an essay on 'Authority and Identity in India' by T.G. Vaidyanathan which seems to me to belong very much to the second of the two modes just mentioned.[13] While one may agree with Vaidyanathan's identification of the guru–shishya relationship as a master paradigm of social

---

sending . . .'. (303). If we agree with Williams that 'a transmission is always an offering, and that this fact must determine its mood: it is not an attempt to dominate but to communicate, to achieve reception and response', we will have to agree that 'active reception and living response depend in turn on an effective community of experience'.

[13] T.G. Vaidyanathan, 'Authority and Identity in India', *Daedalus*,118, 4 (Fall 1989), 157. Interestingly enough Vaidyanathan, himself an English literature teacher, does not in his piece consider the implications of his paradigm in the Indian classroom. In addition to the relevance this article has to my point about the power structure in the classroom, it is worth noting that Vaidyanathan's paper, along with others on theatre, literature, architecture, economics, etc., is part of a special issue on India brought out by *Daedalus* in collaboration with the Ford Foundation. The paper on Indian literature (itself a problematic term/concept) is by Anita Desai, a writer in English.

relationships in India, one is uneasy and often in disagreement with the conclusions drawn from such an observation. Thus:

when the harmony and symmetry of this relationship is broken—as it increasingly is in modern India—the guru-shishya conglomerate splits off into its component parts, precipitating the crisis of authority and identity that is rampant today.

Such gloomy conclusions may be arrived at only if it is assumed that the guru as the prototype of an authority figure is seen as an unquestionably integrated figure (cf. 'Our writers celebrate not the brooding Hamlet or the tormented Oedipus, but integrated figures like Rama and Krishna: for whom wisdom lies in the banishing of doubt.') [14] It appears to me that the guru in academia, specifically in English literature departments, has been trained for too long (and has learnt too well) to project an integrated persona. The student acquiesces in this projection, but the element of belief or faith which could possibly make such a relationship worthwhile is absent. It is a contract that is convenient to both sides and one that is rarely violated by the parties concerned for fear of having to work out a new position. Vaidyanathan argues that 'the guru–chela relationship isn't in the least repressive or authoritative. It is the chela who chooses his guru and not the other way round. It is not a goal-oriented short-term relationship.'

The first statement is clearly not true of our academic situation. The final sentence is, unfortunately, quite true, but is related more intimately to what I would call the elaborate patronage system that characterizes power relations in almost every sphere of our lives in India today; the guru–shishya paradigm is only *one* of its attributes. I have known young faculty members refrain from voicing their objections in public to decisions that they will oppose in private because of the 'bonds' that exist between them and older colleagues who may have taught them and/or facilitated their entry into academia through personal intervention.

This kind of moral obligation may be commended, but it results in the effective silencing of a whole generation of teachers, encouraging them in turn to expect the same kind of loyalties from their chelas. One agrees that there is the 'Indian' who 'pursues not rights but adjustments', but to contend that 'this will lead to social harmony' is surely to

---

[14] Vaidyanathan, 158. One could question, of course, the comparison of Rama and Krishna, clearly divine figures (however human their manifestations) with the all-too mortal figures of Hamlet and Oedipus.

simplify dangerously both the question of rights as well as of what constitutes social harmony, and even to elide the question of whether 'harmony' is our desired social goal: the classroom is the place and the problematic status of English literature the means by which precisely such questions have to be faced.

THE TEACHER AS POLICY MAKER

The preceding sections of this essay have been in the nature of a preliminary survey; I have attempted, in intentionally general terms, to delineate the lay of English literature in India and the position of the teacher in this land. The absence of a sociological profile of 'The Teacher of English Literature' or the case study of any one such teacher is clearly a lack. The question of gender, which I have not explored at all, is one instance of a crucial omission, since a large percentage of English literature teachers (and students) are women. The implications of this sharply sex-segregated labour force in terms of status in the departments, professional mobility, work capacity and commitment to teaching or to one's career and success in unionizing have to be examined if we talk about changes, as they will have to be worked out within existing institutional structures.[15]

This section offers, instead, a rapid overview of this community as represented at a recent all-India seminar.[16] On the basis of the presentations and exchanges in that four-day meet, and keeping in mind changes in national policies related directly to this discipline, I will venture to plot our historical position, in this last decade of the century, and to suggest the possible directions in which we may wish to move in order to make our professions and the discipline more relevant to other, larger

[15] For useful approaches to a possible study dealing with these factors, see 'The Educational System: Gender and Class', in Michele Barrett's *Women's Oppression Today: Problems in Marxist Feminist Analysis* (London: Verso, 1985), 114-51, and more specifically, on 'Women and the Transmission of a Literary Culture', in Terry Lovell, *Consuming Fiction* (London: Verso, 1987), 139-51.

[16] 'Perspectives', 1990. (cf. note 8). The anatomy of a seminar would require first of all, a foregrounding of its sponsors/organizers. The agenda, the presentations and the tone of the ensuing discussions are to a large extent predetermined by the sponsoring institution or body. Thus, for instance, it was not entirely surprising that of the five speakers who were asked to sum up the seminar in question, three were British.

concerns. The relationship between English literature and the English language, for example, needs to be explored not only as an academic topic but as a vital constituent of classroom interaction. Equally relevant are the government's (state and central) policies on language. Recent developments in Uttar Pradesh and Madhya Pradesh, and earlier rumblings in West Bengal about the mother tongue, will have to be taken into account in our search for a new English literature. I believe that the teacher can be effective as a policy maker only if such concerns feed into and even define actual pedagogic practices. Envisaging such an active/activist role for the teacher requires us to situate her/him against the anomie which characterizes the discipline today. Perhaps the most outstanding feature of the study of English literature in India is the status it occupies. It is studied by a minority, but by a substantial portion of the minority which has access to higher education. In the absence of any one of the regional literatures occupying the role or status of a 'national literature', English literature comes to assume, however outrageous this claim may appear, a pan-Indian, national status. Hence the proliferation of departments all over the country, with English literature seen as an indispensable unit of any university, whether in metropolitan centres or in remote rural peripheries where even basic texts may be unavailable. This is one major difference, besides that of the colonial origin of English Studies, between Indians studying English literature and those studying other non-Indian literatures (for example, French, Russian or Japanese), and between Chinese or Slavic literatures studied elsewhere (for example in the USA).

It would *appear* that English literature is a neutral field where students from all regions of India, irrespective of class, creed and caste, would be able to participate on fairly democratic terms. But the reality of the multilingual situation in India and its heterogeneity, quite apart from polarized economic differences, only accentuates the corresponding hollowness of this national front.

From the context of what we could refer to as the 'larger question', the seminar made very clear that apart from ideological divides (which often, although not always, matched with a 'generation gap'), English literature in India, despite the dismal monotony of curricula, teaching methods and evaluation systems, is far from being a homogeneous discipline in the problems faced and resolved by various teachers from the different parts of the country. Besides the standard contrast of the elite versus the provincial colleges and universities (or of the provinces within the metropoles), there are far too many differences in the regional situation of a particular institution with respect to language, the body of literature in that language, the access to and currency of other literatures and arts—popular and classical—the history of its colonial past, the politics of that area, and of course the finances available. Therefore, while the laments of most teachers could be summarized in refrains like 'failing standards', 'increasing numbers', 'not enough English', 'inefficient bureaucracy', and 'government interference', there was little attempt to read these complaints as questions that went beyond the covers of 'English literature'. Incipient questions as to why *so many* people wanted to or simply ended up studying/teaching English literature were ignored, postponed or glossed over. Far more disturbing was the attempt to schematize and separate, in some way, 'their' problems from 'ours'. This was done on the basis of tacit assumptions of who should 'do' English literature and who 'need not' study/teach English. The ease with which such statements were voiced (whether in passing or as the point of an argument) is a matter of concern; they are indicative of the insularity of our own position and the questionable tactics by which we seek to stay within these niches. Uncomfortably close to the development model I had referred to earlier, such casual and confident settlement of 'needs' reveals a strong subtext of power politics. Questions about the function of the teacher and her role in policy-making can only be answered through a problematization of needs, namely who decides whose needs? And on what basis?[17] In the case of English (language more than literature) this is a thorny area that will have to be entered and tackled before we move on to fancy redesigning. Participants in the seminar, though they came from various parts of the country and spoke of problems specific to their locus, were nevertheless an elite minority who, aware of the crisis in the discipline, still responded in piecemeal strategies of 'patching up' and 'enduring' or making cosmetic changes in the syllabi—which only ensured the status quo.

[17]As Nancy Fraser argues in her essay, 'Gender Politics of Need Interpretation', the interpretation of people's needs 'is itself a political stake, indeed sometimes *the* political stake'. *Unruly Practices: Power Discourse and Gender in Contemporary Social Theory* (Cambridge : Polity Press, 1989), 145. This is a statement particularly valid for any consideration of the 'complex and differentiated' societies in the Indian subcontinent. It is therefore essential for us to 'raise and question the tacit norms and the implicit assumptions' which lie behind our 'perspectives' on English literature.

If the teaching of English literature in India reminds one of the Frankenstein mode, seminars such as the one under discussion bring to mind Borges's dreamer/teacher protagonist in 'The Circular Ruins'.[18] After spending his life dreaming up (creating) a 'perfect pupil', the dying man realizes that he too is a creation—somebody else's projection. The space of a seminar offers us the possibility of deconstructing our projected selves in the shadow of Colony and Canon, in the future of national differences. However, instead of coming to terms with these projected selves, the participants responded to papers which provided markers on this projection with 'panic', 'silence' or 'postponement', and more often than not with hostility, since these papers were perceived as an invasion of hitherto safe territories.

Perhaps more dangerous in the long term are the 'positive' responses to the crisis. The repeated advocacy of some kind of an essentialist Indian solution to the English bogey, in phrases like 'the Indian sensibility', 'the Indian mind', 'the Indian weltanschauung' misleadingly suggests that there is an essential Indian and that all the problems endemic to the discipline can be resolved with reference to this elusive Indian. As teachers in classes which are ideally composed of a heterogenous body of students, such a belief would merely replace one hegemonic monolithic dominance (if we wish to see the colonial legacy of English literature in these terms) with another, differing from it only in being of indigenous origin.

The second 'solution' that cropped up with similar frequency was Comparative Literature. The temptation that this garden of delights offers to the teacher are too numerous to be listed. It is both catchy and convenient and enables its practitioners to feel complacent about having included 'Indian' material. Comparative Literature (whatever the literatures compared), may very easily become Comparative Littering, as has indeed been the case with a large number of third world or non-Western courses designed by well-meaning teachers in the West, specifically in North American universities. My point here is that even experiments in Comparative Literature courses (where English is one of many literatures, and hence devalorized) have to be preceded by (i) more interchange/exchanges between English literature teachers and those in

[18] Jorge Luis Borges, 'The Circular Ruins' in *Labyrinths: Selected Stories and Other Writings*, eds D.A. Yates and J.E. Irby (New York: New Directions Books, 1964).

other literatures and disciplines, and (ii) a commitment on the part of the individual teacher to ground herself in other literatures and disciplines, even if this entails considerable investment of time and resources. Equally attractive options are designing courses around, or sprinkling courses with, 'ethnicity'. It is fairly common now to have courses, papers, and dissertations which deal with the 'folk' and the 'popular' in studies of literary texts and films, or which combine theories and/or data from other disciplines. This could really be the promised beginning of a reconstituted Literary Studies, but it cannot be done without a substantial amount of groundwork. Not only does the teacher have to caution students against fashionable ethnicity, but she has the responsibility of learning before she can teach. In view of these demands it is doubtful whether isolated 'positive' alternatives to traditional English literature will serve any useful purpose, unless they are contextualized within a larger agenda.

The question that remains suspended at the end of a seminar such as the one discussed is: To what extent are we as teachers prepared to re-site ourselves if we wish to re-form English literature in India? Offering alternative courses with readings of hitherto excluded or marginalized texts or with new readings of established texts is not a viable proposition for long-term objectives. At best, alternative courses are permitted by authorities as safety valves, and at worst as licence, born of a department's indifference to course content. Much like 'mainstream' (commercial) versus 'experimental' (art) films, these courses are perceived/read by students as existing in a marginalized slot—as interesting but ultimately freak experiments. Similarly, merely replacing first world English literature with third world English literature (spanning the works of Caribbean, African and Fijian writers, for example) is in fact to perpetuate the myth of the three worlds and to erase the differences within the third world.

There are no short-cuts or lucky breaks out of this prison house; only sustained and co-ordinated efforts can dismantle its worn out but petrified structures. English literature teachers all over India share a common burden—of being aliens in their own territories. However, the strategies required to make English literature relevant to our own concerns must be disparate and different in response to our heterogeneous needs. Building on the specific skills and competencies already available in existing departments, and building up skills with specific programmes in mind—programmes that are related to the needs of a particular region and its diverse communities—is one way of moving out of the rut that we are in. Yet another option lies in the conscious cultivation and incorporation of 'interests' into 'occupation' so that related activities (for example, translation) become part of the discipline rather than a retreat from the discipline. While some individuals have already begun to work in this direction, the majority are still thinking in terms of survival and of the short-term rewards that the system provides to those who have managed to advance in the proper fashion.

This paper has perhaps projected a larger-than-life role for the teacher. The purpose of such foregrounding was to draw our attention to the often invisible network of connections that exists between person and system, text and context in the obscure regions of classroom activity. If English literature is indeed being transformed—at home and abroad —into English Studies, it seems pertinent to consider the gap between the roles we as teachers are prepared to play and that we may choose and then prepare to play. The first is a result of conditioning and envisages our own role as that of a catalyst—unchanging but capable of transforming others. The second involves using our alien selves as prisms and filters to explore and understand our historical situation. It is one of the few real privileges that our discipline affords us—a painful but promising way out of canonized readings of our texts and ourselves.[19]

[19] A part of this paper was written for (and circulated at) the seminar on 'The Teaching of English Literature in India', which has itself become the focus of the second section of the present essay. The paper actually presented at the seminar was on a somewhat different, though related, issue, 'Alternative Teaching', which requires to be developed in a separate essay. My thanks to the editor of this volume, and to Lola Chatterji, for their helpful suggestions and comments in organizing disparate strands.

12

The Indian Academic and Resistance to Theory

SUVIR KAUL

At Oxford, Cambridge, Sussex, Birmingham and Kent—to list just a few institutions—sophisticated and innovative work in 'post-colonial' literary criticism is defining this branch of study. Many of the younger scholars in the field are accepting teaching positions in Africa, India, Pakistan, and throughout the 'Third World', attempting to wrest control of pedagogy and scholarship from older conservative scholars, who are still under the spell of F.R. Leavis . . . and who still believe in the possibility of a 'pretheoretical' practical criticism.

—Henry Louis Gates, Jr.,
'Tell Me, Sir, . . . What *Is* Black Literature?'[1]

And so it Came to Pass: When I returned to Delhi University after completing a Ph.D. at Cornell, armed with letters of recommendation from members of my Thesis Committee, I was promptly invited to come and speak to an M.Phil. seminar on Literary Theory. I asked what I should speak on, and over the telephone I was told, without a trace of irony or reserve, that my topic should be 'Structuralism and Post-structuralism'. I was, as might be expected, struck by the magnitude of this assignment, and, in an attempt to narrow it down, asked what the students had been reading. Lentriccia's *After the New Criticism*, I was told, Culler's *On Deconstruction* and Terence Hawkes's *Structuralism and*

---

[1] Henry Louis Gates, Jr., 'Introduction: "Tell Me, Sir, . . . What *Is* Black Literature?"', *PMLA* 105 (1990), 12.

Semiotics. I realized that I was being asked to do a capsule survey, and I did, committing myself to enormous generalizations and simplifications. Fortunately, the students warmed to the subject, the talk became a free-wheeling discussion, and we decided to meet again informally to continue where we had left off. In all this the seminar supervisor, who had invited me, struggled manfully to stay awake—the next day, when I bumped into him, he said he was grateful for my effort, and then, in a remarkably disingenuous moment, he played the naif: 'Tell me', he said, 'don't you find this Post-structuralism very boring?'

I offer this anecdote as a gloss to Gates's scenario of the return of the theoretically-informed native—both to confirm what he says and to remind us that the wrestling match he envisages has scarcely begun. Institutionally and personally, most members of Indian university and college departments of English still doggedly ignore the entire production of contemporary literary and critical theory, and reject especially any examination of the ideology or history of their academic activity. For older academics, this ignorance is sanctioned and justified in the name of Arnoldian and Leavisite models of literary and cultural values; for many younger academics, such ignorance is the result of their restricted exposure to a curriculum and a pedagogy that celebrates the unexamined virtues of 'organic form', 'moral/ethical vision' and 'creative genius', and systematically excludes all other social, philosophical and historical concerns. Further, and this holds true for most of the teaching of English literature in India, most academics and students (both at metropolitan and provincial colleges) are concerned largely with giving demoralized lectures and taking even more demoralizing examinations, respectively—the staple of the university degree then is the 'guide-book', with its miserably written and printed collection of 'solved' past papers and model answers to expected questions.

Thus, even as this essay deals with issues that concern the vast majority of English teachers and students in our country, it should be clear that only a small minority of them is interested in recent theoretical examinations of the problems and presuppositions of literature and pedagogy. Most teachers have no interest in the essays of Culler or de Man or Bhabha; we are encouraged to develop a strictly 'professional', non-academic, even anti-intellectual and sterile concern with the syllabus dictated to us by the university authorities. We do not choose our classroom texts, structure our courses, or formulate the questions that our students answer in the annual university examinations—our alienation is more or less complete, and our classroom instruction, like our general relation to our discipline, often enacts this alienation. Yet, as I suggest later, this very alienation can generate productive energies, provided its pedagogic forms are recognized and its historical, socio-cultural and institutional correlatives articulated and made part of the agenda of our discipline.

This is where 'theory' can be of greatest consequence for us, for the 'theoretical' is often another name for the self-reflexive, for that brief or sustained enquiry into the value-laden assumptions—psychological, cultural, ideological—that structure and lend coherence to any academic discipline. In the case of English literature in India, to think theoretically will necessarily be to think about historical and pedagogic issues, for there is no escaping the colonial provenance of the subject, nor of the fact that the discipline was born of the imperial need to engender the deracinated colonial subject and facilitate the centralized administration of the colonial state. Theorizing this disciplinary history and historicizing the theoretical (or 'pretheoretical') claims of the discipline could be twin routes to a more academically viable and intellectually fertile version of the subject in the decolonized future.

Anecdote Two: The scene is the annual prize-giving function for the best M.Phil. student in the department of English at Delhi University. The awardee reads out her prize-winning paper on theories of language in the seventeenth century, as revealed in contemporary prose treatises and poetical practices. It is a full account, yet one whose assumptions and formulations often beg more questions than they actually address. At the end of her talk, the head of the department, beaming generously, says, 'As this paper proves, and as the Bible tells us, notwithstanding all the pyrotechnics of Husserl and Heidegger, Neitzsche, Derrida and de Man, there is nothing new under the sun.' There has never been any evidence that he is familiar with the work of those he names; what is worse is that the top brass of the department sitting in the audience smile knowingly and approvingly.

I recount this story to remind us that, often, the less-than-benign obverse of academic ignorance is intellectual and institutional coercion. Teachers discourage students from reading certain writers, or encourage them to engage *only* with particular issues. 'Theory' and 'theorists' (witness the list marshalled above) are quickly ruled out of court, even at the level of so-called 'research' degrees at the university. Even in courses on Literary Criticism or Critical Approaches to Literature, the syllabus stops with T.S. Eliot, with 'Tradition and the Individual Talent' or 'What is a Classic?' being offered as the last word on the subject. In Delhi University, there is virtually no M.Phil. course whose list of required readings includes any of the enormously significant, indeed revisionary, critical work being done by feminists, marxists, new historicists or any other variety of post-structuralist critics.

Yet, as the anecdote above shows, the very academics who do not (will not? cannot?) read literary or critical theory think it necessary to deny it value or relevance. The irony of such a situation is too obvious to be missed: those who would wilfully remain ignorant of theoretical developments are themselves coerced by this ignorance into making wildly defensive (and indefensible) claims. Like Bob Dylan's Mr Jones, they know that something is happenin', but they don't know what it is, and this makes them extremely insecure. And yet this unthinking, knee-jerk response to theory is only the latest manifestation of similar reactions in the past. The same academics who would earlier insist that marxist readings of cultural texts belonged properly to a vulgar Sociology and not to a virginal Literature now see in the entire complex, internally differentiated and contestatory corpus of theory a single repudiation of all the glories of the high-cultural literary tradition: the object of their gaze may have shifted, but their myopia remains untreated.

Similarly, those who have been teaching a catechism based on the dogma of 'negative capability', 'primary and secondary imagination', 'spontaneous overflow of powerful emotions recollected in tranquillity', and 'objective correlative', for years now claim it impossible to read the 'jargon' and the neologisms of deconstructive and psychoanalytic, or even marxist or feminist theory. The well-digested critical vocabularies of Romanticism, or of Arnold or Leavis or Eliot, are taken as pre-discursive and self-evident, as belonging to no histories and staking no ideological positions: theirs are the virtues of universal concern and trans-historical and -cultural meaning and value. Any other critical vocabularies, especially those that derive their fundamentals from disciplines other than Literature, and which are of comparatively recent provenance and thus demand an extra effort to learn, are rejected as motivated and partisan. Ultimately (and unfortunately), the entrenched dismissal of theory has more to do with wilful ignorance, academic prejudice and intellectual sloth, and less with an engaged, informed and rigorous response to or rebuttal of competing ideas. What is lacking is a fundamental seriousness or integrity of academic purpose; what substitutes is a series of bad faith, *ex cathedra* pronouncements.

Anecdote Three: A Cambridge professor of English comes to Delhi University to give a talk on a most innocuous-sounding, scholarly theme: 'Shakespeare in the Late Eighteenth Century'. She is introduced by a fellow Shakespeare enthusiast (an Indian professor) who uses her brief introduction to launch a tirade against what she calls 'things modern', anything that is 'of the twentieth century'. Her own interest, she claims, stops with Shakespeare; after that, but more particularly in the 'twentieth century', new-fangled ideas and literatures have disturbed the repose of the literary ages. Many present there wondered what might have provoked this declaration—surely Shakespeare in the Late Eighteenth Century is not a subject looming with a terrifying modernity. The answer lies, as it usually does, elsewhere. The Cambridge professor is slated to give a major public talk the next day on 'Revising the Literary Canon', and that is of course a 'modern', a 'twentieth-century' formulation. Hence our introducer fires her salvoes in anticipation of the literary carnage that is bound to be unleashed by the lethal forces of critical modernity. She herself, of course, does not come to the lecture the next day.

This story might allow me to clarify the position stated in the quotation that begins this essay. While there are some academics in Indian universities whose postgraduate studies in progressive departments of literature have trained them in the various forms of theoretical enquiry, it will be a tremendous overstatement to claim that it is solely, or even largely, their efforts which are challenging the ideologies dominant in these departments. The 'pre-theoreticals' versus the 'theoreticals' (if I can put it like that) is only one of the debates that threaten the established consensus; more immediate are efforts to broaden syllabi to include courses in Indian Writing in English, in Commonwealth Literature, in African and Afro-American Literature, even in English and American Literature post-T. S. Eliot. These decisions about the academic canon of course involve all the issues of language, race, gender, colonialism and the class co-ordinates of cultural production that have so energized theoreticians in the last two decades, but, for the most part, it is not 'theory' that is at the root of demands to expand the curriculum. In fact, such demands are most often the product of the exigencies of academic specialization, and when such new courses are allowed they are usually taught in the same ways, and communicate the same values, as the earlier orthodox courses in English literature. The canon is occasionally expanded, but 'canonicity' and the ideological formation of canons are rarely made the explicit subjects of discussion and enquiry. Similarly, it becomes possible to teach the occasional 'research level' course on Contemporary Black Women's Writing in America without paying any attention to issues of gender and race; or

to study Commonwealth Fiction without being bothered at all about the
provenance of the term 'Commonwealth', or the ways in which this
explicitly post-British colonial designation glosses over the specificity of
literary and cultural issues in the very different countries that comprise
the political Commonwealth. Ultimately, such an expansion of the curriculum does not interrogate, but actually strengthens, notions of the
universal validity of those cultural and literary criteria supposedly best
manifested in the achievement of English literature. To teach literary
criticism as a way of rendering the very *idea* of 'literature' problematic,
as a way of acknowledging the historical contingency of ethical and
social values, as a way of investigating the ways in which linguistic and
semiotic systems construct, *naturalize* and thus mystify cultural meanings[2]—these projects of theory have not yet reached the top of the
pedagogical and academic agenda in Indian universities.

Anecdote Four (which is offered without comment, as one that
Speaks For Itself): A well-known American critic is making the rounds
in Delhi, as he has done a few times before, giving talks on subjects that
he has written on for the past three decades, iconoclastically and ener-
getically before, somewhat less forcefully now. He talks of the theme
of inter-ethnic homoerotic bonding in American literature, of Natty
Bumppo and Chingachkook, of Huck and Jim on the raft. Every time he
talks of the problematic of race, or of an other-than-normative sexuality,
flickers of anxiety run across Indian professorial faces: here is a white
person, with a white beard, and a string of honours and a place in the
sun, talking about issues that are surely best left outside the purview of
our genteel discipline. During the discussion, a miffed voice raises the
question: 'But don't you think, in times to come, people will forget these
minor differences in skin colour. After all, Othello will still be a great
play even if we forget about race, about Othello being black and Des-
demona white, because it is about that most elemental of human pas-
sions, Jealousy.'

[2] For a parallel account of the classroom as 'a productive rather than a
reproductive environment', see Jeffrey M. Peck, 'Advanced Literary Study as
Cultural Study: A Redefinition of the Discipline', *Profession 85* (1985), 51. Peck
pleads 'above all for greater historical consciousness and a more systematic
critical reflection on the institution of literary study, its history and development' (49). Peck's argument stems from his concerns as a teacher of
foreign literatures in America. His pedagogy is based on this experience of
cultural distance; his theory accordingly demands a critical stance towards
the profession of Literature.

This summary and anecdotal account of some aspects of English Studies in our universities must now give way to a more systematic consideration of three essays (Jonathan Culler's 'Literary Theory in the Graduate Program', Paul de Man's 'The Resistance to Theory', and Homi Bhabha's 'The Commitment to Theory') that engage with issues raised by the presence of literary theory within the Anglo-American academy. These essays are representative of recent attempts to examine institutional and ideological resistance to the analytical methods and intellectual priorities encouraged by Literary Theory, and each of them argues (in different ways, of course) for the necessity of a continuous commitment to such revisionary strategies of reading.

However, my analysis will suggest that the assumptions and goals that motivate Culler, de Man and Bhabha ultimately cannot, except partially, enable similar attempts by the Indian student of literature and culture. Even as the work of contemporary theorists, like the three under discussion, has proved useful in articulating our position *vis-à-vis* the 'master discipline' that is English Literary Studies, it is only through a critical engagement with such work that a specific sense of the historical and political dimensions of 'English' in India will emerge. I will argue, that is, for the necessity of a genuine *resistance* to Literary Theory, and thus for the establishment of a critical dialectic that respects the protocols of Theory even as it responds to the urgencies of our pedagogical practices and cultural situation.

In 1979, writing in the Association of Departments of English *Bulletin*, Jonathan Culler put forward a cogent and persuasive argument for the centrality of literary theory to graduate programmes in American universities. Entitled 'Literary Theory in the Graduate Program', this essay suggests that such centrality is demanded by a contemporary situation where 'young teachers will find themselves in situations where it cannot be taken for granted that any educated person will study the great works of English Literature.'[3] Hence, 'confronted with students for whom literature is simply one aspect of their culture, and an aspect with which they are relatively unfamiliar, teachers need to be able to discuss literature in its relations to more familiar cultural products and in its relations to other ways of writing about human experience, such as philosophy, psychology, sociology, anthropology, and history' (213).

---

[3] Jonathan Culler, 'Literary Theory in the Graduate Program', in the Association of Departments of English *Bulletin* 62 (1979), 212. Future references are incorporated in the text in parentheses.

The cultural and pedagogic problems, as Culler defines them, are structurally similar to the problems we teachers of (English) literature face in India. They involve the 'marginal situation of literature within the students' cultures' (213), a marginalization that has been aided by the 'tendency of literary critics to treat literature as a thing apart, something to be studied in and for itself' (214). Culler's corrective response to this predicament is to suggest that teachers be trained to think that the 'distinctiveness' of literature, 'its privileged character', cannot be 'taken for granted, as some kind of given or inherent quality' (214). Thus, pedagogically the 'most strategic approach in graduate courses might be one that does not concentrate on literary works to the exclusion of all else but one that adopts a comparative perspective, comparing literature with other forms of discourse and other modes of representation' (214). In this schema, the 'literary' is understood as one of our 'basic ways of ordering experience'; literary works then 'appear not as monuments of a specialized high culture but as powerful, elegant, self-conscious, or perhaps self-indulgent manifestations of common patterns of sense-making' (217).

Over the last two decades, Culler's ideas, or ideas like these, have exercised a powerful influence on the shape of literary studies in the American academy. Innumerable courses map the relationships between literary and non-literary discourses, and students learn routinely how to read the master texts of philosophy, psychoanalysis and history as riven by the same anxieties about the figurative or performative aspects of language that the master texts of literature are supposed to thematize. As Culler had hoped, students learn about the 'operations of . . . "textuality"' (221), about the transformative powers of rhetorical forms, and in doing so they are confirmed in their understanding of the problematic commonality of our language-based 'patterns of sense-making'.

Is it not possible, then, for us as teachers and critics living and working in Indian universities to assimilate to our needs and purposes Culler's programme for a systematically relevant literary studies curriculum? As I hope my detour through his article has shown, Culler's is an unexceptionable, indeed compelling, analysis and argument. However, there are several reasons why such a translation of concept and programme would prove infructuous. I will reserve an account of the institutional problems endemic to Indian universities for later—now, I should like to go back to Culler's essay briefly, to suggest that it contains in itself one extremely important reason why that which is theoretically and pragmatically powerful in the American (or Western) academy is virtually untenable, even ideologically suspect, here. My reason for highlighting this feature is simple —I believe that it is foundational to Culler's project, and to many others like it, and that it traces, in its intellectual, academic, cultural and historical priority, what remains *for us* a genealogy and tradition of repressive otherness.

For part of Culler's agenda is the preservation and propagation of what he calls the 'central texts of the humanist tradition', neglected in an American academy dedicated to analytical philosophy and clinical psychology. The comparative approach to literary studies and theory is important 'in universities where philosophy departments fail to teach traditional philosophy and psychology departments reject psychoanalysis, producing a situation in which central texts of the humanist tradition—Plato, Descartes, Hegel, Nietzsche, Freud—are neglected, unless they are taught in literature courses' (221). Ultimately then, Culler has two congruent aims: to 'both give literary theory its appropriate place in the discipline of literary studies and offer courses that embody the central concerns of humanistic education' (226).[4]

For the Indian academic, always already shadow-boxing in the postcolonial arena with the legacies of European imperialism, this formulation begs the fundamental question: Whose humanist tradition? What humanistic education? At this point, however, I should like to make clear that I am absolutely not interested in mining Culler's essay for signs of a motivated or unconscious 'Orientalism'. It was written for a particular academy, in response to a particular crisis, and makes no claims to trans-cultural applicability. I chose it for comment only because I believe we can learn much from it—not only about the cultural and academic territories it maps, but also about the limitations of the particular cartographic approach which it so well exemplifies. It is worth noticing that Culler's version of the humanist tradition actually

---

[4] Writing about similar pedagogic and curricular issues, Wayne Booth says: 'The best reason our publics have for supporting the vast machinery of what we call "English" is their belief that we are, after all, the final guardians of what I have called liberal education. They have no discernible reason to support us in producing more books asserting why language does or does not refer to reality, or why critical theory is or is not grounded, or even why the canon should be revised . . . . We must persuade ourselves that our own interests require a visible commitment to liberal education.' 'Reversing the Downward Spiral: Or, What is the Graduate Program *For*?', *Profession 87* (1987), 39.

celebrates such 'humanist' masters as are now read as *critics* of one or other of the foundational principles of liberal or bourgeois humanism.

We need especially to ask these questions when we deal with Culler's particular humanistic genealogy—Plato, Descartes, Hegel, Nietzsche, Freud. Post-structuralist theorists have mined the work of precisely these thinkers in their continuing efforts to problematize and deconstruct the constitutive discourses of Western humanism. Their efforts have produced a corpus of *anti-humanist* discourses and methods which offer intellectually rigorous and ideologically sensitive ways of engaging with the tradition. For those of us who read from the outside, this inside job is particularly seductive, and offers itself as an easy, even necessary way of inserting ourselves into the alternative tradition of those who read oppositionally.

Thus, our problem with Culler's genealogy is not that we are invited to believe uncritically in a humanist tradition, but that we are invited to believe critically in it, to see in its own protocols and logic-systems compelling and satisfying ways of overturning the traditional. Tied as we are by the history and present structure of most of our humanistic disciplines and of our academies, to the conceptual categories, taxonomies, and parameters of the production of knowledge in the Anglo-American West, we need to be suspicious of the 'critical' almost as much as we are of the 'traditional'. Disciplinary bonds do strengthen us, by giving us a trans-cultural academic identity, but also enervate us, by producing a ready-made body of master-discourses which we then reproduce locally. For us, to be professionally committed to such reproduction is to shut our eyes to the historical complicity of philosophy and politics, pedagogy and ideology, culture and imperialism. This continuing history of the humanities is of course even more true of English literature—to teach the subject in post-colonial India without a primary sense of its historical involvement in the legitimation of the imperial presence in India, or even to teach the discipline as the repository of the finest values of a global, transcendent, culture- and history-free liberal humanism, is precisely to perpetuate the ideological delusion whose intellectual claims we should interrogate and whose cultural effects we must combat.[5]

---

[5] In her *Masks of Conquest: Literary Study and British Rule in India* (London: Faber and Faber, 1989), Gauri Viswanathan examines the role of empire in the formation of the curriculum of nineteenth-century English Studies, and concludes: 'Until curriculum is studied less as a receptacle of texts than as activity, that is to say as a vehicle of acquiring and exercising power, descrip-

But I would like to postpone for a while longer our engagement with the social and ideological relations of the teaching of English literature in the Indian university. It would be easy enough to show the ways in which the entire confused enterprise of literary theory would or would not be welcome in departments of English in India, given their conservative political profiles and retrogressive institutional imperatives. Before we do that, however, I would like to take up the essay that gives my paper its title, and whose major theme is 'The Resistance to Theory'. This essay is useful for our purposes not only because it is concerned with the place of literary theory within literary studies, but also because it is written from a point of view that sees theory as incompatible with pedagogy, indeed as ultimately incompatible with any attempt, humanistic or otherwise, to communicate a code or programme of aesthetic, cultural and political values.

In 1981 Paul de Man was commissioned by the Committee on Research Activities of the Modern Language Association to write an introductory essay on the aims and methods of literary theory that would be part of a collective volume entitled *Introduction to Scholarship in Modern Languages and Literatures*. As it turned out, this essay, which de Man characterizes as being about 'why the main theoretical interest of literary theory consists in the impossibility of its definition',[6] was not included in the volume as the editors deemed it unfit to achieve the primarily pedagogical aims of the publication. As we might expect, de Man thematizes this refusal, seeing in it a symptom of the problematic relations that exist between 'the scholarship . . . the theory, and the teaching of literature'. Within the discipline 'such uncertainties are manifest in the hostility directed at theory in the name of ethical and aesthetic values, as well as in the recuperative attempts of theoreticians to reassert their own subservience to these values' (4). For de Man, unlike for Culler

---

tions of curricular content in terms of their expression of universal values on the one hand or pluralistic, secular identities on the other are insufficient signifiers of their historical realities. The nineteenth-century Anglicist curriculum of British India is not reducible simply to an expression of cultural power; rather, it served to confer power as well as to fortify British rule against real or imagined threats from a potentially rebellious subject population' (167).

[6] Paul de Man, 'The Resistance to Theory', in *The Resistance to Theory* (Minneapolis: University of Minnesota Press, 1986), 4. Future references are incorporated in the text in parentheses.

and Booth, theory cannot be recuperated into the service of critical or liberal humanism—a pedagogy that speaks 'in the name of ethical and aesthetic values' will necessarily 'denounce theory as an obstacle to scholarship, and consequently, to teaching' (4). De Man makes his own position quite clear: if indeed theory is an obstacle to scholarship and teaching 'then it is better to fail in teaching what should not be taught than to succeed in teaching what is not true' (4).

Is this then a radical moment that Indian academics in pursuit of theory should cherish and make their own? Caught in a situation where we are always teaching 'what is not true'—the cultural, ethical and aesthetic normativeness of the master-canons of English and American literature—should we not believe with de Man in the inherent opposition between the 'theory' and pedagogy of literature, and perhaps learn 'to fail in teaching what should not be taught'?[7] Herein lies the rub, though, for in de Man's scheme of things, there seems no place for an *oppositional* pedagogy *based on theory*, for that which can be taught is always resistant to, and resisted by, theory. Nor is de Man interested in a Foucauldian demonstration of the micrology of power, in which the pedagogic space might be understood as the arena of sanctioned dissent or opposition, or in the Althusserian sense of the educational system being a primary Ideological State Apparatus.

For de Man, the only 'true' resistance offered is that of theory, but not because it can serve as the chosen discourse of a politically oppositional subject, responding to his or her interests and imperatives. The resistance offered by 'theory' comes from its being that metaliterary discourse which foregrounds, after linguistics, the twin insights that the link between 'word and thing is not phenomenal but conventional' and that 'this gives . . . language considerable freedom from referential restraint, [and] makes it epistemologically highly suspect and volatile, since its use can no longer be said to be determined by considerations of

---

[7] I am here moving de Man's formulation towards an itinerary not that of the original, but it is precisely this kind of an analytic swerve, such motivated misreading (in the strong sense of the term) that I take to be the method of this essay. In fact, at another level, I am advocating a similar strategic and critical response to the texts of contemporary Anglo-American and Continental literary theory as one important way in which we can problematize their assumptions and conclusions and render them useful to the concerns and compulsions of the Indian academy.

truth and falsehood, good and evil, beauty and ugliness, or pleasure and pain' (10). The 'object' (9) of theory is the demonstration of 'literariness' or the 'autonomous potential of language', and of 'literature as the place where this negative knowledge about the reliability of linguistic knowledge is made available' (10).

For de Man this means that the pedagogic and institutional 'resistance to theory is a resistance to the use of language about language' (12); that the 'resistance to theory is in fact a resistance to reading' (15); that the 'resistance to theory is a resistance to the rhetorical or tropological dimension of language' (17). The logic of de Man's argument culminates in his claim that 'it may well be . . . that the polemical opposition [to theory], the systematic non-understanding and mis-representation, the unsubstantial but eternally recurrent objections, are the displaced symptoms of a resistance in the theoretical enterprise itself' (12). The nature of this inherent resistance is also clear—it is predicated on the 'actively negative relationship' (17) of rhetoric to grammar and logic: 'Since grammar as well as figuration is an integral part of reading, it follows that reading will be a negative process in which the grammatical cognition is undone, at all times, by its rhetorical displacement' (17). The resistance to theory, it turns out, is the resistance of language to itself, of the grammatical to the tropological, and vice versa.

De Man's formulations are particularly disturbing in their complete co-optation of the language of resistance into an essentially hypostatized, solipsistic account of 'literariness' and the 'readerly'. When 'resistance' is understood as a purely linguistic, tropological activity, then critical practice is reduced to the elaboration of (its own) cognitive and rhetorical tensions. Also, the possibility of an oppositional pedagogical practice is denied in the absolute polarity that de Man establishes between the pedagogic and the literary-theoretical. Rather than showing what it is 'to fail in teaching what should not be taught', de Man's essay actually tells us that the 'truth' of reading is the simultaneous discovery of the lie of teaching.

Having said that, I will go back to the lie of the land in our classrooms. My pun is deliberate, for the only way we can understand the lie within our classroom activity is to correlate it with the lie of English in our land, mediated through and in our social, civil and educational institutions. That is, our sense of the lie of our teaching must come not from a de Manian understanding of the truth of reading, but from an equally rigorous and incisive examination of the contexts of reading—that is, from analyses of the history and socio-cultural import of English language and literature in India. For us, the forms that resistance to theory take have little to do with tropological instability and everything to do with institutional inertia, intellectual conservatism, and radically unexamined assumptions and presumptions about the place, scope and disciplinary purpose of English literary studies in India.[8]

In this context, theoretical enquiry must define, and be shaped by, the urgencies of our academic, institutional and cultural practices. There is much more at stake than the reading strategies and epistemological anxieties attendant upon a de Manian concern with linguistic and literary theory. Jurgen Habermas writes of 'the crossover points between theory and practice where [disciplinary] self-reflection arises', as enabling a 'dimension' of thought in which disciplines

critically account to themselves, in forms originally employed by philosophy, both for the most general implications of their presuppositions for ways of viewing the world and for their relation to practice. This dimension must not be closed off . . . . Only in it, finally, can we subject to critical discussion both attitudes of political consequence and motives that form the university as a scientific institution and a social organization.[9]   ·

Similarly, Frank Lentriccia argues that the 'study of theory, whether of one's own or the older positions, is a way of studying the involvement of culture in political power and, in the twentieth century, the specific relations of academic criticism and political power'. Thus, 'theory is not the pointlessly specialised activity of disengaged intellectuals; it is

---

[8] In an essay on English Studies in the American academy, William E. Cain bemoans the 'inability of academics to take their discipline as an object of study and reflection. Most of us profess that English Studies are in trouble, even in "crisis", yet we instinctively recoil from any sustained attempt to evaluate the discipline, probe its methods, review and assess its history, explore its rituals and statements of purpose. Literary theory continues to prosper, and to an extent it does sponsor work on the aims of interpretation and teaching. But theory has not caused members of the profession to reexamine their enterprise in fundamental ways. In certain ways it actually hinders and deflects the type of critique of English Studies that we need . . . '. 'English in America Reconsidered: Theory, Criticism, Marxism, and Social Change', in *Criticism in the University*, eds. Gerald Graff and Reginald Gibbons (Evanston: Northwestern University Press, 1985), 86.

[9] Jurgen Habermas, 'The University in a Democracy — Democratization of the University', in *Toward a Rational Society*, trans. Jeremy J. Shapiro (Boston: Beacon Press, 1970), 9.

rather the fundamental obligation to live self-reflexively and even . . . a condition of democratic community.'[10]

In so far as theory is defined as the *critical* engagement with the foundational and functional logic of differing linguistic, cultural and historical practices, its oppositional aims and possibilities are as radical, and as circumscribed, as those of other varieties of the 'hermeneutics of suspicion' (marxism, psychoanalysis, deconstruction, feminism, various forms of ideology-critique). To recognize this, and to examine its implications—as the ongoing debate about the politics of one or the other kind of theory does—is to extend to its varied discourses their characteristic protocols. More pointed for us, however, is the often articulated suspicion that the new languages of theory only speak across, and extend, the divide between the producers and the objects of knowledge. In his *New Formations* article, 'The Commitment to Theory', Homi Bhabha addresses precisely this issue.

Bhabha begins by labeling as 'damaging and self-defeating' the assumption that 'theory is necessarily the elite language of the socially and culturally privileged', and that the 'place of the academic critic is inevitably within the Eurocentric archives of the imperialist and neo-colonial West.'[11] For him the real question is 'whether the "new" languages of theoretical critique . . . simply reflect those geopolitical divisions and spheres of influence. Are the interests of "Western" theory necessarily collusive with the hegemonic role of the West as a power bloc? Is the specialised, "textualised", often academic language of theory merely another power ploy of the culturally privileged Western elite to produce a discourse of the Other that sutures its own power-knowledge

[10] Frank Lentriccia, 'On Behalf of Theory', in *Criticism in the University*, 107-8.

[11] Homi K. Bhabha, 'The Commitment to Theory', *New Formations* 5 (1988), 5. Bhabha's prose, difficult as it is to unravel, is impossible to summarize. Most of the pre-publication readers of this essay suggested that I drop my discussion of Bhabha's essay, on the grounds that the dedicated obscurity of many of his formulations makes his argument difficult to follow, and betrays a contempt for his audience. I have retained this section particularly because Bhabha is read, within the Western academy, as a privileged spokesman for a 'Third World' position (while being largely unknown in India, for instance), and is a good example of the ease with which the 'radical' stance in the Western academy can be perceived as quite its elitist reverse (if only at the level of style) in another context of reception.

equation?' (6-7). As we might expect, his answer is 'it aint necessarily so' (5).

It aint so because, for Bhabha, the very process of 'intervening ideologically' (which is the task of the committed progressive intellectual) is a discursive act, political *écriture* whose dynamics 'require us to rethink the logics of causality or determinacy through which we recognize the "political" as a form of calculation and strategic action dedicated to social transformation' (8). The call to activism 'must acknowledge the force of writing, its metaphoricity and its rhetorical discourse, as a productive matrix which defines the "social" and makes it available as an objective of/for action . . . the political subject—as indeed the subject of politics—is a discursive event' (8). The 'true' political is not realizable as a pre-textual *a priori*, but emerges only in the 'history of the form of its writing', and is 'always marked and informed by the ambivalence of the process of emergence itself . . . within the terms of a negotiation (rather than a negation) of oppositional and antagonistic elements' (8).

A socialist critique then, marked by the act of scription, of *écriture*, will not posit the 'new political object, or aim, or knowledge, as simply a mimetic reflection of the *a priori* principle or commitment', (10) and thereby attempt to confirm its identity as socialist or materialist. It will, on the other hand, articulate itself in the form of a 'translation', an iterated 'negotiation' that will 'overcome the given grounds of opposition' and open up a 'place of hybridity, figuratively speaking, where the construction of a political subject that is new, *neither the one nor the Other*, properly alienates our political expectations, and changes, as it must, the very forms of our recognition of the "moment" of politics' (10-11).

What Bhabha is arguing for, it seems to me, is the concept-logic and methodology of an open ended-dialectic, one that is not subject to what he calls 'the redemptive rationality of sublation or transcendence' (11). No Hegelian (marxist) mode for him, nor any Althusserian 'scientistic' sense that symptomatic readings of the 'nervous tics on the surface of ideology reveal the real materialist contradiction that History embodies' (11). He wishes the 'project of our liberationist aesthetics' to be rid of a 'totalizing, Utopian vision of Being and History that seeks to transcend the contradictions and ambivalences that constitute the very structure of human subjectivity and its systems of cultural representation' (5). His arguments claim not only conceptual or methodological advance, but important political effects: they 'open up hybrid sites and objectives of struggle and destroy those familiar polarities between knowledge and its objects, and between theory and practical-political reason' (11). There is no 'unitary or homogeneous political object' (11) for socialist critique, only the articulation of hybrid political objectives. Further, Bhabha categorically gives up on the idea of a revolutionary class (and indeed on the language of class analysis itself): it is necessary that 'questions of organization are theorised and socialist theory is "organised", *because there is no given community or body of the people, whose inherent, radical historicity emits the right signs'* (12). The *object* of socialist theory then, may be the 'act of determining our specific political *objectives*' (13).

This may seem a perfectly unobjectionable conclusion to arrive at, and in fact what is engaging in Bhabha's argument is the process of 'socialist' argumentation itself—what he gives up on, and what he puts into its place. Bhabha's understanding of the practice of contemporary politics is analogous to Stuart Hall's Gramscian sense that politics is not

an arena which simply *reflects* already unified collective political identities, already constituted forms of struggle. Politics . . . is not a dependent sphere. It is where forces and relations, in the economy, in society, in culture, have to be actively *worked on* to produce particular forms of power, forms of domination. This is the production of politics—politics as a production. This conception of politics is fundamentally contingent, fundamentally open ended. There is no law of history which can predict what must inevitably be the outcome of a political struggle.[12]

Ironically (and this ultimately differentiates Bhabha from Hall), even as Bhabha argues for the hybridity of effects and objectives, for the enunciation and construction of the political, for the iterations, the translations and the negotiations of cognition and recognition, he grounds his case in the universal, generalizable, *necessary* structure of the moment of enunciation, of the act of *écriture*. He is quite aware that he does so, and he offers a partial explanation (partial in that it explains the polemical need for such a ground, but not why the truisms of structuralist semiotics or grammatology should provide an immediately acceptable, or even preferable, foundation): 'This emphasis on the heterogeniety and the double inscription of the political objective is not merely the repetition of a general truth about discourse introduced into the political field. In denying an essentialist logic and a mimetic referent to political representation it is a strong, principled argument against political separatism

---

[12] Stuart Hall, 'Gramsci and Us', *Marxism Today*, (June 1987), 20. See also Hall's 'Blue Election, Election Blues', *Marxism Today* (July 1987), 30-5.

of any colour, that cuts through the moralism that usually accompanies such claims' (12).

It seems to me that the argument against political separatisms, pietistic or opportunistic, must come from analyses of the historical contingencies which these separatisms articulate as their political truth (I am trying here to remain within Bhabha's terminology for the recognition of History as textual *happening*). Those (anti-imperialists) who seek to maintain political-ideological positions based on an 'implacable oppositionality or the invention of an originary countermyth of radical purity' (5) do so not only, or not even primarily, because they possess an 'essentialist logic' and a naive faith in 'a mimetic referent to political representation'. On the contrary, theirs is often the insight that the structure of enunciation itself is doubly agonistic because it is marked by the colonizing logic of the political unconscious (always already inscribed by the language of power as the power of language).

Bhabha understands that the 'enunciative process introduces a split in the performative present', (19) a split that problematizes any claim of 'culture as a knowledge of referential truth' (19), but he fails to consider that this split 'I' (the 'disjuncture between the subject of a proposition . . . and the subject of enunciation', 20), this sundered linguistic and cultural identity, must always speak to a gap that is not only of the performative present but the performed past. Memory and historical experience (which need not be thought of as linear or orderly or evolutionary, but even as a disruptive ensemble of overdetermined traces) have no impact on Bhabha's semiotic account of subject positioning; its structure is proof against their shaping powers. There are moments in his discussion that pay lip service to the 'institutional' constitution of linguistic practice, but he never follows through the implications: 'The pact of interpretation is never simply an act of communication between the I and You designated in the statement. The production of meaning requires that these two places be mobilized in the passage through a Third Space, which represents both the general conditions of language and *the specific implication of the utterance in a performative and institutional strategy of which it cannot "in itself" be conscious*' (20, my italics).

It is this 'unconscious' that is the source of greatest worry for those who would, as Ashis Nandy puts it, 'defy the given models of defiance',[13] for this unconscious has a continuing history too, that of the

---

[13] Dedication in Ashis Nandy, *Traditions, Tyranny and Utopias: Essays in the Politics of Awareness* (Delhi: Oxford University Press, 1987).

colonized and still hegemonized other. Bhabha is sanguine in his faith that the ambivalence, the splitting, of the 'subject of culture' originates in phenomena explained by the general laws of semiotics. I have a less easy understanding of the process; the *agon* of the enunciation of identity is the less than free play of the traces of memory, of repression and imposition, of impacted resistance to the only language (of enunciation) there is, which is always the language of (some one else's) power. Bhabha's concept of enunciation may lead to a 'historical politics of negotiation' (19), but it cannot deny a history of pernicious political (im)positions, no matter how differently they are recovered, 'repeated, relocated, and translated' in and as the present.

Similarly, when Bhabha claims that the 'reason that a cultural text or system of meaning cannot be sufficient unto itself' is because it is 'crossed by the *différance* of writing or *écriture*' (20), he does not worry about the asymmetry of *différance*, which defers not just to temporality, but to the 'invisible hand' that scripts the global equation of knowledge/power. *Différance* may ensure that 'meaning is never simply mimetic and transparent' (20), but I am less sure of Bhabha's claim that 'the splitting of the subject of enunciation destroys the logics of synchronicity and evolution which traditionally authorise the subject of cultural knowledge' (20). What authorizes the 'subject of cultural knowledge', it seems to me, is not only its methodological and narrative paradigms ('the logics of synchronicity and evolution') but its genealogy, in which the congruent discourses of imperialism and humanism (to name only the big guns!) feature prominently. Their historical logic, in all its continuing institutional authority and transformative power, is at stake too, and that suggests to me that the play of self and other, or self as other, is not reducible, even as a heuristic, to the splitting of the subject at the moment of (its) enunciation. Indeed, it is strange to read Bhabha arguing hard against the prescriptive and predictive 'ruptures' of the teleological marxist social text by privileging the single rupture enshrined by semiotic theories of the *general* condition of language.

Bhabha's examples always manifest his belief (not unlike de Man's) that the play, the '"desire of the signifier", the "indeterminacy" of intertextuality' are always 'deeply engaged in the struggle against dominant relations of power and knowledge' (17). The master discourse is always translated and transmuted by its resistant native recipient (incidentally, this is a perception Bhabha never garners from an indigenous record, but from performative fissures in the master discourse). What he is less concerned to show, however, is how the native (discourse) is translated and transmuted, or indeed mauled and mutilated, in this asymmetrical interaction. This leads him to an entirely suspect claim at the end of his essay, when, following Fanon, he describes the liberatory uncertainties of the Algerian anti-colonial struggle:

In the moment of liberatory struggle, the Algerian people destroy the continuities and constancies of the 'nationalist' tradition which provided a safeguard against colonial cultural imposition. They are now free to negotiate and translate their identities in a discontinuous intertextual temporality of textual difference . . . . The people are now the very principle of 'dialectical reorganisation' and they construct their culture from the national text translated into modern Western forms of information technology, language, dress. The changed political and historical site of enunciation transforms the meanings of the colonial inheritance into the liberatory signs of a free people of the future (21-2).

The fact that, so late in the essay, Bhabha can talk of the 'freedom' of people who are making the transition from the colonial to what lies beyond it to construct their own identities, reveals an astonishing opacity to the forms of post-colonial domination, some of which—*modern* Western forms of information technology, language, dress—Bhabha lists himself. Similarly, to talk blithely of 'the people' denies the specificity of domestic class and power relations, which in the post-colonial moment, always take their co-ordinates from the hierarchies and apparatuses of colonial authority.[14] Precisely because there is no easy polarity, and only the illusion of material or significatory rupture, between the colonial and the post-colonial, the cultures and peoples that emerge in, and shape, the transition continue to enunciate the languages—repressive as well as emancipatory—taught to them by their history. The narratives of our 'translated' or 'negotiated' (or even 'imagined') futures are articulated not in discontinuous but in continuous, even if non-serial, time. That is our possibility, and our contradiction.

Earlier, I had said that our pedagogic crises and their resolutions must emerge from the contradictions of our classroom experience. Working out the exact nature of our lived contradictions is, of course, coming to terms with the historically and structurally overdetermined processes that Rajeswari Sunder Rajan has insightfully, and movingly, described

[14] See Aijaz Ahmed, ' "Third World Literature" and the Nationalist Ideology', *Journal of Arts & Ideas* (1989): 117-35, especially 125-6.

in her *Social Scientist* article, 'After *Orientalism*: Colonialism and English Literary Studies in India': 'Having been construed unproblematically as (lesser) members of the community of western readers of western texts, we find ourselves as critics (a) naturalised into the role of western-type critics (b) but suffering from a sense of inferiority or lack of worth as second-order critics (lacking in true language facility, sufficient scholarship, etc.) and (c) experiencing a loss of natural identity and alienation from lived experience'.[15] Sunder Rajan offers a slogan and a programme to deal with this (self) marginalization—she calls 'for a radical politicization of English literary studies, both pedagogical and critical, in India' (31).

For those of us who feel queasy about the conjunction of the words 'politics', 'literature', and 'pedagogy', I would suggest that the lived experience of the relations of power and knowledge in our classrooms (in which we displace our own frustrating conversion into walking, talking dictionaries and paraphrasers of surface meanings into an aggressive, alienating instruction to our students that they are generally deficient because they lack access to the superior mysteries and moralities of English literature) teach us about the conjunctions of power and knowledge outside our classrooms, and about the privileged, indeed co-ordinating, role 'English' has had in the historical construction and continued perpetration of those conjunctions. To rephrase André Bétéille, we need to study Class, English and Power, and thus articulate where our interests—both present ideological motivations and future hopes—lie.

I will close as I began, with an anecdote. Two years ago I attended a

[15] Rajeswari Sunder Rajan, 'After *Orientalism*: Colonialism and English Literary Studies in India', in *Social Scientist* (1986), 31. Gene H. Bell-Villada offers a parallel reading of the Latin American situation: 'Virtually every modern South American critic of repute feels compelled to grapple at some moment or other with the fundamental and monstrous fact: Latin America as product of the West but not of it, as target but never the beneficiary of foreign plunderers. Five successive centuries of control by Spanish, British, French and United States imperialists are the reality always lurking subliminally in any South American discussion of the glories of North American civilization. Though armed with full knowledge and coherent understanding of the West, Latin literati remain ever-conscious of their problematical relationship thereto.' 'Criticism and the State (Political and Otherwise) of the Americas', in *Criticism in the University*, 138.

'Developments in Literary Theory' conference at Hyderabad, and heard a series of papers (and gave one too) on the work of contemporary literary critics and theorists. Most of the papers were descriptive rather than analytic, and offered paraphrase and celebration instead of scrutiny and critique. Much in contemporary theory that is potentially radical or revisionary, or even simply unsettles older strategies of reading or pedagogy , was effaced as the implications of the critical positions summarized were not understood or followed up. The ease with which this recuperative, accommodative process worked was disturbing—as academic after academic offered no intellectual resistance to the linguistic, literary and cultural first principles they enumerated, I wondered if anything would stem this fresh critical tide.

Help came from a somewhat unexpected source when, in casual coffee-break conversation, I asked an MA student who had been diligently attending our seminar sessions whether he found them 'interesting'. His answer was succinct: 'No'. I tried again, shifting my question from the loosely pedagogic to the utilitarian and didactic; did he find them 'useful', I asked. 'No', he said once again, equally sharply and simply. It may have been an initial curiosity that brought him there (though I am inclined to think it was an academic in authority who told him to come), but it was a strange power and fascination that kept him there. His involvement in, resentment of, *resistance to*, the entire process—a process much larger than him, larger than us—took the form of an absolute, resolute denial of interest, worth or value. That denial still resounds in my ears, echoing similar denials that haunt our classrooms, reminding me that we ignore, or worse, suppress, such voices at our own peril.[16]

[16] I wish to thank Ania Loomba, Raji Sunder Rajan and Janadas Devan for their work on this essay.

13

Mapping A Territory: Notes on Framing a Course

MEENAKSHI MUKHERJEE

Among the papers in this volume which highlight theoretical issues regarding critical strategies and the pedagogy of English in India, this empirical paper has a rather precarious place. In fact it is not an analytic study at all, but a brief report relating to the practice—not the ideology—of teaching literature, though I am aware that there can be no practice without theory, however unformulated its assumptions. I attempt here to recount the steps involved in devising a course entitled 'The Novel and Society'—somewhat non-traditional in content and approach—which I taught to MA English students at the University of Hyderabad for three years. I am not suggesting that it was in any way an exemplary exercise, nor that everyone else should try it. My intention here is only to share my experience of an alternative course I designed and taught; it may help others plan new courses in other areas. At the very least, this account can serve as a springboard for discussion.

Like most of the contributors to this volume, I too, for most of my adult and working life, have been beset by doubt and unease about the validity and relevance of the kind of English Studies traditionally propagated in our universities. When the institution is a megalith and when the individual teachers have no say in framing the syllabus, in choosing the texts to be taught, or in organizing the evaluation system, we all have to devise our personal strategies for survival, our secret devices for making life meaningful to ourselves, if not to anyone else. For example, we could dislodge a text from the static context in which it is traditionally set and create dynamic new contexts for it. But these are entirely private enterprises. The other, more aggressive, way of tackling the problem is to try to restructure the syllabus, and that is a public act. We all know that in most Indian universities— and I have worked in five so far—syllabus change is a major operation; the process is elaborate and long-drawn, and the skills needed to be effective in policy-making are vastly different from what a serious teacher generally possesses. But we also know that while restructuring the syllabus is necessary, it is in itself no guarantee of injecting vitality into the system. As a token gesture towards making the literature syllabus 'relevant' to the Indian situation, some eighteen universities have introduced courses in Indian Writing in English. But judging by the syllabi and the question papers set for these courses (there are a fair sample in my collection) I do not see that these courses are doing anything radically different from the older ones. A text is a text is a text, and it is treated as a timeless artefact wrenched out of history. Raja Rao and R.K. Narayan are just new icons added to the pantheon of literary gods to whom our students are required to pay homage. A similar situation obtains in an area which is called Common-wealth Literature, and which is taught in no less than a dozen univer-sities in India. I have serious problems with the term 'Commonwealth Literature', though not with the fresh horizons it opens up. Here I will not get into the details of what I find unacceptable in the term and in the assumption that all non-British English literatures can be lumped to-gether as a single homogeneous entity. All I want to emphasize is that if a new syllabus only sets down a list of texts to be 'done' in class without offering any detailed statement of purpose and objective of the whole course, then, no matter what texts are chosen, one does not go very far from the fragmented, anaesthetized and merely textual approach that has prevailed in the classroom since the fifties, which taught the good student only to be a superior kind of ventriloquist.

After spending a good part of my teaching life in traditional univer-sities, where the syllabus is seen as an immutable document that is almost god-given, revealed once and for all, in 1979 I found myself in a more flexible system. This was at the new University of Hyderabad, and the English department—as indeed all other departments there—had only postgraduate and research programmes. There, among the sixteen courses to be studied by MA students, fifteen were designated by the title (Eighteenth Century Survey, Victorian Fiction, Modern British Poetry, etc.) but the course instructor had the freedom to choose the texts for the course and determine the format and emphasis so long as her plan was approved in the faculty meeting which, in those days, tended to be long and contentious. The sixteenth course was an open slot, with a long list of possible options printed in the syllabus. Each teacher could choose one out of these and teach a course that could be modified to suit her current research interest. An ideal situation, and after years of teaching in a college of Delhi University, and elsewhere, in similarly rigid situations, it seemed almost unreal. How best could I make use of this opportunity?

One of the options listed for this sixteenth course was 'Literature and Society'. I changed it to 'The Novel and Society' to make it more specific, and also because this genre was my special interest. I decided to use Indian texts for this course—not those written in English by Indians—but Indian language novels in English translation, as starting points of our investigations in class. Students were required to read a number of critical books which would provide the theoretical framework. The books listed in this category included those by Lukacs, Raymond Williams, and Lucien Goldman, and several anthologies of criticism that focused on the link between verbal text and social context. Students were also expected to make judicious use of the critical approaches they had earlier come across in their English literature courses. They were familiar, for example, with the work of Ian Watt, whom they had read for their eighteenth-century course, or that of Elaine Showalter, Susan Gubar and Sandra Gilbert, whom they had read for their Victorian fiction course. The general idea was that the new course would attempt to examine the relationship between literary texts and the social processes out of which they emerged.

Getting approval for the theoretical component in the course was easier than getting it for the other part, consisting of the texts. In the faculty meeting there was opposition to the idea of using translated texts in an English MA programme, an objection I was familiar with, because I had taught in Delhi University, where the syllabus-making body is well-known for its opacity on this question. For some reason these objections did not seem to apply with equal force to the teaching of Homer, Sophocles or Brecht. Once this battle was fought and won I was faced with the very practical problem of finding texts of novels in translation that would satisfy the following conditions:

(1) The text should be a major one within its tradition: seminal, formally or thematically significant and influential, lending itself to close analysis and multiple readings; and it should be available in English translation. In India what gets translated and what does not appears to be purely a matter of chance, because the novels seldom get talked about outside their own language constituencies. Most of the major novels from the Indian languages have not yet been translated into English. Locating the right texts for the course was thus the first major hurdle.

(2) The translation should be of a certain acceptable standard. Translation into English has generally been a rather uneven cottage industry in India, and ensuring quality is not easy. In some cases I was compelled to choose a novel that was essentially not major and not central only because the translation had a certain fluency and competence — *Chemmeen*, for example, or *The Wild Bapu of Garambi*.[1] I also wanted the translations not to be all from one or two languages. If the originals emerged from different regions, we could have a greater range of texts to compare and analyse against variations of social pattern. The availability from Bengali was the highest, but I had to look for less easily available novels from some other languages in order to make a balanced whole.

(3) The last and the most important consideration was that the translated text should be available in the market and at a price the students could afford. This is a crucial factor for selecting texts for any course, and I realized why certain standard English novels—and not others—are always prescribed at every university. On another occasion, for a Victorian literature survey course in which I wanted to emphasize certain issues pertaining to women, I tried prescribing Gissing's *The Odd Women* and Elizabeth Barret Browning's *Aurora Leigh*, but found them virtually impossible to obtain. For novels like *Oliver Twist* or *Silas Marner* a choice of editions exists, ranging from Norton editions or Penguin Classics to quite inexpensive local editions. The syllabus makers' decision is substantially affected by these material factors. *Pather Panchali*, a novel I chose for this course, was available in three different translations. I was forced to choose the one that was published in India (hence cheaper), rather than the decidedly better hardcover version published in London.

I taught this course for three years consecutively from 1981 to 1983. In the first year twelve students opted for the course and with some effort it was possible to manage with a few copies of each text and synchronize the reading schedule to allow time for the books to circulate. But in the subsequent years, when the number increased, this arrangement became virtually impossible. The problem of the non-availability of texts was most acute when it came to nineteenth-century novels. Bankimchandra Chatterjee is a major novelist of nineteenth-century India and I wanted to include him in the course, but among Bankim's fourteen novels only *Krishnakanter Will* was available in mod-

---

[1] The texts used for this course are listed at the end of this essay.

ern translation in an American edition.[2] It had to be imported through a friend's good offices and photocopied for the use of the students. From among the other Indian languages, only two nineteenth-century novels were available, and these were both from Malayalam: *Indulekha* by O. Chandu Menon and *Martanda Varma* by Ramana Pillai. The English translation of *Indulekha*, done by one of the author's British contemporaries the year after its publication, had fortunately been lately reprinted in Calicut, and the price was reasonable. The publishers were co-operative and sent copies promptly to the bookshop next to the university.

Incidentally *Indulekha* turned out to be an invaluable text for the purpose of tracing the relationship between a literary text and the society in which it is produced and read—both in its thematic concerns and the mode of representation—but these details are not part of the present discussion. Because of the paucity of nineteenth-century novels that were available I had to come to the twentieth century in search of texts. The most readily available novels were those by Rabindranath Tagore—in those archaic translations published by Macmillan which are unfortunately reprinted year after year without being revised. From the available range of Rabindranath's novels I chose *Gora* and, in spite of a highly uneven translation, it turned out to be a very discussable text in the classroom. It drew us into the non-literary discourses of nineteenth-century Bengal, because of the way the intellectual ferment of the time is woven into the questions of identity, religion and nationality to which the text addresses itself—questions that are in some way or other relevant even today. I can go on recounting the travails of choosing suitable texts, but will refrain here after mentioning that *Godan* had a fate similar to *Pather Panchali*; I had to choose the less satisfactory translation only because it was an Indian paperback and priced low.

The number of texts to be read in class varied from year to year. In the first year the students agreed to read twelve, which became some kind of a record, but in later years this number was reduced because the

---

[2] A number of Bankim's novels were translated in the late nineteenth and early twentieth centuries; none are easily available now. I have been able to trace: *Anandamath*, trans. as *The Abbey of Bliss*, Nareshchandra Sengupta, 1906; *Chandrashekhar*, trans. Dependra Chandra Mallik, 1905; *Krishnakanta's Will*, trans. Miriam S. Knight, 1895; *Visha Vriksha*, trans. as *The Poison Tree, a Tale of Hindu Life in Bengal* by Miriam Knight, with a Preface by Edwin Arnold, 1884; *Yugalanguriya*, trans. P.N. Bose and H.W.B. Moreno, 1918.

quantum of non-fictional reading in history, criticism and theory increased considerably. For a number of reasons, I preferred a larger number of texts than the four or five that are normally prescribed for a course on the novel. A society, at any given time, is characterized by a range and complexity of 'ideas, concepts, hopes, doubts, values and challenges in dialectical interaction with their opposites, serving towards plenitude'.[3] Focusing on just a few texts would assign to them an unwarranted centrality, obliterating in the process the contradictions as well as heterogeneity implicit in a culture. Since there was no well-tried-out canon in the area we were examining, I experimented by varying the texts from one year to the next.

Choosing the texts, writing a descriptive introduction outlining the scope and objective of the course, and providing a bibliography were the teacher's initial tasks. The next concern was how to get the greatest student involvement, and how to get out of the simple lecture method in order to open the texts, via simple lecture method, to the possibility of multiple meanings. The unilateral process which Freire termed 'the banking concept of instruction' —the professor depositing knowledge into the students—was not possible in this course, because it covered uncharted territory where we were compelled to make the maps as we went along, and this had to be a collaborative process.

We drew up a schedule for the whole forty-eight-hour class-time available to us during the semester, and each student opted to introduce one of the novels for discussion by raising the questions and isssues pertaining to it. In the first year this was an ideal arrangement because there were twelve texts and twelve students, and we had twelve weeks at our disposal. In the subsequent years two or more students got together for a joint presentation. Fifty per cent of the grading for the course depended on these presentations, combined with a term paper each student wrote on a different theme. The preliminary drafts of these term papers were read out to the class and discussed, after which the students revised them in the light of comments for written submission. The other fifty per cent of the final grade was decided—as was the custom in the university—by the end-semester examination. We had to arrange for separate sessions for the reading of the draft term papers, because the normal four hours a week did not suffice. In their term papers the students were free to choose texts from any culture they

---

[3] Paulo Freire, *Pedagogy of the Oppressed*, trans. Myra Berman Ramos (New York : Penguin Books, 1972), 73.

wanted—British, Russian, Nigerian, or whatever—but most of them preferred themes where the illustrative texts could be from India.

The lecture method was not abandoned altogether. I did lecture to them: so did other teachers who I roped in every now and then. Two colleagues, one from history, one from sociology, lent solid support. For two texts we had teachers from other literature departments come to our class and offer variant readings. Communication could have been a serious hurdle, but did not turn out so, because the people from the Urdu and Hindi departments who lectured on *Umrao Jan Ada* and *Godan,* respectively, chose to speak in a Hindustani accessible to most people in the class. At the end of the lectures the students asked questions in English or Hindi, and after a while this bilingual dialogue seemed quite a natural thing to happen. Another time a senior colleague from our own department offered a diametrically different interpretation of *Samskara* from what I had earlier attempted, and we argued about our positions in class, hoping the students would join in. They made no interventions at that time, but their discussions and arguments, I learnt, spilled over into the corridors and the canteen after the class ended.

I have no way of knowing whether, as an experiment, the course succeeded: only the students can judge that. Since I came with no previous expectation I had no reason to be disappointed. I learnt a few things in the process of teaching this course. For one thing, I found that when abstract ideas about society and literature become concrete in terms of a culture that they have first-hand exposure to, the students' responses grow more confident.

Second, because very little critical material interpreting these texts was available in English, the students showed more initiative in formulating connections and making observations than they would when they read, say, *Tess* or *Wuthering Heights.* While focusing attention on texts previously untried in the English classroom, and texts that are not circumambulated by critical discourse, it was possible to initiate a dialogic mode of study.[4]

---

[4] 'The pedagogical implication of dialogics seems to be that the unit of study should cease to be the isolated text (or author) and become the virtual space or cultural conversation that the text presupposes'. See Gerald Graff, *Professing Literature: An Institutional History* (Chicago: University of Chicago Press, 1987), 'Dialogic criticism . . . will not try to decide among . . . competing claims or to synthesize opposing theses but will try to imagine and enter their unrealized conversations'. Don H. Bialostosky, 'Dialogics as an Art of Discourse in Literary Criticism', *PMLA* 101 (1986): 792.

The University of Hyderabad being a central university, we had students from different regions of the country rather than only from the neighbouring areas, and this turned out to be an asset. Since the students had access to different languages, diverse social practices, and since some of them were familiar with as yet untranslated novels from several Indian languages, we had a rich pool of resources to draw from. While we were reading *Indulekha,* one of the students from Kerala volunteered to do some reading on the matrilinear system and inform the class about the power structure of the Nair *tharwad,* referring to other Malayalam novels in the process.

Incidentally, it seemed to me that students who had also read some literature in Telugu, Marathi or Bengali, or any other Indian language, were more open to all the texts even if these were not from their own linguistic region, than students whose reading had so far been limited to English literature alone, and who had never read an Indian text before. The response of the English-medium student and the mother-tongue-medium student often tended to be perceptibly different.[5] I would like to make an observation here about the response to one particular novel, *Pather Panchali.* I have also had occasion to teach this novel at an American university, and I find the American student—as well as the Indian student with a predominantly English literary orientation—tends to react sharply to the economic deprivation and poverty that led to Durga's death and Opu's displacement in the novel; whereas the more indigenous student—be she from Andhra Pradesh or Bengal or Kerala—tends to react to the other aspects of the novel, noticing not so much the poverty, which in any case is an ubiquitous presence in India, but, among other things, Opu's sense of joy and wonder at life, and the process of his imaginative growth.

[5] In this connection I would like to refer to a paper by Harish Trivedi, presented at a seminar in Delhi in 1990, in which he makes another point about non-English-medium students of English literature: 'Paradoxically, the profoundest and most enduring literary impact of English literature in India has been through non-English-medium readers/writers who have been firmly rooted in some other, Indian literature. English literature from Shakespeare to T.S. Eliot was eagerly received and creatively internalized by them in India between *circa* 1880 and 1940, and it has arguably transformed not only our literatures but our very notions, for example, of the self, of narrative and of modernity.' During the period Trivedi mentions, and possibly even afterwards, a large number of writers in the Indian languages were students, and subsequently teachers, of English literature.

One of the things I avoided in the course was to make formulations about the Indian novel as a whole, or hold forth on Indianness as a general entity—an issue that has come up with relentless regularity every time I have taught a course on Indian novels in English. The Indian writer who writes in English tends to be more self-conscious about his Indian identity than the Bengali or Hindi writer. What surfaces in Indian language novels—unlike in novels written in English—is the specificity and texture of daily life in a multilayered and heterogeneous society, and not larger colonial or neo-colonial concerns. If literature is part of the social process, then at any given moment the different elements that constitute the process may be comparable in different regions, and both the common patterns and the departures, as manifested in literary texts, are bound to be of interest to us in the larger cultural mosaic of our country—which too is constantly dissolving into new shapes. The attempt in the course that I taught was to proceed from the specific to the abstract, to examine the forces that shape the designs in this mosaic that we inhabit, taking into account the multiplicity of elements that go into the making of a specific text, and also to inquire into the way literature is constituted, and into how it differs from history.

Meenakshi Mukherjee's essay, above, is largely presented in the form in which she delivered it, as a paper at the Miranda House seminar on The Study of English Literature in India. Because of the great interest created by her description of her innovative course, The Novel and Society, a number of questions were put to her after her presentation. We therefore decided to expand the scope of her original paper by conducting the following interview. The questions were framed by the editor, under five broad categories, and Meenakshi Mukherjee provided the answers in writing.

I. PURPOSE OF THE COURSE

Q: You have stated the problems of the current situation of English literature as a subject, especially as it is taught in English departments in India. Did you see your course as offering some 'solutions'—and if so, how are the problems addressed? Secondly, how do you distinguish between the different pedagogic purposes of Indo-Anglian and Indian language-in-translation texts?

MM: In India, for nearly a century, the study of English literature was sacralized, as it were, by removing the entire canon of English literature—from Shakespeare, Milton and Coleridge down to T.S. Eliot—from its social formation, so that it remains pure and permanent, uncontaminated by ideology. New Criticism, which reigned supreme from the thirties to the fifties, and in whose afterglow my generation was brought up in India, tended to treat the literary text as an autotelic unit, isolating it from the complex non-literary co-ordinates of its production. This reinforced and strengthened pedagogic practices extant under the colonial education system, which invested English literature with universal values and a timeless human significance by disengaging it from the circumstances out of which the text has emerged as well as from the ethos in which it was being received.

In recent years this approach to literature has been subjected to some critical scrutiny. A consequence of this interrogation has been the partial dismantling of the rigid boundary between literature and what has traditionally been regarded as 'non-literature'. That colonial discourse can now be a legitimate part of English Studies, overlapping with the realm of History, and that the analysis of gender construction can be appropriated to some extent from Sociology, are two very obvious examples of this territorial expansion. English departments in certain American and British universities are broadening out to encompass Cultural Studies—including within its purview myth, oral narrative, folklore, film theory and even popular forms such as television, comics and pulp fiction. Such things can be done relatively easily in a monolingual culture. In India a similar expansion, though theoretically possible, would be strongly resisted in the English departments because the language of cultural transmission—whether it is high culture or popular culture that is sought to be transmitted—is seldom English. On purely linguistic grounds we tend to exclude a great deal that is vital and immediate if literature is to be seen as an intrinsic part and product of the culture we inhabit. My inclusion of Indian language novels in English translation in the course entitled 'The Novel and Society' was a small attempt to undo this rigid principle of exclusion.

Indians have been writing novels in English off and on for nearly a century. Could these have served my purpose in the course? I do not think so. My reasons for not including them in this course were several, the most arbitrary one being that the students get to read them, or at least know about them, far more easily because some of these novels are prescribed at various stages of their education from the secondary school onwards. But the more pertinent reason for me was that in a course called 'The Novel and Society' the texts written in English by Indians could not be treated in the same way as the novels written in

Bengali, Hindi or Malayalam, because of the very special and, in a sense, artificial, position English occupies in the socio-economic context of the country. Functional English percolates to many levels of life in India, but as a language of creative expression it is limited to the economic and cultural elite of the country.

Since we live in a multilingual society, our literature courses should make our students aware of this very important dimension of our cultural existence, rather then shut them off from it. There is a tendency among our 'good' English literature students to be oblivious of this polyphony, and to live in an illusory, unilingual world. An absurd corollary of this is the belief that 'literature'—meaning the kinds of texts that are analysable with the critical tools taught in the classroom—can only exist in English. I hoped this course, without making it a special issue, could indirectly contribute towards dispelling this unarticulated but widely-hold notion among Indian students of English literature.

II. THE QUESTION OF TRANSLATIONS

Q: 1. You say that what gets translated is a matter of chance, but you have also drawn attention to the 1889 translation of *Indulekha* by a British contemporary of Chandu Menon—so who translates what, and when, are facts, obviously, of some significance. Your preliminary search for texts must itself have thrown up a number of speculations on this subject. Did translation *itself* come up for discussion in the classroom— the actual translation of the text under consideration, or differences in translation, its ideology, its context?

2. There is your invocation of 'good' and 'bad' translations. What are the criteria involved in such discriminations? Does 'good' mean authentic? Close to the original? Or a good standard 'idiomatic' English style?

3. This is a chicken-and-egg question. You point out the paucity of translations as a constraint on syllabus selection, whereas publishers argue that it is academic demand that must stimulate the sluggish translation trade. Has the situation changed somewhat in the past two years, with the availability of more translations—from Penguin India and other new publishers, including women's presses?

4. Among the problems of designing—and then propagating—a course like this must be the rarity of a teacher acquainted with the whole *range* of Indian literatures, or possessing facility in several Indian languages. Your choice of texts could not have been based on a knowledge of only some (as you say, highly selective) texts available in English translation. Would you like to discuss this situation?

MM: Translation—its problems and concerns—was not the focus of this course, but inevitably these questions came up. Studying literature in a society in which linguistic plurality is the norm, we are naturally exposed to translation in its various forms, and it is therefore desirable that we become aware of the challenges and nuances of the task. Our students of English literature also read a considerable amount of European literature in translation, but when they read Kafka, or Dostoevsky, or Flaubert, they do not always seem aware of the fact that these works have also been rendered into English from other languages, and hence are vulnerable to the same distortions, loss or transformations that, say, a Hindi text translated into English is subject to. One of the by-products of this course turned out to be the development of a greater sensitivity in the students to this phenomenon.

Specific textual questions regarding actual translations also surfaced occasionally, specially because for two of the novels we were reading in class—*Godan* and *Pather Panchali*—more than one translation was available. By and large the consensus of the class was that the translator has no right to edit or abbreviate the original unless the omissions are explained and footnoted. Any simplification or dilution of the original for the sake of making the translation smooth or readable was also suspect, because of the implicit assumption that the reader of the translated version is not capable or worthy of entering into the cultural complexity or verbal density that gave the original its literary value. A certain degree of difficulty or strangeness of language seemed acceptable, so long as the effect was not achieved out of the translator's laziness or ineptitude. These were debatable issues, and unanimity was not always achieved even after lengthy discussions.

Most of the translations we used in class were far from perfect. There is a long and unfortunate tradition in India, for which Tagore may have been originally responsible, of the author translating his own books, or letting his well-meaning friends do this as an act of goodwill. This has prevented the growth of professionalism is this area. *Gora*, which in my opinion is a major and seminal Indian novel, has been the victim of this sort of kindly-intended mutilation in the available Macmillan translation. The translator's name has not been mentioned, but the translation has obviously been done by several hands. One of the translators decided, much to the mirth of my students, to refer to the wife of Paresh Babu, whose name is Varadasundari (pronounced Barodasundari in Bengali), as Mistress Baroda. Halfway through the novel, mercifully, another translator discontinued this usage. Such absurdities and inconsistencies are numerous in the present English version. Let us hope that in 1991 when Tagore's work goes out of copyright, more private enterprise will go into the publication of better and more modern translations of his novels.

Contemporary fiction from the Indian languages is not much better served by translation. A few publishing houses including Penguin India, have announced regular translation programmes, but some of their recent releases are merely reprints of old translations, as in the case of Bhisham Sahni's indifferently translated *Tamas*, which had an earlier life as *Kites Will Fly*. Since the target of most paperback publishers is generally the popular market, the texts chosen for translation tend to be topical or sensational. There has been no attempt as yet to produce annotated and well-edited translations of either significant contemporary classics, or older texts of the kind that could be used in the classroom.

The case of *Indulekha* remains atypical. Published in Malayalam in 1889, it was translated into English the following year by an Englishman who knew the author as a colleague. The English version has the author's preface, the translator's introduction, notes and appendices—in short, all the paraphernalia that make an older text useful to the present generation of readers, more so in our case because even the teacher did not have complete access to the original context of the novel.

This relates to the question you asked about the teacher's language competence. I think it is unreal to expect that whoever is teaching such a course should know all the languages from which the books are translated. In fact 'knowing' a language is rather an imprecise description and may not always mean the kind of discourse competence that would enable a person to place a novel in its literary, social and historical context. The teacher would necessarily have to depend on secondary sources—not only literary and social history—but critical studies which lie scattered in old issues of journals like *Indian Literature, Journal of South Asian Literature, Jadavpur Journal of Comparative Literature*, and now defunct periodicals like *Indian Writing Today* and *Vagartha*. I must also add that I sought and received considerable help from colleagues in other departments of literature in my own university, and some ambidextrous friends in other universities who are at home in two literatures.

III. STUDENT RESPONSES

Q: What is the significance of the student responses you have talked about—as well as the *variations* in student responses? How homogeneous is an Indian classroom—especially in a metropolitan/central university—in terms of regional and class composition? This relates also to the problem of how major and irreconcilable are regional differences *among* Indian literatures, and how these might affect students' responses. What is your experience of this?

MM: As every teacher knows, student response to the same course varies from year to year, and each year the course itself gets modified by the kind of dialogue that takes place in class. The classroom in the University of Hyderabad tended to be heterogeneous, consisting of students from many states in India. But the majority were from the southern states. The difference in attitudes, if any, was not between the north and the south, nor between metropolitan and non-urban students; sometimes it depended on whether the students had received their secondary-level education through the medium of English or through their mother tongue. The latter group were accustomed, from an early age, to reading books in a language that was not English, and seemed a little more willing to overlook syntactical lapses in order to get into the spirit of the novel, than were those students whose standards of English were perfected in English-medium public schools. I mention this difference only because you ask about the range of student responses, not to argue that tolerating infelicitous language is any special virtue.

IV. CRITICISM AND LITERATURE

Q: What were the critical tools used in this course? You mention certain (western) 'theoretical' texts which framed the reading of the texts. You also mention in passing an Indian aesthetics reader that would have been helpful had you known of it earlier. You regret in general the paucity of indigenous criticism. Is this because you felt the need for a radically different set of conceptual categories not available in western theory and criticism? How were these dissatisfactions articulated in the classroom? At the same time you also appear to feel that the historical/sociological approach obviates the need for purely theoretical models. Is this so?

MM: There was indeed a great shortage of published material that we could call upon as secondary sources, virtually no critical explications of the texts we could rely on, no available bibliographies to refer to. One positive result of this was a fairly active collaboration between the students and me, and lively discussions in the classroom. There is both a risk and an exhilaration that the teacher experiences when she finds herself learning from students. Students also may have experienced for themselves the excitement of testing the validity of the intellectual framework they were being asked to understand and examine.

This framework, as I have already pointed out, was not significantly different from what they would use in reading British, American, African or any other fiction. Apart from the books of theory mentioned earlier, we also looked at various anthologies that examined the relationship between literature and society, the most useful of which turned out to be one edited by Elizabeth and Tom Burns—I think entitled—*The Sociology of Literature and Drama*. There are many more books of this kind available now than there were at that time, and if I teach this course in the present decade the reading list is going to be substantially different.

You mention Indian aesthetics: if you are thinking of critics like Rajshekhara or Anandavardhana, I do not know how far they would have helped us analyse the complex correlations between ideology and practice that provide the context of literary production in colonial and post-colonial societies. I am willing to be corrected on this point, but what little exposure I have had to Indian aesthetics makes me believe that the application of these theories would be far more useful in the reading of poetry than in the analysis of narrative fiction. What I could have used much more systematically than I did were the occasional critical comments made by some nineteenth and twentieth-century Indian writers, but access to these remain limited because they are scattered in different places, and remain largely untranslated. Rajwade's essay on the mode of representation in Indian fiction was published in Marathi at the turn of the century, but became available to me through Shanta Gokhale's English translation much after I taught this course. Hazari Prasad Dwivedi was another person who thought about fiction, society and modes of narration, but his ideas remain dispersed in different essays in Hindi. There must be many seminal ideas thus available in different Indian languages which need to be put together after they have been translated into English, if we plan to devise similar courses in the near future.

Now that, in response to your question, I try to recount what critical material was available to us, the list does seem woefully inadequate. Some social and literary histories of India were recommended for reading, and I tried to put together in a file all the relevant journal articles and critical pieces that I could lay my hands on. Altogether quite meagre indeed, but neither I nor the students felt particularly handicapped at that time.

V. THE CONTEXT OF THE COURSE

Q: 1. One context—the immediate one—is, of course, the English literature programme as a whole. What connections can be made between
this course and the curricular context within which it was lodged?

2. The context you invoke in the designation of this course is 'society'
(also, implicitly, 'history'). Can you spell out some of the relationships—
and I am aware that these are not only of the text–context variety—that
operate between the novel and society?

3. As a curricular innovation how does this course 'fit' into the
requirements of say the UPSC (civil service) examinations, which so
many students sit for immediately after their MA? How did students
respond to something that may not have been 'useful' in this sense?

MM: The Indian students of MA English are not unfamiliar with the
novel as it evolved as a genre in England since the eighteenth century,
nor are they unaware of the links this genre had with changes in British
society. All that this course tried to do was to alter the cultural parameters of the study to bring it closer to the students' own history and
existential experience. There were consequent changes in emphases and
focus: we pondered over the differences in plot structures, modes of
representation, concepts of self and society, and the possible relation of
these with non-literary determinants, like the colonial history of the
subcontinent, the social hierarchy in traditions, communities, and the
epistemic frames that control values in a culture.

I am afraid I didn't give any thought to how the course would, as you
put it, 'fit' into the requirements of the UPSC exams, nor were the
students of the University of Hyderabad at that time very much oriented
towards these exams. I did not know, in any pragmatic sense, whether
students found this course useful; certainly they would not be required
to teach these texts in the colleges where they might get jobs. This was
an optional course, and the first batch of students could have warned
their successors about the non-utilitarian nature of the course if they had
wanted to. But in fact the number increased in the second year, and in
the third year all but three students in a class of twenty-five opted for
this course. Perhaps the novelty of the enterprise attracted them. I do not
think that everything taught in the MA class becomes immediately useful
to students in terms of their professions and daily tasks. Non-traditional
courses like these will not provide the students with any extra qualification in the present job market. But if they become aware of questions that
make the study of literature more meaningful and relevant to their lives,
the course would have served its purpose.

LIST OF NOVELS USED IN THE COURSE

Krishnakanter Will, Bankimchandra Chattopadhyay (Bengali) 1876, trans. J.C. Ghosh. New Directions, New York, 1962.

Indulekha, O. Chandu Menon (Malayalam) 1889, trans. W. Dumergue, 1890. Rpt. Matrubhumi Printing and Publishing, Calicut, 1965.

Umrao Jan Ada, Mirza Mohammad Hadi Ruswa (Urdu) 1899, trans. Khushwant Singh and MA Husaini. Sangam Books, New Delhi, 1982.

Gora, Rabindranath Tagore (Bengali) 1907. First trans. 1924, Rpt. many times, Macmillan, Delhi.

Pather Panchali, Bibhutibhushan Bandyopadhyay (Bengali) 1929. *The Song of the Road*, trans. T.W. Clark and Tarapada Mukherjee. George Allen and Unwin, London, 1968. *Pather Panchali*, trans. Monika Varma. 2 vols. Writers Workshop, Calcutta, 1978.

Godan, Prem Chand (Hindi) 1936, trans. P.Lal and Jai Ratan. Jaico, Bombay, 1957. *The Gift of a Cow*, trans. Gordon Rodarmel. Indiana University Press, Bloomington, 1968.

Putul Nacher Itikatha, Manik Bandyopadhyay (Bengali) 1936. *The Puppets' Tale*, trans. S.L. Ghosh, edited by Artur Isenberg. Sahitya Akademi, New Delhi, 1968.

Jagari, Satinath Bhaduri (Bengali) 1952. *The Vigil*, trans. Lila Ray. Asia Publishing, Bombay, 1965.

Arogyaniketan, Tarashankar Bandopadhyay (Bengali) 1958, trans. Enakshi Chatterjee. Arnold Heinemann, New Delhi, 1977.

Chemeen, Thakazhi Shivasankara Pillai (Malayalam) 1958, trans. Narayana Menon. Harper, New York, 1962. Rpt. Jaico, Bombay, 1968.

Farewell to the Gods (Marathi title not mentioned), D.B. Mokashi, 1958 (?), trans. Pramod Kale. Orient Paperbacks, Delhi, 1972.

Uska Bachpan, Krishna Baldev Vaid (Hindi) 1958. *Steps in Darkness*, trans. by the author. Orion Press, New York, 1962.

Garambicha Bapu, Shripad Pendse (Marathi) 1965. *The Wild Bapu of Garambi*, trans. Ian Raeside. Sahitya Akademi, New Delhi, 1969.

Samskara, U.R. Anantha Murthy (Kannada) 1965, trans. A.K. Ramanujan. OUP, New Delhi, 1976.

Amma Vantal, Janakiraman (Tamil) 1966. *The Sin of Appu's Mother*, trans. M. Krishnan. Hind Pocket Books, Delhi, 1972.

Chomana Dudi, K. Sivarama Karanth (Kannada) 1967. *Choma's Drum*, trans. U.R. Kelkur. Clarion Books, Delhi, 1978.

Kaadu, Srikrishna Alanhally (Kannada) 1972 (?). *The Woods*, trans. Rajeev Taranath. Vision Books, Delhi, 1979.

14

'History, Really Beginning' : The Compulsions of Post-colonial Pedagogy[1]

TEJASWINI NIRANJANA

I

In Michelle Cliff's novel *Abeng*, set in post-independence Jamaica, one of the crucial locations of subject-formation is the classroom.[2] Mr. Lewis Powell, the schoolmaster of the 'cement-block back room' attached to the stone church of the small market town of Black River, has been teaching pupils from six to fifteen years old in the same classroom for twenty-five years. The room possesses no blackboard, but the children have slates and pieces of chalk to write with. Mr Powell re-

---

[1] Vivek Dhareshwar's obsession with the West Indies led me to Caribbean literature, and helped me elaborate this paper's concerns. David Scott's friendship and generosity allowed me to hear some of these texts for the first time. I am also grateful to Susie Tharu, and my students at the University of Hyderabad, especially S.V. Srinivas. Thanks to Rajeswari Sunder Rajan for invaluable editorial assistance, and to Kumkum Sangari, Jasodhara Bagchi and Sibaji Bandyopadhyay for useful critical comments at the Jadavpur University Comparative Literature seminar on Colonialism and Literature, where this paper was first presented.

[2] Michelle Cliff, *Abeng* (Trumansburg, NY: 1984). For a discussion of the school as an apparatus of colonial power in Caribbean literature, see Vivek Dhareshwar, 'Self-Fashioning, Colonial Habitus and Double Exclusion: V.S. Naipaul's *The Mimic Men*', *Criticism*, vol. XXXI, no.1 (Spring, 1989), 73-102.

ceives teaching manuals from the governor's office, which in turn obtains them from the education department of the colonial office in London. The manuals stress reading, writing, simple arithmetic, the history of the English monarchs, and the history of Jamaica as it pertained to England.

The manuals also contained instructions for teaching literature: Mr. Powell was told to have the younger children read poems by Tennyson, the older ones, poems by Keats—'supplied herewith'. To see that all in the school memorized the 'Daffodils' poem by William Wordsworth, 'spoken with as little accent as possible; here as elsewhere, the use of pidgin is to be severely discouraged'. The manual also contained a pullout drawing of a daffodil, which the pupils were 'encouraged to examine' as they recited the verse.

Mr. Powell received the exact same manuals year after year. For twenty-five years he had been told in the same words and by the same methods what he was expected to impart to his students ...

The manuals were oblivious to any specific facts about the nature of Mr. Powell's class. No doubt the same manuals were shipped to villages in Nigeria, schools in Hong Kong, even settlements in the Northwest Territory—anywhere that 'the sun never set', with the only differences occurring in the pages which described the history of the colony in question as it pertained to England.

Probably there were a million children who could recite 'Daffodils', and a million who had never actually seen the flower, only the drawing, and so did not know why the poet had been stunned. (84-5)

Later in the novel, Kitty, one of the protagonists, thinks about the time when she used to go to school:

The only thing English that Kitty remembered from Mr. Powell's school was that silly poem 'Daffodils', about a flower she had never seen, which he had made them learn by heart, and one of the children had colored a deep red like a hibiscus. The red of a flame. (129)

II

This paper has its beginnings in a course I offered two years ago, almost by default, on African and Caribbean literature. Before this I had taught, among other things, traditional English literature, especially the works of those figures inextricable from the very name of 'poetry' or 'literature' in our context—Wordsworth, Keats, Shelley and company.

We are familiar with the angst of the English teacher who, like Mr Powell but perhaps in more exalted surroundings like the university, is compelled to discuss daffodils, interminably. One could, I suppose, change that verb 'discuss' to 'deconstruct' in order to alleviate the angst and provide a grander self-description for the task of the teacher. One could also thereby bring to visibility the traces of colonial discourse from Shakespeare to Conrad, using the techniques of post-structuralism in combination with the historical materialism of critics like Raymond Williams. Given a good library and some initiative, it is not too difficult to produce this kind of reading of canonical English texts. Neither is it impossible to unearth texts which have been excluded from the canon, and make a case for putting them in. If the institutional set-up and resources permit innovation, it may even be possible, for example, to have students of Romanticism read broadsheets, folk-songs, letters and evangelical tracts along with *The Prelude* or *The Ancient Mariner*, so that their notion of what constitutes legitimate subject-matter for Eng. Lit. is at least temporarily widened.

Reading English texts through *their* history, however, has been made increasingly possible only by research undertaken, and techniques honed, in the metropolitan countries, since 'original' work in the area by scholars living in the third world is hampered by severely restricted access to metropolitan archives. In any case, we should ask what we accomplish by a historical materialist reading of canonical texts—a project which is ultimately limited by its very 'safeness'—unless we can make visible the mutually intersecting histories of those texts/worlds and ours. Some English teachers in India, if only at the university level, who are fortunate enough to be able to make a 'choice' in the matter, have seen the study of and research into what has been obnoxiously termed 'Commonwealth Literature' as an alternative means of coping with their post-colonial situation. Very often, however, 'Commonwealth' writing helps merely to swell the canon and provide another set of recuperative and assimilative readings which emphasize the 'universality' and 'timeless concerns' of the texts. In its unproblematic coalescing of Australian, Canadian, West Indian, African and Indian writing as equally post-colonial, the field of Commonwealth Literature occludes by the very principles of its constitution the asymmetrical relations of power between metropolitan countries and the so-called third world. It is only too obvious that, although there are some non-Western scholars working in the area, institutional power in the field of Commonwealth Literature rests with the metropolitan countries. Witness the proliferation of numerous Western 'experts' on third world texts (as on third world politics).

What might appear as a challenge to the existing canon of English Studies is effectively domesticated in English departments through 'compulsory' courses in Commonwealth Literature, which now has a canon of its own, constituted according to the strictest criteria of sophistication, complexity and multi-layeredness (often merely asserted but sometimes demonstrated by means of the most impeccable New Critical and nowadays post-structuralist techniques). The point I am trying to make is that hardly anyone questions the *need* for a canon of great texts and consequently the compulsion to teach it in a particular way. The demand to be included or accommodated within the existing paradigm obviously does not pose any kind of threat to the paradigm itself, since it never questions the criteria which determine exclusion in the first place. We must ask, therefore, *how* one reads or teaches, for a questioning of the need for a canon will lead inevitably to the question of what one looks for in a text, or rather how one weaves a text into classroom practice. My argument is that while we *must* insist on teaching non-metropolitan texts, we should resist their incorporation into the canon by refusing to employ customary ways of reading.

In the course I taught, I had included some West Indian poetry and a play (Derek Walcott's *Pantomime*), Wole Soyinka's *Death and the King's Horseman*, and Chinua Achebe's *Things Fall Apart*. As pre-reading for the course, I had assigned a chapter from Edward Said's *Orientalism*, extracts from Aime Cesaire's *Discourse on Colonialism* and Albert Memmi's *The Colonizer and the Colonized*, a chapter from Ngugi wa Thiongo's *Decolonising the Mind*, Gabriel Garcia Marquez's Nobel Prize lecture, 'The Solitude of Latin America', Salman Rushdie's essay, 'Outside the Whale', and Chinweizu on the *West and the Rest of Us*. Although I had attempted to teach English literature along the lines suggested by materialist critics, and also in other ways that might undermine New Critical obsessions with the words on the page, I was quite unprepared for the challenges presented by the West Indian and African texts. I am not suggesting that some intrinsic quality in these texts prompted certain kinds of readings. That would be to capitulate once more to the tyranny of the iconic text and its hermetic closures. Rather, the questions we were preparing to ask, or reiterate, in our own post-colonial context seemed to come into a particular conjuncture with these Caribbean or African works to produce the readings in my class that were political rather than aesthetic. Our questions, or the coinciding of our 'interests' with those of other third world writers, had to do with the critique of colonialism, the formation of identity and the assertion of what Frantz Fanon called national culture, the attempt to recover lost traditions or to rewrite history, the politics of language in the colonial and post-colonial contexts, the problem of subject-formation and education, and the tradition versus modernity debate centred around the status of the West and the Rest.

The conjuncture of text and questions confronted me with pedagogic choices which were ultimately choices of theory as well. The fact that the West Indian poets, novelists and playwrights, for example, seemed to be attempting to write 'a history of the present'[3] meant that we could not simply see 'history' as yet another theme in their work, although the reduction to thematic analysis and consequently the production of the self-contained text are very often tied up with the anxiety to explain, to close or to conclude that is an imperative of the classroom rather than of literary theory. Students often get justifiably impatient with what they see as vacillation or indecisiveness (what theorists call 'indeterminacy'), demanding instead a total accountability.

Even as we risked papering over real differences between the complex negotiations of specific societies with their particular pasts, our awareness of a shared history, and our appreciation of the attempts to come to terms with colonialism forced our attention away from the aesthetic to the political dimension in reading the third world texts, making us seek assonance and dissonance not in poetic form but in the realm of culture, politics and history. To put it somewhat differently, the weight of interpretive traditions which for metropolitan texts offer structures and allusions stemming from genre rather than world did not overdetermine our strategies of reading these Caribbean and African texts, enabling us instead to place the text more firmly amidst material and social practices instead of in a purely literary tradition.

III

Using examples from some of the West Indian texts read in the course, I shall try to suggest what prompts the post-colonial conjunctures I have referred to. In the work of playwright and poet Derek Walcott, for instance, we encounter a notion of history which is linked to the question of what V.S. Naipaul has made notorious as 'mimicry'. For Naipaul, 'nothing has ever been created in the West Indies, and nothing will ever be created'.[4] He condemns the West Indian, and by extension all post-

---

[3] The phrase is from Michel Foucault, *Discipline and Punish: The Birth of the Prison* (Harmondsworth: 1982), 31.

[4] Quoted in Derek Walcott, 'The Caribbean: Culture or Mimicry?', *Journal of Inter-American Studies and World Affairs*, 16:1 (February 1974), 8-9; henceforth CM.

colonial subjects, to imitation, lack of originality and mimicry. In response, Walcott suggests that 'Nothing will always be created in the West Indies, for quite a long time, because what will come out of there is like nothing one has ever seen before'.[5] Walcott argues that mimicry is 'an act of imagination', perhaps even of 'endemic cunning'.[6] It is, therefore, both 'defense' and 'lure'. Mimicry is a matter of repetition, but not of the same, since all creation is repetition. One cannot say that the New World imitates the Old World, for there is 'no line in the sea which said, this is new, this is the frontier, the boundary of endeavour, and henceforth everything can only be mimicry'.[7] Walcott's prodigious energies are poured into a devastating critique of what he calls the 'anthropological' notion of mimicry. How do we deal with a question like 'When did the ape become human?' What can we do, he asks, with the image of the last   ape applauding the first man? Science cannot distinguish between 'the last ape and the first man', and since there is no 'memory or history of the moment when man stopped imitating the ape', 'everything is mere repetition'.[8] Likewise, there is no memory of the moment when the Old World person (the African slave, for example), crossed over to the other side of the mirror so that every action of his or her now became 'a parody of the past', an imitation.

In the character of the ex-calypsonian Jackson in the play *Pantomime* (1980), Walcott expands this notion of mimicry and its connection to a practice of writing history.[9] Set in post-colonial Tobago, *Pantomime* has for its protagonists a British hotel owner, Harry Trewe (formerly a music-hall actor), and his West Indian servant Jackson Phillip. The tourist season is beginning, and Harry wants to set up some entertainment for the guests. He proposes a pantomime about Robinson Crusoe, with himself as Crusoe and Jackson as Friday. Walcott's play teeters precariously between farce and seriousness, between a complete dismissal of 'history' and a persistent questioning of it. Jackson the servant is in no way overawed by his white master, yet he constantly draws the attention of the audience to the relationship between colonizer and colonized. As they rehearse for the pantomime, Jackson improvises some dialogue—Friday to Crusoe:

[5] CM, 9.
[6] Ibid., 10.
[7] Ibid., 8.
[8] Ibid., 7.
[9] *Remembrance and Pantomime : Two Plays* (New York : 1980).

Jackson (giggling):

For three hundred years I served you. Three hundred years I served you breakfast in ... my white jacket on a white veranda, boss, bwana, effendi, bacra, sahib ... in that sun that never set on your empire I was your shadow, I did what you did, boss, bwana, effendi, bacra, sahib ... that was my pantomime. Every movement you made, your shadow copied ... (stops giggling)

and you smiled at me as a child does smile at his shadow's helpless obedience, boss, bwana, effendi, bacra, sahib, Mr. Crusoe. Now ... (trancelike drone)

But after a while the child does get frighten of the shadow he make. He say to himself, That is too much obedience, I better hads stop. But the shadow don't stop, no matter if the child stop playing that pantomime, and the shadow does follow the child everywhere; when he praying, the shadow pray too, when he turn round frighten, the shadow turn round too, when he hide under the sheet, the shadow hiding too. He cannot get rid of it, no matter what, and that is the power and black magic of the shadow, boss, bwana, effendi, bacra, sahib, until it is the shadow that start dominating the child, it is the servant that start dominating the master ...

(laughs maniacally)

and that is the victory of the shadow, boss.

(normally)

And that is why all them Pakistani and West Indians in England, all them immigrant Fridays driving you all so crazy. And they go keep driving you crazy till you go mad. In that sun that never set, they's your shadow, you can't shake them off. (112-13)

At one point, when Jackson kills the hotel parrot—he says it choked on prejudice—and throws it at Harry's feet, Harry proclaims that shadows can only imitate. It's been done before, in *The Seagull*, in *Miss Julie*; there's nothing original in the gesture. Does the feeling of belatedness, I asked my students, produce both imitation and original? Does the sense of inferiority and repetitiveness result from an acceptance of the historiography of colonialism? And is the seemingly identical gesture in a completely different historical context exactly the same gesture?

Although Jackson is more interested in dramatizing the politics of the present, what the colonized sometimes do in response to the assault on their history is to assert the glories of their civilization and demand a return to the past. But, says Walcott, 'a return is ... impossible, for we cannot return to what we have never been'.[10] We have no way of

[10] CM, 7.

establishing what really happened, no way of determining the purity of origins. To search for one's history is to confront the 'Medusa of the New World', which paralyses the post-colonial into inaction.[11] To avoid being limited to condemnation or justification (attitudes forced on us by traditional modes of writing history, according to Walcott), the West Indian must see the 'degraded arrival' of the slaves in the New World as 'the beginning, not the end of our history',[12] an idea shared perhaps by another West Indian writer, Edward Kamau Brathwaite, whose major collection of poems is titled *The Arrivants*. It is not Crusoe or Columbus who kneels on New World soil and makes it holy, for to accept this vision of history is to proclaim unproblematically the virtues of progress:

The vision of progress is the rational madness of history seen as sequential time, of a dominated future. Its imagery is absurd. In the history books the discoverer sets a shod foot on virgin sand, kneels, and the savage also kneels from his bushes in awe. Such images are stamped on the colonial memory . . . these hieroglyphs of progress are basically comic. History-as-Enlightenment or as Progress can be written only through the construction of a homogeneous Other who can be inserted into that history. Only by writing this kind of history can colonialism create the original as well as the imitation.[13]

As Jackson's repartee demonstrates, the miming of the images of progress transform them into ludicrous emblems of colonial domination. Mimicry becomes a weapon that ridicules and subverts even as it repeats. As George Lamming shows us, Caliban appropriates the language of Prospero 'as Prospero, and appropriated his labour, thinking to appropriate his being', not realizing that Caliban survives, changing forever the meaning of Prospero's language.[14] What Walcott's notion of mimicry helps reveal is the pomposity of the concept of originality, which is seen as a prerogative of the first world. Once we stop seeing history merely as 'progress', perhaps we can also begin to perceive the historicity of 'originality', to see its complicity with projects of colonial domination. History in the old sense is 'irrelevant' in the Caribbean, says Walcott, 'not because it is not being created, or because it was sordid; but because it has never mattered'.[15] What does matter now is the need for

---

[11] Walcott, 'The Muse of History', in *Is Massa Dead?*, ed. Orde Coombs (New York : 1974), 2. Hereafter MH.

[12] MH, 6.

[13] Ibid., 6.

[14] George Lamming, *The Pleasures of Exile* (1960; rpt. London : 1984), *passim*.

[15] CM, 6.

amnesia, for the loss of history, which would enable 'imagination' as 'invention'.[16] I do not think Walcott is arguing simply for an erasure of the past; rather, in using the trope of amnesia, he seems to refer to the futility of recovering the past as it really was, a task that doesn't matter because it isn't possible. Surely the post-colonial needs history, but history that enables, that does not cripple. Positing a monolithic, homogeneous cultural identity would curtail possibilities instead of opening them up. Which is why Walcott is intent on showing the diffusion and heterogeneity of origins, demonstrating not what Foucault would call 'inviolable identity' but the 'dissension of other things' and their 'disparity'.[17] At least this is what Walcott constantly does in his poetic practice, searching for 'descent', not in order to erect 'foundations', but to fragment 'what was thought unified' and show 'the heterogeneity of what was imagined consistent with itself'.[18]

The recognition that there is no single ancestor, no single origin, and therefore no single history is the contention of the nation-language poet Louise Bennett.[19] Let me quote a poem by her in full to show the relentless logic of her satire:

BACK TO AFRICA

Back to Africa Miss Matty?
Yuh no know wa yuh dah sey?
Yuh haffe come fron some weh fus,
Before yuh go back deh?

Me know sey dat yuh great great great
Gramma was African,
But Matty, doan yuh great great great
Grampa was Englishman?

Den yuh great granmada fada
By yuh fada side was Jew?
An yuh grampa by yuh mada side
Was Frenchie parley-vous!

But de balance a yuh family

---

[16] Ibid.

[17] Michel Foucault, 'Nietzsche, Genealogy, History', in *Language, Counter-Memory, Practice*, trans. Donald F. Bouchard (Ithaca, NY: 1977), 142. Henceforth NGH.

[18] NGH, 147.

[19] *Jamaica Labrish* (1966; rpt. Jamaica: 1989).

Yuh ole generation
Oonoo all bawn dung a Bun grung
Oonoo all is Jamaican!

Den is weh yuh gwine Miss Matty?
Oh, you view de countenance,
An betweens yuh an de Africans
Is great resemblance!

Ascorden to dat, all dem blue-eye
Wite American,
Wa great grampa was Englishman
Mus go back a Englan!
Wat a debil of a bump-an-bore,
Rig-jug an palam-pam!
Ef de ole worl' start fe go back
Weh dem great granpa come form!

Ef a hard time yuh dah run from,
Teck yuh chance, but Matty, do,
Sure a weh yuh come from so yuh got
Someweh fe come back to!

Go a foreign, seek yuh fortune,
But no tell nobody say
Yuh dah go fe seek yuh homelan
For a right deh so yuh deh![20]

The idea of an authentic past or an inviolate origin is shown to be an impossible fiction for anyone who takes history seriously.

In the poem 'Names', Walcott talks of how his race 'began as the sea began,/with no nouns, and with no horizon'.[21] 'Have we melted into a mirror,/leaving our souls behind?' he asks, 'The goldsmith from Benares,/the stonecutter from Canton,/the bronzesmith from Benin'. The West Indian is cut off from the past:

Behind us all the sky folded,
as history folds over a fishline,
and the foam foreclosed
with nothing in our hands
but this stick

---

[20] Ibid., 214-15.
[21] *Collected Poems* (New York : 1986), 305-8. Hereafter CP.

to trace our names on the sand
which the sea erased again, to our indifference.[22]

It is perhaps the same sea which is the 'grey vault' enclosing all the martyrs and monuments and battles of the West Indian, 'Bone soldered by coral to bone,/mosaics/mantled by the benediction of the shark's shadow' during the Middle Passage, in the poem 'The Sea is History'. The tragedies and devastations of colonial history are, in Walcott's Biblical parody, not History but Lamentations, or the New Testament, or Emancipation. It is only now, in the midst of the bellowing bullfrogs, 'the mantis, like khaki police' and 'the furred caterpillars of judges', only now

. . . in the salt chuckle of rocks
with their sea pools, there was the sound
like a rumour without any echo

of History, really beginning.[23]

As the poet and historian Edward Brathwaite puts it,[24]

. . . we who have achieved nothing
work
who have not built
dream
who have forgotten all
dance
and dare to remember

the paths we shall never remember
again . . .[25]

Just as Walcott believes that the challenge to the old way of writing history will aid the West Indian 'in the arduous enunciation of a dimmed alphabet, in the shaping of tools, pen or spade', which is indicated by 'the whole, profound sigh of human optimism, of what we in the archipelago still believe in: work and hope': 'It is out of this', says Walcott, 'that the New World, or the Third World, should begin'.[26]

---

[22] Ibid., 306.
[23] 'The Sea is History', ibid., 367.
[24] *The Arrivants* (Oxford : 1973). Hereafter TA.
[25] TA, 13.
[26] CM, 13.

IV

If we were to speculate briefly on what attracted late-twentieth-century Indian students to these Caribbean texts, we might be too hasty in saying it's a question of simple identification. What the students saw here was the possibility of reading differently, a possibility opened up both by these texts and by the questions we put to them. While the texts extended and illuminated our concerns, our readings allowed us to see how our concerns might be somewhat different. Although the unique experience of colonization in the West Indies, manifested for example in the question of language, precluded what I have called simple identification, the issues addressed by Walcott and others put under interrogation our own understanding of the problem of the past and the homogeneity of origins. Most crucially, since the characterization of the third world as the realm of imitation is deeply formative of our very subjectivity, we felt it important to speculate on and challenge the notions of originality and mimicry.

At the research level, more and more 'bright' students are turning to Indian, African and Caribbean literature—the young middle- and upper-middle-class women who are traditionally English department students, as well as young men, mostly from relatively underprivileged backgrounds, who don't seem to feel oppressed by third world texts, as they do by metropolitan ones. They are beginning to believe, as one student expressed it, that their knowledge need not be discounted in their engagement with texts. 'What more can you say about *The Waste Land* ', he said. 'You are told exactly what to think. But in the case of non-Western literature, the possibilities are immense.'

Hitherto, the attraction of metropolitan texts for students was to be located in their signaling of a culture, the most trivial manifestations of which tended to become the objects of our most inarticulable desires. To put it differently, the hankering after electronic gadgets and foreign cosmetics is transfigured, in the realm of art and literature, into the longing for Impressionist prints or a theatre programme from Stratford-on-Avon. Reading Joyce's *Ulysses* or Eliot's *Four Quartets* sets us apart, and above, those who are dying for a bottle of Chanel perfume, even as we fail to recognize that we participate in the same economy of desire and fantasy, dream the same dreams of the metropolis, share the same striving for 'distinction'. In the nineties, however, with the rapid expansion of the Indian middle class and the greater availability of consumer goods, the old displacement of desire from the economic to the cultural

realm doesn't function in quite the same way. Consequently, the metropolitan texts seem to be losing their strength as cultural signifiers, or as
cultural products scored through with the economic.

Increasingly, students seem unwilling to be disempowered by metropolitan texts, for the cultural aggressiveness of the Indian middle classes
is turning them—as they constitute themselves as, and create, new
markets—towards non-Western texts in search of legitimation. It would
be misleading, however, to see the attraction for third world texts as
motivated merely by a politically dubious neo-nationalism. The texts are
read and refracted in directions which exceed the attempted appropriation by contemporary nationalism, and are prompting English department students to question not only their own position of privilege but
also the exalted status of their discipline in our post-colonial setting.

Some argue that we should be suspicious of third world texts that are
becoming available to us only because of the metropolitan rapid-growth
industry promoting cultural difference. But to say that we won't read
Ngugi or Brathwaite because they are published by Heinemann or OUP
is a poor kind of choice, for our own engagement with these texts cannot
be totally controlled by metropolitan publishing imperatives. Another
problem is that the lack of access to the histories of Africa or the
Caribbean might lead to an easy domestication of their texts. While it is
important to teach third world texts in *their* histories (and the accumula-
tion of material would be slow but not impossible), I would contend that
not having ready access to the histories is no reason for refusing to teach
the texts. Given the global spread of colonialism, systems of domination
have often been structurally similar, and their representations in literary
texts are capable of being compared. That third world texts compel
students to foreground the political is surely, at least, a beginning. When
we make the demand for African or Caribbean history, what we come
up against is our enormous ignorance about these areas. And, as students discover, it is not an ignorance that can be overcome by merely
checking out the appropriate books from the library. In the first place,
very little relevant material is available; in the second place, even what
exists has been produced in the metropolis, and is structured by its
needs and anxieties. Confronting this appalling lack of material, I think,
allows us to ask questions regarding the production and dissemination
of knowledge about the third world, while it also forces us to devise
alternative lines of communication, however limited.

Perhaps what we need to ask, in the phrase made famous by Ngugi
and others at the University of Nairobi, is whether English departments

should be abolished.[27] Since most of us are not in positions of institutional power that would make such a move possible in the near future, perhaps we need to be asking *what* it is we want to teach in English departments and *how* we can teach it. I believe a study of some Caribbean and African texts, not to mention Indian writing in translation and in English, would raise significant questions for both literary theory and pedagogic practice. The whole ambivalent enterprise of teaching English in India could perhaps be re-evaluated, deflected and re-inflected through the reading of post-colonial texts. The challenge to English literature in our cultural context needs to be seen as part of a larger process of critical evaluation and the creation of resources. The task is going to be complicated, the questions difficult to formulate, calling for a new kind of construction.

Here is a poem by Dennis Scott that seems to point towards the nature of the task:

CONSTRUCTION 12

Sometime in de greathouse wall
is like a thumb mark de stone,
or a whole han.
Granny say is de work sign, she say
it favor when a man tackle de stone, an mek
to tear it down, till de mortar tek de same shape
as him han. But I feel say
is like sumaddy push de wall up
an hole it dere until de brick dem dry
out. Now dat is hard.[28]

[27] Ngugi wa Thiong'o, *et al.*, 'On the Abolition of the English Department', in Ngugi, *Homecoming* (1972; Westport, 1983).
[28] *Uncle Time* (Pittsburgh : 1973), 12.

15

Dissimilar Twins: Language and Literature

RUKMINI BHAYA NAIR

Academic disciplines, as we know, progress by policing their boundaries. Although interdisciplinary work is currently fashionable, a great deal of such activity is predicated on the recognition of territorial differences. The goals, problems, methods, and consequently the ideologies, of literary criticism and linguistics appear so (distressingly) divergent that any attempt to bring them together seems doomed to failure. Literary criticism, with English literature as its prototypical object of study, has had a distinguished pedigree in India; its aristocratic status is attested by the hierarchies that it has spawned. Linguistics, on the other hand, an upstart discipline by all accounts, apparently offers just a crude bag of tricks, which temporarily may amuse, but hardly can impress, the sophisticated *afficionados* of literature.

This paper will not try to unpack that poor prestidigitator's apparatus.[1] It will resist the temptation to put on display the contributions to contemporary analyses of style made by Jakobson, Halliday, Sinclair, Burton, Austin, Searle, Wilson and a good many other linguists as well as philosophers of language. Distinguished as these thinkers are, it is difficult to place their innovations in perspective until the uneasy relationship between literary and linguistic studies is explored in more

[1] A version of this paper was read at the British Council–Jawaharlal Nehru University seminar entitled 'Perspectives on the Teaching of English Literature in Indian Universities', held in Delhi from 29 April to 3 March 1990. However, the paper appears in print here for the first time.

excruciating detail. The Indian subcontinent has had a great tradition in which theories of grammar have come excitingly close to being theories of text.[2] Yet the works of Bhartrhari, Panini or Abhinavagupta are as marginal to the teaching of English literature in our universities as are the ideas of the present day linguists mentioned earlier. This is especially surprising when we recall that several of the conundrums we fail to resolve in our English literature courses are specifically linguistic in nature. Linguistic competence,[3] however vexed the definition of this phrase, is a necessary, though not sufficient, condition for literary immersion. However, we all agree that language proficiency in English is obviously not to be ideologically equated with fluency in Gujarati, Tamil or even another foreign European language like German. English was a colonial and is now an elite tongue; it is a conduit to power, influence and the dominant 'Western world'. Any *literature* that is premised on prior knowledge of so privileged a *language* is bound to have problematic implications. Readings of great, 'universal' texts such as those of Shakespeare and Dickens are constrained by the linguistic contexts in

[2] Grammars of languages are in general kept rigidly separate from grammars of text or discourse in modern Western linguistics. In fact, many mainstream linguists today would vehemently deny that there can *be* an abstract grammar modelling discourse structure. The tradition of Indian linguistics seems to have followed a less compartmentalized ideology; it had extremely sophisticated grammatical rules, comparable in some ways to the arsenal of current linguistics, but nevertheless appeared to combine notions relating to 'text grammar' with those relating to 'sentence grammars'. As J.E.B. Grey puts it, supporting his argument from the *Mahabhasya* and the *Paniniyasiksa*, '*homo phoneticus indicus* was no mere cross-sectioned larynx sited under an empty cranium . . . ; on the contrary, the whole man, belly, head and heart, produced voice.' See *Bulletin of the School of Oriental and African Studies* 22 (1959). The possibilities of this 'holistic' perspective, attributed to ancient Indian linguistics, may be worth investigating in our present approaches to critical theory.

[3] Chomsky introduced this phrase in *Aspects of the Theory of Syntax* (M.I.T. Press : 1965), making a distinction between grammatical 'competence', which is part of intrinsic human ability, and 'performance', which differs from individual to individual, community to community. According to Chomsky, a linguist is primarily concerned with explaining the former, abstract ability, but there is considerable disagreement among linguists on the validity of Chomsky's views. Compare also Saussure's similar langue/parole distinction, and see above on the difference between sentence grammars and text-grammars.

which they occur. When a multicultural society fails to exploit, indeed suppresses, its many languages in order to respond appropriately to a particular literary tradition, then that literature, whatever its intrinsic merit, however seductive its grace, is as alienating as the language in which it is written. In post-colonial societies, linguistic dilemmas logically precede literary ones; and it is for this reason that the present paper examines literary issues from a linguistic standpoint.

Ground-clearing is essential before path-breaking can begin; but, like most essays that start from first principles, and assume, moreover, a programmatic (pro-grammatical?!) stand, this one runs the risk of being both irritating and dull, since it must state the obvious in order to understand the obscure. In the following paragraphs, I will attempt to (a) categorize some traditional *functions* of literary criticism; (b) describe these functions further as *modes of response* to literary texts; (c) argue that a *systematic set of contrasts* found between literary modes and linguistic methods reveals the distinct *ideological orientations* of the two disciplines; (d) discuss possible ways in which the ideological presuppositions of linguistics, as well as its analytic tools, may be used to teach English literature in a more precise, conscious, and therefore perhaps *politically liberated*, space.

In my treatment of (a) and (b), that is, the functions and modes of literary criticism, I will invoke two familiar Shakespearean metaphors—the monument and the stage. Literary texts (past, present, potential) may be visualized easily as *monuments* for which literary critics make themselves professionally responsible. The critical community, which I will compare to a well-trained, informed, and superior *best audience*, is taken to fulfil several functions. My somewhat idiosyncratic effort at characterizing and systematizing these functions is presented below.

1. SIGN-POSTING — pointing to the monument, telling others about the text

2. EXPLAINING — elucidating mysteries, interpreting, teaching the text

3. PRESERVING — restoring the monument, canonizing the text

4. COMPARING — evaluating, contrasting relative textual merits

5. DEFINING — theorizing about the text, formulating ISMS

6. DISCOVERING — finding new monuments, adding to the canon

7. DESTROYING — erasing claims of canonical status, discouraging audiences/readership

8. EMULATING — becoming the monument itself, being, replacing the text

Any paradigmatic characterization, such as the eight-point charter just sketched, is likely to border on parody, be 'parodygmatic' in fact. But caricature serves certain ends better than a likeness. From the list of critical functions, a number of inferences can be drawn.

First, as the conical representation insinuates, by far the largest number of literary critics perform deictic and guiding functions. Teachers of English in Indian universities, as elsewhere, generally situate themselves in relation to function 2 but, since this pedagogic activity naturally involves some theorizing as well as some evaluative criteria, they are often comfortable with all the functions 1–5. Indeed, it is on the interestingly ambiguous area occupied by function 5 that I believe we must focus attention, because there are good grounds for assuming, in the terminology of Catastrophe Theory,[4] a 'structural break' in this region, the region of theory. For pedagogic purposes, 'ISMS' initially formulated by others in different contexts (new criticism, poststructuralism, as well as theories in the traditions of Indian poetics), may apparently be painlessly borrowed in the service of this fifth function. But painless borrowing, as modern economics has taught us, often leads to a debt-trap and to a crisis of confidence. Not only does theoretical borrowing in a merry *ad hoc* manner possibly indicate intellectual dependence, it constitutes 'theorizing' only in a very feeble sense, if at all. In fact, such theoretical weakness, if it continues, may effectively block our passage for a long while yet to the last three functions listed, that is, finding new monuments to add to the canon, disputing canonical claims and, in certain cases, becoming part of the canon.

Although I am aware that such a statement sounds pompously alarmist, I would still like to put it to you that our whole passage to intellectual freedom, '*svaraj* in ideas' as K.C. Bhattacharya memorably phrased it,[5] may be what is at stake here. Therefore, it is crucial to examine our relationship to this troubled and seemingly remote area of theory from scratch; but it is equally important not to misconstrue my argument here. I am not claiming that we have nothing to learn from others, nor that we must not 'borrow from the West' (indeed I believe

[4] The mathematicians Rene Thom (see, for example, 'Le role de la topologie dans l'analyse semantique', in Pottier, ed., *Semantique et Logique*, 1974), and Jean Petitot ('On the Linguistic Import of Catastrophe Theory', in *Semiotica* 74-3/4 1989) have worked extensively on the applications of Catastrophe Theory to language situations/linguistic structure.

[5] *Indian Philosophical Quarterly*, October-December 1984.

strongly that intellectual inheritance can come from (m)any sources). Still less am I advancing the chauvinistic hypothesis that the Sanskrit literary theorists and grammarians have said it all before and said it better (I have no doubt at all that it is as difficult, or more, to borrow from ancient Indian scholarship, as from recent 'other' traditions). I am simply stating the paramount importance of asking our own questions, as acutely as possible, before we cast around for suitable pedagogic theories. Second-*hand* theories are fine, in my opinion, but not second-*best* ones.

The starting point of every theory is a set of problems and no one is in a better position to formulate our problems than ourselves. This crucial point seems to me to be insufficiently appreciated by the community of English literature teachers in our country. 'Theory', as Lentricchia and MacLaughlin have recently put it, 'is contested territory'.[6] There is no easy route to theoretical confidence; it is imperative to fight over theories, to squabble seriously about the relevance of existing theories to our particular circumstances of reading, before we can claim them for our own. This seems to me to be one reason why a school of thought like Deconstruction, which has made such waves outside our shores, hardly induces a ripple here. Although the *term* is widely, and loosely, used by us, we have not really bothered to question its context of production, its genesis in a carpentering culture in which the mechanical imagery of plank by plank construction dominates.[7] Yet, our collective unwillingness to raise this sort of query about cross-cultural

---

[6] *Critical Terms for Literary Study*, ed. Lentricchia and McLaughlin (University of Chicago Press : 1990), 2.
[7] Researchers into cultural differences in perception have noted that 'certain illusion figures, such as the Muller-Lyer and the Sanders parallelogram, did not evoke such strong effects in cultures where rectangular objects and arrangements were rare, as in those more "carpentered" cultures where such phenomena abounded. The more carpentered the cultures in which the observers lived, the higher their susceptibility to these illusions'. (Section on 'Perception : Cultural Differences' in *Oxford Companion to the Mind*, ed. Gregory, 602). Thus, my allusion to the metaphor of 'deconstruction' as arising out of a carpentered culture may have some support from psychological studies in vision, undertaken in a very different context. Again, I should like to plead that the interdisciplinary approach yields results here. Practising linguists are much more likely than literary critics to be interested in this sort of research, coming up with insights that might prove useful to English studies, but are difficult for literary theorists to discover on their own.

salience keeps us forever in the 'our-problems-their-solutions' bind that is so typical of a country still colonized in the mind. This is not, in my view, a mere *meum-teum* point. Theories can be taken over or rejected, but it smacks slightly of absurdity to take on *problems* willy-nilly. Unless we struggle to articulate our particularized, historically situated, problems for ourselves, our theories will remain hand-me-downs not *worth* quarrelling over, and our texts imposed. Conversely, to ask authentic questions is also to commit ourselves to a genuine engagement, first and foremost, with theory. Later in this paper I will argue that the discipline of linguistics helps us towards the framing of such questions.

Of course, it is always possible to claim that, in bringing 'third world writing' to English literature courses, we are automatically 'discovering' new monuments and inventing new canons, that is, fulfilling the sixth and seventh functions without much reference to the fifth. In other words, a healthy activism and pragmatism may justly preclude any airy-fairy concern with theory. But it is my contention that the mere addition of a Ngugi or a Naipaul text to the traditional syllabus signifies little if we teach these authors without discussing the ways in which they significantly differ from a Dickens or a Dryden. It is here that theory, which makes of the literary text an arena for the articulation and solution of problems, is essential. In this sense, and in this special circumstance, to be an indigenous critical theorist is perhaps to be the most subversive kind of activist. I hope to show, by the end of this paper that taking theory—and in particular some versions of linguistic theory—seriously may have intensely practical consequences in the classroom. In the following paragraphs, I am going to argue for a movement from (linguistic) theory to (literary) text, rather than the classical pedagogic route from text to theory, with the proviso that I shall be discussing not so much any *specific* linguistic theory here as the *ideological presuppositions* of a cluster of modern linguistic theories that have entered the Indian classroom.

The eight heirarchical functions of criticism suggested earlier could be understood as learned and learnéd modes of response to a text. It is these modalities of response that render a text 'literary'. Language abilities, we have come to believe with Chomsky, *pace tante viri*, are innate; literary sensitivity, on the other hand, has to be mastered. We do not come genetically equipped with literary antennae, hence our cultural environment plays a near total role in teaching us to recognize the 'literariness' of texts. The English literature classroom in Indian universities is one such well-defined cultural context in which pre-selected texts are placed before us, sign-posted as it were, explained with the help of earlier deified generations of critics, positively evaluated in terms of other non-canonical texts, and thus raised to full glory before the bemused eyes of students. By the time our students reach their final Honours year, or in exceptionally recalcitrant cases their final Masters, they have so internalized the received explanations, comparisons, definitions and deifications that their own linguistic awareness is silenced or suppressed. I accept in part the argument that this process is not peculiar to the Indian situation but is characteristic rather of the fashion in which any discipline is institutionally acquired. However, a special poignancy attaches to a context where the vast majority of students and teachers are bi- or multilingual; yet in the environment of the English classroom this often becomes a source not of strength, but shame. Ironically, the typical English literature teacher is guilty of perpetuating a lotos-eater syndrome in which the classroom becomes an island where we can forget whence we came from and the destination we seek; it becomes the perfect habitat for intellectual laziness, camouflaged as elite liberalism.

Linguistic approaches may well provide an antidote to this particular and very widespread malaise of English departments. It will not do to retort, as English teachers often do, that anyone interested in studying Gujarati or Kannada could betake themselves to the appropriate departments, and anyone interested in comparing English genres to Russian ones should take shelter under a Comparative Literature umbrella, because the tools of linguistics are universalistic not in the accepted sense that a Shakespeare text is, but in the sense that they make no *a priori* distinctions between literary and non-literary texts and, furthermore, no theoretical/disciplinary distinction between English literature and other literatures. If linguistic tools are of any use at all in the literature classroom, it is because they provide a descriptive vocabulary which enables certain *basic questions* to be raised about the *relevance of language competence to judgements of literariness*. This technical apparatus helps problematize anew those issues of canonical worth that remain intrinsically uncontentious within a classical literary programme. The value of linguistics as a scientific discipline for literary studies today is its refreshing power to *resurrect the naive queries* which historically institutionalized and continuously reiterated literary modes of response have all but succeeded in obliterating. The object of study, as it is constituted in contemporary linguistics, is in ideological terms very different from the literary object of study, and has correspondingly different theoretical implications.

Some of the most obvious of these divergences are recounted, as briefly as possible:

(i) In literary studies, the object of interest is typically a *text* that is socially authorized, sanctioned, privileged, *legitimized as literature*; in linguistics, the object of inquiry is usually a *grammatical structure* such as a sentence, clause, word or morpheme, productions *without any particular social significance*.

(ii) In essence, the literary text is considered *unique*, extraordinary, an unpredictable feat that cannot be repeated by others; the linguistic structure, in contrast, is in principle ordinary, *necessarily reproducible* by any competent speaker of a given language.

(iii) The literary text, depending on cultural context, is generally either *written or committed to memory*, that is *preserved* for the pleasure and benefit of repeated re-readings/tellings: the grammatical form, however, is mostly studied in terms of the *oral utterance*, which is *ephemeral* and inconsequential for the long-term future.

(iv) The literary text is considered primarily a *non-utilitarian* object; it provides *aesthetic* satisfaction above all; the oral utterance, the object of study favoured by grammarians, is in the main geared to achieve some *immediate function*. It is a structure for transmitting *information*, a speech-act.

(v) Creativity in a literary text is *convention-governed;* such a text depends for its success on members of a community recognizing the norms of a particular genre and inspired departures from it. But creativity in a linguistic sense is taken to be *rule-governed*, it consists in a single person's ability to construct and recognize an infinite number of grammatical utterances and discard ungrammatical ones.

(vi) The literary text, despite protestations by authors to the contrary, is regarded as a *conscious performance* by a person who is practising her craft; the grammatical utterance, in spite of stumbling attempts by speakers to explain their competence, is supposed to be a projection from *subconscious knowledge* that a person does not even know she has.

(vii) Representations in a literary text focus on the *mimetic* and *external words-to-world* relationship, while any grammatical structure is governed by the *categorical* and *internal words-to-words* relationship.

These beliefs (it is important to stress that they are *not necessarily facts*), held by literary critics about texts and by linguists about grammar, result in professional differences of methodology and, as I have insisted before, in modes of response. Three such major consequences for the orientation of the two disciplines, both in search of a language to describe language yet pursuing these meta-goals in diametrically opposed ways, are discussed below.

(a) Beliefs about the authority, uniqueness and historical durability of already canonized literary texts lead in classical literary criticism to *originality of interpretation* and *felicity of expression* being almost as highly prized in a literary critic (Pater, Leavis, Fiedler) as in an author. This is why I argued earlier that a critic's highest success was arrived at that magical moment when audience metamorphoses into actor, that is emulates (mimes?) literary qualities so closely that she literally becomes part of the canon itself.[8] Since the linguist believes she studies ordinary language structures that are ephemeral but reproducible, the qualities valorized in linguistics are seldom originality and expressiveness but rather *replicability of analysis*, evidence that the explanatory tools and methods proposed will extend to a large set of cases and can be used *repeatedly*. This is the sense in which linguistic methods are egalitarian: they are *wilfully blind* to social, non-structural distinctions between privileged texts and plebeian utterances.

This brings us to another set of beliefs about the convention-governed, mimetic and consciously produced literary texts which affects the methodological practices of literary criticism in two further ways.

(b) In mainstream linguistics, the *stylistic features* of a text are considered relatively unimportant as a consequence of the belief that the communicative purposes and expressive semantic properties of a text are trivial by-products of its structure. Although it is true that linguistics has developed a useful vocabulary for the description of grammatical patterns in literary texts, it is paradoxical that this 'applied' aspect of

[8] English literature courses are replete with works of literary criticism which are read as Literature with a capital L, rather than as commentaries on literature. This imposing list includes Dryden's *Essay of Dramatic Poesie*, Johnson's *Lives of the Poets*, Coleridge's *Biographia Literaria*, Pater's *Essays in Criticism*, Arnold's *Culture and Anarchy*, not to mention the contributions of Hazlitt, Lamb, Carlyle, and of the presiding deity of the early twentieth century, Eliot. It is hard to believe that any of these writers would have been displeased to learn that the writing they had proffered as criticism has eventually become literary canon, because, as I have maintained, the boundary between literary criticism and creative writing is indistinct. Both share ideological presuppositions, and not only does criticism aspire to the condition of literature, it is, paradoxically, the main instrument by means of which other criticism is *made* literature.

linguistics is quite peripheral within the linguistics classroom itself. Thus *genre studies*, which are extrapolations of broad stylistic categorizations, form an inconsequential part of a linguistic curriculum, even one which has a course or two in 'stylistics'. In contrast, literature departments subsist on genre studies; the 'novel', the 'epic', the 'lyric' can be the epistemic staples of literature in ways that the linguistic ideology of micro-analysis of grammatical content simply will not allow. If linguistics tools are to be used for closer reading of literary texts, this limitation in their designing must be understood; they provide a rigorous vocabulary for the description of sentence and discourse, but, overtly at least, are silent about text and genre. This equivocal silence within linguistics about written genres is in my view a possible site for theoretical interrogation, where the overlaps between literary studies and linguistics may be profitably examined.

(c) Unlike linguists, literary critics standardly attempt to place a text in its historical context. Knowledge of the social conventions, the communicative status, the properties which led a text to being preserved in a culture, feed into literary studies and make a large space for *diachronic scholarship* within English literature departments (the 'period' and the 'century' specialists). Since language competence, in contrast, is believed by linguists to be guided by internalized, subconscious rules, knowledge of social conventions is considered relatively unimportant in formulating definitions of grammatical constructions.[9] Historical consciousness is thus deliberately excised out of much contemporary linguistic analysis, with the result that the burdens of history, of postcolonialism, etc., are simply shrugged off by the practising linguist. In its intense concentration on 'the moment of enunciation' modern linguistics effects, as it were, the renunciation of history; it visualizes all languages, in ideological terms, existing in a coterminous, *synchronic* arena, without political boundaries. Of course, this is not the way the world functions, but it *is* the way this discipline creates its object. Few Indian linguists agonize about referring to data from Hindi, English, Swahili and Gujarati all in the same classroom, because, sanitized as

---

[9] My use of 'linguists' here might come under fire for homogenizing the discipline of linguistics, for being reductionist, as it were; but my reference point is simply the dominant paradigm in linguistics today, which is unquestionably 'Chomskyan', despite strong rearguard action. 'Most' is therefore a qualitative epithet, as much as a quantitative one, in my usage. See also footnotes 2, 3 and 12.

data and shorn of their pasts, these languages all illustrate similar 'facts' about human competence. How this cavalier disregard of history may be refashioned for liberating ends that indeed have to do with 'universal' notions of linguistic competence will concern us now in the last section of this paper.

It may be argued that, since neither genre nor period nor any particular language is ideologically privileged in linguistics, it offers a uniquely democratic point of entry into the complex debates about canon and the status of English literature in India today. But is a democracy that is amnesiac, mechanical and very pragmatic necessarily desirable? My controversial, but I think not uncommitted, answer must be—yes.

The reasons are painfully simple. Within a linguistics classroom, the oral utterance and everyday language is reified. The 'text' (Shakespeare, Aristotle, Eliot) is nowhere in sight; instead the student's own linguistic knowledge, powerless as it is and poor as it may be, becomes a plausible 'text' which can be placed centrestage. Although the college/university classroom has intimidating institutional dimensions which tend to deny or reduce the existence of other contexts of learning, other classrooms, the ideology and the disciplinary beliefs that the teacher brings with her can, to a large extent, counteract this setting/siting. It has often been the experience of an English literature student, that her powers of expression fall far short of her understanding; the English teacher's normative response in this situation is to comment that the student lacks 'expressive skills, is unable to write well' (c.f. again the critical function of text emulation). Within the linguistics classroom, there is little or no praise for this sort of expressive command of language. As an altogether desirable result, the student from the mofussil town or the provincial university is arguably much less at a disadvantage. A university professor recently remarked to me that the few linguistics students in her university were mostly 'literature dropouts'. To me, the place that such castaways—'rejects' particularly from English literature—find within linguistics departments is heartening, and not necessarily indicative of low intellectual standards. Rather, linguistics creates a different and less daunting discursive space for students who do not have what Alok Rai has called 'a gabbling familiarity with the English tongue'.[10]

The dialogue that students have with a linguistics teacher is, from the very beginning, oriented in a certain direction by the goals of this

[10] At the seminar mentioned in footnote 1.

discipline; in the Indian context, it veers almost inevitably towards the reach and scope of bi/multi-lingualism. Hence, questions about the registers of speech, the implications of structural similarity yet cultural differences between languages are often naturally raised and nurtured within the linguistics classroom. It is my belief that, in the multilingual contexts of India, we have a tremendous advantage in being able to insert, should we have the will to do so, very immediate, real, political, concerns about language, into the traditional English literature curriculum. For example, an elite institution like the Jawaharlal Nehru University (JNU), New Delhi, has left the boundaries between literature and linguistics flexible, so that first year MA students may take initial courses in linguistics; yet this programme is an anomaly because in the courses at JNU the theoretical foundations of the two disciplines, their areas of ideological divergence and convergence, have, perhaps deliberately,[11] been left unexamined. This leads inevitably to a *laissez faire*, 'lazy fare' doctrine of a sort little different from the traditional lotos-eater syndrome I mentioned earlier. Even if it were possible to follow JNU's lead and establish Papers I and II as, say, 'An Introduction to Linguistics' and 'Linguistics and Literature', in various degree colleges this would hardly work if English literature teachers maintained their current *attitudes* towards linguistics and language studies.

English literature teachers have two great and haunting horrors. The first is a horror of *'mechanical tools'* insensitively applied to 'transcendent' literary texts. What can we possibly have to gain from such soulless analysis,[12] exclaim the teachers in a chorus of bewilderment. The second horror is the related one of *oversimplification* and *reductionism* that literature teachers see as a corollary of linguistic discourse.

Provocative though it sounds, I am tempted to describe these two inhibiting horrors as strategic 'feminine' (not *feminist*, indeed quite the opposite!) constructions of the literary enterprise. A deep ignorance of 'machinery' and a concomitant inability to manage simple mechanical activities is part of the prison of the bourgeois female; likewise, the typical bourgeois female has 'irreducible' mystic qualities foisted on her

---

[11] I have to admit that I have no 'hard evidence', of the type usually considered mandatory in a discipline like linguistics, for this conjecture.

[12] The Chomskyan paradigm of linguistics, mentioned in footnote 9, takes as its model the discipline of classical physics, in which deductive hypotheses are offered, revised, and/or rejected to resolve 'problems' posed by the data. Problem-solving, therefore, is a 'core' concept in this sort of linguistics.

that mask her lack of power over the world that she is a part of. The vast majority of literary critics construct themselves as 'female' in this special sense. They are determinedly anti-mechanical and resistant to most enabling simplifications; moreover, they have actually schooled themselves to be *proud* of this attitude, with the result that they face some of the classical disablements of the bourgeois female self, not the least of these being the internalization of complicated rhetorics about the (male?) 'power' of literature and a resultant disavowal of theory.

The literary 'text', as it has typically been characterized within literary studies, is specifically invested with the power to 'defamiliarize' the world and 'decondition' the reader via the linguistic means of metaphor, irony, wordplay, etc. Yet there is little that is mystical about this enterprise. On the contrary the tools of linguistics (notions such as 'semantic deviance', 'subcategorization', 'syntactic versus lexical ambiguity', scope of NP/VP, suprasentential connectives, etc.) might enable both students and teachers to shed a false reverence for the text. Despite the instability and indeterminacy of texts being much discussed topics in literary theory, the practice in our classrooms is still to preserve, by and large, a respectful distance between the humble reader and the hallowed text.[13] What linguistics as a discipline does is provide a hardy vocabulary for the description of the relationships between the language(s) we ourselves speak (even if it isn't English) and the literary dialects of a George Eliot or a T.S. Eliot. The study of linguistics forces upon the reader of literature the assumption that the ambiguities/ analogies/ seductions inherent in a literary text are rooted in everyday language, that they are, paradoxically, part of the grammatical apparatus which the reader brings to the text. This is an enormously enabling insight, particularly with respect to a colonial language, which English has been to us. To find a vocabulary that applies the same technical terminology to one's own poverty-stricken language *and* to Shakespeare's, radically renegotiates the gap between ordinary language and literary language, between English literature and other litera-

---

[13] Rushdie's 1990 Herbert Read Memorial lecture, 'Is Nothing Sacred?', reveals how deep-seated this reverence for the literary text can be, even among post-modern writers. For, in that essay, he proposes to substitute religious texts, such as the *Koran*, with what are to him equally holy — the divine texts of literature. Literary texts may be 'secular', but to most readers, not excluding those like Rushdie, who seem to have shaken off several other mental shackles, they are still, in some mysterious way, sacrosanct.

tures. I believe this enterprise is important enough for English teachers in India, and perhaps even elsewhere, to seriously consider casting aside what I have described as their gendered stance towards the literary text.

Linguistics may be characterized as a workaday discipline. Its mechanics have to be tediously learnt step-by-step (maybe I should say mastered!). However, the teacher of English literature who has enough humility and industry to stick the course may find some communicative rewards, especially with those non-metropolitan, non-elite struggling students of English who have been so willy-nilly excluded from the debates we conduct about the place of English literature and language in our country. Arising out of the discussion earlier in this paper, there are five specific areas where I think I see enough convergences between the ideologies of linguistics and English literary studies in India today, for there to be conversation on a common curriculum. These are

(a) genre-studies (e.g. narrative theories)
(b) translation studies
(c) the study of oral *vs.* literal speech/texts
(d) gender studies
(e) close reading of texts

In each of these areas, there is a rich and rigorous and, in my view, liberating set of linguistic theories available to literary theorists, which may well assist us discover and inscribe new monuments, and boldly erase parts of the existing canon. It must be part of our long-term goal in reformulating syllabi to document these theoretical resources,[14] but the polemic of this particular paper does not, cannot, include the onerous task of documentation. So I will simply end by recalling the metaphor implicit in the title of this paper—dissimilar twins. However different these twins, English language and English literature, may seem, it would be unfortunate, even tragic, if we did not recognize their close

---

[14] In this connection, it may turn out to be rewarding to address the question of an appropriate critical terminology, given the current Indian socio-political context. Lentricchia and McLaughlin's list of twenty-two critical terms (see footnote 6) includes 'race', 'ethnicity', 'canon', 'ideology', 'discourse', but does not consider, for example, 'translation', 'language/ language conflict', 'tradition' or 'colonial/post-colonial', which terms (and others) might generate as much discussion in our country, if cognizance is taken of our multilingual/multicultural background. Of course, this is only by way of a very preliminary, tentative suggestion, requiring considerable debate before it takes shape as a viable critical enterprise.

affinity. The same historical processes engendered them both,[15] and if one reminds us of our complex past, the other shows us our confused present. For the sake of a clearer, less collusive future, which we surely owe our students, not to mention ourselves, I believe we must not easily give up now on either twin, either discipline.

[15] See Gauri Viswanathan's *Masks of Conquest* (London: Faber, 1989) for an impressively detailed account of some of the historical antecedents that established English — the language, and its literature — in India.

16

The Burden of English

GAYATRI CHAKRAVORTY SPIVAK

I am honoured that my colleagues at Miranda House have invited me to deliver the first V. Krishna Memorial Lecture.[1] I did not know her. I have, however, felt enough of her presence from conversation with her friends to have a sense of her and to want to greet her prematurely absent shadow. This is my greeting, on a theme that binds our lives together: the *burden* of English studies in the colonies. She and I were both students of English literature in a colonial and post-colonial situation. She had the added experience of teaching in that context, an experience I am just starting to acquire. Here is something we had in common— a burden. I use the word 'burden' in at least its two chief senses. First the content of a song or account. In this case, expanding the metaphor, the import of the task of teaching and studying English in the colonies. And, secondly, a singular load to carry, in a special way.

I am not speaking of English language policy but of the teaching, specifically, of English literature. Let me start with a passage from *Decolonizing the Mind* by the Kenyan writer Ngugi wa Thiong'o to show how much, in spite of obvious differences, the predicament of the teaching of English literature in post-colonial India has in common with the situation, say, in post-colonial Kenya:[2]

A lot of good work on Kenyan and African languages has been done at the Department of Linguistics and African languages at the University of Nairobi....They ... acknowledge the reality of there being three languages for

---

[1] This paper was delivered in a shorter form at Miranda House, Delhi University, in February 1987. I thank Gyan Prakash for giving the present version of the paper a first reading. I dedicate the paper to Maitreyi Chandra.

[2] Ngugi wa Thiong'o, *Decolonizing the Mind: The Politics of Language in African Literature* (Portsmouth, NH: Heinemann, 1986).

each child in Kenya, a reality which many patriotic and democratic Kenyans would now argue should be translated into social and official policy. Kiswahili would be the all-Kenya national and official language; the other nationality languages would have their rightful places in the schools and English would remain Kenyan people's language of international communication. But I am not dealing so much with the language policies as with the language practice of African writers.[3]

I, too, am dealing with practice, not policies. But I am not dealing with the language practice of Indian writers either. To repeat, my topic today is the situation of Indian teachers of English.

What is the basic difference between teaching a second language as an instrument of communication and teaching the same language so that the student can appreciate literature? It is certainly possible to argue that in the most successful cases the difference is not easy to discern. But there is a certain difference in orientation between the language class-room and the literature classroom. In the former, the goal is an active and reflexive use of the mechanics of the language. In the latter, the goal is at least to shape the mind of the student so that it can resemble the mind of the so-called implied reader of the literary text, even when that is a historically-distanced cultural fiction.

The figure of an implied reader is constructed within a consolidated system of cultural representation. The appropriate culture in this context is the one supposedly indigenous to the literature under consideration. In our case, the culture of a vague space called Britain, even England, in its transaction with Europeanness (meaning, of course, *Western* Europe), Hellenism and Hebraism, the advent of Euramericanism, the trendiness of Commonwealth Literature, and the like. Our ideal student of British literature must so internalize this play of cultural self-representation that she can, to use the terms of the most naive kind of literary pedagogy, 'relate to the text', 'identify' with it. However naive these terms, they describe the subtlest kind of cultural and epistemic transformation, a kind of upward race-mobility, an entry, however remote, into a geo-political rather than merely national 'Indian'-ness. It is from this base that R.K. Narayan can speak of 'English in India' as if it were a jolly safari arranged by some better-bred version of the India Tourist Board and,

[3] Ngugi, *Decolonization*, xi.

conversely, it is also upon this base that a critical study of colonial discourse can be built.[4]

It is with this in mind that many decolonized intellectuals feel that the straightforward ideal of teaching English literature in the theatre of decolonization continues the process of producing an out-of-date British-Council-style colonial bourgeoisie in a changed global context.

I am not suggesting for a moment that, given the type of student who chooses English as a field of study in the general Indian context of social opportunity (whatever that might be), this kind of ideological production is successfully achieved. The demand for a 'general cultural participant' in the colonies has at any rate changed with the dismantling of actual territorial imperialism. Today, the student of English literature who is there because no other more potentially lucrative course of study is open to him is alienated from his work in a particular way.

It cannot be ignored that there is a class-argument lurking here, although it is considerably changed from my student days in the mid-to-late fifties. The reasons why a person who obviously takes no pleasure in English texts chooses English Honours are too complex to explore here. At any rate, the class-value of the choice of English Honours is gendered, and is different according to the hierarchy of institutions—in the metropolitan, urban, suburban and rural centres. The same taxonomy, as it operates among students of English literature as a Pass subject and the teacher's accommodation within it as Brit. Lit. becomes less and less normative, is much more demographically and politically interesting. I have not the skills to study it, and so will turn to a more literary-critical topic and return to the 'implied reader'.

The implied reader is imagined, even in the most simple reading, according to rudimentary or sophisticated hypotheses about persons, places, and times. You cannot make sense of anything written or spoken without at least implicitly assuming that it was destined for you, that you are its implied reader. When this sense of the latent destiny of the texts of a literary tradition is developed along disciplinary lines, even the students (mostly women) who come to English studies in a self-consciously purposive way—all students at Miranda House would have to be included here—might still be open, under the best circumstances, to an alienating cultural indoctrination that is out of step with the historical moment. This becomes all the more dubious when the best of them become purveyors of native culture abroad.

---

[4] R.K. Narayan, 'English In India', in *A Story-Teller's World* (New Delhi: Penguin India, 1989), 20-3.

I should like to look first at a few literary figurations of this alienation. I want next to plot some ways of negotiating with this phenomenon. As I have already suggested, this alienation is a poison *and* a medicine, a base upon which both elitism and critique can be built. The institutional curriculum can attempt to regulate its use and abuse.

I will discuss a few literary figurations of the gradual cultural alienation that might become a persistent accompaniment to the successful teaching of English literature in India. I employ the word 'figure' here from the word 'figurative' as opposed to 'literal'. When a piece of prose reasonably argues a point, we understand this as its *literal* message. When it advances this point through its form, through images, metaphors, and indeed its general rhetoricity, we call it figuration or figuring-forth. Rhetoric in this view is not mere *alamkara*. The literal and the figurative depend upon each other even as they interrupt each other. They can be defined apart but they make each other operate.

Indeed, literature might be the best complement to ideological transformation. The successful reader learns to identify implicitly with the value system figured forth by literature through learning to manipulate the figures, rather than through (or in addition to) working out the argument explicitly and literally, with a view to reasonable consent. Literature buys your assent in an almost clandestine way and therefore it is an excellent instrument for a slow transformation of the mind. For good or for ill. As medicine or as poison, perhaps always a bit of both. The teacher must negotiate and make visible what is merely clandestine.

To emphasize my point that the assent the implied reader gives to literature is more than merely reasonable, indeed perhaps clandestine, my first example is a text where I am perhaps myself the type-case. To make of 'myself', written into a cultural text, the example of alienating assent, is a direct challenge to the hegemonic notion of the 'willing suspension of disbelief', still an active orthodoxy coming via such influential figures as the Anglo-American T.S. Eliot and I.A. Richards, and the Euramerican Herbert Marcuse.

It is not a text written in English, although many of you have read it in a rather indifferent English translation. It is the short story 'Didi' (1895) or 'The Elder Sister' by Rabindranath Tagore.[5] My point here is to illustrate how the implied reader is drawn into patterns of cultural value as she assents to a text, says 'yes' to its judgements, in other words reads

---

[5] Rabindranath Tagore, 'Didi', in *Galpaguchchha* (Calcutta: Visva-Bharati, 1975), vol 2. The translations are my own.

it with pleasure. When we teach our students to read with pleasure texts where the implied reader is culturally alien and hegemonic, the assent might bring a degree of alienation.[6]

It is a simple story. Shoshi is the only daughter of an elderly couple. Her husband Joygopal is hoping to inherit their property. The old couple have a son in late middle age. After their death, Shoshi takes her orphaned infant brother to her bosom almost in preference to her own sons. Joygopal, enraged by the loss of his inheritance, does everthing to take it away from the orphan boy, and indeed tries to precipitate his death by neglecting a serious illness. At this point, the English magistrate for the area comes on tour. Shoshi delivers her brother over to the magistrate. She soon dies mysteriously and is cremated overnight.

I have read this story many times. I am not only its implied reader, but its *successful* implied reader. Even after all these readings, my throat catches at the superb sentimental ending: 'Shoshi had given her word to her brother at parting, we will meet again. I don't know where that word was kept' (290). This assent is so strong, in other words, that the analysis of it that I will now begin and that I have performed before cannot seriously interfere with it. This is why literature is such an excellent vehicle of ideological transformation. For good or for ill. As medicine or as poison.

It is, for women of my class and inclination (*pravritti*), a major ingredient in the centring of the subject that says 'yes', first to reading, and then to reading something, so that more of that subject can be consolidated and sedimented; so that it can go on saying 'yes', indefinitely.

(There are different systems of representation that operate centring for different classes or *varna*-s, different inclinations. And the weave is interrupted with the patchwork of intervention and contingency. To give an example of a different class, a different history, a different set of inclinations: it is 'religion' thrown into the potential sign-system of 'citizenship' as concept and metaphor that wins the assent of the young woman whose class-family-*pravritti* insert her into the Rashtriya Sevika Samiti.)

How then is my assent given to this story? To what do I assent? How

---

[6] I have given a historical account of this alienation outside the classroom in 'Once Again A Leap Into the Post-Colonial Banal', paper delivered at the Davis Center for Historical Studies, Princeton University, 1 March 1991, forthcoming in *difference*.

am I, or indeed how *was* I, historically constructed as its implied reader so that I was able to read it with pleasure within my cultural self-representation?

As you know, many of Tagore's short stories are *about* emancipated women. This story is about a village woman whom love for her brother emancipates to the extent that she can see that the impartial white colonial administrator will be a better *ma-baap* than her self-interested Indian kin. Yet, as a woman, she cannot choose to give herself over to him. Does she choose to remain behind? Or is she, for herself, a prisoner of the patriarchal system from which she delivers her brother by assigning the Englishman as her father? (This is, of course, a central patriarchal theme, this giving of the name of the father to the Englishman, for the issue is inheritance and the passage of property.) At any rate, the implied reader, whose position I occupy for the moment as the daughter of upper-middle-class female emancipation in urban Bengal, cannot be sure if Shoshi chooses to remain with or is a prisoner of patriarchy, and, indeed, still cannot be sure where she stands within this situation. This must remain what Meenakshi Mukherjee has called an 'interesting but elusive and unverifiable statement' for the moment. I will speak of the thrill of ambivalence later. Here all I need to say is that, in order to assent to the story, to derive pleasure from a proper reading, one must somehow see the entire colonial system as a way out of indigenous patriarchy.[7] I have written elsewhere about the cultural politics of this conviction in the matter of the abolition of the self-immolation of widows in 1829.[8]

As we know, in most of his prose writings Rabindranath is not simply telling a story or making a point but also fashioning a new Bengali prose.

---

[7] David Hardiman comments on the peasants' misplaced belief that the British would give them direct access to vengeance as justice (discussion after 'The Peasant Experience of Usury: Western India in the Nineteenth Century', paper delivered at the Davis Center for Historical Studies, Princeton University, 12 April 1991). In response to my query to Hardiman, as to whether there is any documentary evidence that indigenous collaborators with the colonial authorities saw through this peasant belief, Gyan Prakash advises me to look in Bengali tract literature. Until I can undertake that research, I mark this place with the question: what are the cultural politics of Tagore's rhetorical representation of this belief or faith, at a later date, and on the woman's part?

[8] Spivak, 'Can the Subaltern Speak?', in Cary Nelson and Lawrence Grossberg, eds., *Marxism and the Interpretation of Culture: Limits, Boundaries, Frontiers* (Urbana: Univ. of Illinois Press, 1988).

You will therefore accept the suggestion that the texture of the levels of prose plays a strong part in the fabrication of the implied reader's assent.

Tagore endows only Shoshi with full-fledged subjectivity. It is in the service of building that subject that Tagore deploys that stunning mixture of Sanskritized and colloquial Bengali that marks his writing of this period.

There is some cultural discrepancy in creating Shoshi as the subject-agent of a romantic love or *prem* that is still not the legitimate model of the cementing emotion of the institution of the Indian marriage. Rabindranath brings this about through an expert manipulation of the model of *biraho* or love-in-absence abundantly available in classical Sanskrit. Any careful reader will see the marks of this in the construction of Shoshi's subjectivity.

The discrepancy involved in the Sanskritization of Shoshi's subjectivity as the agent of *prem* is never treated ironically by Tagore. It is in the interest of constructing her as the subject or agent of *sneho* or affection that a benevolent irony makes its appearance, but always only at the expense of her brother Nilmoni. There are many instances of this. I will quote a tiny (transliterated) fragment simply to remind myself of the pleasure of the text:

krishokay brihat mastak gombhirmukh shamborno (chhele ti)

This fantastic collection of epithets, reading which it is almost impossible to depart from pure Sanskrit phonetics, is a measure of the registers of irony and seriousness with which Tagore can play the instrument of his prose. The available English translation, 'the heavy-pated, grave-faced, dusky child', is, of course, hopeless at catching these mechanics.

Why read a high-culture vernacular text as we think of the burden of teaching English? Let us backtrack. The goal of *teaching* such a thing as literature is epistemic: transforming the way in which objects of knowledge are constructed. One such object, perhaps the chief object, is the human being, inevitably gendered. It is always through such epistemic transformations that we begin to approximate the implied reader. In our case, the approximation is mediated by the new vernacular literatures secreted by the encounter described, for this writer with a profound imperialist irony, as 'the Bengal Renaissance'. That particular mediation has been commented on *ad nauseam* and is indeed a cliché of Indian cultural history. Like most clichés, this one has become part of the 'truth', of Indian cultural self-representation. And in the fabrication of this truth, Tagore's role is crucial.

Some of Tagore's most significant epistemic meddlings are with women. Women constituted by, and constituting, such 'minds' become the culturally representative 'implied reader'. Therefore the problem of the teaching of English literature is not separated from the development of the colonial subject. And women being notoriously the unfixed part of cultural subjectivity as it is represented by men, the construction of the feminine subject in colonial vernacular literature can give us a sense of the classroom moulding of minds preserved in literary form. To read vernacular colonial literature in this way, as preparing the ground for, as it is prepared by, British literature in the colonies, is to challenge the contrast often made, in 'Western' colonial discourse studies, between 'Western' literature as 'central', and Third World literature—in this case 'Indian' (!)—as 'marginal' or 'emergent'. Expanding Ashis Nandy's idea of the 'intimate enemy', or my own notion of 'violating enablement', it seems more productive to consider the heterogeneity on both sides.

In order to make systemic changes, we need systemic taxonomies. In that conviction, we must repeat that two discontinuous ways in which the opposition centre/margin or dominant/emergent is undone are gender and class. Thus it seems important to look at Tagore's participation in the project of epistemic transformation by way of a rural woman. This is more interesting in the business of the construction of the implied reader precisely because Shoshi, the central character, does not belong to the class of women who will read the story felicitously, 'in its own time'. This class-separation allows for a feeling of identity-in-difference which seems a much more flexible instrument of epistemic transformation as a site of negotiations. What happens when an exceptional underclass woman is herself a creative reader of British literature will be considered in the next section.

Shoshi is developed as an agent of romantic love in elegant Sanskritic prose in descriptive third person with no hint of indirect free style.[9] In other words, rhetorically she is given no access to a Sanskritized subjectivity. In her case, what will be shown is the subordination of love or prem for her husband to affection or sneho for her orphan brother. The entire network of *Indian* patriarchy, including colonial functionaries, would like to keep Shoshi in the gendered private sphere, as her husband's adjunct. Shoshi enters the public sphere by establishing direct

---

[9] For the importance of the assignment of reported, direct, and indirect speech and style, see V.N. Volosinov, *Marxism and Philosophy*, trans. Ladislav Matejka and I.R. Titunik (Cambridge: Harvard Univ. Press, 1986), part III.

contact with the British colonial authority and chooses to re-enter the patriarchal enclosure. She is destroyed by this choice.

Keeping within the allegory of the production of the colonial subject, with something like a relationship with the implied reader of British literature, we see the orphaned brother as the full-fledged future colonial subject, mourning his sister—his personal past—but encircled by the sahib's left arm, the right implicitly pointing to a historical future. But it is Shoshi who supplements the picture, choosing to remain in the static culture, while sending the young unformed male into the dynamic colonial future. A gendered model, this, of the colonial reader, not quite identical with the 'real' reader and therefore, in a patriarchal system of reckoning, more like a 'woman'.

How, then, can we construct a model of the woman or man of the urban middle class, themselves woven and patched as well by the same strands, of the same stuff, reading in the exciting identity-in-difference frame of mind, the subject laid out in the pages of the story? A richly constructed, richly praised female subject who chooses to remain within the indigenous patriarchal structure; with confidence in the magistrate as foster-father, another mark of her heroism. This is the complex of attitudes that is the condition and effect of any appropriate reading of the story. The structure survives; Madhu Kishwar will not call herself a 'feminist' because the word is too much marked by the West, but will work for (other) women's rights.[10]

The magistrate is constructed as a subject who might be privy to the thrill of this ambivalence. The possibility is lodged in this exchange: 'The saheb asked, "Where will you go." Shoshi said, "I will return to my husband's house, I have nothing to worry about." The saheb smiled a little and, seeing no way out . . .'

By contrast, the neighbour Tara, who opposes husbands if they are scoundrels at the beginning of the story, and roars out her rage at the end, is displeased when Shoshi leaves her husband's house to look after her sick brother: 'If you have to fight your husband why not sit at home and do it; what's the point in leaving home? A husband, after all' (288).

The magistrate (Brit. Lit.) (perhaps) understands best of all that Shoshi must sacrifice herself to her own culture, but takes charge of Nilmoni (the indefinite future). A crude but recognizable model of what

<hr/>

[10] Madhu Kishwar, 'Why I Do Not Call Myself A Feminist', *Manushi* 61, Nov.-Dec. 1990.

the 'best' students manage—saying 'yes' and 'no' to the Shoshi-function, as it were—in our Brit. Lit. classes.

I want now to show how this necessarily limited and divided assent to implied readership is parodied in Kipling's *Kim*, within five years of the publication of 'Didi'. Thus it is particularly necessary not to differentiate British and Indian literatures as 'central' and 'marginal' today, in a benevolent spirit; that is a mere legitimation by reversal of the colonial cliché whose real displacement is seen in the turbulent mockery of migrant literature—Desani or Rushdie. Here is Kipling's

Hurree Chunder Mookerjee, . . . an MA of Calcutta University, [who] would explain the advantages of education. There were marks to be gained by due attention to Latin and Wordsworth's *Excursion*. . . . also a man might go far, as he himself had done, by strict attention to plays called *Lear* and *Julius Caesar*; the book cost four annas, but could be bought second-hand in Bow Bazar for two. Still more important than Wordsworth, or the eminent authors Burke and Hare, was the art and science of mensuration. . . . 'How am I to fear the absolutely non-existent?' said Hurree Babu, talking English to reassure himself. It is an awful thing still to dread the magic that you contemptuously investigate to collect folklore for the Royal Society with a lively belief in all the Powers of Darkness.[11]

What Tagore is performing in the narrative, through the epistemic transformation of the central *female* character, as a productive and chosen contradiction: self-sacrifice to culture while bequeathing the future to the colonist *in loco parentis*; Kipling describes in this minor male character as an unproductive contradiction: bondage to a superstitious and mercenary indigenous culture while mouthing sublime doctrine, the distinctive failure of the colonial subject. (We know that Kipling understood the good Indian in an earlier, feudal semiotic; and was incapable of bringing to life an Indian woman as subject or agent of profound inner change.)

At least two kinds of points can be made here. By contrast to Kipling—of course Kipling is an interested choice on my part—Tagore's complicated and complicit structure remains preferable as a mode of assent in the colonies. In the frame of indigenous class-alliances and gendering it becomes dubious. The activist teacher of English can negotiate this only if she works to undo the divide between English and vernacular literatures laid down in our institutions. The teacher can use her own native language skills and draw on the multi-lingual skills of

[11] Rudyard Kipling, *Kim* (New York: Viking Penguin, 1987), 210-11.

the students in class. More important, Departments of Modern Indian Literatures, the Departments of Literature in the State Vernacular, and Departments of Comparative Literature must work together so that the artificial divide between British and Native is undone.

I should like to make clear that I am not *conflating* British and colonial/Commonwealth literatures. Nor am I suggesting a collapsing of boundaries. I am proposing that the complexity of their relationship, collaborative/parasitical/contrary/resistant, be allowed to surface in literary pedagogy. They are different but complicit. I will recite this refrain again, for it is a common misunderstanding.[12]

As contrast to Tagore's class-divisive gendering I will draw on Binodini Dasi's *Amar Katha* (My Story).[13] To contrast Kipling's dismissal of the agency of a productive contradiction to the colonial subject, I will point at Tagore's *Gora* as a counter-*Kim*.[14]

Gora ('Whitey'—the word applied to the British tommy is here a perfectly acceptable diminutive from Gaurmohan) appeared five years after the publication of *Kim*. The heroes of both novels are Irish orphans of the Indian Mutiny, turned Indian. But there the resemblance ends. Gora becomes both a nationalist Indian and a tremendously orthodox Brahmin. At the end of the novel he finds out that he is not only not a Brahmin, but not even a Hindu or an Indian by birth. It is then that he realizes that he is most truly Indian, because he chooses to be so. His realization is embedded in a discourse of woman. First his identification of India with his (foster) mother who, unlike his (foster) father, did not observe caste difference: 'Ma, you have no caste rules, no loathing, no contempt. You are my India.' Then the summons to the hitherto spurned untouchable servant: 'Now call your Lachchmia. Ask her to bring me a glass of water.' And finally the Mother's request to him to acknowledge

---

[12] For an example of such a misunderstanding, with reference to the relationship between philosophy and literature, and based on minimal documentation, see the chapter on Derrida in Jurgen Habermas, *The Philosophical Discourse of Modernism: Twelve Lectures* (Cambridge: MIT Press, 1987).

[13] Binodini Dasi, *Amar Katha o Anyanyo Rachona*, eds. Saumitra Chattopadhyaya, *et al.* (Calcutta: Subarnorekha, 1988). Translations mine. For a reading of this text in the context of women's autobiographies, see Partha Chatterjee, 'In Their Own Words? Women's Autobiographies in Nineteenth-Century Bengal' (forthcoming).

[14] Rabindranath Tagore, *Gora*, in *Rabindra Rachanabali* (Calcutta: Viswa-Bharati, 1955), vol.6. Sujit Mukherjee is supervising a new translation of *Gora*.

the love of the emancipated Brahmo heroine, expressed obliquely as a request to summon a male friend: 'Gora, now send for Binoy' (572).[15] Rather different in historical 'feel' from Kim O'Hara with the Lama on a hilltop, the end of *Kim*.

If I were commenting on the thematics of the half-caste as 'true' Indian, I should contrast this figure with Mahasweta Devi's Mary Oraon, and again the registers of class and gender (and of course coloniality and *post*-coloniality) would come into play.[16] But contrasting it to Kipling's Irish-as-Indian hero, one would have to notice there the feudal, and here the nationalist axiomatic; the codified past as opposed to a possible dynamic future. Kim's return is acted out again by E.M. Forster's Fielding; their futures are not seriously marked by the colonies. For Gora agency is bestowed by the colony as nation. The theme of choice is important here as well.

But Gora is not a divided subject in the same way as Shoshi. If he chooses a return to culture, he is also the inheritor of the future. The theme of sacrifice is less ambivalent and therefore less interesting in Gora. The colonial reader is as race- and gender-divided from Gora as she would be class-divided from Shoshi. And from that race- and gender-distanced position, the system of representations she assents to is again not quite accessible to the staging of her own identity, but this time 'from below', not, as in the case of the indigenous woman, 'from above'.[17] The cultural choice and bequest of the future can inhere in the same fantasmatic character: the white man turned Indian by choice.[18] The development of readership thrives in the difference and deferment staged between hero and reader, whether from above or below. In a former colony, the institutional teacher of imperialist and colonial litera-

---

[15] I am grateful to Ranes Chakravorty for reading out this paragraph to me, when my own *Gora* was inaccessible, and the library did not have one.

[16] Mahasweta Devi, 'The Hunt', in *Women in Performance*, V.i.

[17] The elegantly staged representation of Sarada Devi as the rural woman denoting cultural choice and victory in the general text of imperialist seduction is a complex variation on the thematics we are discussing. Swami Gambhirananda, *Srima Sarada Devi* (Calcutta: Udbodhan, 1st. ed. 1954), 1-6.

[18] There are a handful of prominent whites of this genre who receive a great deal of publicity (on a less exalted register, like middle-class husbands who cook). They offer an eagerly grasped standby for cultural representation as alibi. One thinks of their role in Richard Attenborough's *Gandhi* and, more recently, in the conception of the hero of *Dances With Wolves*.

ture can open this space of difference only by way of persistently undoing the institutional difference between that literature and the literature(s) in the mother-tongue(s). It is then that the active vectors of these differences, negotiating gender, class, and race, would begin to appear.[19]

Let us now consider a performance of this undoing, in the very house of performance, during the colonial era. I am referring to the Calcutta professional theatre at the end of the nineteenth century. To give an example of the undoing of institutional difference I will quote from Binodini's *Amar Katha* at length:

> Girishbabu [the eminent actor Girishchandra Ghosh (1844-1912)] taught me with great care the performance of parts. His teaching method was superb. First he explained the essence [*bhab-bhava*] of the part. Then he would ask us to memorize it. Then when he had time he would sit in our house, with Amrita Mitra, Amritababu and others, and tell us the writings of many different British actresses, of eminent British poets such as Shakespeare, Milton, Byron, Pope, as if they were stories. Sometimes he would read the books aloud and explain. He taught various moves and gestures [*hab-bhab*] one by one. Because of this care I started learning the work of acting with knowledge and intelligence. What I had learnt before was like the cleverness of parrots, I had experienced little. I had not been able to say or understand anything with argument or reasoning. From now on I could understand my own performance-selected part. When big British *actors* or *actresses* came I would be eager to see their acting. And the directors of the theatre would accompany me with infinite care to see English theatre. When we returned home Girishbabu would ask, 'How was it?' (33-4)

Here indeed is teaching to perform. Men teaching women the trick of the 'inside' of their captors, as the captors themselves code that 'inside', with instruments supposedly generated in a deeper 'inside', for general decipherment in an 'outside', the British audience, who supposedly

---

[19] The artificial separation between colonial (roughly British) and neo-colonial (roughly US), migrant and post-colonial, covers a wide field. Howard Winant, for example, makes the claim that '*in the postmodern political framework of the contemporary United States, hegemony is determined by the articulation of race and class*'. Howard Winant, 'Postmodern Racial Politics in the United States: Difference and Inequality', *Socialist Review*, XX.i, Jan.-Mar. 1990, 137; emphasis author's. 'Postmodern' is used here in the to me unsatisfactory sense of neo-colonialism, as being not only after the phase of modernization, but also entering a phase after orthodox socialist radicalism. A curricular re-constellation as is being proposed here might have broader implications than one imagines.

possess 'insides' that are resolutely considered quite different from those held by these men and women. But the devout colonial subject, decent dupe of universalism, thinks to learn the trick perfectly. The performance of the teaching and of the learning is not mere mimicry. Deliberate, canny, wholesale epistemic transformation is what we are witnessing here. This is not the *Natya Sastra* warmed over. The idea that apprenticeship with the West introduces analytic learning in place of rote learning is a sentiment that thoroughly informed the debates on education in the nineteenth century and continues to this day: it was heard in February 1991 from an Indian woman dancer who learnt her stuff from an old-fashioned Indian male master but went on to collaborate with a European male director whose method was not unlike Girishbabu's.[20]

A later passage allows us to sense how completely the principle of reasonable learning affected the episteme:

I had no taste for other topics of conversation. I liked only the accounts of the great British actors and actresses that respected Girishbabu gave me, the books he read to me. When Mrs. Sidnis [Siddons?] left theatre work, spent ten years in the married state and then returned to the stage, where in her acting the critics noticed what fault, where she was excellent, where lacking, all this he read and explained to me from books. He would also tell me which British actress practised her voice by mingling it with birdsong in the woods, this too he would tell me. How Ellen Terry dressed, how Bandman made himself up as Hamlet, how Ophelia dressed in flowers, what book Bankimchandra's *Durgesh-nandini* imitated, in what English book *Rajani* found its idea [*bhab*=thoughts], so many things of this nature, I do not know where to begin. Thanks to the loving care of respected Girishbabu and other affectionate friends, I cannot recount how many tales by what great English, Greek, French, and German authors I

---

[20] For a sober accounting of the debates, see J.P. Naik and Syed Nurulah, *A History of Education in India* (2d rev. ed., London: Macmillan, 1951). The recent reference is to Samjukta Panigrahi, discussion after lecture demonstration with Eugenio Barba, at the Conference on Inter-Cultural Performance, Bellagio, 20 February 1991. The denigration of 'rote' learning as opposed to 'analytic' knowing is no longer as clearly on the agenda and shows evidence of an unquestioning ideological (and therefore often unwitting) acceptance of nineteenth-century imperialist universalism. The project would be to re-inscribe the presuppositions—of knowledge before understanding—proposed in some Indian Speech Act linguistics which challenge British Speech Act theory. Bimal Krishna Matilal, 'Knowledge from Linguistic Utterances', in *The Word and the World* (Delhi: OUP, 1990).

have heard. I did not only listen, I collected ideas [*bhab*=mood] from them and reflected upon them ceaselessly. As a result of this my nature [*shabhab-swabhava*] became such that, when I went to visit a garden, I did not like the buildings there, I would search out the secluded spots resplendent with wild flowers. I would feel that perhaps I lived in those woods, ever-nurtured by them! My heart would throw itself down as it witnessed beauty so intimately mingled with every plant and bud. It was as if my soul would start to dance with joy! When I sometimes went to a riverbank it would seem as if my heart would fill with waves, I would feel as if I had played in the waves of this river forever. Now these waves have left my heart and are throwing themselves about. The sand on the banks of the river at Kuchbihar is full of mica, most lovely, I would often go alone to the riverbank, which was quite far from my living quarters, lie down on the sand and watch the waves. I would feel as if they spoke to me (35-6).

The rhetoric of this extended passage lays out the construction of the colonial subject as contradictory implied reader of the imperial text. Binodini was indeed receiving an education in English and European literature in a way that no university student does. To be sure, to learn to read well is to say 'yes, yes' to the text, if only in order to say 'no', in other words to perform it, if only against the grain. But between that general sense of performance and the narrow sense of performing in order to simulate there is an immense difference in degree. Binodini was not obliged to get her information right, the proper names are often masked. (Ellen Terry comes out 'Ellentarry' in Bengali, a single word; and 'Ophelia' inhabits the same register of reality as Mr Bandman and Mrs Sidnis.) Yet here we see the difference between knowing and learning. She identifies with Bankim, the master-creator recognized as the successful colonial subject by the very *babu*-culture of Bengal that Kipling mocks. If Bankim had taken the *bhab* of British literature, so would she; he to write, she to interpret through performance. Reading-in-performance *is* a species of writing, as Bankim himself recognized:

One day Bankimbabu came to see the performance of his *Mrinalini,* and I was playing the part of 'Manorama' at that time. Having seen the part of Manorama being played Bankimbabu said: 'I only wrote the character of Manorama in a book, I had never thought to see it with my own eyes, seeing Manorama today I thought I was seeing my Manorama in front of me' (36).[21]

[21] For the contrast between Binodini's testimonial and Tagore's literary representation of the insulted wife playing, precisely, Manorama, see 'Giribala', in *Galpaguchcha.*

The public sphere of professional theatre and the private sphere of
the self interpenetrate in the longer passage in a clearer and more intense
model of what can happen in the classroom. In the consummate rhetoric
of this gifted craftswoman, the epistemic simulacrum is obstinately
sustained. The translator has taken care to preserve every 'as if', every
'perhaps'. (It would have been possible to construct the Bengali sentences without them.) It is not a 'real' nature that Binodini imagines as the
place of eternal nurture. It is rather the planted woods in a garden-
house. In the passage about the waves, the *location* of the waves is made
nicely indeterminate; but in fact the waves, ostensibly the vehicle of
union, preserve separation between river and heart, displacing if from
figure to figure. This rhetorical effusion does not break step with the
ritual language celebrating her dead protector within which the autobiography is framed. It seems appropriate that we, in search of a model
for the colonial subject as implied reader, should be implicated in the
reader function of this thoroughly benevolent and utterly dominant
male.

Binodini was no rural subaltern. In her own words:

I was born in this great city of Calcutta, in a family without resource and
property. But not to be called poverty-stricken, for, however painfully, we
scratched together a living. . . . My grandmother, my mother, and the two of
us, brother and sister (14).

A family of women, quite within the other discursive formation that
can look upon marriage as a socio-economic institution of exchange for
consumption:

our sufferings from poverty increased, and then our grandmother perpetrated
a marriage between my infant brother of five years and a girl of two and a half
[the play between infant—*shishu*—and girl—*balika*—is her own] and brought
home a negligible quantity of ornaments. Then our livelihood was earned
through the sale of ornaments.

It is not only the play between shishu and balika that signals that
Binodini—writing at the age of forty-seven, after her brilliant and
thwarted attempt at staging herself, in every sense, as female individualist—is still unemphatically at ease with the pragmatic patriarchal
culture that thwarted her; although her expressed sentiments will not
draw from it. The next few sentences quietly emphasize this; for it is the
love [sneho] of the older women rather than the unconsummated child
marriage that remains in memory: 'My grandmother and respected
Mother were most affectionate [*snehomoyee*]. They would sell the orna-

ments one by one at the goldsmith's shop and give us all kinds of food stuff. They never regretted the ornaments'.

The brother died soon after the marriage. What happened to the child bride deprived of her ornaments for the subsistence of the other women? We cannot know. But there can be no doubt that the tragedy of feminism is played out not only in the obvious and visible masculist suppression of Binodini's ambitions, but also in the widening gap betwen the obscurity of the unremembered child widow and the subtle and layered memoir of the autobiographer.[22]

The male suppression of the competitive female is a poignant story, where the politically correct judgement is trivially obvious, but it is not the only story in coloniality. The feminist has the dubious task of marking the division in womanspace. Tagore may have found it difficult to stage the estranged wife Shoshi as the full-fledged colonial subject, insert her fully into the contradiction of implied readership, make her the agent of both sneho and prem, but the prostitute-performer Binodini straddles the gap with ease. In prostitution, sublated through performance upon the colonially-fractured stage, the old lesson in lasya is destroyed and preserved on another register as prem.[23] Although Binodini is bitter and contemptuous about the men's refusal to let her own a part of her beloved Star Theatre, and indeed to keep their promise of preserving her proper name by naming it 'B-Theatre'—curious synecdoche, known only to the knowing—her extraordinary language of exalted devotion to her dead protector, her companion in the long years after her departure from the stage, rings with greater affect, as does the explicit (auto-) eroticism of her singular love poems, where the agency

---

[22] It is not to denigrate feminism to point out that feminist ambition in the colonial nineteenth century must involve competition and class-ambition. For a discussion of this in the Western context, see Elizabeth Fox-Genovese, *Feminism Without Illusions: A Critique of Individualism* (Chapel Hill: Univ. of North Carolina Press, 1991). Here too the relationship between the colony and the West is complex, not merely oppositional. The fact that powerful men suppressed Binodini's ambition points at another complex relationship between feminism and the critique of capitalism.

[23] The connection between the dramatic representation of lust and drama proper is available in reverse in Damodargupta's *Kuttinimatam*. See Mandakranta Basu, '*Lasya*: A Dramatic Art?', in Bimal Krishna Matilal and P. Bilimoriya, eds., *Sanskrit and Related Studies* (State Univ. of New York Press, forthcoming).

of the male lover is only present to the extent that it is necessary for the topos of male inconstancy. Marriage may be an institution that crumples when the woman is epistemically fractured, but residential (rather than itinerant) prostitution can be re-coded as a peculiar liberty. How far do we want to take this as an allegory of colonial reading?

In the Brit. Lit. classroom today, an answer might be concocted in terms of Hanif Kureishi's *The Buddha of Suburbia*.[24] The shifts are: a century in time, coloniality through post-coloniality to migrancy, a literary representation by a male author who 'read philosophy at King's College, London' (jacket blurb). Here too an uncomfortable opposition between native and migrant can be undone or put under erasure (crossed out while leaving visible).[25] Again, not conflation; perhaps the very shock of the re-constellation lets 'truth'-s flash forth.

The central character Karim will not be allowed to be English, even as Binodini was not allowed to be entrepreneurial-professional-individualist, although she carried bricks on her head for the building of the theatre, and he is

Englishman born and bred, almost ... Englishman I am (though not proud of it), from the South London suburbs and going somewhere. Perhaps it is the odd mixture of continents and blood, of here and there, of belonging and not, that makes me restless and easily bored (3).

This is the flip side of Binodini's restless self-separation on the glittering sand of the Kuchbihar river; the style difference may be between Romanticism and existentialist modernism (small e, small m: *Catcher in the Rye, Under the Net*), rather than only that between India and Britain. Let the student notice that Karim, as he learns performance from British and American directors, is being asked to be 'Indian', or portray migrants favourably. He must dye his skin browner (his mother is working-class English) as he is given Mowgli's part in Kipling's *The Jungle Book*, and produce 'an Indian accent', which he finally, during performance, begins to 'send up' with occasional lapses into cockney. Yet outside the theatre he lives in the incredible violence of racism in contemporary London, which is also vividly described in the novel.

Karim's father, a Muslim, becomes a Buddhist from do-it-yourself books and finds fulfilment with an 'artist' woman. Yet there is real good

[24] Hanif Kureishi, *The Buddha of Suburbia* (New York: Viking Penguin, 1991).
[25] Sensitively argued in 'Location, Intervention, Incommensurability: A Conversation with Homi Bhabha', *Emergences* I (1989).

sense in him, real unworldliness, and there is love between them, however sweetly sexist.

Dominant British society shuttles between racist violence and approval of the 'real' Indian. Once again, it is the productive epistemic fracture of the colonial, post-colonial, hybrid subject that is denied. The expectations are Kipling's Mowgli, or the Buddha of Suburbia. The transformation of the Father is given in the third person. Let us consider what the son says, in the first person, about learning to act.

'India' is an imagined ingredient with material vestiges here, important in the survival technique of the fabrication of a hybrid identity. With a different political impulse from the malevolent racist British underclass, or the benevolent racist British artist, we too would like to keep alive the divide between 'real' Indian and migrant 'Indian'. Without collapsing the difference, what if we attended to the fact that Binodini's imagined 'England' and the representation of Karim's imagined 'India' are both 'created' under duress? We would begin, then, to plot an alternative literary historiography. Binodini thought of the duress as imaginative freedom. We are not surprised that Karim is represented as creatively happy when he puts together his stage Indian. The intimate enemy, a violation that enables. The teacher of British literature in the former colonies must look at this phenomenon carefully, to let the differences appear in their entanglements.

Here, then, are the passages from *The Buddha of Suburbia*. Karim is re-thinking the Indian character, having been criticized for his initial negative representation of an Indian immigrant:[26]

At night, at home, I was working on Changez's shambolic walk and crippled hand, and on the accent, which I knew would sound, to white ears, bizarre, funny and characteristic of India (188).

He is at his father's best friend Anwar's funeral. (The two had come to Britain from Bombay many years ago.):

There was a minor row when one of the Indians pulled out a handy compass and announced that the hole hadn't been dug facing in the right direction, towards Mecca ... But I did feel, looking at these strange creatures now—the Indians—that in some way these were my people, and that I'd spent my life denying or avoiding that fact. I felt ashamed and incomplete at the same time,

---

[26] The criticism comes from Tracey, a politically mature African-British woman. In our classroom, we would have to develop the point of this criticism, significantly different from the desire of the white.

as if half of me were missing, and as if I'd been colluding with my enemies, those whites who wanted Indians to be like them. Partly I blamed Dad for this. After all, like Anwar, for most of his life he'd never shown any interest in going back to India. He was always honest about this: he preferred England in every way. Things worked; it wasn't hot; you didn't see terrible things on the street that you could do nothing about [this is contradicted by the graphic descriptions of racist violence in London]. He wasn't proud of his past, but he wasn't unproud of it either; it just existed, and there was not any point in fetishizing it, as some liberals and Asian radicals liked to do. So if I wanted the additional personality bonus of an Indian past, I would have to create it (212-13).

How very different from the 'uncreative' sacrificial choice thrust upon the rural woman or the unfetishized choice of a culture without the bonus of a past accessible to the 'white migrant' imagined in the colonial context! Again, leisurely classroom consideration of the difference will make it appear how the representation of 'race', of 'gendering', of 'religion/culture', construct the chain of displacements upon which these examples may be plotted. 'Nation' and 'class' relate to these links on other levels of abstraction.

For Binodini, the professional theatre had promised an access to feminist individualism which residential prostitution denied. Down along a chain of displacements, casual prostitution and the stage have become confused for Kureishi's character Karim, although in the 'real' world professional prostitution still has a confining relationship to the media. At any rate, the identity forged in the theatre had come to organize Binodini's own staging of her identity in honourable residential prostitution recalled in later life. 'The acting bit of her lost its moorings and drifted out into real life'.[27] There is no such bleeding over in the representation of Karim. The character who plays the sexual field is the Paki. When he 'wants the additional personality bonus of an Indian past', he reverses the demands of his protector, and 'creates':

There were few jobs I relished as much as the invention of Changez/Tariq ...

---

[27] Martin Amis, *London Fields* (New York: Harmony Books, 1989). I quote this from a trendy English novelist somewhat bloody-mindedly, because Amis too is in a world transformed by migrants. His villain is 'multiracial' in his choice of women. But the staging of identity in migrancy is not Amis's burden. Hence this sentence about life and acting does not attach to a *multiracial* character. They remain victims. Our best students will have to come to grips with the fact that the epistemic fracturing of the colonial reader is no longer a marginal event.

I uncovered notions, connections, initiatives I didn't even know were present in my mind ... I worked regularly and kept a journal [*Amar Katha?*]; ... I felt more solid myself, and not as if my mind were just a kind of cinema for myriad impressions and emotions to flicker through. This was worth doing, this had meaning, this added up the elements of my life. And it was this that Pyke [the director] had taught me: what a creative life could be ... I was prepared to pay the price for his being a romantic, an experimenter. He had to pursue what he wanted to know and follow his feelings wherever they went, even as far as my arse and my girlfriend's cunt (217).

Karim is a character in a book. The fact that this passage about creativity and the discovery of a coherent identity is much less gripping than Bindoini's passage about divided self-creation, cannot be taken as representative of the difference between the colonial reader's longing for the metropolis and the migrant's fancy for his roots. It is simply that our students might be encouraged to place it on that chain of displacements that will include *Gora*, and *Kim*, and *The Jungle Book*. Through attention to the rhetorical conduct of each link on the chain, the student might be encouraged, to belabour the by-now-obvious, neither to conflate nor to oppose, but to figure out gender and class difference in complicity. I draw attention, again, to the moment when the half-caste tribal woman in 'The Hunt' fabricates identity for the object (rather than the individualist subject) by intoning a word that would allow the indigenous exploiter to be constructed within the script of Oraon performance. Mahasweta offers a link in the chain away from migrancy into subalternity.

What I am suggesting, then, is that, in the post-colonial context, the teaching of English literature can become critical only if it is intimately yoked to the teaching of the literary or cultural production in the mother tongue(s). In that persistently asymmetrical intimacy, the *topos* of language learning, in its various forms, can become a particularly productive site. I am not speaking here of becoming an 'expert' of the mother-tongue, for the benefit of those who are thoroughly ignorant of it in the metropolis, a temptation to which many of us have given in. I am speaking of a much less practical thing: becoming 'inter-literary', not 'Comparative', in the presence of long-established institutional divides and examination requirements. It is a kind of homeopathic gesture: scratching at the epistemic fracture by awkwardly assuming a language to be an 'epistemic system' and staging a collision between Kipling and Tagore, Didi and Binodini, 'Mary Oraon', and 'Karim'. The authority of cultivating the felicitous implied readership is questioned in such teaching and learning. Any number of 'correct' readings can be scrupulously taught here, with some degree of assurance that the reader's space of the mother-tongue will secure the quotation marks by way of repeated colonial and post-colonial encounters, among them the one in the classroom.

Great clumps of topics are pulled up with this style of teaching: access to subjectivity, access to the other's language are among them. Such topics allow us to float into Commonwealth Literature, even without access to the various native traditions or emergences. The peculiar authority in this floating reading is of the contingent reader who *might* have that access. An interruptive authority, for the text is in English.

Let us consider an example: the last scene of Nadine Gordimer's *July's People*.[28]

Successful black insurgency in South Africa. A family being protectively steered into the village of their former servant, July. Barriers falling, people learning about being human, the nature of power, being gendered, the master-servant dialectic. The emergence of July's proper name—Mwawate—in itself the kind of topic that rocks the centralized place of the 'implied reader'. As if Man Friday should have a history. When people have been pared down a good bit, we encounter an event impossible to conceive earlier in the book. Mwawate speaks to his former mistress, the central character in the book, in his own language, with authority, dignity, and irritation. I will first quote the preparatory moments: 'She knew those widened nostrils. Go, he willed, go up the hill to the hut; as he would to his wife ... The only way to get away from her was ... to give up to her this place that was his own ...' (152).

Then a furious exchange in English about why had he stolen little things; why had she given him only rubbish; why had he accepted rubbish; almost farcically resembling what Jan Niedersen Pieterse has called 'the dialectics of terror': '*Not* discussed is the *initial* ... terror, which includes the institutional violence of the denial of ... human rights and [of imperialist] occupation'.[29]

[28] Nadine Gordimer, *July's People* (New York: Viking Penguin, 1981).

[29] Jan Niedersen Pieterse, *Israel's State Terrorism and Counterinsurgency in the Third World* (Kingston, NECEF Publications, 1986), 4. My extrapolations refer to the specific case of Israel and Palestine. Again, the student can link the international press with autobiography, Brit Lit., and vernacular literature if the teacher fills in Pieterse's passage. The pedagogic interest is, always, to globalize and politicize the burden by pointing at linked differences rather than divisive turf battles.

It is in response to this frustrating exchange that Mwawate speaks:

You—he spread his knees and put an open hand on each. Suddenly he began to talk at her in his own language, his face flickering powerfully. The heavy cadences surrounded her; the earth was fading and a thin, far radiance from the moon was faintly pinkening parachute-silk hazes stretched over the sky. She understood although she knew no word. Understood everything: what he had had to be, how she had covered up to herself for him, in order for him to be her idea of him. But for himself—to be intelligent, honest, dignified for *her* was nothing; his measure as a man was taken elsewhere and by others. She was not his mother, his wife, his sister, his friend, his people. He spoke in English what belonged in English:—Daniel he's go with those ones like in town. He's—join. The verb, unqualified, did for every kind of commitment: to a burial society, a hire-purchase agreement, their thumbprints put to a labour contract for the mines or sugar plantations (152).

Gordimer is playing a whole set of variations on the topos of languages as epistemes. To begin with, the imperious gestures, of the pronominal address as imperative: 'You'. But even before that, and surreptitiously, the sudden incursion of Mwawate's 'inside' into the novel: 'Go, *he willed*' (emphasis mine). It remains paratactic—cannot be staged as becoming syntactic in the hands of this white author woman writing about a female white protagonist, precisely because both are painfully politically correct. The sentences can start only after that enabling shifter, 'you', (staged by the writer as) pronounced by the imperfect speaker of English. Put this on a spectrum of contemporary artists using this topos in many different ways: Toni Morrison, J.M. Coetzee, Guillermo Gomes-Pena, Jamelie Hassan.[30]

In the hands of a radical Creole writer like Gordimer, the implied black reader of a white text cannot be in a subject-position, not even a

[30] I have discussed this cluster in 'War as Culture', to be submitted to *Critical Inquiry*. Lars Engle makes a persuasive case for this passage as the characteristic irruption of the Freudian 'uncanny'. Lars Engle, 'The Political Uncanny: The Novels of Nadine Gordimer', *Yale Journal of Criticism* II.ii (1989), 120ff. I think, however, that it is more fruitful to consider the 'uncanny' as inhabiting the past and the present and the future—always under the skin of the familiar everyday—rather than only a 'post-revolutionary' future conceived as a future present in sequential narrative time. I also think that we should take note of 'July's real name. The uncanny lurks under the skin of the everyday as Mwawate always lives in the skin that is always called July by his masters.

compromised one like Shoshi's. The text belongs to the native speaker.
But the rhetorical conduct of the text undermines and complicates this a
lot. The desire of the radical native speaker is in that sentence: 'She
understood although she knew no word'. How fragile the logic of that
sentence is; there are no guarantees. It is as if the white magistrate in 'The
Elder Sister' should enunciate the desire for understanding Shoshi's
ambivalence, which the writer as classed male colonial subject articulates by way of the representation of his slight smile. And, in Gordimer's
text there is the strong suggestion that rather than understand the
'burden' of Mwawate's words, the peculiar situation of being addressed
by him in his tongue produces in her an understanding of a narrative of,
precisely, the infelicity of their communication. His measure was elsewhere. 'He spoke in English what belonged in English'.

Just as Mwawate's subject-space is syntactically inaccessible in the
rhetoric of the novel, so is the dubious assertion of 'understanding'
unmoored from the passage that tells you *what* she understood. And, in
addition, the man speaking his mother tongue—the other tongue from
English—is deliberately distanced by a metonym with nature: Mwawate flickering, adjacent to the moon and the parachute silk clouds. Put
this on a spectrum with the neat divisive locatives of nature and mind
in Binodini's *self*-staging!

What is it that Mwawate says in English? It is the matter of public
organizations: 'he's join'. This is not a 'mistake', just as Dopdi Mejhen's
'counter' is not.[31] In its profound ungrammaticality, it undoes the dominant language and pushes its frontiers as only pidgin can. Put this calm
approach on a spectrum with Kipling's mockery, Rushdie's teratology,
and Tagore's colonial prose.

It is not possible for an 'expatriate English professor', as Madhu Jain
described me in the December 1990 issue of *India Today*, to produce a
thick analysis of the burden of English teaching in India. Let me remind
my readers that I have not attempted to comment on the importance of
English as an international medium of exchange. The statistics on Pass
and Honours English students will have to wait.[32] All I seem to have
done is offered impractical suggestions: to undo the imported distinction between centre and periphery as well as some indigenous institu-

---

[31] See Spivak, ' "Draupadi" by Mahasveta Devi', in *In Other Worlds: Essays
in Cultural Politics* (New York: Routledge, 1987).

[32] I am in correspondence with appropriate officials in India, and hope to
follow this up with on-site inquiries.

tional divisions by looking at literature as the staged battleground of epistemes.

It may not be altogether as impractical as it seems, at first glance, to the embattled local teacher. I am speaking, after all, of disturbing the arrangement of classroom material as well as our approach to them. Predictably, this would be against the interest of the student, who would have to sit for an examination that expects ferocious loyalty to a colonial curricular arrangement. (This is an argument we daily face, *mutatis mutandis*, in terms of bilingualism in the United States; in the sixties and seventies it was Black English). Can one share the dilemma with the students while preparing them for the regular exam papers? A time-honoured strategy of politicization through pedagogy. The counter-argument here is the cynicism of students in a demoralized society, where English learning does not occupy centrestage; also the difficulty of learning the language for those students who would be most susceptible to such politicization. (In the United States, this translates, as imperfectly as all translations, to the justified cynicism of the urban underclass student towards the smorgasbord of Cultural Studies.) Alas, the answers to that one are lost or found, lost *and* found, in the transactions in the classroom. It is to the most practical aspect of our trade that I dedicate these ruminations.

Would such a technique of teaching work outside modern literature? And if so, with Adivasi creation-myths and the reclaiming of 'African' mythic traditions by writers and film-makers of contemporary Africa? Or only with *Beowulf* and the *Mahabharata*? One looks forward to an alternative literary historiography of postcoloniality critical of the hierarchical imprint of 'the Commonwealth'.

17

Landmarks in Official Educational Policy: Some Facts and Figures

Compiled by LOLA CHATTERJI

1823 *Appointment of Committee of Public Instruction* in Bengal. Raja Ram Mohan Roy requests the Governor-General, Lord Amherst, to set up a college 'promoting a more liberal and enlightened system of instruction embracing natural philosophy' and the sciences, instead of the proposed Sanskrit College in Calcutta.

1835 *Macaulay's Minute* in favour of institutionalizing 'English Education'. Followed up immediately by the passage of the English Education Act under Governor General William Bentinck.
    Available public funds to be used for setting up English-medium educational institutions.

1854 *Wood's Despatch*
    Charles Wood, Lord Halifax, President of the Board of Control (of the East India Company) recommends a co-ordinated system of education, the establishment of a Department of Education, and the setting up of universities in Presidency towns. This results in selective higher education for training future administrators, imparted through the medium of English, and in 'useful and practical' education for the rest of society, imparted through the vernaculars, thus confirming indigenous patterns of social stratification.

1857-87 *Establishment of universities* in Calcutta, Bombay, Madras, Lahore and Allahabad.

1882   *Indian Education Commission*
Set up to review progress of education. In its Report (1884), the Commission recommends improving primary and elementary education, and confirms university policy. Social stratification widens.

1902   *Indian Universities Commission*, leading to

1904   *Indian Universities Act*

The Viceroy, Lord Curzon, tightens government control over university and college administration, and provides funds for setting up laboratories and museums.

1913   *Resolution of Educational Policy*
Recommends need for establishing new universities, including residential institutions. Six more universities set up during the period 1913-20.

1917-19   *Calcutta University Commission Report*
Bulky evidence critical of the quality of students graduating from the university is submitted.

1919   *Montagu–Chelmsford Reforms*
Recommends introduction of far-reaching constitutional changes, including demarcating functions of the centre and provinces. Education comes under the respective ministers for education in the provinces.

1925   *Inter-university Board* established.

1935   *Government of India Act*
Further measures adopted for provincial autonomy, making local bodies responsible for education.

1949   *Constitutional Position of English*
Under 'Official Language' (part XVII) of the Constitution of India, Hindi in the Devanagari script is provided as the language of the Union with the proviso that English will continue to be used for the first fifteen years for the purposes for which it was being used previously. At the expiry of this period an official language commission would be set up to review the position.

1948-9   *University Education Commission*
Set up under the chairmanship of Dr S. Radhakrishnan.
In its Report (1951), which dealt comprehensively with the

issue of the medium of instruction, English was not considered desirable for these reasons: (i) it is a negation of
democracy since it divides the Indian people into two nations: the few who govern, and the many who are governed;
(ii) it is educationally unsound to use a foreign language.
Hindi is recommended as the medium of instruction, the
Devanagari script to be reformed and used for this purpose.
The study of English to continue.

1956   *Report of Official Language Commission.*
Regarding the use of English, notes that literacy in English
constitutes 6.41 per cent of total literacy, and 1.06 per cent of
that of total population. Recognizes its value as 'pipeline'
within the country and 'window' to the rest of the world;
recommends its continuance as the language of the law-
courts and in the administration of justice. Therefore recommends that there should be no restriction on its use for all or
any official purpose of the Union.

1957   *Kunzru Committee Report*
Set up by the newly formed University Grants Commission
(UGC). Its recommendations regarding the use of English in
the universities include the following: (i) that the change
from English to an Indian language as the medium of instruction at the university stage should not be hastened; (ii)
that even when a change in the medium of instruction is
made, English should continue to be studied by all university students; (iii) that the teaching of English should be
given special attention in the pre-university class (a three-
year degree course was proposed to be set up in place of the
four-year undergraduate course functioning in most institutions); (iv) that the teaching of English literature should be
related to the study of Indian literatures in order to stimulate critical thinking and writing in the Indian languages; (v)
that it is in our interest that English be retained as a properly
studied second language at the university level.

1960   *Committee of Experts* under the chairmanship of G.C. Banerjee set up by the UGC to examine issues involved in the
teaching of English.

1961   *Report of Working Group*, set up by the UGC regarding the
switch-over from English to an Indian language as medium
of instruction, observes that the change-over should not be

hastened and that English shall be retained as the alternative medium. Group asked to offer 'advice . . . in bringing about an orderly change . . . consistent with the maintenance of standards.'

1961   *Three-Language Formula*

Conference of chief ministers of states recommends the following pattern of language study, involving study of three languages in schools:

(a) Regional language, or mother tongue when different from regional language

(b) Hindi, or any other Indian language in Hindi-speaking areas

(c) English, or any other European language.

This measure not uniformly adopted.

1963   *Official Languages Act*

English adopted as associate official language of the Union without any time limit.

1964-6   *Education Commission Report*

Set up under the chairmanship of Dr D.S. Kothari. Recognizes the language question as one of the most complex and intractable of India's post-Independence problems.

Recommends the use of regional languages as media of instruction. Not in favour of single-language medium, whether Hindi or English. Notes the occurrence of riots in Tamilnadu over attempts to popularize the use of Hindi. Nevertheless recommends both Hindi and English as link languages, while recognizing that English cannot serve as a link for the majority. Confirms Three-Language Formula and recommends the third language be studied from the point of view of national integration.

Use of English to continue as library language and channel of international communication; *therefore* no student to be considered as qualified for a degree, unless she has acquired a reasonable proficiency in English; all teachers consequently to be bilingual.

Recommends special units to be set up for teaching English as a language skill, as distinct from teaching it as literature. English to be the medium of instruction in all major universities because of their all-India character.

Switch-over to regional languages as medium to be achieved within ten years. Position to be reviewed in due course.

1967   *Official Languages Amendment Bill*

Seeks to give statutory recognition to Jawaharlal Nehru's assurance regarding the continued use of English as long as the non-Hindi speaking people do not desire a change.

Resolves to promote the spread of the Hindi language, and recommends that an intensive and comprehensive programme be prepared and implemented for this purpose; at the same time, that arrangements be made for the study of a modern Indian language, preferably one of the southern languages. Compulsory knowledge of Hindi not required for selection of candidates for Union services and posts; therefore non-Hindi-speaking persons would be required to know English. English translations to be attached to all official communications in Hindi.

Report on Study of English in India by Study Group set up by the Ministry of Education under the Chairmanship of V.K. Gokak.

Endorses Three-Language Formula. Recommends investment in reading material in regional languages.

English to be studied at the college level as language skill; nevertheless, canonical literary texts proposed for study.

1968   *National Policy on Education*

Embodies recommendations of Kothari Commission Report. Emphasis on the need to inculcate democratic values and national integration. Uniformity in courses of study, evaluation procedures and number of years to be spent at each stage of educational process sought. The study of regional languages to be encouraged, and provision made for textbooks; the study of English to continue as alternative language and as medium of instruction at institutions of higher learning.

1969   *P.B. Gajendragadkar Report*

Recommends administrative changes bringing about greater centralization in university affairs.

Banaras Hindu University Report

P.B. Gajendragadkar heads inquiry committee set up to review serious breaches of discipline. Regarding medium of instruction, strongly recommends change-over to regional languages while leaving the pace and methods to the university system. Endorses Kothari Commission's recommendations regarding the use of English.

1976   Constitutional amendment places education in Concurrent List.

1979   *Hospital and Other Institutions Bill*
Proposes the abrogation of fundamental right under Article 19 of the Constitution to form associations for purposes of collective action.

1986   *National Policy on Education and Plan of Action* (NPE & POA)
Popularly described as the New Educational Policy, it reviews the 1968 National Policy. Reviews slow progress in the implementation of some basic recommendations and emphasizes the need for a 'dynamic' approach. Highlights the following areas for attention: the consolidation and expansion of institutions; the development of autonomous colleges and departments; the redesigning of courses; the training of teachers; strengthening research; improvements in efficiency of the system; the creation of structures for co-ordination at state and national levels; mobility; vocationalization. Suggests de-linking degree requirement for employment wherever feasible. No mention of medium of instruction in its chapter on Higher Education, but development of English Language Training institutions encouraged. POA recommends the establishment of Navodaya Vidyalayas, schools set up in rural areas with the objectives of identifying and promoting excellence. Thus, centralization and creation of elite institutions further widens gap between favoured minority and under-privileged majority, contradicting the basic avowed aim to democratize and bring about equality of opportunity.

1989   'Angrezi Hatao' movement in UP represents antagonism to English.

1990   Punjab militants insist on the use of Punjabi in all official transactions and in the media. Echoes language riots in Tamilnadu against the use of Hindi in 1963.

1990   *Acharya Ramamurti Commission Report*

Commission set up to review NPE & POA entitles its report 'Towards an Enlightened and Humane Society'.

Criticizes the exclusion of the poor from the educational process; decries elitism and Navodaya Vidyalayas and the tardy pace of implementation of vocational avenue requirements.

Endorses the recommendations of 1986 NPE regarding: regional languages; the three-language formula; the development of Hindi and Sanskrit; foreign languages, including English. Suggests measures to ensure uniform and rationalized implementation by merging bodies concerned with similar objectives: e.g. Kendriya Sansthan, Central Institute of English & Foreign Languages, and Central Institute of Indian Languages. 'Pending ultimate switch-over to the media of regional languages and Hindi for purposes of higher education, English will continue to be a vital medium for universities and colleges.' Observes that eleven English Language institutes exist, but that standards vary and that the overall standards of English are going down. Recommends a further use of technology for language development.

1991   Meeting of Central Advisory Board of Education recommends setting up sub-committee to study Ramamurti Commission Report by end April. Pleads for raising the level of expenditure on education during the Eighth Plan to 6 per cent of national income, without which the objectives of restructuring education and ending illiteracy by 2001 cannot be met.

SOME STATISTICS

Literacy and proficiency in English

Overall literacy rate— 36.23 per cent of population (1981 Census Report)
    Literacy in English 6.41 per cent
    Literacy in English of total population 1.06 per cent (Report of Official Language Commission 1956)

, According to other estimates approximately 3 per cent of population are English-speaking bilinguals, i.e. about 20 million people. (B. Kachru, *The Indianization of English*, Delhi : OUP, 1983.)

STUDENT ENROLMENT

All students at college and university level study English; for those doing professional courses, and for most post-graduate courses, English is the medium of instruction.

Enrolment in higher education 3.5 million students (1984-5 figures of Seventh Five Year Plan Report).

This figure declined to 3.1 million in 1987-8.

Number of universities 157; deemed universities 19.

National Laboratories 27 (1963).

Number of colleges 8856 (1986-7).

FINANCIAL OUTLAY

Outlay on education in Seventh Five Year Plan Rs 6383 crores (non-plan outlay of this comprises Rs 5200 crores).

Plan outlay for 1990-1 Rs 865 crores, 2.86 per cent of total outlay.

Non-plan outlay Rs 794 crores, 1.23 per cent of total outlay.

In the First Five Year Plan, the share of education was 7.86 per cent of the total outlay.

India ranks 115th in the world in terms of investment in education as a percentage of GNP.

Amongst countries with populations of 10 crores and above, India ranks second last (Bangladesh ranks last).

Source: Ramamurti Report.

PRESS AND PRINT MEDIA IN ENGLISH (UP TO 31 DECEMBER 1989)

Total:	5634
Distributed as follows:	
Dailies	197
Bi-weeklies	15
Weeklies	536
Fortnightlies	433
Monthlies	1899
Quarterlies	930

Annuals	1112
Other	512

Roughly a third of all published books and a fifth of all periodicals are in English.

ELECTRONIC MEDIA

Approximately 2 per cent of time is given to English Language programmes and news on state-controlled radio and television.